EUROPEAN POLITICAL, ECONOMIC, AND SECURITY ISSUES

GREECE

ECONOMICS, POLITICAL AND SOCIAL ISSUES

EUROPEAN POLITICAL, ECONOMIC, AND SECURITY ISSUES

Additional books in this series can be found on Nova's website under the Series tab.

Additional E-books in this series can be found on Nova's website under the E-book tab.

European Political, Economic, and Security Issues

Greece

Economics, Political and Social Issues

Panagiotis Liargovas
Editor

Nova Science Publishers, Inc.
New York

Copyright © 2012 by Nova Science Publishers, Inc.

All rights reserved. No part of this book may be reproduced, stored in a retrieval system or transmitted in any form or by any means: electronic, electrostatic, magnetic, tape, mechanical photocopying, recording or otherwise without the written permission of the Publisher.

For permission to use material from this book please contact us:
Telephone 631-231-7269; Fax 631-231-8175
Web Site: http://www.novapublishers.com

NOTICE TO THE READER

The Publisher has taken reasonable care in the preparation of this book, but makes no expressed or implied warranty of any kind and assumes no responsibility for any errors or omissions. No liability is assumed for incidental or consequential damages in connection with or arising out of information contained in this book. The Publisher shall not be liable for any special, consequential, or exemplary damages resulting, in whole or in part, from the readers' use of, or reliance upon, this material. Any parts of this book based on government reports are so indicated and copyright is claimed for those parts to the extent applicable to compilations of such works.

Independent verification should be sought for any data, advice or recommendations contained in this book. In addition, no responsibility is assumed by the publisher for any injury and/or damage to persons or property arising from any methods, products, instructions, ideas or otherwise contained in this publication.

This publication is designed to provide accurate and authoritative information with regard to the subject matter covered herein. It is sold with the clear understanding that the Publisher is not engaged in rendering legal or any other professional services. If legal or any other expert assistance is required, the services of a competent person should be sought. FROM A DECLARATION OF PARTICIPANTS JOINTLY ADOPTED BY A COMMITTEE OF THE AMERICAN BAR ASSOCIATION AND A COMMITTEE OF PUBLISHERS.

Additional color graphics may be available in the e-book version of this book.

LIBRARY OF CONGRESS CATALOGING-IN-PUBLICATION DATA

Greece : economics, political and social issues / editor, Panagiotis Liargovas.
    p. cm.
  Includes index.
  ISBN 978-1-62100-944-3 (hardcover)
  1. Financial crises--Greece. 2. Greece--Economic conditions--1974- 3. Greece--Economic policy--1974- 4. Greece--Politics and government--1974- 5. Greece--Social conditions--1974- I. Liargovas, Panagiotis G., 1963-
  HB3807.5.G74 2011
  330.9495--dc23
                    2011040285

Published by Nova Science Publishers, Inc. ✛ New York

CONTENTS

Preface		**vii**
Chapter 1	Introduction *Panagiotis Liargovas*	**1**
PART I: ECONOMIC ISSUES		**9**
Chapter 2	Stabilization and Reform in a Statist Regime, 1974-2011 *Panos Kazakos*	**11**
Chapter 3	Perennial Structural Problems in Modern Greek Economy *Panagiotis Evangelopoulos*	**33**
Chapter 4	The Political Economy of the Greek Crisis Revisited: Economic Growth Versus Political Development? *Pantelis Sklias*	**71**
Chapter 5	Euro and the Twin Deficits: The Greek Case *Nikolina E. Kosteletou*	**87**
Chapter 6	Is a "Bad Bank" Solution for a Possible Future Greek Banking Crisis? *Panagiotis Liargovas and Spyridon Repousis*	**115**
Chapter 7	An Assessment of Business and SME Growth Policies Applied in Greece in the 1994-2002 Period *Constantinos Ikonomou*	**129**
Chapter 8	The Common Agricultural Policy's Effects on the Agricultural Sector in Greece and Its Environmental Impacts *Antonios A. Vorloou and Joanna Castritsi-Catharios*	**163**
PART II: POLITICAL ISSUES		**175**
Chapter 9	The Political Economy of the Greek Crisis: Collective Action Perspectives *Panagiota Manoli*	**177**

Contents

Chapter 10   The Greek Economic Crisis: A Trigger for Public Administration Reforms?   **197**
Stella Ladi

Chapter 11   Anti-Money Laundering and Anti-Fraud Methods to Detect and Prevent Occupational Fraud in the Greek Public Sector   **209**
Panagiotis Liargovas and Spyridon Repousis

Chapter 12   Info-Communication Globalisation and the Global Info-Cash (GIC): A Practical Way for Greece to Emerge from the Crisis   **221**
George K. Gantzias

Chapter 13   Greek Foreign Policy Since the End of World War II   **237**
Charalambos Tsardanidis

PART III: SOCIAL ISSUES   **251**

Chapter 14   Unions and Labor Market Organization in Greece   **253**
Stella Zambarloukou

Chapter 15   Corporate Social Responsibility in Greece: Current Developments and Future Prospects   **273**
Skouloudis Antonis and Evangelinos Konstantinos

Chapter 16   Greek Youngsters' Perceptions of Modern Greeks: An Exploratory Study   **291**
Chrysa Tamisoglou

Chapter 17   Depiction of the Role of Women on the Island of Evia (Greece): A Significant Fishing Area   **303**
Joanna Castritsi-Catharios and Steriani Matsiori

Index   **313**

PREFACE

Greece is at a critical juncture of its recent history. The economic policies of the last three decades have brought it close to bankruptcy. Much of the debate about Greece's current problems has focused on the short-run management of the crisis. This book contributes to public debate by bringing into discussion important economic, political and social issues which have played a major role in preventing Greece's transformation into a modern capitalist economy.

Chapter 1 - Greece is experiencing an unprecedented economic crisis. In fact, Greece experiences the historic failure of the post-democratic developmental model, a model based on extensive statism, weak institutions, lack of credibility in economic policy, non-implementation of structural reforms, political clientelism and non-respect of the rule of the law.

Chapter 2 – This chapter deals with the politics of economic stabilization and reform in Greece and addresses questions already raised in the literature. The focus is specifically on the changes in economic and social policies characterized by a transition from statist designs to ambivalent liberal reforms. Thereby, the authors do not address one policy field alone but look at a number of core issues or policies that include fiscal discipline, product and labor market reforms, privatization, pensions and environment. The analysis, covering the entire time span from 1974 on to the present, is a tale of an ultimately failed liberal adjustment. To explain it the authors apply mainly soft public choice approaches about interest-based behavior; (institutionalist) references to path–dependent political norms and practices and formal rules of the game; and, inevitably, ideas, while allowing for the impact of multilateral arrangements and crisis as external inducements to reform. The course of things and the exemplifications the authors provide invite to a reexamination of the ultimate balance between institutionalized coordination mechanisms of the EU and domestic forces.

Chapter 3 - Structural economic problems are chronic in modern Greek economy, resulting in emergence of a generally inefficient institutional economic framework that is financed through a dramatically expanding public deficit and debt and supported by a strong continental currency, the euro. In this chapter the author examines how this unfortunate state of economic affairs of the Greek economy worsened from 2004 when the conservative government was elected. Although the conservative government realized some crucial reforms, privatizations and public-private partnerships, neither it completed them nor it expanded them in the main institutional structure of the Greek economy and finally it failed to organize a new type of economy based on the robustness of private sector and supported by an efficient and operational public sector.

The author concludes in his analysis that the Draconian austerity measures of the new socialist government are unlikely to succeed if the new economic authority does not limit dramatically the size of the public sector and does not restore the economic rationality in Greek economy on the path of Classical Economic Liberalism.

Chapter 4 - The assessment of current macroeconomic indicators of Greece justifies the critical situation of the country. However, the normative neoclassical framework of analysis does not provide an adequate insight and explanatory basis of this situation since it does not consider the historical context within which this phenomenon has been taking place. The author argues that we are currently facing a unique paradox. On one hand, current reality is that of a state battling to avoid default. On the other hand, the economic performance of the past 30 years contrasts this reality.

In this chapter, the major principles of new institutional economics and international political economy are applied in a historical context in order to provide the necessary tools to capture contemporary economic and political reality in Greece.

The Greek crisis can be seen as the result of inadequate institutional building and poor political performance during the last 30 years. Europeanization and modernization of the 90's have not been supported by the necessary institutions. Incomplete measures of the EMU mechanism have exacerbated the situation. High economic performance did not coincide with the low level of political and institutional development in the country. It is shown empirically that the lack of political and institutional development is a causal factor of the Greek crisis which could have been prevented otherwise.

Chapter 5 - Since the beginning of 2010 and as a result of the debt crisis in the eurozone and specifically in Greece, fiscal imbalances have been at the center of interest. Related to these imbalances are imbalances of the external sector, which are equally important, as they need financing by net inflows from abroad. Financial integration and the euro have been blamed for the sharp deterioration of the Greek Current Account deficit, during the last two decades. In this chapter, we show that the increase in external deficit is related to the expansionary fiscal policy. The twin deficit hypothesis is empirically verified for the period 1991-2010. The relationship has distinct characteristics for the period after the country became a member of the eurozone. In the context of a portfolio model it is shown that the fiscal budget, but also interest rate fluctuations, growth and competitiveness have an important role for the determination of the Current Account. Empirical investigation is realized with panel data from Southern eurozone countries. All of them have Current Account deficits. It is found that not only fiscal policy of these countries affects their Current Account deficits, but also fiscal policy of the eurozone surplus countries of the North has a role to play. Interdependence among the countries of the eurozone suggests that fiscal policy can be used for the elimination of external disequilibrium within the eurozone.

Fiscal policy should be coordinated but not uniformly applied. Consequently for the case of Greece as well as for the other eurozone countries with deficits, the improvement in their fiscal situation will have a beneficial influence on their CA deficit, if accompanied by a combination of favorable changes in the net private savings, competitiveness, interest rates and also fiscal adjustments in eurozone countries with surpluses.

Chapter 6 - This chapter examines the "bad bank" solution for a possible future Greek banking crisis which might originate by the accumulation of non-performing loans in banks' loan portfolios. "Bad bank" solution in Greece is apart from all a funding problem and it is not the best solution to be implied because the Greek economy and the Greek banking sector are in a very weak fiscal position. Greek enhancement programme of €28 billion was not enough to stabilize the Greek banking sector and offer sufficient funding in the Greek economy. In order to prevent possible future liquidity crisis, there is need to improve liquidity buffer (safe assets) of the Greek banking sector which means higher capital adequacy standards to limit liquidity risk and implement better risk management. A combination of mergers and acquisitions would be the best solution.

Chapter 7 - This chapter synthesizes the picture of Greek state, regional and local policies supporting business and SME growth between 1995 and 2002, incorporated within the broader EU Cohesion and Regional Policy framework. Then, it introduces a new microeconomic methodology to assess their national-level impact. Synthesizing the picture of policies for business and SME growth is a difficult task for any state, as they have to be contextualized first. Hence, a more general introductory discussion is held on main useful points for evaluating business and SME state-support policies: their different origin, focus and targets, what is often seen as a policy fragmentation, the policy interaction and timing, the need to distinguish between recipient and non-recipient firms and other issues that are discussed and taken into account in policy assesment studies (as from [1] to [12]). Assessing the effects of state-level policies on business growth should investigate their particular association, by focusing especially on policy recipients. If policies target at the broader change of local and regional environments, a focus should be given on the role of these environments, by taking into account at the same time that firms receive influence from their more specific rather than the more general, external environment, as discussed in organization theory ([13],[14],[15]). A large representative sample of SMEs is used, surviving between 1995 and 2002. Data are collected from different sources. Business level data are drawn from the Greek VAT database. Information on the local and regional environment is collected from the respective local and regional accounts. Policy status information is drawn from the Greek Integrated Information System. Business growth is measured as cross-sectional change between the final and initial year. After removing growth outliers, the means and medians of assisted and non-assisted firms are compared. By matching these results with those found in the OLS and ANOVA models produced that make use of dummies, a conclusion is reached on the positive policy impact on business and SME growth. The models high-light the significance of capital and labour variables, as suggested in neo-classical theory and expected from various readings in literature. As several of the local and regional level variables are not found to significantly associate with business growth variables, the overall success of policies in delivering business growth is put under question. More intense changes at the local and regional environment are needed or changes focusing more upon business and SME growth outcomes. Furthermore, more study is needed to shed light on the causes of limited success. The use of new assesment methods and tools (as those found in [2] to [12]) could reveal the needs in institutional building, in developing and using local and regional instruments and mechanisms, emphasizing the delivery of more successful business and SME growth outcomes.

Chapter 8 - The Common Agricultural Policy (CAP) has been many times quoted as one of the most important drivers for the agricultural sector in the European countries and its adverse effects on the environment. Various approaches have been used to investigate the actual links between the two. In this research effort the use of datamining techniques have been used in order to determine what are the links, if any, between the funding provided by the CAP to Greece during the 2nd Programming Period (1994-1999) and the changes in the agricultural sector during that period and in particular the environmental effects of the programs. The results indicate that the three larger financial programs were having some impact to agricultural production. These programs were the Less Favored Areas program, the Farming Investment Plans program and the New Farmers' program. All this programs were funded in Greece by Measure 1.1 of the 2nd Community Support Framework (CSF) for Greece. The main field of environmental investment for the Farming Investment Plans was drop irrigation but this amounted only to 2% of the total investment plans for the whole of the country. On the other hand, no direct linkage with the agricultural production of the three Accompanying Measures of the EU CAP was observed. These Measures were the Organic production program, the Rare Animal Breeds Preservation program and the Reduction of Nitrates Pollution program. Although these programs are more directed towards environmental protection, their limited impact is hardly surprising since these three programs have a narrow scope with regard to areas affected as well as funds provided. The results confirm that the link between the CAP and the agricultural sector size exists but the actual impact of the environmental reform of the CAP during the 90s had hardly any effect in Greece since it was largely underfunded.

Chapter 9 - This chapter looks at the political economy of the Greek crisis arguing that it exemplifies a collective action problem. Emphasis is placed on the domestic and European levels of policy as they have become increasingly interlinked especially since Greece's eurozone membership. Long before the outbreak of the 2008 global financial turmoil it was argued that the international financial architecture needed strengthening and better regulation. The 'domino' effect of the American mortgage crisis displayed the uncertainty over how the global financial market runs and the vulnerability of exposed deeply indebted, economies. As for Greece, at least three decades of undermining public interest and reckless borrowing led the country to an explosive combination of alarming levels of budget and current account deficit. The country's political system proved unable to implement much needed stabilization programs bringing the country's economy in a near collapse in spring 2010. The Greek crisis is definitely an economic and sovereign debt crisis in its expression but it has deeply intertwined political and social ingredients. At the European level, the crisis tested the EU's ability to take swift and efficient action to prevent contagion and hold the eurozone together.

Chapter 10 - Greece initially signed a Memorandum with the European Commission (EC) and the European Central Bank (ECB) that was followed by further agreements in order to get financial assistance and to avoid a total collapse of its economy following the severe international economic crisis. The Memorandum and the subsequent agreements, apart from its suggestions for the economy, offer detailed steps for structural reforms that affect all public services in Greece. One of the most important aspects of the structural reforms is the reduction of the size of the state. This chapter applies Hall's framework of policy change and claims that Greece is facing the possibility of a paradigm shift in its administrative structure. Empirical data from current public administration reforms such as the local government reform 'Kallikratis' and the transparency reform 'Cl@rity' are discussed in order to evaluate the process up to now and whether a new coherent model exists.

Chapter 11 - According to the General Inspector of Greek Public Administration, only one per cent of corruption in the Greek public sector is detected and Greek state fraud losses from corrupted public servants are estimated to 20 billion Euros annually. This is a great amount if we bear in mind that since May 2010, the European Union, the European Central Bank and the International Monetary Fund, approved a joint, 110 billion Euros financing package to help Greece ride out its debt crisis, revive growth and modernize the economy. This chapter examines occupational fraud in the Greek Public Sector and suggests the steps that can be taken to avoid and combat it. It has become clear in the anti - money laundering field that having co-equal programs "to know your customer" and "to know your employee" are essential. Implementing a Know Your Employee program and methods from anti - money laundering and anti - fraud field, relevant with fictitious payments to employees, administration of Greek public sector can detect and prevent occupational fraud. Using direct and indirect methods such as behavior profile of employees, Benford's Law, job rotation, segregation of duties and others, administration of Greek public sector can restore a climate of mistrust and reduce occupational fraud. The authors' proposals offer important solutions for political analysts, politicians and society as a whole.

Chapter 12 - Nowadays digital transactions are part of our everyday life. The info-communication globalisation becomes a fact of life for civil society worldwide, involving many actors – politicians, activists, non-governmental organisations, info-communication firms, software providers and political parties. This raises obvious questions for the role of new communications technologies, the recent Greek crisis, the info-communication public sphere, participatory democracy and the digital form of currencies. As the info-communication public sphere gets more complex and chaotic, regular citizens/users/consumers are gaining access to digital entertainment, information and education anywhere and at anytime.

This chapter examines and analyses the role of the info-communication globalisation in recent Greek crisis. It introduces the info-communication public sphere and the participatory democracy as analytical 'tools' to examine the Greek crisis. Moreover, it analyses the Greek crisis together with the recent crisis in the USA. Finally, it strongly recommends that a practical way for Greece and the USA to emerge from the recent crisis is: to switch off the physical form of the Euro and dollar currencies, i.e. the cash payments using different currencies such as the Euro and the Dollar and switch on the digital form of single currency the Global Info-Cash (GIG), i.e. the info-cash payment using the digital subdivision of the Global Info-Cash, such as Info-CashGR and Info-CashUSA.

Chapter 13 - The liberation of Greece from Nazi occupation in October 1944 gave birth to hopes that the country would find its pace and a new era would emerge despite the disasters brought by the war. These hopes were soon gone when, in December 1944, the first battles began in Athens between the forces of ELAS (Greek People's Liberation Army), and the British forces and Greek armed groups supporting the legitimate government of George Papandreou. This civil war which lasted until 1949, as well as the real commencement of Cold War in 1947 that is connected to the Greek civil war, have marked Greek foreign policy in a decisive manner. Greece had no other option but to join the West. This purpose of this chapter is to make an assessment of Greek foreign policy since the end of World War II.

Chapter 14 - The chapter focuses on understanding the main driving forces behind union and labor market organization in Greece. It concentrates on the period since the fall of the dictatorship in 1974, up to the present, but were necessary references are made to earlier periods. The particular characteristics of labor market formation and union organization are examined in light of the distinctive model of economic development followed in Greece and its turbulent political history. Greece has evolved during the post war period from a poor agricultural country to a modern service economy. The cost of this rapid change has been a highly segmented labor market and poor institutionalization of union organizations.

Chapter 15 - The objective of this chapter is to provide an overview of Corporate Social Responsibility (CSR) in Greece and denote challenges that need to be met in order to further promote socially responsible business behaviour in the domestic economy. Drawing from prior literature, the analysis is built around three basic questions in relation to the Greek context: How is CSR perceived by Greek business professionals? How is CSR practiced in Greece? And how strategic CSR can help overcome the downturn the Greek economy faces nowadays? The extant empirical work suggests that, while CSR in Greece appears to be developing, there is still scope for improvement and further diffusion of relevant practices. While some of the patterns shaping CSR in Greece have been analysed, much work still remains to be carried out in extending and deepening our knowledge in this part of Europe.

Chapter 16 - This chapter reports the findings of exploratory research conducted in Greece aiming to identify what image the Greek younger generation has of modern Greeks. Nearly 200 children aged 12-15 participated in this research depicting modern Greeks' internal (psychological and personality) and external (physical) features. The methodological approaches used for data collection were focus group interviews and human figure drawing. Children were asked to draw a representative Greek person regardless of gender and to depict as many as possible internal and external traits in their drawings. Afterwards, they were stimulated to discuss their drawings in groups and to express their perceptions of modern Greeks. The findings of this study indicate that the younger generation perceives the national self through a critical lens attaching to modern Greeks not only positive characteristics but negative as well. They underline the direct link with ancient Greeks, the view that modern Greeks can rightfully be considered as European and the superiority of the national self in relation to some other nations. They point out that modern Greeks develop rather racist attitudes in regards to specific countries. The participants of this research also underline how social and political circumstances influence them in terms of the way they perceive their national self and suggest what should be changed in the social and political context in order for modern Greeks to develop a better state and national profile.

Chapter 17 - The role of women (and specifically those involved in the fisheries) on the island of Evia (Central Greece), the second biggest island in the country, was depicted through an extended survey. Evia is a significant fishing area, in terms of fishing fleets and number of fish farms. The field research was based on semi-structured interviews and on the usage of proper questionnaires. These were addressed to professional fishermen, owners of fish farms and conversion plants, women occupied in fish farms, local associations and local cooperatives.

The data collected refers to the economic situation of the family, the structure of the family, the social status and the educational level. Care was taken that the interviewed were covering a minimum of 5% in each category. Data was also used from the last National (Greek) census. The women on the island of Evia play a secondary role, in relation to males, in all fields of activity. The majority of fishermen's wives is not employed, but belongs to the category of assisting spouses. They have a lower educational level than their husbands, and their participation in public affairs is very limited. The women who are working do so, mainly in the primary sector (most commonly in the fisheries), and secondarily in the tertiary sector, usually in tourism or in the service field (in the urban areas). In fish farming, women are working independently from their husband's involvement in the field. Most of the women

(59%) are workers, 27% are clerks in the offices and 14% are technological or scientific staff. In the cooperatives, the role of women is also secondary: they do not participate in the administration, being mainly involved in the production and marketing of the products.

In: Greece: Economics, Political and Social Issues
Editor: Panagiotis Liargovas

ISBN: 978-1-62100-944-3
© 2012 Nova Science Publishers, Inc.

Chapter 1

INTRODUCTION

Panagiotis Liargovas[*]
University of Peloponnese,
Department of Economics, Tripolis, Greece

Greece is experiencing an unprecedented economic crisis. In fact, Greece experiences the historic failure of the post-democratic developmental model, a model based on extensive statism, weak institutions, lack of credibility in economic policy, non-implementation of structural reforms, political clientelism and non-respect of the rule of the law.

THE EXTENSIVE STATISM

I deeply believe that the state has an important role to play in the economy. In particular, the state must intervene and provide solutions whereas the markets fail, in areas such as public safety, defense, etc. But the state should not replace the market. It should regulate the market, but not being itself a player within the market. Over the past thirty years we have seen the Greek state in various roles:

- To participate in the production of agricultural products, industrial products (clothes, weapons, chemicals, submarines) and services (air, rail, hotel, gambling, casinos, banking)
- To impose maximum prices on a number of basic goods
- To control the entry and exit of new entrepreneurs in several professions

The managers of State Organizations and Enterprises (SOEs) were (and still are) usually frustrated politicians, who used to manage these SOEs not according to market criteria (e.g. efficiency), but based upon political considerations aiming at their future election in the Greek parliament.

---

[*] E-mail address: liargova@uop.gr

Until recently, concepts such as "competition", "entrepreneurship", "efficiency", "effectiveness", "profitability" and "competitiveness" were inexistent in the public dialogue, and if one claimed them, he/she immediately had the "curse" of being "neo-liberal".

WEAK INSTITUTIONS

Institutions are the most valuable assets of a society. Only when institutions function, the state operates effectively and serves the interests of its citizens. However, in the years after the dictatorship, there were not strong institutions in Greece. Or if there were institutions, these were not well designed. Some noticeable examples include the Greek National Statistical Authority (which was converted into a data manipulation tool), the lack of competitive markets and the frequency of new tax laws.

Moreover, good formal institutions were either not implemented or altered in practice. A typical example is the provision of the Constitution regarding expropriations. Its non-implementation contributed to a general liquidity of property rights. In its turn, this affected the inflow and the quality of Foreign Direct Investments in Greece. Another example is the creation of independent administrative authorities. Although these are the most important institutions worldwide, in Greece, there is some disharmony between them, caused by the differences in their legal status. Only some of them were established constitutionally (The Data Protection Authority, the National Council for Radio and Television (NCRTV), the Hellenic Authority for Communication Security and Privacy, the Ombudsman and the Independent Council of Personnel Selection (ASEP). Others, e.g. the Hellenic Competition Commission, the National Telecommunications and Post Commission (EETT) are not. For the latter ones there are several doubts about their real independent status, since their heads are appointed by the government and not by the parliament.

The process of accession of Greece into the EMU, however, has forced Greece to implement a number of institutions as well as fiscal restrictions. For example, Greek governments were supposed to achieve the targets of the Stability and Growth Pact, to participate in "mutual monitoring" and to provide relevant data to Eurostat. They were also pledged to implement three Regional Development Plans and draft budgets. But the EU financial rules were not as strict as the monetary rules. Countries like Germany and France did not respect them, thus paving the way for similar abuses in others countries, like Greece and their replacement by other informal "institutions" such as clientelism and rent-seeking.

THE LACK OF CREDIBILITY IN ECONOMIC POLICY

A common practice of governments in recent years in Greece is time inconsistency, i.e. the lack of correlation between pre-election announcements and post-election measures. An example of this practice is the pre-election announcement not to impose additional taxes. To justify this inconsistency, the ruling parties usually claimed that before the elections they thought that the situation was different compared to the one they found after the elections. The final result was that private operators were surprised and confused and the government used to lose its credibility, which is one of the strongest tools of economic policy.

THE NON-IMPLEMENTATION OF STRUCTURAL REFORMS AND CLIENTELISM

All previous years there was no decisive political will to implement structural reforms. Politicians used to behave as entrepreneurs, operating rationally, thus serving primarily their own interests, i.e. maximizing the political profits i.e. votes. They were in a constant interaction with all kinds of vested interests and used to overlook the "public interest". Clientelism played also a significant role in strengthening this interplay between politicians and vested interests. Entrepreneurs had requests for selective protection and support mechanisms whereas workers had requests for special benefits. So everybody had close relations with the state, because the state was the main "client". And politicians had more votes and sometimes illegal economic benefits. The socialist governments of the '80s played an important role in the consolidation and legitimation of this situation and also cultivated the illusion that the state support and protection would continue in the future, perhaps with other means.

THE NON-RESPECT OF THE RULE OF THE LAW

Another black spot of modern political economy in Greece is the lack of respect towards the laws e.g. non-application of anti-smoking law, the occupation of streets, public schools and universities by a group of people during a political demonstration. The right of free expression should be respected but not at the expense of other citizens. The rule of law has been considered as one of the key dimensions that determine the quality and good governance of a country.

But since 2009, the Greek economy was affected by the world financial crisis. The crisis affected the public sector and the real economy. It soon turned to a debt and liquidity crisis. Despite its negative effects on the real economy, it is safe to say that the current economic crisis creates conditions of "creative destruction" in the Greek economy and society. The purpose of this book is then to shed some light on this aspect of Greek life. The structure of the volume is as follows.

In the first section seven chapters approach the Greek economy from a mainstream and a political economy perspective, offering an outline and an overview of the current economic crisis as well as an analysis of significant economic sectors in the Greek economy.

In particular, *Panos Kazakos* deals with the politics of economic stabilization and reform in Greece. The focus is specifically on the changes in economic and social policies characterized by a transition from statist designs to ambivalent liberal reforms. The analysis, covering the entire time span from 1974 on to the present, is a tale of an ultimately failed liberal adjustment. He explains this by applying mainly soft public choice approaches about interest-based behavior; (institutionalist) references to path–dependent political norms and practices and formal rules of the game; and, inevitably, ideas, while allowing for the impact of multilateral arrangements and crisis as external inducements to reform.

Panagiotis Evangelopoulos concentrates on the most recent economic policies since 2004 when the conservative government was elected. Although the conservative government realized some crucial reforms, privatizations and public-private partnerships, neither it completed them nor it expanded them in the main institutional structure of the Greek economy and finally it failed to organize a new type of economy based on the robustness of private sector and supported by an efficient and operational public sector. He concludes that the austerity measures of the succeeding socialist government are unlikely to succeed if the new economic authority does not limit dramatically the size of the public sector and does not restore the economic rationality in Greek economy on the path of Classical Economic Liberalism.

Pantelis Sklias supports that the normative neoclassical framework of analysis does not provide an adequate insight and explanatory basis of the current crisis since it does not consider the historical context within which this phenomenon has been taking place. According to him, the Greek crisis can be seen as the result of inadequate institutional building and poor political performance during the last 30 years. Europeanization and modernization of the 90's have not been supported by the necessary institutions. Incomplete measures of the EMU mechanism have exacerbated the situation. High economic performance did not coincide with the low level of political and institutional development in the country. It is shown empirically that the lack of political and institutional development is a causal factor of the Greek crisis which could have been avoided otherwise.

In her contribution, *Nikolina Kosteletou* examines the relationship between fiscal and current account deficits. She shows that the increase in external deficit is related to the expansionary fiscal policy in Greece and in other Southern European countries. The twin deficit hypothesis is empirically verified for the period 1991-2010. It is found that not only fiscal policy of these countries affects their Current Account deficits, but also fiscal policy of the eurozone surplus countries of the North has a role to play. Interdependence among the countries of the eurozone suggests that fiscal policy can be used for the elimination of external disequilibrium within the eurozone. Fiscal policy should be coordinated but not uniformly applied. Consequently for the case of Greece as well as for the other eurozone countries with deficits, the improvement in their fiscal situation will have a beneficial influence on their CA deficit, if accompanied by a combination of favorable changes in the net private savings, competitiveness, interest rates and also fiscal adjustments in eurozone countries with surpluses.

Panagiotis Liargovas and Spyridon Repousis examine the "bad bank" solution for a possible future Greek banking crisis, which might originate by the accumulation of non-performing loans in banks' loan portfolios. A "Bad bank" solution in Greece is apart from all a funding problem and it is not the best solution to be implied because the Greek economy and the Greek banking sector are in a very weak fiscal position. Greek enhancement programme of €28 billion was not enough to stabilize the Greek banking sector and offer sufficient funding in the Greek economy. In order to prevent possible future liquidity crisis, there is a need to improve the liquidity buffer (safe assets) of the Greek banking sector which means higher capital adequacy standards to limit liquidity risk and implement better risk management. A combination of mergers and acquisitions would be the best solution.

Konstantinos Ikonomou synthesizes the picture of the Greek state, by looking at regional and local policies supporting business and SME growth between 1995 and 2002, incorporated within the broader EU Cohesion and Regional Policy framework. Then, he introduces a new microeconomic methodology to assess their national-level impact. Assessing the effects of state-level policies on business growth should investigate their particular association, by focusing especially on policy recipients. The models highlight the significance of capital and labour variables, as suggested in neo-classical theory and expected from various readings in literature. As several of the local and regional level variables are not found to significantly associate with business growth variables, the overall success of policies in delivering business growth is put under question. He suggests changes at the local and regional environment or changes focusing more upon business growth outcomes. The use of new assessment methods and tools could reveal the needs in institutional building, in developing and using local and regional instruments and mechanisms, emphasizing the delivery of more successful business growth outcomes.

Antonis Vorlou and Joanna Kastritsi-Catharios use datamining techniques to determine the links, between the funding provided by the CAP to Greece during the 2nd Programming Period (1994-1999) and the changes in the agricultural sector during that period and in particular the environmental effects of the programs. The results indicate that the three larger financial programs were having some impact to agricultural production. On the other hand, no direct linkage with the agricultural production of the 3 Accompanying Measures of the EU-CAP was observed. The results confirm that the link between the CAP and the agricultural sector size exists but the actual impact of the environmental reform of the CAP during the 90s had hardly any effect in Greece since it was largely underfunded.

In the second section of the volume the focus is turned on the political issues affecting Greece. Emphasis is given to the political explanations of the Greek crises, the necessity of administrative reforms as well as to cultural issues.

Panagiota Manoli looks at the political economy of the Greek crisis arguing that it exemplifies a collective action problem. Emphasis is placed on the domestic and European levels of policy as they have become increasingly interlinked especially since Greece's eurozone membership. Greece's political system proved unable to implement much needed stabilization programs bringing the country's economy in a near collapse in spring 2010. According to the author, the Greek crisis is definitely an economic and sovereign debt crisis in its expression but it has deeply intertwined political and social ingredients. At the European level, the crisis tested the EU's ability to take swift and efficient action to prevent contagion and hold the eurozone together. With so many players (national governments, European institutions, the ECB, credit rating agencies, interest groups and so on) and diverse interests and preferences it is not all surprising that the initial response to the Greek crisis (a solution orchestrated by Brussels) was a sub-optimal one. Still, the management of the financial crisis points to the role of politics, or the lack of it.

Stela Ladi applies Hall's framework of policy change and claims that Greece is facing the possibility of a paradigm shift in its administrative structure. Empirical data from current public administration reforms such as the local government reform 'Kallikratis' and the transparency reform 'Cl@rity' are discussed in order to evaluate the process up to now and to investigate whether a new coherent model exists.

Panagiotis Liargovas and Spyridon Repousis examine occupational fraud in the Greek Public Sector and suggest the steps that can be taken to avoid and combat it. It has become clear in the anti - money laundering field that having co-equal programs "to know your customer" and "to know your employee" are essential. Implementing a Know Your Employee program and methods from anti - money laundering and anti - fraud field, relevant with fictitious payments to employees, administration of Greek public sector can detect and prevent occupational fraud. Using direct and indirect methods such as behavior profile of employees, Benford's Law, job rotation, segregation of duties and others, administration of

Greek public sector can restore a climate of mistrust and reduce occupational fraud. Their proposals offer important solutions for political analysts, politicians and society as a whole.

George Gantzias, focuses on the role of the info-communication globalization in recent Greek crisis. It introduces the info-communication public sphere and the participatory democracy as analytical 'tools' to examine the Greek crisis. Moreover, it analyses the Greek crisis together with the recent crisis in the USA. Finally, it strongly recommends that a practical way for Greece and the USA to emerge from the recent crisis is: to switch off the physical form of the Euro and dollar currencies, i.e. the cash payments using different currencies such as the Euro and the Dollar and switch on the digital form of single currency the Global Info-Cash (GIG), i.e. the info-cash payment using the digital subdivision of the Global Info-Cash, such as Info-CashGR and Info-CashUSA.

The last chapter of this section, written by *Charalambos Tsardanidis* makes an assessment of Greek foreign policy since the end of World War II. The liberation of Greece from Nazi occupation in October 1944 gave birth to hopes that the country would find its pace and a new era would emerge despite the disasters brought by the war. These hopes were soon gone when, in December 1944, the first battles began in Athens between the forces of ELAS (Greek People's Liberation Army), and the British forces and Greek armed groups supporting the legitimate government of George Papandreou. This civil war which lasted until 1949, as well as the real commencement of Cold War in 1947 that is connected to the Greek civil war, have marked Greek foreign policy in a decisive manner. Greece had no other option but to join the West. Greece's membership of the EU was meant to guarantee a number of important advantages for its foreign policy.

The third section of the book includes chapters related to social issues such as labor, corporate social responsibility, images of Greek younger generation and the role of women.

Stella's Zambarloukou chapter focuses on understanding the main driving forces behind union and labor market organization in Greece. It concentrates on the period since the fall of the dictatorship in 1974. The particular characteristics of labor market formation and union organization are examined in light of the distinctive model of economic development followed in Greece and its turbulent political history. Greece has evolved during the post war period from poor agricultural country to a modern service economy. The cost of this rapid change has been a highly segmented labor market and poor institutionalization of union organizations.

Antonis Skouloudis and Konstantinos Evangelinos provide an overview of corporate social responsibility (CSR) in Greece and denote challenges that need to be met in order to further promote socially responsible business behaviour in the domestic economy. The extant empirical work suggests that, while CSR in Greece appears to be developing, there is still scope for improvement and further diffusion of relevant practices.

Chrysa Tamisoglou reports the findings of an exploratory research conducted in Greece aiming to identify what image the Greek younger generation has of modern Greeks. The findings of this study indicate that the younger generation perceives the national self through a critical lens attaching to modern Greeks not only positive characteristics but negative as well. They underline the direct link with ancient Greeks, the view that modern Greeks can rightfully be considered as European and the superiority of the national self in relation to some other nations. They point out that modern Greeks develop rather racist attitudes in regards to specific countries.

The last chapter by *Joanna Castritsi-Catharios and Matsiori Steriani* examines the role of women (and specifically those involved in the fisheries) in the island of Evia (Central Greece), the second biggest island in the country, through an extended survey. The women in the island of Evia play a secondary role in relation to males in all fields of activity. The majority of the wives of fishermen is not employed but belongs to the category of assisting spouses. They have a lower educational level against their husbands while their participation in the public affairs is very limited. The women who are working do so in the primary sector mainly (most commonly in the fisheries) and secondarily in the tertiary sector, usually in tourism or in the field of services (in the urban areas). In the fish farming, women are working independently of their husband's involvement in the field.

PART I: ECONOMIC ISSUES

In: Greece: Economics, Political and Social Issues
Editor: Panagiotis Liargovas

ISBN: 978-1-62100-944-3
© 2012 Nova Science Publishers, Inc.

Chapter 2

STABILIZATION AND REFORM IN A STATIST REGIME, 1974-2011

Panos Kazakos[*]
University of Athens, Department of Political Science
and Public Administration, Athens, Greece

ABSTRACT

This chapter deals with the politics of economic stabilization and reform in Greece and addresses questions already raised in the literature. The focus is specifically on the changes in economic and social policies characterized by a transition from statist designs to ambivalent liberal reforms. Thereby, we do not address one policy field alone but look at a number of core issues or policies that include fiscal discipline, product and labor market reforms, privatization, pensions and environment. The analysis, covering the entire time span from 1974 on to the present, is a tale of an ultimately failed liberal adjustment. To explain it we apply mainly soft public choice approaches about interest-based behavior; (institutionalist) references to path–dependent political norms and practices and formal rules of the game; and, inevitably, ideas, while allowing for the impact of multilateral arrangements and crisis as external inducements to reform. The course of things and the exemplifications we provide invite to a reexamination of the ultimate balance between institutionalized coordination mechanisms of the EU and domestic forces.

INTRODUCTION

Greece is assessed as a case of unstable stabilization and unfinished reform [1], leaving the country without defenses against the 2008-2009 financial crisis and recession. This is even more important, considering that Greece joined the euro zone in 2001.

Greece experienced significant political and economic changes since 1974. To understand what happened since 1974 we divide the whole era in two periods: the first one

---

[*] E-mail address: Pan41kaz@otenet.gr.

ended in 1989-90; the second covers the rest of the time to the present crisis (2010-2011). We begin with explaining the initial situation in the late 70's and early 80's. The following section outlines the mounting difficulties of the populist management of the economy during the 80's. Populism has been associated with a strong expansion of state interventionism by the socialist movement (PASOK). The third section gives a short account of the admittedly hesitant, politically difficult and ultimately unsuccessful attempts to stabilize the economy and reform policies since the beginning of the 90's up until 2008-10 and explains how they interacted with European integration. A section then focuses on the current fiscal and economic crisis 2009-11. The final section raises some more fundamental questions about the tensions between international economic environment and domestic factors. Understanding what went wrong is potentially of some academic and political importance.

TRANSITION TO DEMOCRACY AND EXPANSION OF STATE INTERVENTIONISM IN THE LATE '70S

After the collapse of the dictatorship (1974), democratic governments had to cope with a set of difficult problems- the military defeat on Cyprus, the first oil crisis and the multiplications of expectations for better economic conditions. So far as the economy was concerned, the then governing party of new Democracy, a coalition of centre-right forces, extended state interventionism through harsh nationalizations and rapidly increasing public expenditure. The size of the state grew from roughly 33% (1973) to almost 40% of the GDP (1981). The course was expected to consolidate democracy against rising anti-capitalist sentiment reflected in the rise of the Panhellenic Socialist Movement (Pasok) under A. Papandreou [2].

After the breakdown of the authoritarian regime 1967-1974 Greece experienced an astonishing renewal of its post-war statist economic policy paradigm. The process was paradoxically led by the New Democracy party (ND) that declared itself as radical liberal[3][4]. The government of K. Karamanlis drew from some past successes: The post-war statism was initially associated with high growth and remarkably low inflation rates. Later on however, roughly since the end-70's it proved unable to generate growth. After the second energy crisis in 1979 and during the 80's the Greek economy slipped in a prolonged stagnation period, characterized by increasing unemployment, budget deficits, debts and inflation rates as well as worsening productive structures ("de-industrialization").

While reviving post-war statism, the Greek government accelerated integration in the EU and applied in 1975 for full membership without waiting for the full implementation of the Association Agreement of 1962 that entailed transitional provisions extending until 1984. Overlooking some economic and social realities, Prime Minister Konstantinos Karamanlis considered membership as an additional instrument to consolidate the 1974 restored Democracy and as best serving the long-term security interests of Greece. He also linked membership to the survival of the economic model of market economy in the country.

The Commission, however, was rightly concerned over Greece's ability to adapt. According to its opinion presented to the Council in January 1976:

"The Greek economy at its present stage of development contains a number of structural features which limits its ability to combine homogeneously with the economies of the present member states."[5]

To implement the necessary institutional and structural changes, even with the Community's support, would be a very complex and demanding task. Therefore, the Commission recommended a transitional period of some years "before the obligations of membership, even subject to transitional arrangements, are undertaken" (Ibid: 10).

Greece did not accept the opinion of the Commission and pressed ahead for a quick decision on full membership. The Accession Treaty was signed in May 1979 and entered into force on 1 January 1981.

THE SITUATION IN THE '80S: STAGFLATION

In October 1981, shortly after accession, the socialists (PASOK) achieved a sweeping electoral victory. Whilst in opposition the party rejected membership, seeing it as a major obstacle to socialist aspirations As it had declared before assuming governmental responsibilities, EU accession "will consolidate the peripheral role of the country as a satellite in the capitalist system; will render national planning impossible; will seriously threaten Greek industry; and will lead to the extinction of Greek farmers" [6][7]

In government, however, the socialists recognized to a certain degree international political and economic realities but they implemented contradictory policies: They decided not to leave Union in which competition was the norm and at the same time applied extensively traditional socialist instruments.

The socialist governments that dominated the scene until 1989, implemented on the whole, but with a short-lived stabilization effort in 1985-6, economic policies with strong populist characteristics: They increased social expenditure particularly for pensions, nationalized further parts of the Greek industry and banking sector, extended government "guidance" in key sectors, experimented heavily with central planning methods, expanded worker's participation in state owned enterprises and public employment[8]. In 1983 the government established the so called Industrial Restructuring Organization (IRO)– a public holding group for ailing enterprises- and brought under IRO control a big number of private firms for restructuring purposes partially with illegal methods. For many years the IRO managed the firms poorly, absorbed a lot of money and simply subsidized heavily otherwise not viable firms, which were kept in a quasi-public status and exhibited deteriorating performance.

Statism took new forms and penetrated worryingly both the economy and the society. In institutional terms and policy orientation, Greece diverted from its partners in the EU.

Associated with expanding statism was an excessively expansionary macroeconomic policy throughout the '80s. As the OECD commented "the most spectacular and probably the most damaging feature" of the macroeconomic management during the last decade was the steep increase in the public sector deficit[9]. But, supply stagnated. Prominent among the factors responsible for the weak responses to growing demand for goods and services fuelled by fiscal deficits and the influx of EU resources, were initial wage increases and a political climate unfavorable for private initiatives. In the late '80s and early '90s Greece was caught in a stagflationist trap.

In the late '80s budget deficits and public debt expanded worryingly, based on the mistaken crude keynesian assumption, that they would lead to growth recovery. The budget deficit increased from 2.6% GDP (1980) to 16.1% (1990). At the same time inflation jumped again up to 20.4 percent (1990) after a short-lived stabilization period. Total public debt rose from 28.6% GDP in 1980 to 80.7% GDP in 1990[10].

Professor J. Spraos, a leading economist of the Greek Diaspora saw Greece suffering under the so-called "Dutch disease" experienced by the Netherlands during the natural-gas boom there in the '70s. In Greece easy money came not from natural resources but from the EU, whose resources kept the exchange rate high and inflation up, thus putting the rest of the economy under additional pressure. De-industrialization was the result[1].

JOINING THE UNION ON THE ROAD TO EMU: STABILIZATION WITHOUT REFORM

In the meantime the ambitious EU-program to create an internal market by abolishing a whole range of protectionist controls and other practices with similar effects was progressing and rapidly creating a new economic environment. Moreover, in 1991 the Treaties were reformed to establish an economic and monetary union (EMU). Both, internal market and EMU reflected a new, essentially liberal (or monetarist) consensus among European governments. Greece had formally subscribed to it. "Nominal convergence", by which was meant the fulfillment of the so-called "Maastricht criteria" of low inflation, deficit reduction etc as a precondition for participating in the monetary core, became an immediate target in the EU.

In Greece a broad consensus between the major political forces in Greece has been established in the 1990s, that Greece should join EMU (Euro-land) at the earliest possible date. Political reasons seem to have played a crucial role in forming this consensus. The political leadership was (and remains) convinced that only through the EMU participation can the country have a say in important community policy sectors "on an equal footing" with the other member states as Prime Minister K. Simitis repeatedly argued. Participation would also send a clear signal to third countries that Greece is indeed a part of the European gravity centre. Prestige and national identity considerations may also have played a role[11][12]. Since World War II Greece has always seen itself as integral part of the European project and this would be endangered if the country could not join the new ambitious step in the history of integration. But, certainly, economic considerations, for example, to halt the cost of borrowing, cannot be overlooked [13].

Together with the disappointing experience of the '80s, the developing legal and institutional framework of the EU exercised strong pressures to remold economic and social policies and limit the scope for old tailored state interventionism. In the new European (and indeed international) environment the tendency has been for regulation in privatized sectors to replace state administration and public ownership, and for competition to replace multiple forms of protection and monopoly building [14][15].

---

[1] See reference in Panos Kazakos (2001), p. 402.

There has been however an apparent tension between political consensus for the EMU on the one side, and every day politics, on the other. The politics of adjusting to the EMU environment were characterized by inconsistencies and delays. Many forces worked to preserve the status quo.

Early De-Etatization Plans

The first stabilization attempt (1991-1993) failed despite the generous support of the EU in the framework of an agreed stabilization program. The program aimed at both, restoring macroeconomic balance and initiating deep structural adjustments. The centre-right government under Prime Minister K. Mitsotakis (1990-1993) and its economic policy core envisaged, as they put it, an ambitious "de-etatization of the economy". They encountered however broad and strong opposition from organized interests in and around the giant state apparatus and from a public opinion still impressed by the populist promises of the '80s. However the government had succeeded in halting the slippery road to bankrupsy, in accomplishing limited privatization and in stemming the rapidly deteriorating financial position of the pension system.

By that time, the pension system deficiencies had already become apparent and, indeed, threatening. The pension system was extremely complex, fragmented and financially unsafe. The contribution of revenues from employers and employees were (and, despite changes, still are) insufficient to pay for the current (and expected) level of pensions with the resulting deficits financed by the budget. The system distributed state subsidies inequitably, as an official memorandum later pointed out, and gave rise to disincentives for labour mobility, savings, normal retirement and compliance with the contribution rules. Its bureaucracy "often leads to services deficient in quality" and high costs[16]. The variable geometry of the pension system had of course its origins in the particular circumstances of the '50s and '60s as well as in the clientelistic practices of the country.

The 1991 pension reform included sharp increases in contributions rates which placed Greece among the countries with the highest non wage labour cost, eliminated the link of pensions to wages and tightened invalidity eligibility. Through these measures the pension system gained a temporary breath.

Further, public enterprises posed particular problems to the economy. According to an estimation of the Ministry of National Economy it comprised in 1997 nearly 50 enterprises and employed about 130.000 individuals, equivalent to 6 per cent of wage earners. Most of them operated often inefficiently and offered unsatisfactory services or products in terms of cost and quality. They became a burden not only for the state budget, but also for the rest of the economy. In a special feature included in the 1998 country report the OECD located the sources of the poor performance in the pricing policy of the enterprises, in the inflexible labour arrangements and high labour costs, in the extraction of monopoly-power rents by the unions operating in the public sector and in critical investment lags [17].

The poor financial performance of public enterprises required financial assistance from the central government, equivalent to nearly half of Greece's large debt burden (with the latter amounting to nearly 110 per cent of GDP at end-1997). Behind this pathology worked strong clientelistic links between party functionairs, party controlled unions, interested private suppliers with political connections and the government [18].

The liberal-conservative government (1990-1993) initiated a first round of measures to slim down the public enterprises sector. Some initiatives were brought to a positive end (for example the big cement producer AGET has been successfully transferred to private hands) but the whole program of "de-etatization" came to a halt as early as 1993. Several factors were responsible for this early failure, among them the instability of a government which could only count on a marginal majority, a still unfavorable public opinion, internal tensions in the governing party between liberals and conservatives, serious policy design mistakes as a result of lacking experience and an aggressive opposition, dominating the unions of the public sector and still promising to renew the populist politics of the '80s. The etatist tradition in all its versions had deep roots and was sustained by multiple institutional arrangements and informal practices.

Stabilization with Limited Reform and Euro Zone Entry: 1994-2000

A new attempt primarily aiming to stabilize the economy, was vigorously pursued after 1996 by the new prime minister K. Simitis and brought a small but temporary miracle at the stabilization front [19].

On the way to the single currency zone the Central Bank legislation and statute was amended to comply with the Treaty requirements. The prime objective of the Bank of Greece became to ensure price stability as member of the ESCB. The Bank obtained for the first time in the post-war area an independent status.

By the end of 1999 Greece appeared to have re-established macroeconomic balance and fulfilled the Maastricht-criteria as laid down in the Treaty of the EU[2]. Fiscal discipline had been attained although it remained fragile and inflation had been brought in 1999 to the lowest point of 2% (CPI) in almost 30 years to go up again afterwards. Also, growth outstripped the euro area average since 1996 thus achieving real convergence measured in terms of per capita GDP[20]. Growth benefited from the large resource transfers from the EU through the Community Support Framework 1994-1999, lower interest rates and the influx of immigrants that lowered labor costs. Additionally, Greece seemed to improve its overall competitiveness as measured in the World Competitiveness Yearbook. The country ranked 30th (2001) against 36th in 1997 and was now in a comparatively better position than Portugal and Italy [21].

Additionally, some necessary reforms have been implemented on the way to the introduction of euro despite widespread resistance. Liberalization mainly in the telecommunication and banking sector has progressed well. In the telecommunications sector, the privatization limit for the public operators has been lifted and the whole sector is open to competition since early 2001. The banking sector was also liberalized during the '90s in compliance with EU regulation associated with the internal market. The result has been an accelerated restructuring and concentration of private banks and the privatization of some public or state controlled banks.

On 9 March 2000 the Greek government felt in a position to request a re-examination of its convergence situation and, thus, opened the procedure by which the Council could decide

---

[2] See Article 121(1) of the EU-treaty (Maastrict) as well as protocol No 21 on the convergence criteria referred to in Article 121.

on the admission to the single currency of a member state with derogation. After positive assessments by the Commission and the ECB[22], Greece became in June 2000 a full member of the monetary core of the Union dominated by a European Central Bank and promoting the issue of a single currency.

Greece's achievements on the road to the Euro-zone are all the more remarkable as both its budget deficit and inflation rate were at the start (1994/5) four times higher than in the euro-zone member states just a few years earlier and were coupled with stagnation. However, uncertainties overshadowed the convergence project. After Euro-zone accession, Greek fiscal policy seemed to loosen again. A first EU audit in 2002 resulted in a limited upward "correction" of official data about deficits and debts but a second one in 2004/5 revealed more serious problems with official data and extensive "creative accounting" by the government[23]. Moreover, Greek fiscal position was considered to be unsustainable on the long run [24]. The country's Achilles' heel was the underlying structural and institutional problems.

The euro-zone accession was the culmination of ten years of effort to keep pace with the most ambitious integration project of the EU. From a political point of view the success should have meant that the political system of Greece would henceforth need to work inside a more narrowly defined action field, defined by the Growth and Stability Pact and competition in the internal market.

Amidst broad euphoria [25] the government recognized that[3]

> "the success of macroeconomic policies depends on, inter alia, the smooth functioning of individual markets: the goods, services, capital and labour markets [...] To ensure that the Greek economy remains dynamic and competitive in the new economic environment, we will pursue a prudent fiscal policy, and undertake all the necessary structural reforms to improve the functioning of markets and increase the potential output of the economy so as to ensure high rates of growth with low inflation [26]"

However, many of the reform measures adopted in the last half of the 90's were the result of compromising with the strong unions of the public sector, which in turn make it impossible to achieve declared goals. For example, the so-called partial privatization (sell of minority shares) did not lessen the control of the union-party-ministerial bureaucracy upon the enterprises nor diminished the influence (through party links) of privileged suppliers. Two attempts to restructure Olympic Airawys failed [27]. The labour market law adopted in December 2000 increased bureaucracy, not flexibility in the labour markets. And the planed fusion of the pension funds of the bank sector would in fact weaken the general Social Insurance Foundation (IKA) by taking out of it the pension funds of private banks and consolidating already existing pension privileges of the state bank employees.

Similar observations can be made with regard of the government-party-business relationships. The new European environment has indeed generated more intense competition in many sectors, but in crucial sectors individual firms or groups gained privileged access to public construction and procurement through a combination of clever political connections,

---

[3] In an optimistic mood, the first Stabilization and Growth Program reiterated that "...the entrance of Greece in the euro zone from January 2001 marks the start of a new era for Greece by creating the right conditions for sustainable growth." Hellenic Republic- Ministry of National Economy and Finance "The 2000 Stability and Growth Program", Athens, December 2000Ibid, p. 19.

electoral grants, control of mass media and ownership of popular sport clubs, thus. Reforms, such as partial privatizations have not changed much in the way the system works.

The Day after: Greece in the Euro-Zone: 2001-2009
It is broadly accepted that EMU has wide implications even in policy areas that remain in the responsibility of national governments and have not been directly addressed by the Maastricht Treaty such as labour markets policy, state productive activities and social policy. EMU and the EU as a whole have acted as a powerful catalyst for domestic reform in all member countries. The debate at EU level ran under the heading "conditions for the success of EMU".

Modernization Abandoned: 2001-2004
Greek officials have recognised, in philosophical as well as practical terms that Greece, stabilisation apart, was after Euro-zone entry faced with the additional challenges of stepping-up the structural reforms required to prepare the economy for the demanding competitive environment of monetary union. [4]

The Bank of Greece resumed regularly the debate on structural adjustment *inter alia* on the occasion of its Annual Report [28] [5]. In the Bank of Greece reports, successive governors (N. Garganas, Lucas Papademos, G. Provopoulos) called for accelerated structural reforms in order to cope with the challenges generated by the EMU membership. Structural changes, they reiterated again and again, were necessary if the country wanted to cope with the challenges of stable money (the Euro) and to maintain a high growth rate and create more jobs. They particularly stressed, that the government needed to open up key markets, implement consistently privatizations, upgrade the education system and create a favourable environment for business. N. Garganas, the deputy-governor of the Bank of Greece, sees structural adjustment as closely interrelated with the need of coping with eventual shocks. [6]

But, after the introduction of Euro, discipline weakened. In many ways the discipline effect of the euro system proved to be greater when applying for membership in the Euro-zone than afterwards. Greece continued to experience over-indebtedness despite EMU commitments and despite agreement among experts that mounting public debt imposes large costs on present (through interest rates) and future generations. Deficit reduction on a sustainable base was repeatedly postponed and the state of public finances regularly obscured through creative accounting. The lowest deficit was 3.2% in 1999!

Reforms were watered down or abandoned. The pension system is a good example to illustrate reform delay. According to the OECD, the Greek system was in a far more shaky position than in higher income countries as illustrated in the present value of *net* (uncovered by contributions) future pension liabilities of the order of 200% of GDP[29]. The socialist government recognized that changes could not be postponed for long. The Government reassured in the "Stability and Growth Program 2000-2004" that the reform of the social security system, "in light of the adverse demographics forecast for the medium-term", was on

---

[4] Speech of the minister Yiannos Papantoniou in a conference organized by the Bank of Greece, on 16 June, 2001 in honour of the accession to the euro zone, *Athens News*, 17 June 2000.
[5] Bank of Greece *Annual Report of the Governor 2000*, 2005, 2007, 2008, 2009, Athens, and earlier issues.
[6] See his address on *" Integrating Greece into the Euro Area: The challenges ahead"* at the "Athens Summit 1999", 18 September 1999, mimo.

the agenda for immediate action[7]. It had twice, in 1998 and 2000, commissioned studies to prepare the ground for a deep reform. The first study, conducted under the lead of Prof. Spraos has been quickly withdrawn after sharp reactions of the unions and party segments, arguing that the study reflected a "neo-liberal" spirit already tested in General Pinochet's Chile! The second study, commissioned to the British Government Actuaries had not a better receive inside and outside the government camp. The study was completed in March 2001 and was followed by a formal proposal of the minister Tassos Giannitsis to the social partners.

The report of the British Government Actuary's Department concluded in a rather cautious phrasing that the Greek pension system needs from a long-term point of view more than "parametric" changes. On this basis of a report [30] the labour minister T. Yiannitsis presented proposals that left basic features at the heart of the Greek pension system untouched. He rejected diluting the public character of the system or introducing of privately-financed provisions for old age or limiting the so-called pay-as-you-go principle. Instead, the government proposed a prolongation of working life to 65 years for men and women and even for those working in hazardous professions, a lowering of the pension benefits (as percentage of the wage) and cutting the number of public pension funds, which produces red tape and covers big inequalities in the pension benefits [31].

The Labour Confederation, led by representatives of the public sector unions, rejected any negotiation on this base and met the government on the streets. After an impressive protest demonstration, the biggest for many years, and a general strike on May 17, 2001, the whole procedure was stalled[8]. Leading party and government figures denounced the proposal as "neo-liberal". The Unions presented lastingly an alternative defending essentially the status quo[32] and demanding more transfers from the budget. The project failed. The efforts to reform Greek pension system would be resumed only six years later, in 2007 [33].

Another telling example was a bill on labour market reform that the government passed in December 2000 through the parliament. The bill tackled the remaining impediments to part-time employment but it also includes mandatory premiums and detailed limits for overtime work. It also limited the discretion of the management in handling questions of over-time work. The Federation of Greek industrialists criticized that the bill increases labor cost by roughly 14% and that it was counter-productive in view of the demanding preparations of the firms for the transition to the euro currency.

Things changed after the fiscal crisis of 2010 (see below) confirming somehow that an economic crisis is likely to induce necessary reforms.

"Reinventing the State" Fails: 2004-2009

In 2004 the liberal-conservative ND came back to power promising *inter alia* to fight corruption and to "reinvent the state". On both promises the record was poor. Between 2002 and 2004 there has been evidence of widespread misreporting of deficit and debt data by the Greek authorities. Following it, the Commission demanded a revision of many data. The significant revision that followed after 2004 has been heavily contested by the socialists but did not resulted in a significant improvement of the quality of data and the institutional framework.

---

[7] Ibid, p. 24.
[8] See newspaper reports from 20th April 2001 onwards.

Under a deficit excessive procedure it also reduced deficits approaching the limit established by the GSP. On the reform front, the government attempted to lower taxes acting in a rather liberal spirit and under the responsibility of the minister of the economy G. Alogoskoufis. But in 2007 deficits began to climb up again because public revenues and expenditure came out of control as a consequence of underlying structural deficiencies (malfunctioning tax authorities, widespread tax evasion, loose legal procedures, corruption, waste in public works and so on). Clientelism flourished.

Even before the 2009 recession, Commission projections had shown that accumulated debt and demographic developments made fiscal sustainability an acute challenge and required both bold fiscal consolidation programs and reforms of social protection. Therefore, Greece appeared to be *"a high long-term risk with regard to the long-term sustainability of public finances"* [34].

Under liberal-conservative rule Greece made some progress in privatizing state-owned enterprises. Two public enterprises producing gargantuan deficits were privatized (Olympic and Commerce Bank) even though with high costs (unreasonably high compensation for 'voluntary' redundancy, taking over existing pension rights and so on) and minority shares of the Telecommunication Company were sold.

Broader reform plans remained unfinished. The laws establishing evaluation procedures for the Universities were not implemented. A new attempt in 2007 to reform the fragmented pensions system emphasizing the merge of a great number of funds generated mainly formal rearrangements. The funds retained their autonomy.

Then, the state of public finances worsened rapidly in 2009 as the crisis reached Greece. The ND-government deployed discretionary measures to counter recession. It implemented a combination of instruments- relaxation of tax collection, tax reductions aimed at stimulating the replacement of old cars, cash transfers to weak groups and expansion of state employment.

The policy response revealed either unjustified optimism with regard to the potential of fiscal activism or confusion and electoral considerations. Thereby the Greek government followed a broader trend in Europe where Governments enacted several rounds of activist fiscal policy during the recession 2008-9, mainly expenditure increases either to save banks or to stimulate the economy. This led to a serious deterioration of fiscal deficits and rapid accumulation of debts in Europe (and elsewhere) [35]. But Greece experienced the most striking deterioration of its fiscal position due to the unfavorable initial conditions. In 2009 the deficit increased from around 6% to 15.5% of GDP and the accumulated debt to over 126% of GDP (see table 1).

The already alarming "sustainability gap" worsened. The government overlooked academic warnings about the effectiveness of fiscal activism and important suggestions for the policy design. The result was that the Council formally regretted the renewed problems in the Greek fiscal statistics in October 2010.

On the whole, policy performance during the last decade was disappointing. Fiscal deficits present a telling story. Greece has not run a balanced budget before and after the introduction of the Euro. The least deficit was -3,2% of GDP in 1999. Debt accumulation went on despite some attempts to bring it under control (see figure 1). The country accumulated debt more than any other member state of the euro zone and until 2009 neither "soft" pressure from the EU nor academic warnings seemed to be taken seriously.

Table 1. Main features of country forecast - Greece

	2009		Annual percentage change						
	bn EUR Curr. prices	% GDP	92-05	2007	2008	2009	2010	2011	2012
GDP	233.1	100.0	3.0	4.3	1.3	-2.3	-4.2	-3.0	1.1
Private consumption	174.4	74.8	3.1	3.1	3.2	-1.8	-4.1	-4.3	0.6
Public consumption	45.4	19.5	2.6	9.2	1.0	7.6	-9.0	-8.5	-6.0
Gross fixed capital formation	40.1	17.2	4.3	5.3	-7.6	-11.4	-17.4	-7.5	-2.6
of which: equipment	17.9	7.7	8.6	21.9	6.2	-12.2	-13.0	-7.3	-3.1
Exports (goods and services)	44.3	19.0	6.3	5.8	4.0	-20.1	0.6	5.1	6.0
Imports (goods and services)	69.5	29.8	5.8	9.8	4.0	-18.6	-12.0	-4.4	-1.6
GNI (GDP deflator)	226.7	97.3	2.8	3.3	1.0	-1.8	-4.3	-3.1	1.0
Contribution to GDP growth: Domestic demand			3.4	4.9	0.9	-2.2	-8.0	-6.0	-1.0
Inventories			-0.1	1.3	0.8	-2.1	-0.1	0.1	0.3
Net exports			-0.4	-2.0	-0.5	2.1	3.9	2.9	1.8
Employment			1.2	1.7	0.2	-0.7	-2.8	-2.6	0.1
Unemployment rate (a)			9.9	8.3	7.7	9.5	12.5	15.0	15.2
Compensation of employees/head			7.9	6.2	6.8	2.3	-1.8	-0.2	0.1
Unit labour costs whole economy			6.0	3.7	5.7	3.9	-0.4	0.1	-0.9
Real unit labour costs			-0.2	0.6	2.4	2.7	-3.2	-1.4	-1.3
Savings rate of households (b)			*	*	*	*	*	*	*
GDP deflator			6.3	3.1	3.2	1.2	3.0	1.5	0.4
Harmonised index of consumer prices			*	3.0	4.2	1.3	4.6	2.2	0.6
Terms of trade of goods			0.0	0.8	-3.3	1.0	1.0	0.1	-0.6
Trade balance (c)			-15.2	-19.7	-20.5	-16.4	-13.1	-11.1	-10.3
Current account balance (c)			-6.3	-15.7	-16.4	-14.0	-10.6	-8.0	-6.5
Net lending(+) or borrowing(-) vis-à-vis ROW (c)			*	-13.5	-15.0	-12.9	-9.5	-6.7	-5.1
General government balance (c)			-6.5	-6.4	-9.4	-15.4	-9.6	-7.4	-7.6
Cyclically-adjusted budget balance (c)			-6.5	-7.7	-10.5	-15.2	-7.4	-4.1	-4.7
Structural budget balance (c)			*	-7.5	-9.7	-14.2	-7.7	-5.3	-6.0
General government gross debt (c)			97.7	105.0	110.3	126.8	140.2	150.2	156.0

(a) Eurostat definition. (b) gross saving divided by gross disposable income. (c) as a percentage of GDP.

A Lost Decade after Euro-Zone Entry?

Greece's fiscal build up was part of a broader trend in advanced economies and that during the period 2007-2010 the increase in real terms of debt in Greece has been rather moderate when compared with what happened in many other countries such as Spain, United Kingdom and United States (see figure 2)[36]. Still, Greece was near default on its external debt in 2010 and its problems seem to be more difficult to cope with. One reason is that the country already had accumulated high debts prior to the crisis and that fiscal profligacy for decades went hand in hand with diminishing competitiveness.

Greece allowed wages to increase much faster than productivity after 2000. Unit labor cost left all other countries of the eurozone far behind, thereby loosing competitiveness. Public sector wage formation set the tempo! Calculations by the Bank of Greece showed that unit labor cost increased between 2000 and 2008 by 28% against less than 2% in Germany [37]. Competitiveness declined constantly since the entry into the eurozone.

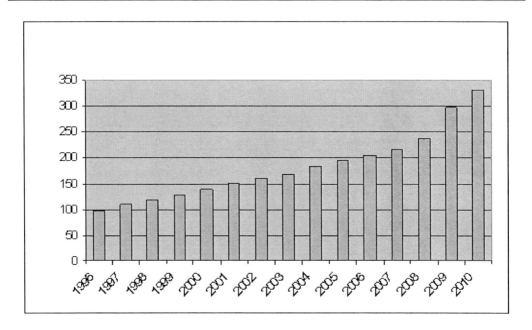

Figure 1. Greece. Accumulated debt 1996-2010. in billion Euros.

Greece also neglected long-term productivity and other structural aspects. Its production structure concentrated on relatively labor intensive sectors confronting competition from low wage countries. Innovation lagged behind. So, Greece saw a threatening build-up of external imbalances which reached levels of around 15% GDP. It became more and more apparent that policy choices were bad. A more fundamental rethink was urgently needed.

Again on the supply side, the country remained unattractive for foreign business trying to invest (see figure 3). There were and still are many reasons why this happens, from corruption and bureaucracy to the difficulties of obtaining secure property rights on land, impunity of corrupt corners in politics and administration and prevailing anti-liberal ideas. Successive conservative (2004-2009) and socialist governments (2000-2004, 2009-10) had realized all this had to be changed timely, but many reform designs remained on paper.

Wage formation in the pace setting public sector, inefficient use of resources by state authorities colluding with privileged firms, regulation protecting insiders and so on, all associated with rent-seeking games, went undisturbed on. At the same time other pathologies of the broader public sector became acute - bureaucratic chicanery, poor quality of public services (health, education etc) and corruption in an environment where none was brought to account and law was badly implemented. Throughout the '90s and 00s corruption appeared to thrive as International Transparency insisted [38].

All this made the country vulnerable to an eventual external shock.

The Role of the EU

It has been often argued that EU arrangements have worked as external inducements to reform[39]; that they increased "the state's domestic capacity to act in relation to major problems of structural adjustment, by weakening the position of opponents of reform"[40], or convinced political elites and other domestic players of the legitimacy of liberal reforms.

Admittedly the influence of the EU explains repeated reform run-ups and some successes. Also, issues of fiscal discipline and liberal reform were put on the domestic agenda as a consequence of the institutionalized discourse and (soft) coordination in the EU. But this external inducement had limits before and after the introduction of Euro. Both medium-term stabilization programs (1985-87, 1991-93) agreed on IMF like conditionality terms (EU financial assistance on the condition that the Greek government implements an anti-inflationary policy package) have failed and were early abandoned. The *longer-term* convergence process cum reform in the 1990s turned out to be fragile and was reversed after the introduction of Euro. In the decades before and after EU-entry, stabilization and reform run-ups have been stalled or were quickly followed by setbacks (1987-90, 1993-1994) or periods of uncertainty (1995-1996 and, again, 2001-2004 and 2007-2009) due to the resilience of domestic factors (see below).

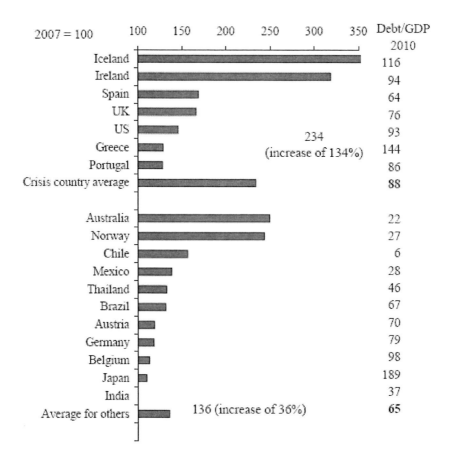

Notes: Unless otherwise noted these figures are for central government debt deflated by consumer prices. *Sources:* Prices and nominal GDP from International Monetary Fund, *World Economic Outlook.* For a complete listing of sources for government debt, see Reinhart and Rogoff (2009) and Reinhart (2010).

Source: Reinhart, Carmen and Rogoff, Keneth *A decade of debt*, CEPR, WP 8310, April 2011.

Figure 2. Cumulative Increase in real Public Debt Since 2007, Selected Countries.

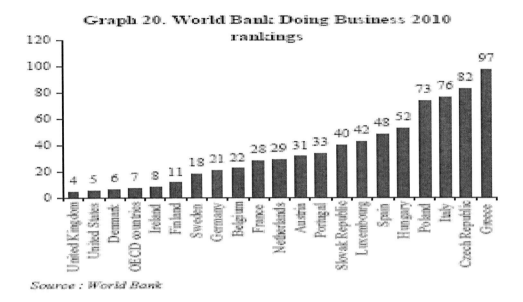

Figure 3. World Bank: Doing business 2010 rankings.

It is the debt crisis and deep recession in Greece, not EU coordination that seems to induce a decisive swift away from the institutions and practices of statism and rent-seeking. However, under conditions of crisis EU (and other international) arrangements regain force through an unprecedented policing of economic policy!

THE OUTBREAK OF THE DEBT CRISIS IN 2010 AND THE EU/IMF RESCUE PLAN

On October 5th 2009 the socialists returned to power after wining a landslide victory by promising to reverse the alleged austerity of the ND government. In fact the predecessors implemented strongly expansive fiscal policies in their efforts to stop recession. The socialists also promised to grant more social benefits, to re-nationalize privatized enterprises etc. "There is money" insisted G. Papandreou during the poll campaign.

Naturally enough, the new socialist government announced new social expenditure, abandoned plans of the predecessor to increase revenues and imposed additional burdens to business (in the form of backdated "exceptional contributions" beyond normal taxation). The first Budget was based upon unrealistic growth assumptions and wishful thinking– as Commission and Council alike assessed. The rating firms began to lower their rating on Greek bonds. Despite some *late* efforts of the government to reduce deficits, the "spreads" climbed to high levels and made it impossible to refinance debts (see figures 5 and 6).

In spring 2010, Greece had no alternative but to seek help from the EU and the IMF and in May 2010 it became the first country in the eurozone to ask for a bail-out from the EU and the IMF. Ireland and Portugal followed. The international "arrangement" with IMF and EU rescued Greece from an outright and chaotically default. 30 billion euros were provided by the IMF and 80 billion by eurozone member states over a 3-4 years period.

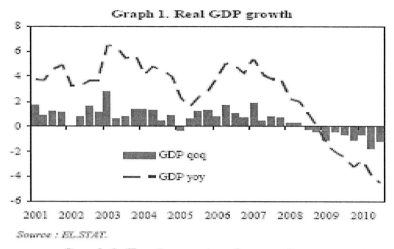
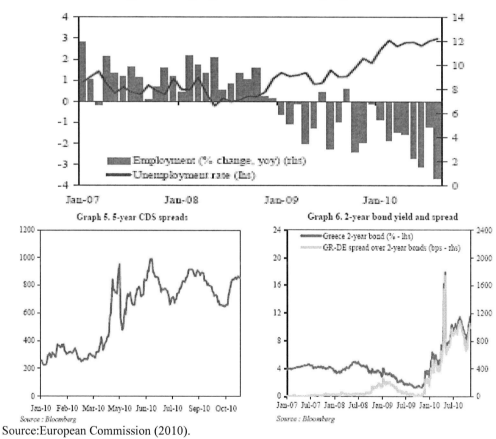

Source: European Commission (2010).

Figures 4a and 4b. Real GDP growth, employment and unemployment rate.

The amount was made available under the strict condition that Greece implements a three-year program based on the commitment to turn a large primary deficit into a large primary surplus. The program laid out a long list of expenditure cuts and structural reforms. It included radical tax changes, cuts in public-sector pay, labor market deregulation, other market opening measures (for example in the energy sector), privatization, and pension reforms[41].[9]

The Agreement requires close reviews of the economic adjustment program for the quarterly disbursements of aid. The three-year plan implied a radical change in the practices and institutions of governance and a radical re-orientation away from statism and pseudo-liberal arrangements towards liberal policies. The swift would predictably encounter resistance on the pact of all those profiting from the status quo. But the situation revealed some the deficiencies of the EMU regime [42].[10]

A serious defect of the fiscal austerity was that it did not rely as it should on expenditure cuts and trimming the state. Broader academic research and empirical evidence suggest that countries, relying primarily on cutting government expenditure rather than increasing tax revenues, are more successful in consolidating public finances and returning to growth [43]. Instead, a good part of the Greek austerity package concentrated in increasing direct and indirect tax rates. This proved to be self-defeating because it deepened recession and undermined the expected increase of tax revenues. There is an explanation why the Greek government made this choice of instruments against academic warnings. It *links the choice of instruments with* broader rent-seeking and clientelism [44].[11] Politicians regard the public sector as a space to accommodate individual clients, organized interests, and big business by targeted spending. Because some targets of the adjustment plan have been missed (see below), the government presented in May 2011 a new medium-term (five-year) plan of fiscal reform and deficit-cutting measures to be implemented over the next years despite growing dissent inside the socialist party. In addition the plan included an ambitious programme of privatisations and state property sales worth 50 billion euros to be carried out over the 2012-2015 period. Doubtless, it is a positive step. However, to implement the real estate part of the program the government has first to create the necessary institutional structures for the development of real estate assets, which will be the basis of this amount. This may take much time if we consider legal problems in Greece and that privatization is not backed by a political consensus.

Assessing Reform a Year on

One year on the results are again mixed [45]. It is true; the public deficit has been reduced by impressive 5 percentage points of the GDP which is generally considered to be a big step. But, the government (and the plan) originally had announced a deficit of fewer than 9% for 2010. This has finally reached 10.5% of GDP and the deficit reduction in 2011 failed. It is in some distance from original targets. Because GDP decreased more than predicted in 2010 by 4,5 % and it is feared that it will fall by 3,5% in 2011, fiscal consolidation rendered more difficult than expected.

---

[9] All documents -the Memorandum of Economic and Financial Policies (MEFP), the Memorandum of Understanding on Specific Economic Policy Conditionality (MoU) and the Technical Memorandum of Understanding (TMU) are annexed to Greek Law 3845/2010.

[10] Early version of the theory of optimum currency areas implied (under certain assumptions) the centralization of a significant part of the national budgets, the establishment of automatic transfers in cases that some member states suffers a negative shock and, by extension, more "political integration". See inter alia discussion in Paul de Grauwe The economics of monetary integration, Oxford University Press, 1994. There is by now a rich but inconclusive debate about the link between monetary and political integration. Anyway the situation of the Euro-zone is unique since there is a shared currency without a state.

[11] K. Peven Arin, Viera Chmelarova, E.Fees and Ansgar Wohlscchlegel (2011) emphasize on the role of corrupt politics.

On the other side unit labour cost is already falling due to the recession. Internal devaluation seems to work. Exports are rising and tourism seems to profit from both wage restraint and widespread unrest in the Arab world. Further some useful reforms have been achieved after the agreement on the IMF/EU rescue package in May 2010. The government transformed the statistical service into an independent agency to cope with the credibility problem of its statistics, and passed a law concerning many services (layers, pharmacists, engineers, etc) and abolishing administrative prices and restricting market entry. Independent sources had calculated the benefits that opening the services markets could bring to Greece [46].

A major step in summer 2010 was the pension's reform. It included an adjustment of the parameters of the main pension funds [47]. The reform increased the retirement age, cut generous benefits to high income earners, simplified the highly fragmented pension system and established a new model combining a minimum "national pension" with characteristics of a capital based system. Preliminary studies showed that the reform has significantly reduced the projected increase in pension spending. To ensure further improvement the authorities will now cut entitlements in the funds for supplementary pensions.

Liberalization of labour markets has progressed somehow. In December 2010 the Parliament passed a bill on labour relations. The bill seemed to tackle a main impediment to flexibility by permitting wage negotiation at the level of the firms wage deviation from sector or general agreements. The government has cut red-tape for new business. Parliament approved fast-track investment legislation simplifying procedures and accelerating deadlines for approval of strategic investment projects. Additionally the government eliminated legal barriers to the full operation of one-stop-shops in 2011. Now, it plans to create a unified public sector payroll in which dozens of discrete benefits handed out by various ministries over the past decades would be cut or streamlined, resulting in net civil servant salary reductions of 25 percent or more in some cases. Resistance to many economic reforms and fiscal consolidation is once again strong with the result that implementation lags behind schedule. Overall, reform has been restrained (until mid 2011) despite progress in cases we have just outlined. In crucial sectors such as privatization, public services (health, tax authority other), opening of the energy market and liberalization of professions were swallow and their implementation poor or questionable. Even the bill that seemed to liberalize labour markets included several brakes to the implementation of the new rules, for example prior setting-up of a union in interested firms, monitoring agreements by a normally anti-business oriented Department of the central government etc. Equally, the services liberalization did not seem to work in practice until May 2011. With time passing by, there is growing awareness that the adjustment task does not harmonize with the workings of the political system.

EXPLAINING REFORM DELAYS AND FISCAL CONSOLIDATION PROBLEMS

As just briefly outlined, evidence indicates that reform in Greece has been often fragmented, incoherent and domestically negotiated rather than based on established wisdom. These characteristics invite to political economy explanations pointing to interest-based behavior, weak institutions, underlying norms and dominant ideas [48],[49],[50],[51], [52].

These factors, obeying to logic of their own, prevailed at long last over European commitments and efficiency considerations.

Greece is indeed an obvious case for testing the relevance of the Olsonian Hypothesis that stable societies tend to accumulate special interest organizations continuously, with the result that their impact upon economic policy formation becomes greater. Broad coalitions such as political parties and workers' federations become less able to adhere to more general interests. In times of change, necessary adjustments enhancing efficiency and promoting a flexible re-allocation of production factors are stalled, delayed or blurred. Influential interest groups (unions, business organizations, etc.) emerge as pro-status quo forces co-determining the potential for reform [53].[12]

In particular, we argue that political processes, if exposed to traditional clientelism in non-trust societies, as is the case in Greece, are more vulnerable to pressures from domestic forces pursuing short term distributional gains or defending diverse acquis. Traditional clientelism *increases the number of "veto players"* (to use a key-word coined by G. Tsebelis, properly re-defining it to embrace strong informal players and channels of influence) and this is negatively related to the potential for policy innovation and the political capacity to actively respond to external challenges [54]. Accenting to the top, clientelism may also be associated with government fragmentation, weak rule of law and other pathologies.

On several occasions, it has been argued that the role of the labour movement tends to be reduced in the present phase of European and global. This may be generally correct, but *public sector* unions retain enough capacity to influence government decisions. In Greece union membership has decreased in the private sector, but remained high in the public sector throughout the period we deal with [55].[13] As providers of vital monopoly services, for example city transport, they can disturb painfully normal economic activities in the big cities of the country Athens and Thessalonica. Moreover, public sector unions dominate the General Confederation of Greek Labour. In 2001, 33 out of 45 members of the General Council of the Confederation came from public sector unions (public administration, public or publicly controlled economic enterprises, state banks). Most of them were also active members of political parties. Within the socialist party, they had built a strong and comparatively homogeneous power block that denounced any substantial reform as "neoliberal".

Indeed, they have a lot to defend. The public sector has achieved advantages far bigger than the private sector. Public sector employees earn, on average, a half more than their private-sector counterparts and enjoy "generous" advantages in terms of working time regulation, workload, paid holidays, accountability), pensions coupled with early retirement rules and many more. The unions oppose vigorously any move to more accountability. It has been almost impossible to discharge incompetent or corrupt employees. In 2007 Marietta Giannakou, the education minister in the last ND-government lost her seat at the next election because she insisted on accountability for teachers and professors. Her predecessors shared the same experience.

Business interests, particularly those of construction firms and other big suppliers, are no less influential. Although the EU has intensified competition in many sectors, in some of them (e.g. construction, transport, energy) individual firms or entrepreneurial consortia have

---

[12] Mancur Olson (1982); see too Petrakis (2010) for an application of this theory to the Greek case.

[13] 77.8% Union membership is in the public sector 77.8% , while average union participation in Greece is around 31.3% . See General Confederation of Greek labour wage earners and Unions in Greece (in Greek), Athens, 1995, p. 2. Petraki-Kottis and Kottis (1997) gave lower figures.

preserved privileged access to the state. The deals are often non transparent. Access is achieved through a combination of personal networks, control of mass media and ownership of popular sport clubs. Past changes of the law governing tenders to make it compatible with EU regulations do not seem to have changed much in the way the system works.

In Greece, it is not uncertainty that causes broad resistance to reforms or a broader *ex ante* societal bias against them, as it might generally be the case [56], but almost complete *certainty* about their distributional consequences. Reforms attack long established rents and rent-producing institutions and networks for political exchange.

Last but not least, ideological preferences are closely intermingled with clientelism and state-centrism in Greece (and elsewhere). They justify dominant practices. In Greece concepts like competition, transparency, flexibility, accountability, responsibility, employability, productivity etc have been demonized as neo-liberal devices, as Costas Simitis a former MP belatedly recognized [57]. A deep rooted anti-market bias is fuelled all the time by most mass media, which in turn work in an overblown sector and depend on external resources for survival.

However, most of these ideas and practices are now challenged.

The Greek government (as well as other governments) are being forced to cut back public spending, to halt debt accumulation, and to restore competitiveness. Public sector unions, professional associations in heavily protected and regulated activities, even individual big business enjoying privileged access to the government respond with repeated strikes and other actions against both, austerity and reform. But, due to the scale of the debt crisis and the threat of a chaotic default the pressure to consolidate public finances, to overhaul regulation and to increase efficiency, combat corruption and even insert the spirit of innovation in the public sector is likely to continue in the future. A second wave of reforms is almost inevitable under conditions of crisis.

But, sustaining such a course demands political-institutional modernization[14] that might best serve the transition from a state-centered rent-seeking society into an open and competitive one.

REFERENCES

[1] Simon Tilford and Philip Whyte *The Lisbon Scorecard IX*, Centre for European Reform, London (2010).

[2] Panos Kazakos *Between State and markets: Economic policies in post-war Greece 1944-2000 [Ανάμεσα σε κράτος και Αγορά: Οικονομικές πολιτικές στην μεταπολεμική Ελλάδα 1994-200]*, Patakis, Athens 2001, ch. 4, p. 293ff.

[3] Evanthis Hatziwassiliou *Greek liberalism. The radical current 1932-1979 [Ελληνικός φιλελευθερισμός. Το ριζοσπαστικό ρεύμα 1932-1979]*, Patakis, Athens 2010.

---

[14] In Greece the new Constitution, finally adopted in 2001, did not come up with the broadly recognized need for innovative changes nor introduced any numerical rules to limit fiscal discretion of the government. It has rather broadened the scope for executive discretion and microeconomic rule-free interventionism in matters such as land use and environmental protection by restricting independent judicial control and by loosening strict provisions of the constitution. In a sense constitutional reform provided the parties with new domains to apply clientelistic practices, thus compensating them for the restrictions arising from EU rules and procedures. We call it 'the substitution effect". For the future George Tsebelis concept of veto players properly redefined may provide practical guidance. See George Tsebelis (2002).

[4]   Mark Dragoumis *The Weg to liberalism Centre of Liberal Studies [Πορεία προς τον φιλελευθερισμό]*, Papazissis, Athens 2010.

[5]   Commission der EG *Opinion on the Greece's application for accession*, Brussels, 1976, p. 8.

[6]   Kevin Featherstone *Socialist parties and European integration-a comparative history*, Manchester University Press, Manchester 1988, p. 178.

[7]   Lyrintzis, Chr. *West European politics* 7/ 2, 111 (1984).

[8]   OECD *Greece, economic survey 1988*, Paris, 1989.

[9]   OECD *Greece, economic survey 1989-1990*, Paris 1991, p. 13.

[10] Ministry of National Economy: *The Greek Economy 1960-1997. Long-term statistical series*, Athens 1998.

[11] *Financial Times*, 15.11.1996.

[12] Johannes Pakaslahti: *Does the EMU threaten European Welfare?* Working paper , June 1997, p. 47.

[13] L. Tsoukalis "Greece in the EU: Domestic reform coalitions, external constraints and high politics', in Mitsos, A./ Mossialos,E (eds): *Contemporary Greece and Europe*, Ashgate, Aldershot 2000, pp 37-51, p. 40.

[14] Giandomenico Majone " The rise of the regulatory state in Europe", in Mueller,W./ Wright, V. (eds): *The state in Western Europe, retreat or redefinition?*, Frank Cass,Ilford Essex, 1994, 77-101.

[15] Giandomenico Mayone "The future of regulation in Europe," in G. Mayone (ed) *Regulating Europe*, Routledge, London 2000, pp 265-283.

[16] Ministry of Labour relations *The Greek response to the questionnaire on the pension system* , Athens, march 2001, mimo, p. 5 ff. SN 5367/00 (SOC).

[17] OECD *Greece, economic survey 1997-1998*, Paris, 1998, pp 93-159.

[18] J. Mylonas and Isabelle Joumard: *Greek public enterprises: Challenges for reform*, OECD economics department working paper No 214, Paris May 1999.

[19] Panos Kazakos *West European Politics*, 5, 900-918 (2004).

[20] European Commission *European Economy, statistical annex*, Brussels, Spring 2007.

[21] Ministry of Economic Development 2001, *The competitiveness of the Greek economy*, (in Greek), Athens, 2001.

[22] Commission of the EU "Convergence Report 2000", *European Economy*, No 70/2000, Brussels 2000, p. 91ff, p. 98.

[23] Eurostat *Report on the revision of the Greek government deficit and debt figures*, 22 September 2004. IMF *Greece, Article IV consultation. Concluding statement of the Mission*,14 September 2004.

[24] OECD Greece, economic survey 2009, Paris 2009, p.36ff.

[25] Christodoulakis, N.: "The Greek economy converging towards EMU", in Mitsos, A./ Mossialos,E (eds): *Contemporary Greece and Europe*, Ashgate, Aldershot 2000, pp 93-129.

[26] Hellenic Republic- Ministry of National Economy and Finance *The 2000 Stability and Growth Program*, Athens, December 2000, p. 19 and 24.

[27] Kevin Featherstone and D. Papadimitriou, *Manipulating rules, contesting solutions: Europeanization and the politics of restructuring Olympic Airways*, Paper presented to the Joint Sessions of the European Consortium for Political research, April 2005.

[28] Bank of Greece *Annual Report of the Governor 2000*, 2005, 2007, 2008, 2009, Athens.

[29] OECD *Greece, country report 1996-7*, Paris 1997, p. 66.

[30] Government Actuary's Department, United Kingtom: *Review of retirement pension system . report on financial estimates for parametric and structural changes*, Athens, April 2001(published by the Greek Government).

[31] Labour Ministry: *Summary report and proposals of the labour Ministry on the reform of the social security system*, Athens, 19 April 2001 (mimo).

[32] INE/GSSE : *Study of the Social Security System in Greece.* Athens, April 2001 (in Greek).

[33] G. Kazamias and D. Papadimitriou *The limits of external empowerment: EMU, technocracy and reform of the Greek pension system 1996-1998*, Paper for the Political Studies Association – UK 50th Annual Conference, London, 10-13 April 2000.

[34] *European Commission Sustainability Report 2009, European Economy* No. 9/2009, p. 106.

[35] Carlo Cottarelli and Andrea Schlaechter *Long-term trends in public finances in the G-7 economies*, IMF Staff Position Note (SPN /10/13), September 1 2010, p. 3ff.

[36] Reinhart, Carmen and Rogoff, Keneth *A decade of debt*, CEPR, WP 8310, April 2011.

[37] Bank of Greece Monetary policy 2009-10, Athens, November 2010.

[38] Transparency *International Corruption perception index*, 2010 and earlier issues. See too World Economic Forum, *The Global Competitiveness Report 2004-2005*, Macmillan, 2004 and successive issues.

[39] Loukas Tsoukalis *National Interest* 55, 73 (1999).

[40] K. Dyson, and K. Featherstone *South European Society and Politics*, 1(2), 275-6, 295-6 (1966).

[41] IMF Greece: Request for stand-by arrangement, Country report No 10/111, May 2010.

[42] Francesco Paolo Mongelli *'New' views on the optimum currency area theory: What is EMU telling us?* European Central Bank, Working Paper No 138, April 2002.

[43] Alberto Alesina and Silvia Ardagna *Large changes in fiscal policies: Taxes versus spending*, NBER Working Paper No 15438, October 2009.

[44] K. Peven Arin, Viera Chmelarova, E.Fees and Ansgar Wohlscchlegel *Journal of Public Economics* 95, *521-530, (2011)*.

[45] IMF Greece: Second review on the stand-by arrangement, Country Report No. 10/372; European Commission The economic adjustment programme for Greece. Third review, Occasional Paper 77. Winter 2011.

[46] The Institute of Economic and Industrial Research (IOBE) and the Hellenic Centre for Research and Planning (KEPE).

[47] European Commission *The economic adjustment programme for Greece. Second review.* Occasional Paper No. 72. December 2010, p. 20ff.

[48] Mancur Olson *The rise and decline of nations- Economic growth, stagflation and social rigidities*, Yale University Press, New Haven and London, 1982.

[49] James Buchanan, Collected Works. Vol. 1, The logical foundations of constitutional liberty, Liberty fund, Indianapolis 1999.

[50] Guy Peters *Institutional theory in political science. The 'new institutionalism'*, Continuum, London 1999;

[51] Dennis C. Mueller (ed) *Perspectives on public choice*, Cambridge University Press, Cambridge 1997.

[52] Williamson, J. (ed) *The political economy of policy reform*, Institute of International economics, Washington, DC, 1994.

[53] Panagiotis Petrakis *The Greek Economy. Challenges [Η Ελληνική Οικονομία: Προκλήσεις]*, Papazisis Publishers, Athens 2010.

[54] George Tsebelis *Veto players. How political institutions work, Princeton University Press, Princeton 2002.*

[55] Petraki-Kottis and A. Kottis *Labour Market Studies: Greece*, European Commission, Brussels 1997, p. 55.

[56] R. Fernandez and D. Rodrik, *American Economic Review*, 81/5, 1146-1155, (1991).

[57] Kostas Simitis *Thoughts about progressive governance [Σκέψεις για μια προοδευτική διακυβέρνηση]*, Polis, Athens 2008, p. 21,25,26.

In: Greece: Economics, Political and Social Issues
Editor: Panagiotis Liargovas

ISBN: 978-1-62100-944-3
© 2012 Nova Science Publishers, Inc.

Chapter 3

PERENNIAL STRUCTURAL PROBLEMS IN MODERN GREEK ECONOMY

Panagiotis Evangelopoulos[1]
University of Peloponnese,
Department of Economics, Tripolis, Greece

ABSTRACT

Structural economic problems are chronic in modern Greek economy, resulting in emergence of a generally inefficient institutional economic framework that is financed through a dramatically expanding public deficit and debt and supported by a strong continental currency, the euro. In this chapter I examine how this unfortunate state of economic affairs of the Greek economy worsened from 2004 when the conservative government was elected. Although the conservative government realized some crucial reforms, privatizations and public-private partnerships, neither it completed them nor it expanded them in the main institutional structure of the Greek economy and finally it failed to organize a new type of economy based on the robustness of private sector and supported by an efficient and operational public sector.

I conclude in my analysis that the Draconian austerity measures of the new socialist government are unlikely to succeed if the new economic authority does not limit dramatically the size of the public sector and does not restore the economic rationality in Greek economy on the path of Classical Economic Liberalism.

INTRODUCTION: PRIOR TO 2004. DEAD-END MODERNIZATION

Up until 2004, under the leadership of Costas Simitis, the prevailing doctrine in the Greek economy was that of modernization. Costas Simitis took over where the short-lived second government of Andreas Papandreou had left off, initiating his own rule for a long ensuing period and undertaking to establish a New Modernizing Greece under a New Modernizing PASOK. The new PASOK of Costas Simitis was structured around the central idea of

---

[1] E-mail address: panos@evangelopoulos.gr

modernizing all of Greek society. Just as the PASOK of Andreas Papandreou had used the word "change" when for the first time the socialist party came to power in Greece in 1981, so "modernization" now acquired a special significance for PASOK. And just as Andreas Papandreou did not succeed in changing Greece, so Costas Simitis did not succeed in modernizing it.

On the contrary, for all the modernizing rhetoric, which had assumed Manichaeistic proportions in the way it carried out the tasks of government in all sectors, the country was eventually led into a serious impasse, with incalculable harm being inflicted on the country in the course of its strategy for the new century that had already arrived.

The greatest problem for the modernizing PASOK was its ineffectiveness in reorganizing, indeed its inability to reorganize, Greek society as a whole, reshaping its structures through reconstruction and activation of all the forces with the potential to carry through such a difficult and daring undertaking. The institutions of a society are what give it its character and activate it.

The new PASOK did not dare to embark on significant institutional reforms with the capacity to lead not only to dramatic change but also to basic improvement in the internal structures: political, social and economic, of our society. It depended on a stagnant public administration and an endless labyrinthine bureaucracy that would enable it to claim that it was reforming something which, the more it depended on it the less it influenced it, and the more it left it as it always had been, if not considerably worse. Striking examples of this dead-end politics are the debt-ridden Kapodistrias reform plan and the debt-ridden National Health System.

Neither the new municipalities nor the older municipalities were strengthened in any way. No solution was offered to the problem of bureaucracy. Local authorities did not transform themselves into instruments of orderly decentralization. There was no reduction in the costs of central government subsidization and no relief from the suffocating grip of state interventionism in the planning of local public works projects.

The new National Health System did not succeed in resolving the great paradox that while resources for health were increasing, owing to increased contributions at all levels from all health insurance subscribers, at the same time administrative deficits of the participating units were also increasing, as were shortages and lack of necessary resources for carrying out the tasks of health care facilities.

The National Health System established by the old PASOK of Andreas Papandreou and subjected to would-be modernization by the new PASOK of Costas Simitis, in George Papandreou's late PASOK of today finds itself on its last legs, recalling the fall of the Soviet Empire, when against a grim backdrop of shortfalls and inadequacies a number of hospitals were led to closure, leaving the populace to its fate as far as health care was concerned.

In this essentially dead-end situation, whatever the superficial successes achieved such as Greece's entry into the Eurozone and the holding of the Olympic Games, which led to the commissioning of the great public-sector infrastructural works, Costas Simitis' modernizing PASOK handed over the reins of government in 2004 to New Democracy, and to the youngest ever prime minister in Greece's history, Costas Karamanlis.

THE THESSALONIKI INTERNATIONAL FAIR AS TRANSMISSION POINT FOR GREEK ECONOMIC POLICY

The term Political Economy was emphatically marked by David Ricardo in his celebrated work "Principles of Political Economy and Taxation" at the beginning of the 19th century [1]. The value of the definition of Political Economy put forward by this great exponent of classical liberal economics may be judged from the guidance it provided, by virtue of its theoretical analysis of the laws of economics, to the then fledgling science. It helped economists to formulate policy clearly derived from economic criteria. Hence the term Political Economy, whose objective was to promote enterprise profits through reduction of taxation while at the same time achieving improvement of the wages to labor on the basis of the economic progress of the system.

However long the period of time may seem that separates us from those days, it is no paradox to argue that we once again face the same economic policy planning dilemmas. The Thessaloniki International Fair (TIF) has won recognition as an institution for formulation of economic policy, both for the government and for the opposition. From the rostrum of the Thessaloniki International Fair policies have been proclaimed that have changed our economic policy-making landscape. It would not be unjust to say, indeed, that the change has been for the worse, not for the better. From the Thessaloniki International Fair nationalizations have been proclaimed, socialization programmes have been initiated, all for the sake of appeasing socialist *parti pris* and promoting facile solutions for flourishing enterprises whose profits are required to be handed on to the people or to used to support failing enterprises whose losses must be covered by the decrepit state budget.

Similarly attributable to the political economy of the TIF is the large-scale squandering of economic, political and social resources that reached its zenith in the 1980s and put Greece back decades in terms of infrastructures, responsible social policy and education. This manna from heaven of massive social waste that can be traced back in one way or another to the rostrum of the TIF came as a blessing to a certain kind of parasitical economic opportunism. It objectively fostered it, undermining efforts at productive long-term wealth creation and collective prosperity. But above all it had the effect of aiding and abetting the present-day rent-shark stratum, these being the key opponents of reform and reformers in today's society [2][3][4]. But as the moment of crisis approached, the Cassandras began to be vindicated, and the impasse into which the country had been driven by the economic policies of social waste became impossible to ignore, the same people who had caused the crisis started to implement the most inequitable and harsh economic programmes of financial austerity, imposing collective punishment on society as a whole, fair and unfair, conscientious workers and idle privileged, worker bees and drones.

Hermaphroditic political economy of this type has always tended to come to the fore during much-noted periods of political downturn, when the government is taking a beating in the polls, bearing the brunt of popular disillusion and disapproval or facing crucial electoral contests. It was in precisely this way that the former Prime Minister Costas Simitis in his last year in office became a hostage to the rostrum of the TIF when, despite his munificence towards his potential voters, the proxy campaign mounted by his successor George Papandreou went down to a humiliating defeat. And so it was that the then leader of the opposition and now Prime Minister George Papandreou was given the task of ascending the rostrum with a plan for a national pension of 400 euros a month. How paradoxical, hollow and absurd all this sounds today when everyone has realized that this kind of Political Economy of the TIF, dictated by cheap electoralist competition, has led to the worst economic crisis our country has known in its recent history, bringing it to the very brink of catastrophe, i.e. bankruptcy.

Greeks don't want to see the country's economy transformed into something like a latter-day *prytaneum* with their political representatives competing over who will offer the most attractive handouts. Modern political economy requires development through implementation of a properly planned programme of privatizations, simplification and reduction of taxation, without consideration of the source or provider of income, but also with restructuring of the insurance system to secure full rights for the insurance client in managing his contributions.

The TIF is able today to formulate and put into practice a different kind of modern political economy which will not turn out unemployed workers with truncated pension rights and will not permit the state to see itself, and be seen, as life saver-cum-underwriter of hand-to-mouth subsistence. The demand to be placed on our economic policy should be imprinted on the consciousness of the population: the ongoing restructuring provides opportunities for benefits much greater than the mediocre gains to be expected from state welfare provision and protection.

THE PERENNIAL PATIENT AND AHE OPTION OF PRIVATE SECTOR DEVELOPMENT

The Greek economy some time ago embarked on a profound and painful process of redrawing the boundaries between the public and the private. Despite the fact that this process never acquired its full momentum, it did – slowly, gradually, with numerous interruptions and short-lived conjunctural backslidings – lead the country towards a more developed mode of functioning of the private sector, with numerous associated benefits. But the public sector has continued to be disproportionately large, and – even worse – to be in very bad shape, burdening the Greek economy as a whole, with its inefficiency, its inflexibility, its inbuilt inertia and lack of rationality.

These must be the conclusions of every alert and perceptive citizen, confirmed by the declarations of almost all politicians on the subject of the Perennial Patient, not to mention the more daring formulations of analysts who refer quite explicitly to certain characteristics of the Greek state sector that are reminiscent of Soviet Russia shortly before its collapse. It is true that we bear considerable responsibility for this situation but we have an even greater obligation to reverse it. Our only possible hope for assistance in this difficult undertaking lies in the development of a profounder awareness in the Greek community of the superiority of private organization over public and bureaucratic modes of operation. The supremacy of the private over the public for the organization of markets must achieve general recognition, with the realm of the public elevated to the lofty plane of supervision and control.

Prominently displayed on the flag of the New York University is the epigram "A Private University in the Service of the Public Interest". This is a grand truth that has come into the possession of all the democratic communities of the world, inherited from the father of economic science Adam Smith [5]. His charismatic formulation of the invisible hand which through the free market brings absolute harmony between the manifold private interests and the overall public interest symbolizes the way in which capitalism has managed to flourish throughout the world for centuries, mastering with all the force of its dynamic the two basic problems of production and distribution of wealth. When markets are allowed to operate without impediment they comprise a self-regulating order embodying the consummate synthesis of political and economic liberalism, as analyzed by the New Austrian school of economists with Ludwig von Mises and Friedrich Hayek (Nobel 1974) as their most distinguished representatives [6][7][8]. The self-regulation achieved by the markets ensures the optimum productive outcome, in a democratically organized state, exercising effective political control and reinforcing the network of social protection in potent alternative ways, eschewing the monolithic operational modes of the state, with all the bureaucratic inertia they entail.

In the past in Greece we opted for the public as against the private. In the 1970s, under the pressure of advancing socialism, we chose nationalizations. In the 1980s, when the entire world was being swept by privatizations, we intensified the socializations. The result was huge deficits and exorbitant public borrowing that landed us in debts equal to the entire GNP and even more. Ill-considered actions of an out-of-control public sector which, like the biblical monster Leviathan as characterized by economists of the public choice school, and notably James Buchanan (Nobel 1986) consumed every dynamic element in the Greek economy [9]. When at the beginning of the 90s the liberal Mitsotakis government embarked upon privatizations, albeit slowly, there was an outcry against them and he was undermined. When at the end of the 90s the modernizing Socialists finally came to understand the virtues of the market and of privatizations, they implemented them but were ashamed to give them the name of privatization and called them denationalizations.

When our political leaders are presented as perspicacious communicants of what is right and proper, they behave like enlightened despots, attempting to impose policies of whose correctness they themselves have been convinced, though public opinion has not. This is the greatest challenge of the present conjuncture: to persuade public opinion of the importance of changes favoring the private, and to generate the corresponding enthusiasm. Let them at long last allow the private to flourish at the hard core of the Greek economy, in its full significance and above all under its correct name.

IN THE DEFICIT VICE

Bread and circuses were the most popular form of politics pursued in Ancient Rome by political demagogues, the dictators of the day, and even by the last emperors, for the sake of winning shallow and short-lived support from the people, with the economic strength of the empire as the collateral. When we find ourselves faced with problems like that of the public sector deficits it should therefore be impermissible for any political leadership to prefer, instead of dealing with the problems in a rational manner through level-headed management, to choose the logic of the auction sale, while at the same time embellishing its image for the mass media and so for the people.

Greece's economic problem in the present conjuncture results from the pressure of economic demands being exerted from many different quarters on a state that is financially unable to satisfy them. There is of course the great ethical question of pre-electoral promises by government which nowadays come across as stale verbiage that, without having any real impact, nevertheless serve further to strengthen the demands and turn them into urgent requirements, albeit rhetorical, that make it possible for the government to be censured, even if only morally, in the eyes of the public. But in this way the implication of the deficits in the ongoing political controversy exacerbates the economic problem as such, magnifying even further the distance from fiscal equilibrium.

The deficit vice is a sui generis instrument of economic torture that prevents economic policy from cultivating the fertile ground that is needed for indispensable reforms to go forward, for the necessary restructuring to be carried out, so that market forces can be activated to organize production of goods and services, in an effective and profitable way, so that all the factors of production may reap the benefits. We in Greece, by contrast, every time that the controversial political demand is put forward for restructuring of the economy: modernization under Simitis, reform under Karamanlis, choose to impose political disarmament on the most enlightened protagonists for freeing our economy from the deficit vice. We then throw them into the Kaiada , as the Spartans did with deformed children, only to discover that what has been acquired through great effort has once again been dissipated or consigned to a kind of fiscal black hole [10].

Instead of this well-trodden path, this failed political reflex of reiterating again and again throughout the entire post-junta historical period exactly the same scenario of substantial groups of working people and pensioners in the public sector petitioning and demanding, we must opt for another course of resolutely abandoning this vicious circle of claims on, and exactions from, a state that is incapable of meeting them. An unwavering and stable policy of fiscal control would be the most promising means for extracting the economy from the deficit vice. Fiscal control for the purpose of balancing the budget would introduce rationality into the actions of politicians and public functionaries [11]. The balanced budget is the parameter within which the limitations of our collective activities must be established. Fiscal control means maintaining a check on the observance of limits, but it also promotes transparency and the ethical sense that should accompany the rule of law.

It is essential for management of our fiscal policy to adhere to clear directives radically different from what has prevailed in the past. The publicly-owned corporations that are so skilled in generating deficits: the Athens Urban Transport Organization, the Greek railway company OSE, must revise their pricing policy, their provisioning policy, their investment programming policy.

Hospitals should publish balance sheets and be subject to genuine controls. Public enterprises should be transferred to the private sector employing new and innovative methods. The technology of privatization should be further specialized so as to incorporate the new knowledge that has been developed in the course of three decades of privatizations globally. The budget should win back its former prestige in the face of challenges and political maneuvering and it should become implanted in the consciousness of citizens that it comprises the country's supreme, unquestioned constitutionally underwritten annual fiscal map from which there can be no deviation at any of the different rankings of the public sector.

Thus, through the methods of fiscal regulation and the introduction of balanced budgets we will release our economy from the deficit vice and liberate our democracy from the bonds of grandiose false promises which always lead in the direction of mistaken collective choices.

NAVIGATING BETWEEN SCYLLA AND CHARYBDIS

In the period between 2004 and 2008, like a latter-day Jason of the Argonauts, George Alogoskoufis tried to navigate his ship - the Greek economy - between Scylla and Charybdis. The mythical narrows bordered by these rocks were impassable because of the violent turbulence of the sea and the powerful cross-winds. Under these difficult conditions George Alogoskoufis attempted to secure a safe passage, making our economy, the Argo of the present-day, as robust and seaworthy as possible. He combined a program of mild fiscal adjustment with a policy of spectacular post-Olympic Games economic growth in Greece. But he was not successful. The dangerous rocks closed again before the Argo had time to negotiate the dreaded straits. George Alogoskoufis lost the battle for control of public expenditures. Although Costas Karamanlis and George Alogoskoufis triggered early elections in 2007 to secure a mandate for fiscal controls, when they won them they opened the floodgates to the tidal wave of deficit and debt. For one more time in the economic history of the Hellenic republic the voracious Greek Leviathan had succeeded in swallowing up what economic liberalism was attempting to rescue.

But a safe passage between Scylla and Charybdis retains its urgency today for the Greek economy. However uncertain the prospects for a positive outcome owing to the conditions prevailing at the outset, nevertheless as part of a comprehensive strategy, with well-thought-out objectives and skilful handling of the tools of economic policy, it would be possible to put the Greek economy successfully on track towards increased productivity, with exploitation of dynamic relative advantages and overcoming of chronic weaknesses and distortions with their origins primarily in state regulation of markets, in bureaucracy, in syndicalist organizations and the imperialism of parties.

It is not enough today merely to reiterate criticism of the mistaken nationalizations of the 70s and the socialization and political party domination of the 80s. It is however important to note, and emphasize, that the mild and slow liberalization of our economy that is being attempted today does not suffice to hold the economy on a steady course between Scylla and Charybdis. Rather than cutting wasteful public expenditure we have chosen to indulge it while providing additional funding through raising Value Added Tax and introducing other indirect charges. Instead of giving power to the management to reduce salaries and curb the privileges of loss-making publicly-owned corporations, we allow them to stagnate, maintaining - and even propagating - the heavy deficits and extensive losses. We argue that the station master or the engine driver of the OSE railway company is poorly paid, whereas in fact what he is doing is contributing in the ways indicated above to the miserable decline of the Greek railways. Many examples could be cited of the widespread economic irrationality pervading both the central core of the public sector and the public sector in a wider sense. There are unfortunately no positive developments to be detected, despite the rhetoric and whatever efforts are being made, which remain half-finished or fruitless.

On the other hand we have a systematic undermining of the reforms, assuming a number of different guises equally inauspicious for the changes that are being attempted. The same phenomenon was to be seen during the most recent period of government by New Democracy from 2004 to 2008. New Democracy's insistence on prioritizing an ill-defined humanistic central policy plank introduced vulnerability into every change that it might seek to undertake. The most justified component of New Democracy's economic policy, the proposed simplified taxation system with measures for tax relief, was greeted by accusations from powerful public opinion leaders of excessive zeal for the interests of the plutocracy. I did not hear anyone arguing that blanket reductions in company taxes and distributed profits reinforce the stock market, strengthen the position of shareholders, extend the institution of company proprietorship to wider layers of the population, in this way creating a broader base for the theory and practice of popular capitalism, the optimal organizational structure for free economies and open societies.

Instead of that, the PASOK of George Papandreou, when it was still in opposition, was supporting the most ill-documented critique and recommending a complex and bureaucratically discriminatory policy of incentive taxes that had been tried by all the preceding PASOK governments and had failed miserably. As part of the attempt by PASOK to come up with new economic ideas, aimed apparently at attracting votes without too much trouble, one proposal put forward was for a constitutionally guaranteed minimum income. But we all know from the political economy of neo-liberalism that when poverty is subsidized, it persists, and – what is worse – it proliferates and expands. On the other hand payment of a guaranteed minimum wage entails unsustainable costs, both fiscal and transactional. Registering and classifying the economically weaker, organizing safeguards against misuse, establishing the necessary instrumentalities for provision of the benefit, supervising and regulating of everything involved, all these factors conspire to make the guaranteed minimum income a fiscal torpedo and a totally counterproductive economic and social measure.

It is imperative that our economy, whatever failed endeavors there may have been in the past, should – by forging a steady and determined course – successfully negotiate a passage between Scylla and Charybdis. This is feasible only through adoption of economic liberalism. With the opening and freeing of markets and institutionalization of profit as the driving force for development of our enterprises, we will very soon see a wider distribution of profits that will in turn function as a catalyst for reform, delegitimating in the popular consciousness our anachronistic statist past.

An Inadequate Incomes Policy in Consequence of an Over-Inflated Public Sector

The government's incomes policy is obliged to adhere strictly to the tight constraints imposed by the economic downturn, as epitomized – and illustrated – by the figures for the public debt and the size of the fiscal deficit. In any case it is the coziness of the wage increases and the large-scale mass public-sector appointments introduced in the past by party imperialism and unconstrained and irrational political competition that has led us into the deficit morass. Another factor behind the deficits is the multiplicity of unmonitored decision-making centers in the public sector generally, but also very specifically. Greece is still to be numbered among the countries where the public sector has enormous weight in economic life and whose decisions on which wages policy will be followed have an effect on the lives of a significant sector of the working populations. Under these circumstances incomes policy, though sidelined in the more up-to-date advanced economies since the 1980s, in Greece continues to play a critical macro-economic role. Although the question currently under consideration is how best to handle incomes policy, I would like to focus more on the real losses to working people, the reason for which is delay in the reforms which could on the one hand make government incomes policy a factor working tacitly for the system and on the other substantially upgrade the level of prosperity of public sector workers.

Throughout the entire post-junta period, with the exception of the first four years in office of the PASOK government, the pre-electoral periods and the period between 2004 and 2008, government incomes policy has been restrictive. Its aim has been not so much to hold down overall levels of consumption, the bulk of which involves imported goods, with all the negative repercussions that implies for the trade balance (this is in any case a conventional view that is challenged by modern macro-economic studies) as it is above all to bring under control the high fiscal deficit. But, this not an achievable objective. However, small the increases, the fiscal expense of the salaries of public employees will remain high, something in no way conducive to reduction, or even restraint, of the fiscal deficit. This great army of public and quasi-public employees in the wider state sector in Greece outmaneuvers every serious endeavor to introduce rational macroeconomic management of the fiscal deficit via methods compatible with the objective. In the face of this well-entrenched status quo what are required are policies of structural change, the cornerstone of which is a radical overturn in the asymmetrical development of the public sector at the expense of the private, which just happens to be the source of all funding for state activity.

Elaboration of an economic policy aimed at turning around this asymmetrical relationship must necessarily be based on an accelerated and clearly defined program of privatizations. If this process can be implemented imaginatively by politicians, with working people consciously won over, a multitude of benefits will ensue for all. There will be significant relief from the fiscal deficit, in real terms, and incomes policy will cease to be controversial and underfunded. Together with the money that will be saved through reduction in overall numbers, particularly of workers in the semi-public sector, the state will be able to proceed with significant wage increases, above all benefiting public functionaries. Ultimately the greatest benefit to emerge will be for the economy as a whole, because there will be a considerable rise in the productivity of labor, with an attendant redistribution of human resources, and all within the logic of the new relationship that will emerge between public and private sectors.

In contrast to everything said here, we observe organizations of public functionaries behaving maximalistically as if they were unions of industrial workers. A strike by workers does damage in the short term to the profits of the company, in the long term also weakening the position of the workers. A lengthy strike in the education sector does damage in the short term to the government, in the long term also affecting the education of younger generations. The asymmetries that characterize our economy are unfortunately now spreading over the whole spectrum of social life and this is the greatest obstacle to be confronted by all of us who place ourselves in the camp of the reformers.

THE SUBORDINATION OF POLITICS TO CORRUPTION

When its basis is the liberal project, politics as organized collective management of the common affairs of a democratic community aims to provide a foundation for individual prosperity, and to expand it. To depart from the form and focus on the essence, the individual does not sign the constitution for collective organization of the society but when he goes to cast his vote at regular intervals he gives a clear mandate on the type of policies he wants to see pursued within a framework of good government and respect for the law. The emergence of corruption, and indeed of a multi-dimensional kind, leads to loss of the criterion of politics, in fact to its collective rejection.

It is no coincidence that historically corruption has brought down great leading personalities, has led to ostracism even of just and able politicians, has wiped empires off the map and led to the downfall of systems of political organization and ideologies that have in other respects sought to foster high ideals. Every encounter between politics and corruption ends in humiliating and miserable defeat for politics. Corruption starts with institutions being eroded by a few skilful practitioners, people with a considerable talent for opening holes in what has been prescribed by the rules and regulations. The payoff for them is the securing of significant advantages to the detriment of the majority who respect and support the legal order. From that point on, imitation by admiring onlookers, along with co-optation of key people for the purpose of closing deals against the public interest, suffice to bring down the barriers upholding the rule of law, with a resulting deluge of corruption that poisons everything in public life. Henceforth every political effort to bring change, modernization and reform will be engulfed in a mire of corruption.

The drastic curbing of corruption should be the major political objective of any government because it is only then, firstly, that its primary political tasks can be strengthened and made credible and, secondly, that suitable conditions can be created for consolidation and successful implementation of the changes brought about by its collective action. Despite this undeniable fact, because of the dynamics of society, even democratic governments find themselves faced by unexpected crises as a result of corruption scandals. In such cases governments are overcome with embarrassment, which is metamorphosed into negligence and profound guilt when it transpires that people dependent on them have contributed to the emergence of a corruption scandal. This is the most crucial phase of the policy-making process, which if it leads - on the one hand - to paralysis of the work of government and - on the other - to a hectic pursuit of the culprits, will succeed neither in restoring transparency nor in getting any political work done: the only effect will be perpetuation of the stagnation of a country that is slowly sinking into a morass of corruption.

The management of crises generated by such instances of corruption scandals usually involves something like a witch hunt, including immediate and arbitrary removal of possible culprits, the imposition of draconian penalties, adoption of extremely harsh restrictions, and establishment of a multitude of new repressive mechanisms and committees, authorities and other bodies of pre-emptive regulation. This is precisely the solution chosen by the Soviet Union to rescue really-existing socialism. Developed democracies have another way of dealing with corruption. Their central concern is to reform the institutions that have been found wanting in dealing with corruption, to oblige them to function with transparency, to make them answerable for their actions, participatory in their mode of operation, open to new organizational conceptions, transforming their collective structures through a new emphasis on individual responsibility and individual input. The greatest strength of liberal democracy is its focus on the individual as key vehicle for undertaking initiatives, both in private life and in the public realm. If we proceed with these reforms to crack the carapace of state power that keeps people separated from management of institutions, then corruption will no longer find a refuge among financial adventurers and speculators.

Corruption is a challenge and requires answers. The experience of our country from the time of Koskotas through the stock exchange bubble to the junk bonds affair of more recent times only serves to highlight our failure to introduce politics to the winning side. We must therefore wean ourselves from the habit of off-the-cuff denunciation and the traditional and ineffective tactic of massive sanctions and turn responsibly to the shaping of institutions that can provide significant opportunities for the achievement of individual progress, without having to bring in police sirens or practices already resorted to by the corrupt.

THE ABOLITION OF COLLECTIVE BARGAINING

It is true that collective bargaining is an established institution in Greek society for fixing salaries and the daily wages of workers. We are in fact at this time living through a long-protracted process of negotiating the percentage increase in salaries and wages between the General Confederation of Workers of Greece and the various employers' associations: a process which perhaps given the political, economic and social conditions in the country appears unlikely to produce results. But is this the only problem or are there other much deeper contributing factors that only serve to highlight the impasse and complicate the emergence of some settlement that could at least be tolerably acceptable to the two sides without exposing them to condemnation from the members they represent?

To obtain some idea of the real dimensions of this subject it may be useful to present a brief rundown of the changes that have taken place in the labor market in a modern dynamically changing economic climate which, despite the crisis - or perhaps because of it - demands new methods and new conceptions, not only for management of the labor market but also for its evolution on a course parallel to the strengthening and primacy of market forces and the new global division of labor that has in consequence merged. It is not defensible on the one hand to lament the steady diminution in our international competitiveness because of the corresponding fall in labor productivity and on other the hand to surrender the key mode of remuneration to collective bargaining, which has the key responsibility for non-linkage of salaries with productivity, i.e. incentive with effort, cause with effect.

Let us be more explicit. Collective bargaining aims at securing a minimum wage for the great mass of workers that would be better than what an individual worker could obtain from the employer on his own. But this automatically generates a counter-mobilization of employers, who come out against collective bargaining with the same, if not greater, force than that of the workers. The outcome of collective bargaining therefore depends in the final analysis on specific considerations that in no way guarantee more satisfactory wages for workers. International experience in fact indicates that the final agreements are almost always unjust to workers because collective agreements by their nature end up at a lowest common denominator that is inferior to what various sectors, but above all workers in certain individual companies, would be able to achieve. The demand for freedom of upwards wage flexibility in particular sectors or individual enterprises is not special pleading because the impact of the collective labor agreement - political, economic and social - is so great that it readily empowers the individual employer to entrench himself behind it and exclude from its provisions only the handful of executives whose salaries are in any case established by free negotiation on the labor market. This is a particularly damaging consequence of collective bargaining. The most talented can enjoy the benefits of the free labor market while the less talented, but nevertheless noteworthy and capable, must accept downward leveling and make do with the meager wages of the collective agreement.

If the salary level achieved via collective bargaining agreements is lower than what might achieved through negotiations by individual enterprise or individual worker, what makes them entirely unsuitable is their violation of the *sine qua non* for development and progress: the inseparable link between payment and productivity. The collective labor agreement confronts the great mass of workers as a single entity. It cannot make distinctions between the specific contributions of individuals, with the result that it prescribes for a worker a level of wage rise entirely unrelated to his efforts as an individual and to the results he might achieve in terms of more rapid completion of work and/or improvements in working methods: criteria that are decisive for more economical and better production of goods and services.

So collective bargaining and thus collective labor agreements do not ensure better payment for workers, and at the same time they also sever an important connecting link for development with its origins in the labor market, namely the link between pay and productivity. But if these two factors shatter the image of collective bargaining as panacea and all-purpose instrument for establishing wage levels in our society, the key factor weakening and offsetting all our comparative advantages and dismantling our most basic economic structures is the distorted (non optimal) allocation of the labor component in the various productive tasks it is called upon to perform, owing to the flawed messages being sent out by a labor market dominated and controlled by collective bargaining. Wages fixed, as a result of collective bargaining, asymmetrically with the productive contribution of the labor they recompense shift the labor component to sectors and businesses that are unable to maximize their output, so that surplus labor comes to be employed in loss-making activities, with corresponding labor shortages in profitable enterprises. This tragicomic situation has become typical of almost all sectors of the Greek economy and/or enterprises in Greece. It constitutes an impediment to economic reform in general and to every competitive and profitable business initiative in particular.

It is therefore time for us to realize how necessary it is to make the break from outdated procedures for establishing wage levels, particularly when it comes to our own economy, for all serious studies of the Greek economy indicate that our comparative advantages - the dynamic elements – are concentrated in the service sector, where the labor coefficient plays a decisive role in determining productivity and competitiveness, more so indeed than technology. Given, then, that the technological level and the level of technological expertise is in no way lagging in Greece, perhaps because of the country's wealth of social resources but also because Greek workers are in general very well-trained, we must leave the labor market free to determine wages commensurately with workers' contribution to productivity in a regime of free negotiation, above all on an enterprise basis, and with each working person separately. If this takes place on a mass basis we will very soon see a rational shift of the labor coefficient from loss-making enterprises and low-profit public-sector organizations to profitable activities with high levels of return. We will then start to be able to speak seriously about development, combining such measures with other supplementary political actions we will need to initiate to lay the foundations for radical reconstruction of our economy. There is no lack of profit-making enterprises in our country. What is holding them back, and in some cases stopping them altogether, is the political system, with its overall backwardness in introducing new institutions and new ways of solving the problems arising from the - in any case - continual reshaping of our community in a dynamic and ever-changing global environment.

THE TECHNOLOGY OF REFORM

The crucial difference between liberals and conservatives is the former's concept of transforming the established order of things in favor of simultaneous expansion of the space for defending freedom in politics, in the economy and indeed in society as a whole. We underline the difference to show how the movement of change cannot be restricted just to one area of collective action, but also that it should not be implemented in a retrograde manner that will lead to it rebounding on its initiators, further strengthening the status quo. The most significant means, or rather the most effective technique, for effecting the transformation in a democratically organized society is to ensure that any regression taking place should also have a forward momentum to it, in other words that it should move with two steps forward and one step back.

Two steps forward to change things and one step back to make it feasible for the necessary concessions to be implemented. They are necessary on the one hand to assuage the anxieties of conservative circles, and on the other to help consolidate the changes and have them assimilated by the wider, less dynamic, mass of the community. This procedure for implementing change is compatible with Democracy: it normalizes conflict, providing the opportunity both for the minority and for the majority to reform, to inform themselves of the real dimensions of the changes and contribute to a qualitative synthesis with the new that is inexorably displacing the old.

The significance of this method of change, which has its origins in the classical liberal tradition dating from the beginnings of European Enlightenment, is observable throughout the entire course of the transformation of Europe into a constellation of modern democratically-organized states. It is the method of wise liberal reform, and its influence is so great that it made an impression even on Lenin. Faced with the chaos of revolutionary change that had been engendered by the implementation of war communism, the Bolsheviks under his leadership rapidly resorted to a reintroduction of the market and small-scale property via the renowned New Economic Policy.

The reform policies that New Democracy chose to adopt between 2004 and 2009, in conjunction with a discourse of middle-of-the-road politics, aimed at introducing orderly change at a regulated rate, through a technique of smooth adjustments by society to the new conditions that were emerging. But the undertaking ran into trouble: the government's time-scale, it soon became evident, amounted to two steps back and one step forward, with the result that the reforms became bogged down. The middle-of-the-road target audience, with its inhibitions, held the government hostage, discouraging it from acting, turning delay of reform into paralysis of reform. Instead of mobilizing the young, dynamic layers of society, New Democracy attached more importance to the political center, renowned for its inertia, which functioned like quicksand, swallowing up even the most intelligent and courageous reform proposals. Across-the-board tax reductions, abolition of the state monopoly in higher education, privatization of public infrastructure, the opening of closed professions, reform of the health system and reconstruction of the insurance system, which is on its last legs – all these are issues of prime importance; some of them going ahead rapidly, others slowly with signs of progress, others again are waiting to be dealt with after the elections.

If to all this we add the unacceptable tug-o-war over specification of the time for the next election, then this elevation of tactical maneuvering over the charting of a firm strategic course (which should be the concern of government) reduces the institutional leverage of the new governmental style and sounds the death knell for reform. The continual tactical zigzagging undermines the ability to forge successful strategy, effacing reform objectives, which become easy prey of the unfavorable political conjuncture. In the final analysis, and in practice, changes of tactics replace the changes that should be introduced in a strategy of reform.

The political and social arena in Greece is not the most favorably disposed towards liberal reforms. To counter this asymmetrical difficulty, rather than idealizing the middle ground, which is anything but an ally when it comes to implementation of reform, we should choose to create dynamic consensus groupings of informed citizens who are fully aware of what they are defending and how the benefits from reform are disseminated to the people as a whole. This will enable reform to proceed, conceding a step backwards to the opponents of change and facilitating two steps forward by the progressives.

THE SPECIALIZATION OF REFORM

Today in Greece there are few who do not perceive the enormity of the reforms we are called upon to negotiate if there is to be continuation of the development of our economy, mobilization of our society, upgrading of our constitution. In the new four-year period that is opening before us, the reforms are the greatest challenge, and one which is to be met through resolution of the chronic problems that beset our country and keep it tied to the worn-out structures of the past, whose wellspring is the conservative state interventionism of the 70s and the leveling socialist egalitarianism of the 80s.

But there are also brazen examples of the culpability of the politicians we followed. Camp beds in hospitals, money-stashed bribe envelopes, kickbacks, bankrupt state-owned corporations, illegal building activity, an uncompleted land register, a non-existent forest registry, bureaucracy and corruption: these are just a few examples of the well-established vicious circle that must urgently be broken. The national health system, educational reforms, changes in town planning and the tax code, economic policies aimed at stabilization, along with numerous other institutional measures that have been taken, have all had as their foundation inspired high-level public management. But the measures have failed, because as it turns out there is an inherent inability to co-ordinate the different hierarchies that undertake the execution of public works, because of the promotion of private interest, because of the (large) number of people generally - and government officials specifically - involved in the management of public concerns. Reform policy must therefore acquire new foundations. Public management must be disconnected from those sectors of the public realm that could function better if based on the institution of private property and the mechanism of the market.

The world that has already come into existence and has started to make its moves globally is displacing discredited public-sector management on ever more major fronts. This is not happening because of imposition of a unilateral ideological position but because private property and the market prove to be more effective and more secure. The state is hard put to it to rescue the social insurance system, and taxation, even when decidedly progressive, has not significantly reduced income inequalities or overcome poverty. The intentions of the theoreticians of state intervention are doubtless genuine, but the results achieved by the politicians who implement the theories are something entirely different, in fact diametrically opposed, even in their mildest variant, which is evidently the social democratic one. The kind of politics that undertakes serious reform cannot content itself with short-term measures of bandaging the wounds inflicted through the inadequacies of state intervention and bureaucracy. It must embark on something fundamentally different, opening the way for new - non-state - institutions, for education, for insurance, for economy, for public spaces and resources.

Such reform politics will most likely provoke conflict between the new and the old, but that is the inevitable reaction to any courageous initiative that seeks to solve problems and break new ground. If Thatcher had not closed the coal mines thirty years ago and sacked thousands of miners, today Great Britain would be an economy in decline, racked by poverty and debt. Our coal mines refuse to accept the status of bankrupt state-owned corporations, and we keep them in operation to weigh us down, sowing disillusion for our future and blocking progress when we attempt to introduce intelligent and innovative strategies.

In Greece of the early 80s everyone had visions of how they were going to establish socialism. Nobody then would have believed that within two decades not only would the state-owned corporations be private but the banks would be also, above all the National Bank. But today, having overcome many obstacles and charted what has proved to be a difficult course, we have a different Greece. The reforms still lie ahead of us however. Introduction of the system of private insurance policies, the turn towards social assistance only for those in genuine need, the establishment of private universities, the introduction of competition between hospitals and clinics, expansion of private motorways, introduction of ownership titles to neglected public space, the opening of refuse management to the market. These are all fundamental and exemplary instances of the politics of reform. A reform in which the state frankly perceives its weaknesses and leaves space for the potentialities of the market perceives its weaknesses and leaves space for the potentialities of the market.

ECONOMIC STRATEGY

The Greek economy finds itself at a strategic turning point for the achievement of significant objectives. It is the crucial period that has been anticipated in the strategy of the prime minister and the minister of national economy, all possible adjustments already having been carried out to the measures and the instrumentalities that make the strategy a feasible proposition. What is sought in parallel to this is assistance in realizing the objectives that focus attention on the strategic element. There is also a desire to achieve linkage with, and assimilation of, the conflicting and centrifugal parameters that necessarily coexist in an innovative policy-making endeavor.

Very often the terrain of economics resembles a war zone. The army is led onto the battlefield after preparation for the specific conditions of the war it will be required to confront, including a testing of the battle-readiness of the opponent, with a view to striking at his most vulnerable points. Clausewitz [12], the theorist of war, puts forward the view that outcome of the way will be decided by the key battle, if prior to its being fought we achieve optimal co-ordination of the forces we control. Deflection from proper co-ordination on account of mistaken signals from the ranks, loss of co-ordination because of dense fog or unexpected diversionary fire: all this can cause the best-thought-out strategy to unravel. These are precisely the dangers that threaten present policies: failure to maintain proper co-ordination of the reforms because of intra-governmental frictions, because of harsh reaction from those who are beneficiaries of the status quo and therefore comfortable with it, because of diversion of the opposition into maximalistic polemic.

We are precisely at the turning point between fully-fledged development of economic strategy through unfolding of developmental policies based on the freeing of markets and the pioneering role of the private sector. This crystal-clear picture of our fundamental objectives becomes blurred when at the crucial movement of its application criticism starts from inside. This is the most serious of blows, devaluing the whole undertaking in the eyes of distrustful public opinion. It is like losing half the battle. The other half of the battle is left to be taken over by the noisy demonstrations of the oppositionists, who see yet again how close they are to thwarting the reform and the modernization of our country. It was in exactly this way that the change to the insurance system was blocked under Simitis, not to mention numerous other of the major and/or minor changes of which Greece is so much in need.

In this unexpected situation brought about by the cumulative interaction of intra-governmental frictions and harsh reactions from organized groups against the reforms, the official opposition always gets itself implicated in a fatal manner. The official opposition is dazzled by a brilliant future and dogged by a retrograde past. The greatest lesson learnt by the governing PASOK party is that a liberal economic policy is the only program that can get the economy of the country moving and stir the energies of its most productive members. But today it is again making mistakes because instead of pursuing rapid reform immediately it prefers excessive taxation and the draining of incomes. This has two significant and very negative consequences. The first is diminution of the credibility of political discourse and the second the conjoining of its polemic to the reactions of the organized groups and the intragovernmental frictions, all of which together conspire to place in jeopardy the prospects for successful outcome of the needed reforms.

A direct consequence of the above is undermining of the image of the terrain on which the economic strategy is to unfold. It is transformed into something uncertain and inconclusive from the viewpoint of the initial calculations. If we factor in to this such centrifugal and anomalous elements as reduced competitiveness, excessive borrowing, public debt and the heavy deficits of the state-owned corporations, we can perhaps better begin to understand the magnitude of the effort that must be made to overcome all these obstacles that are holding us back from our progress into the 21st century.

In this difficult conjuncture where on the one hand there is a clear, certain and coherent strategy for the economy and on the other a particularly inhospitable, not to say dangerously thorny, terrain for implementing it, where hostile political, social and trade union protagonists compete for influence, the ultimate outcome is in no way a foregone conclusion. Its success can be assured only if it can be explained to citizens why they should identify with it and why the reforms should be defended. Only if they can be persuaded and the broadest possible consensus attained will the liberal strategy succeed. The battle for the economy is not a battle between the government and the opposition. It is a battle for the country's prosperity.

THEORY OF PRIVATIZATIONS AND THEIR SIGNIFICANCE

The problem is not just that Greek political life rests on decaying foundations that have been corroded by the gloomy developments of our days, stamped by the influence of "small people in great positions". There is also an even more urgent need for us to orient both our thoughts and our political practice to the controversial subject of institutional reforms that can change the country's structures and free it from the scourge of the corruption that comes with the big state, big newspaper editors, big journalists. What we need to do is focus on the real problems, and in particular turn our attention to privatizations as a structural change in the organization of our economy for the freeing of the healthy and vital forces of our country with a view to generating expanded development and ensuring its diffusion as widely as possible, with a particular emphasis on the humbler strata of society.

Property rights play a basic role in establishing the foundations of the type of economic organization that will prevail in a society. When private property is strengthened and harmonized with the rule of the free market and the democratic control of legal regulation, there is a maximization of the effectiveness of the productive mechanism and a multiplication of the opportunities for wider distribution of wealth with the minimum of bureaucratic management. I provide detailed analysis of this in my book "Property and the Market"[13] and in my articles "Towards a Synthesis of Theories of State Failure" (2007)[14] and "Institutional Failures of Socialism" (2009) [15]. Ronald Coase (Nobel 1991) has shown that the free market and private property minimize the overall social cost, which is key factor in successful economic organization [16]. It is wrong to overlook and ignore the high cost of operational frictions generated by the mechanisms of government and the perennial failures to be observed in the attempts at regulation carried out by the labyrinthine bureaucratic mechanisms which, instead of the solutions for which they have been designed, ultimately produce chain reactions of dis-functionality.

Historically, societies of large-scale planning have failed, and indeed miserably. This is due to the fact not only that they have not succeeded in producing the wealth that capitalism bestows upon societies by virtue of an automatic propulsive mechanism. It is also because they have been literally brought to their knees by the task of distributing what little they do produce under the pressure of the voracious needs of the administrative structures and the hierarchy of large-scale planning. The mind of the majority no doubt goes to the recent societies of real socialism but one might also examine the ancient water-centered societies of Mesopotamia and Egypt and the way they systematically bankrupted themselves in all the phases of the various dynasties. After 8000 B.C., when the great agricultural revolution took place, our world began slowly to change, albeit with long intervals of retardation or stasis. This has undergone a dramatic change in the last five minutes of history, from the 18th century A.D. until the present, with an incredible explosion of production, population growth and technological development. Douglas North (Nobel 1993) has shown that this happened because the capitalist mode of production established effective rights of property, which multiplied the fruits of human effort at an unexpectedly great and accelerating rate [17] [18] [19].

Capitalism was not invented as a system of social organization by any thinker or philosopher. Nor was it imposed by any political or economic authority. It emerged spontaneously as part of a quest by human beings for effective organization and, on each occasion, in every new phase, it has organized itself, amid attempts both to help it and hinder it, within a process of anonymous, multi-faceted and multiform experimentation. While capitalism developed the joint-stock company to resolve problems of proprietorship in a more demanding and complex world, really-existing socialism responded with the *soviet*, the *solkhoz* and the co-operative. The superiority of capitalism resides in its superior institutions, with the effective ownership rights they entailed. Milton Friedman (Nobel 1976) in his book "Capitalism and Freedom" showed that freedom is the perennial force within capitalism, leaving it up to people to select the proprietorial rights that further their prosperity [20].

In Greece we must implement an ideology of privatizations if their dynamic is to become something feasible and the practice they have adopted up to the present day upgraded. The results to date are by no means negligible. The stage for privatizations was set some time ago by modernizing socialists. The show goes on, with new political protagonists, but the public that approves of what is being done is undoubtedly very small numerically, and shows no sign of becoming larger.

THE POLITICS OF PRIVATIZATION

In the series of my arguments on privatization I am presenting here, I propose to concern myself with the practices we are pursuing. This is necessary if we are to see what led us to embark on this experiment for changing the organization of our economy, how it has evolved and how it is intensifying today. This is by way of a prelude to examining, in the chapters to follow, the dynamics of privatization, above all in the last chapter, which will deal with the necessity of defending the ideology of privatizations before a large and critical mass of citizens, so as to be able to achieve significant reduction in adjustment costs and consolidate the concept of the predominance of the private over the public. The reality is that this is the only solution, not only for reviving our economy but also for defending the position of the country generally, in a difficult, demanding and extremely competitive globalized world in which countries are inevitably divided between up-and-coming countries that harness the power of the free market and marginal and excluded countries, excluded because of their links to socialism and statism.

At the beginning of the 90s the Mitsotakis government opened the way, consciously and clearly, for privatizations. With its starting point the ideology of liberalism and the collapse of really-existing socialism, together with reminders of the crumbling condition of the Greek economy bequeathed by the Socialists of the 80s, he embarked on a strategic program of privatizations, spearheaded by the two most single-minded liberal politicians of the post-junta period, Andreas Andrianopoulos and Stefanos Manos. But the effort was in vain. The abortive Papandreou government that followed, with Gennimatas as Finance Minister, suspended the privatizations and renationalized the urban public transport system. It was patently a step backwards. Today we are in a position to reflect on our responsibility as we gaze in awe at the astronomical deficits registered by the celebrated public transport system and the financial maelstrom it has generated in Greece, appreciating finally that there can be no effective public management of business enterprise.

The Simitis governments turned a new page, albeit less for the country than for Greece's *sui generis* socialism. The manifestly pro-European orientation of the modernizing socialists and the need to meet the corresponding requirements led to the country under the leadership of Simitis, however much through need rather than ideological persuasion, implementing a program of privatizations underpinned by controlled gradual equitization of state-owned instrumentalities and enterprises. Slowly, timidly, the Socialists were discovering the volatile components of liberalism. For the first time the equitized enterprises were observed to be generating profits rather than burdening us with deficits. On account of the profits, they were injecting tax receipts and dividends into the budget while at the same time through sale of shares the state was earning very significant extra income which on account of the depth and the extent of the equitizations could acquire a permanent character.

So lo and behold, the socialists had become partisans of the market, moreso than the liberals! But this applied only for the leadership group and the enlightened middle class, and they did not understand that with the exception of their own hangers-on, the people were not supporting them. They never made any effort to explain to the electorate the benefits and the virtues of the free market and, zealous converts as they were, did not say anything of the dangers. As a result, when – not without a sizeable dose of arrogance – they punted on the most fallible element in capitalism, the stock exchange, they were engulfed in a disaster, along with those who had followed them blindly, more persuaded of the possibilities of profits forever than of the institutional and other longer-term benefits of economic reorganization (such as the prospect of achieving, in the course of a protracted process of realignments and readjustments that would secure comparative commercial advantages for Greece within the framework of international competition, increased productivity of labor and better returns on invested capital.)

The Free Market cannot be part of an economic experiment or be imposed socially through economic sorcery. On the contrary, in conjunction with democracy and the rule of law, it gives rise to superior polities, with rational political organization, a robust economy and a cohesive society. The road of privatization is long and difficult and must be followed with persistence. It is the road of virtue, which does not have the attractive power of the road of vice. But at its conclusion it provides satisfaction for all: it brings results. It is the desideratum, to be pursued in a better organized and more rational manner than the New Democracy reform governments have succeeded in accomplishing. This is something I propose to investigate in the next section.

THE NEW DEMOCRACY PRIVATIZATIONS OF THE 2004-2009 PERIOD

New Democracy's coming to power in 2004 was inevitable and offered the prospect of new impetus to the worn-out program of denationalizations they had inherited from the modernizing socialists. Basing their strategy primarily on equitization, the latter were trying the patience not only of their supporters but also of themselves. On the one hand they could see the obvious benefits of the market for development of the economy and strengthening of the budget; on the other there was their political inability to see the project through, and their aversion to any attempt to make it attractive to large numbers of the people. But the same affliction, more or less, is to be observed in the broad base of the New Democracy party and is part of the inherent make-up of most of its activists. This is the most serious difficulty with this great change we have been trying for the last two decades to bring about, in favor of private organization of our economy.

New Democracy's term in office got under way in mid-spring 2004, when the global business cycle was already on the upswing. International capitalism had again worked its magic. It had left behind it the traumas of the technological bubble and the attack on the Twin Towers, drawing a larger number of new emergent economies into a hectic phase of global development. The key protagonists were China and India. In such an ideal environment the Finance Minister George Alogoskoufis seized the opportunity and organized a differentiated and effective program of denationalizations. Naturally the denationalizations were at the heart of the New Democracy program, but given the weaknesses emphasized at the start nobody was in a position to predict the ultimate outcome in terms of the extent and the depth of the changes, if they did not reflect the clear preferences of the Prime Minister Costas Karamanlis and the direct actions of the Finance Minister George Alogoskoufis.

The politics of privatization at the global level from the 1980s, when it was initiated under the leadership of Reagan and Thatcher, to the present day has undergone a considerable evolution. On the one hand it has brought about essential changes to the structures of the present-day economic world, on the other it has matured as a science, so that today it both provides us with effective and up-to-date technology that remedies chronic budget deficits and secondly puts at the disposal of the economy profit-making businesses that generate wealth, provide work and yield tax revenues. In the light of all this, New Democracy attempted to harmonize the philosophy of the social centre, bastion against the pressures from its popular base, with the inevitable developments that were required to take place in the market so that the country could acquire economic dynamism. The undertaking was in no way easy or straightforward, but it was successful. New Democracy's privatization programme did not content itself simply with continuing the equitizations of PASOK. It assumed other forms, such as direct sale in the case of the Emporiki Bank, or increase in share capital with a view to maximizing it through buyouts, in the case of the National Bank.

The New Democracy party, and George Alogoskoufis personally, were the target of vehement criticism. On the issue of the Emporiki Bank there was internal upheaval inside PASOK with the expulsion of Papantoniou. But this was a storm in a teacup. The National Bank made a great entrepreneurial leap forward, totally freed from the restrictions that had previously been imposed by the state. It was an unqualified success story with benefits that have now started to become measurable. Something that for decades was considered altogether impossible, privatization of the National Bank, became a reality, in the most successful and discreet way. The sale of the Emporiki Bank was likewise a complete success and the benefit to the general interest offered by the proceeds from it became immediately evident in the rise of its price on the stock market. The Emporiki was a big bank with numerous weaknesses, all of them kept nourished via the umbilical cord of the state. Today it is a big private bank, with a dynamic future and powerful underpinnings that make it a stable, indeed an unshakeable, option, even in the midst of the credit squeeze we are currently experiencing.

With a unique mastery that may be glimpsed from the above examples, George Alogoskoufis pursued simultaneously virtually every opportunity for denationalization. He abolished the minimum 34% public ownership requirement and the 5% requirement for voting rights, proceeding immediately to extend equitization to the telephone company OTE, the Hellenic Postbank and the Agricultural Bank, and indeed at the peak of the business cycle. He moved with precision, and rapidly, pre-empting the negative conjuncture that was to follow, pouring revenue into the public treasury, stimulating the market, providing new opportunities for reorganization of denationalized former public sector companies. If the privatization of OTE is brought to fruition, there will be radical changes to the economic map of Greece, and the prospects for privatization of virtually all sectors of the economy currently under the control of the feudal state-owned corporations harbours, water, electricity) will gain further momentum.

The occasion for the next stage of mass privatizations in all the forms demanded by present-day technology was to be provided with the commencement of a vigorous new upswing in the commercial and financial cycle that would overshadow today's highly negative conjuncture, vindicating those who believe in markets and are not daunted by their dramatic fluctuations. In any case today's credit bubble is not very different from the technological bubble that preceded it: neither in its explosiveness nor in its attractiveness, so that the majority, including the most specialized, will seek to take it in hand. This is the magic of markets: they punish the arrogant exponents of the status quo and open the way for those who are brave enough to embark on new entrepreneurial adventures!

THE ROLE OF PRIVATIZATIONS IN CONFRONTING THE CRISIS

In the preceding sections I attempted to analyze the gradual transformation of the Greek economy away from being state-controlled to being a decentralized private enterprise economy. Despite the fact that progress has been slow, with many retreats and strange mutations, the end result has been significant and undoubtedly positive for our economy.

One need only reflect on where we would be today, in the rearguard of developments, in a closed circuit of misery and underdevelopment, if we had remained with a state-controlled banking system, a state-controlled, monolithic and monopolistic telecommunications network, with a plethora of enterprises from shipyards, oil refineries, cement works and so on, all state run, party-controlled and bureaucratic. Twenty to thirty years ago all these enterprises were run by commissars, by supervising social councils manned by representatives of the companies' staff associations, trade union federations, technical chambers, even local government. Everything but the market. The result was that the formerly great state-owned corporations became bogged down in wretched, but boundless, competitive corporate loss-making, in budget deficits and accumulated debt.

But this is the picture of our economy as it was up until the 80s, not today, and it is our liberal transformation that has played the decisive role in this. It is a new world, whose day has just begun to dawn, and we who live in it have a long road ahead of us, necessitating intensification of our endeavors to impart to the practice of the privatizations we have been pursuing over the last decades a clear dynamic that can reduce the uncertainties and the dangers and multiply the benefits with their widest possible proliferation at every level of the social scale. This is the greatest political and social responsibility yet, elevating our liberal transformation into a new chapter in the nation's history, determining our country's future course.

It is a future that will be judged between the two poles that define the terrain of application of the dynamic of privatizations. On the one hand uncertainties and dangers and on the other the diffusion of benefits. Should the uncertainties and the dangers be dealt with effectively, however great the benefits are that emerge, the prestige of market liberalism will fade if they are not disseminated as visible and tangible economic rewards to broader layers of the population and, as far as possible, also to lower-income groups. If, again, we adopt a one-dimensional approach to dissemination of the initial benefits, pursuing old-style distributive policies, in the interest of impulsive political confrontation or naïve manipulation of electoral clientele, then the uncertainties and the dangers, which always arise in the course of the never-ending movement of capitalism, will sweep away our achievements, however significant and durable they may appear to be today.

The dynamics of the privatizations must counter pose the new benefits of dissemination to the many to the spoils surrendered to a few entrenched speculators. To open the harbors to competition, to new investments, to new employment opportunities. To put energy in the hands of competing networks employing a variety of different resources. A nightmarish future for energy is not far off if we remain in today's morass of the Public Power Company, the General Confederation of its staff and lignite.

To make the traditional water supply networks private so as to develop the necessary multiformity in their infrastructural muscle that will boost profits to provide funding for the necessary new investments, which must become a reality immediately because of the dramatic urban growth.

To salvage from the sea bottom the state-owned shipwrecks such as the railway company OSE, the urban public transport systems and all the other odds and ends of the public sector. To reconstruct all the regional airports of the Greek mainland and the Greek islands on the model of our showpiece Eleftherios Venizelos airport, which must undergo the best and most immediate exemplary privatization. Each year Greece welcomes from abroad a number of visitors larger than its entire population. It is unjustifiable that it should lack up-to-date regional airports. If the private sector twenty years ago had moved into the airports it would already have developed ultra-modern infrastructures with the sums of money that are being made available by the millions of arrivals from other countries. The same should be done immediately with rubbish disposal. It is futile to expect the public administration, central or local, to manage it using antiquated landfill technology. In the modern world rubbish is one of the basic resources for energy production and the private sector is more than ready to undertake it, and impatient to do so!

Many other examples could be cited of opportunities, and the list of feasible privatizations potentially beneficial to the public is literally endless. We must therefore support the political leadership's moves in that direction and succeed in enabling the people to sense the enormity of the changes and moving even further ahead. Without hesitation, without prejudices, without inhibitions.

THE FATAL MISTAKE OF TAX SAFARIS

Right from the beginning of the post-junta period all Greek governments demonstrated a remarkable enthusiasm for imposing taxes, stemming from a pernicious illusion that this would enable us to deal, effectively and conclusively, with the problems of the fiscal deficit and public debt. But reality, miserably and repeatedly, thwarts the great architects of taxation campaigns in the Greek economic life of recent years and it is remarkable how Greek politicians, and indeed economists, become trapped in the single-minded pursuit of increased revenue when expenditures are increasing exponentially, surpassing all reasonable boundaries.

In the 70s in the midst of global crisis and stagflation we tolerated harsh austerity measures, upper limits on profits, price controls of every kind, administrative and bureaucratic regulations, nationalizations. State paternalism in all its glory! In the 1980s we distinguished ourselves through dismantling fiscal structures across the board. Nothing could bring us down to earth. Not the successive devaluations of our national currency, not the emergency taxes on profits, not the extremely burdensome general taxation, not the skyrocketing debt, not the administrative restrictions on imports and drastic cutbacks in trade. The state gigantism made us proud, as did the the petty-bourgeois nirvana of permanency, of the salary acquired without effort and without responsibility, fully underwritten and guaranteed by the public sector.

In the turn towards change of the 80s and 90s something momentous occurred, even by the standards of the overloaded fiscal structures in Greece. In the New Democracy/Communist government of 1989 and even more so in the ensuing grand coalition government, all the parties – each in the ministries they controlled, embarked upon a veritable orgy of spending. The public profile of the then Prime Minister, eminent academician and economist Xenophon Zolotas, was somewhat tarnished, not by his age but by the enormity of the ecumenical Greek fiscal free-for-all of that time. In the very brief liberal interlude of the Mitsotakis prime ministership at the beginning of the 1990s, the government attempted to rationalize public finances. It proposed reduction in the size of the state, and indeed reduction to its central hard core, promoting the principle of the pensioning off of two civil servants for every one appointment, along with extensive privatization of state activities. But its numerical weakness in parliament and the lack of unanimity on principles led to the premature fall of the Mitsotakis government over a privatization that it had been elected by the people to carry out. All of this should serve as a warning to us today to be circumspect in our political actions, as the government at that time was not, when the heavy special tax on petrol which was thought to have the potential to generate, for the first time, a primary fiscal surplus not only did not improve public finances but on the contrary had extremely negative, inflationary, consequences, ruining and discrediting the policy of price deregulation.

Greek economic policies since the fall of the junta are a story of repeated mistakes arising out of an uncritical and ostentatious enthusiasm for taxing and out of the fallacy that implementing such a policy will serve to counteract our fiscal disequilibria. It was on this basis that the unpopular, unjust and irrationally modernizing objective taxation criteria were introduced. While contributing to a certain recovery in tax receipts and facilitating our entry into the Economic and Monetary Union, not even they – before they were abolished - provided enough revenue to finance the subsequent Armageddon of state expenditures and benefits in addition to servicing the astronomical public debt. And so arose the paradox that New Democracy, which had advocated tax reductions, started its term in office by increasing taxes. Admittedly this was followed by a lull, accompanied by a gradual but very significant reduction in tax rates which, together with successful privatizations in certain crucial areas, ushered in a period of upturn in the Greek economy, a rise in business expectations, a very important simultaneous increase in investments, consumption and GNP, but above all an opening of Greek enterprises to international markets which for the first time since the fall of the junta imparted to our economy an aggressive outward-looking character.

But good news in Greece has a brief lifespan. Expenditures were never brought under control. The public debt under New Democracy in 2008 shot up to reach a record figure of 250 billion euros and, faced with the threat of Greece finding itself under renewed European fiscal superintendence, the finance minister was obliged once again to climb the Golgotha of increasing taxes. This time he did it in a more tragic manner. He came into conflict with his own central idea that a well-governed democratic state is characterized by generally mild taxation of the middle strata and very low or no taxation of the economically weak. But, as if this wasn't enough, through over-taxation of dividends he embraced the programmatic principle of PASOK for heavier taxation of distributed profits. This policy in particular could justifiably be entitled "copy and paste"! We appear to be only a step away from the profound philosophical principle of socialists that there should be taxation too of the air we breathe! In any case this is what seems to be implied by the desire to tax the surplus value of shares and stock options.

No consideration was given to arguments that dividends are already taxed through a very heavy overall tax exceeding 40%. What indeed do dividends stand for that they should today face one of the heaviest rates of taxation? What is the problem with dividends? They are usually generated by the best-run companies, the joint-stock companies, and they comprise the last very small remainder that is left after all the charges – operating expenses, taxation, social costs and so on – are subtracted. And of course in some years they are not even distributed. The overtaxing of dividends is an unhealthy and in every way mistaken policy. We send the wrong signal to all investors who in recent years have ventured out into the perilous seas of the Greek economy. But above all we undermine the idea of people's capitalism, which wants to see the citizen playing a leading role in the stock exchange, as a long-term proposition, participating directly in the idea of company property, with a stable and lightly taxed divided as a minimum benefit.

The same applies for surplus value. After the collapse of share prices at the turn of the century and given today's stagnation, what defensible political principle can justify taxing what surplus values have been generated? What is the margin of risk that we call upon investors to undertake if they bring their capital to the Athens Stock Exchange and we tell them that the only thing sure is that they will be taxed? The market is in a bad shape: there is negligible turnover while at the same time competing international transaction platforms and other organized national stock markets are eager to appropriate whatever legacy remains from entrepreneurial activity in Greece. In the face of this harsh, relentless reality it is incomprehensible that we should be proceeding to tax surplus value from the purchase and sale of shares.

It appears that ultimately I will be one of the few to defend the freedom of trading stock options. When a leadership group, of directors and top executives, takes over responsibility for a business and achieves a take-off, with spectacular profits, promoting innovations in organization, production and sales, it is morally deplorable for the shares accruing to the protagonists of this magnificent endeavor to have to be divided between themselves and the state bureaucracy. If we want to have profitable companies managed by capable executives we should not tax stock options or they will go to other countries and we will be deprived of precious human assets. Of course improper behavior vis à vis the exercise of stock options is to be observed in the market in some cases. But even here sole responsibility for regulation is in the hands of the general meeting of shareholders and the market itself. In the event that some successful and avaricious cadres might wish to cannibalize the shares they have generated, the market itself will discredit this.

To conclude, the taxation practices that have been implemented can have only detrimental effects. If the frenetic rate of increase in state expenditures is not brought decisively under control, even this crushing taxation will not be enough to deal with the crisis. Greeks today do not want a Leviathan state but a Democracy which can liberate the country's productive forces, with lower taxation and burgeoning profits.

RENT SEEKING IN THE GREEK ECONOMIC DRAMA

The austerity measures of the new Greek socialist government of Mr. George Papandreou are unlikely to succeed if even this government that has replaced the conservative government of Mr. Kostas Karamanlis does not bridle the iniquitous, idle, and totally inefficient Greek public sector. In essence the new austerity measures are neither far-reaching nor comprehensive enough to be able to deal with Greece's dire fiscal situation[2].

An appropriate title for the new austerity measures of the Greek government would be "Economic Policy at Gunpoint", to paraphrase the title of Andreas Papandreou's book "Democracy at Gunpoint", which he wrote when he was fighting the dictatorship in Greece in the late 1960s. Andreas Papandreou, father of today's prime minister George Papandreou, was a radical socialist, both as an academic economist and as a politician, ruling Greece as prime minister in the 1980s and for a few years in the 1990s [21][22][23][24].

It was the statesman Andreas Papandreou that started the fiscal crapulence in Greece in the post-Second-World-War era. He escalated both the fiscal deficit and the debt to huge levels[3] while brutally socializing factories, shipyards, refineries, utilities and expanding the public sector to an enormous size. Ironically, in pursuing these policies the socialist Andreas Papandreou was only following, albeit in a more radical way, the broad program of nationalizations that had been established by the conservative Konstantinos Karamanlis. And there is perhaps a similar irony to the fact that the Konstantinos Karamanlis who ruled Greece in the 1970s was the uncle of the more recent former prime minister Kostas Karamanlis who ruled the Greece from 2004 to 2009 and left Greece in an unprecedented fiscal mess.

The third irony, if not the great paradox that brought Greece to the threshold of default, is that it was from the socialist Andreas Papandreou that the young conservative Kostas

---

[2] According to Eurostat in 2009 Greece's public deficit was 115.1% of GDP and the public deficit 13.6% of GDP.

[3] In 1981 Andreas Papandreou took over a public debt amounting to 29.7% of GDP and in 1990 when he lost the elections handed over a public debt that came to 80.7% of GDP. But even this very high percentage seriously underestimated the level of public debt as it did not include the unpaid state collateral awarded to numerous state companies, public corporations and public utilities. It was ruinous public debt that caused the first modern Greek fiscal crisis in 1993.

Karamanlis imbibed his worst lessons in economic theory and his worst policies as a practicing politician. From the beginning of his term in office as a young and fresh Greek prime minister, Kostas Karamanlis, nephew of Konstantinos Karamanlis, led the country on a course of state gigantism that absorbed like a sponge all the revenues accumulated from five years of successful privatizations, with total public expenditure dramatically increasing without political or economic limit. As with Andreas Papandreou, in Kostas' Karamanlis hands the vast Greek public sector became merely a tool for his re-election and for consolidation of his political position.

The fourth irony, and the fatal mistake of Kostas Karamanlis, was that prior to the elections of October 2009 he announced a freeze on salaries of public sector employees. Faced with the state of emergency in Greece's public finances, in the eleventh hour, Karamanlis spoke the truth! But nemesis came from the people who had been hired, explicitly or implicitly, in the public sector. His followers, his political "army", his political "clients", to use the terminology of rent- seeking theory, did not follow him.

Modern Greece possesses all the characteristics of a deeply rent-seeking society Mark Jackson (2005, p.282) argues that the net welfare cost of successful rent seeking activity is remarkably underestimated [25]. Parente and Prescott (2000, p.145) estimate that if we remove institutional barriers, nations can produce gains 1000 or 2000 percent [26]! Politicians work as brokers in a system of political clientelism. They expand the public sector, exchanging jobs for votes. On the other hand they push the private sector into bed with the public sector, assigning to the former secure profits, privileges and finally explicit and legally established rents[4]. On the basis of this trade-off between political and economic rents, farmers are enriched through subsidies and workers' unions negotiate collective agreements fixing wages much higher than can be justified on productive grounds.

In short, rent-seeking behaviour is chronic in modern Greek society, resulting in emergence of a generally inefficient institutional economic framework that is financed through a dramatically expanding public deficit and debt and supported by a strong continental currency, the euro. Although it could not have been Greece that Douglass North had in mind, I feel impelled to underline his words on the future of democracies: "The pluralist control of the state which emerged from the struggle of workers, farmers, and business groups has produced the disintegration of the earlier structure of property rights and replaced it with a struggle in the political arena to redistribute income and wealth at the expense of the efficiency potential of the Second Economic Revolution."(North, 1981, p.185)

What a lesson for all future and potential expansionist politicians, though it cannot be asserted that this is something unprecedented in modern Greek history. The names of Greek rulers change from Karamanlis to Papandreou and back again[5], the nominal political direction changes between conservatism and socialism, but the size of the state remains stably excessive, not to say anomalous, and fiscal conditions are worsening exponentially!

On the other hand today's prime minister George Papandreou, son of Andreas Papandreou, who had promised salary increases, Keynesian warming of the economy and redistribution of income, finally as winner of the elections decreased salaries and drastically

---

[4] I do not include bribes and corruption that comprise the dark side of the modern Greek economy.

[5] The political phenomenon of democratically elected leaders establishing family political dynasties that last for two or more generations is something that can be seen not only in countries like Greece, India, Pakistan, or Argentina but also in the USA. It is yet another feature of the institutional development of contemporary democracy that undoubtedly deserves examination.

cut public expenditure. This George Papandreou the younger, since his grandfather of the same name was prime minister in the 1960s, plays the leading role in the modern Greek Fiscal Tragedy, imposing draconian measures to pay for the sins of his father Andreas Papandreou and his father's "best student" Kostas Karamanlis, with very heavy consequences. I hereby take the opportunity to predict that these austerity measures will meet the same fate as the notorious Laws of Dracon that were applied in ancient Athens. The austerity of Dracon's Laws was symbolized by their being written not in ink but in blood. They restored order to ancient Athens but were finally reformed by Solon. The spirit of Solon's Laws was such that they brought harmony without austerity and coercion, ushering in the Golden Age of ancient Athens[6]. Modern Greece is evidently destined to relive the hardship of Dracon before being able to hope for a deliverance akin to that brought by Solon.

The Global Public Debt Crisis is Keynesian

The public debt crisis that has erupted in Greece is an excellent point of departure for us to examine the potentially dramatic consequences of unbridled public borrowing for the future of all democratic countries. What has happened in Greece is already beginning to happen in a number of the world's most developed and powerful democracies. My assertion is that what lies behind the abandonment of economic rationality in management of the public finances of developed democracies is the predominance of Keynesian ideas, both in the immediate post-World War II period and in our day, with the resurgence of outdated and anachronistic Keynesianism as the most suitable economic policy for effective handling of the global financial crisis.

In the democratic West in the immediate aftermath of the Second World, despite the alternation in office of conservative and progressive governments, economic policy was constructed and exercised on the basis of Keynesianism. Whether social democrats or conservative paternalists, politicians were devotees of Keynes and Franklin Roosevelt, and they flooded the most up-to-date and developed democracies that had ever been seen in human history with continuously high fiscal deficits that went on accumulating ever greater, ever more pyramidal, ever more unsustainable public debts. It is no coincidence that the Republican Nixon who succeeded the Democrat Johnson, the American political architect of the Socialist great society, proclaimed that "we are now all Keynesians"!

These inauspicious developments in the West prompted the great free market philosopher and Nobel Prize-winning economist Hayek [30] to write his book "The Road to Serfdom", analyzing and highlighting the existing danger for the democratic West that Social Democracy and conservative paternalism could be the Trojan Horse for destruction of our liberties and their unconditional surrender to statism and bureaucracy. On the other hand the Nobel Prize-winning free market economist James Buchanan [31] with his celebrated and prophetic book "Democracy in Deficit" warned as early as 1977 that Keynesian deficits not only represent a clearly ineffective long-term policy but are also the key ideological lever for

---

[6] Bitros and Karayiannis, (2008), Bitros and Karayiannis (2010) and Karayiannis and Hatzis (forthcoming) (see [27][28][29]) show how it was high individualist moral values that decisively determined the social norms, the free institutions and the rule of law that in the period following Solon's reforms minimized the social transaction cost, advanced free enterprise and generated the rapid economic growth and general wealth of classical Athens.

undermining the integrity of the supreme social contract, the Constitution, and ultimately the self-sufficiency, autonomy and independence of the Republic.

If to the two abovementioned contributions we add those of all the other great free market champions of the 20th century, Milton Friedman, Ronald Coase, Gary Becker, George Stigler, Vernon Smith - all Nobel Prize-winners - but also many other classical liberals in scholarly disciplines other than economics, it becomes possible to state unequivocally that only the classical liberals have emphasized in the most resounding fashion that the progress and stability of Democracy has its basis in the limited and frugal state, which rather than allowing itself to be eroded by high public deficits and heavy public debts is duty-bound to uphold and defend individual rights and extend the liberties of individuals and the self-regulating institutions brought into existence by free individuals, such as the market, price mechanisms, competition, property rights, contracts and agreements, the rule of law and the eternal and permanent moral conventions and customs that in the long course of history have come to embody the great virtues of social co-operation and intercourse.

The great classical liberal thinkers of the 20th century overturned the historical trend towards social-democracy. With the powerful momentum that characterized them, their ideas overwhelmed and then overturned the traditional state paternalism in the conservative parties and finally won over their social democratic opponents politically, with the coming to power of Thatcher and Reagan who, in a series of dynamic reforms, restored development and progress to the democratic West, overcoming the stagnation and checking the inflation that had been so symptomatic of the post-war domination of the West by Keynesian policies of deficit and debt. The Political Economy of Classical Liberalism has thus led to a general discrediting of Keynes and Roosevelt and the elevation of Hayek and Friedman in academia, and Thatcher and Reagan in politics.

The Political Economy of Classical Liberalism has once again led the world into exceptional progress and economic growth, this time on a scale unprecedented, with continual and successive waves of innovation that through the mechanisms of the free market have been disseminated automatically to the whole planet, abolishing all borders and casting aside all obstacles, from simple tariff walls to the once impregnable iron curtains of every species of communism.

Notwithstanding all this, with the outbreak of the global financial crisis, the Political Economy of Classical Liberalism has once more been targeted as responsible. It has been openly inculpated and dropped like a hot brick, while its most significant and up-to-date scientific accomplishment, the efficient market theory, has become the butt of ironic remarks, even in academic circles[32]. As a result, the global economy is being surrendered to the same old-fashioned, anachronistic Keynesianism that has led to the greatest global public debt crisis ever, to which Greece constitutes a mere footnote, the only anxiety it induces being that of the collapse of a section that could pull down the great walls of public debt that have been erected in the USA, in Japan, in the United Kingdom, in Italy, in Spain and other major countries of the global economic system.

The reappearance of Keynesianism in consequence of the global financial crisis and the electoral victory of the principal social-democratic political representative of our times, Barack Obama, is what I would give the name "The Great Regression". As I analyzed in Economic Affairs, December 2009, "The 1930s and the Present Day – Crises Compared"[33], there can be no greater offence against democracy and economic rationality than the pyramidal public borrowing bring pursued by Obama, funded so profusely by the most blatant and unbridled monetary policy ever implemented by the FED, by the greatest imaginable zealot for printing fresh money, its director Ben Bernanke. If the post-war Keynesian policies of deficits and the generation of debt led to the collapse of Bretton Woods and stable exchange rates, the post-global-financial-crisis expansionism and out-of-control Keynesian fiscal and monetary policies will lead to total lack of credibility for state paper money (fiat money) and the return of the gold standard of Classical Liberal Political Economy, as a new, technologically innovative medium of exchange.

In generating this global scenario of mountains of state debt to be accumulated by the world's greatest economies, Greece is paradoxically playing a leading role on the front pages of the world's largest and most reputable newspapers, as if it is the key protagonist. In reality of course it is merely a negligible afterthought, which for all that happens to be the critical weight on the scales, determining the direction (euro or dollar) and velocity with which one side will hit the bottom. If Obama is succumbing to the Greek problem of public debt, he is doing so because he brought the public debt of the United States to the maximum constitutionally permissible point, which is only a step away from the most shattering bankruptcy in the economic history of human civilization. If Papandreou remains excluded from the markets, the position of Obama vis à vis his creditors is no less problematic. He is required to justify the devaluation of the dollar and the flood of new bonds that his creditors must absorb to keep alive the debt-ridden American public sector.

Today's well-mannered social-democrats are under siege from the results of the actions of theirs that have emerged from implementation of their mistaken ideas. Perhaps they revere Keynes and Roosevelt, but application of their ideas and policies has led them into the impasses of today. Today's well-mannered social-democrats, like the well-mannered feudal lords of the old times, are up to their eyes in debt and deficits, and thus bereft of the traditional Keynesian economic tools for stimulating effective demand and reheating the economy. Under siege, trapped and disarmed, they are unable to deal with the crisis: all they can do is await their final downfall.

Stability versus Expansionism

On the contrary Germany is the counterexample of USA. Germany despite the difficulties and the challenges that it has faced in the decade now ending, Germany has managed through strict discipline both in the workplace and business world and in its governmental policy, to become the first among the developed economies to overcome the serious economic crisis and display significant and stable growth, along with an impressive fall in the rate of unemployment. Despite the fact that the German economy and fiscal system suffered relentless blows from the crisis, with quite a few banks still licking their wounds, as it were, Germany has recovered and is showing the way forward to a rational and stable upturn.

So, how was this remarkable German recovery achieved? In a particularly tough economic environment swept by the global crisis but also a tough monetary environment, with the Euro undergoing constant revaluation, rallying again and again against almost all other currencies, Germany continues to excel as an exporter and to achieve trade surpluses, economic growth and reduction in unemployment. The German success is attributable to the undeniable fact that it has never surrendered to the logic of bloated fiscal deficits, pyramids of accumulated public debt, and has never permitted the European Central Bank to become the printing press for cheap state money. Whatever the difficulties, Germany opted for fiscal and monetary stability. From the outset it chose sacrifice and effort so as to reap the rewards that all of the rest in the European periphery want in the form of long-term loans to secure their survival.

When I cite Germany as an example, my objective is of course not to compare it with Greece or other weak links of the European periphery, but with the USA. Uncontrolled expansionism[7], fiscal and monetary, from the Obama/Bernanke duet[8], is going to have dramatically negative consequences.

Gold will continue breaking one record after another in its skyrocketing upward trajectory. Prices of commodities, with first and foremost oil, but also metals, agricultural products from that white gold cotton to cereals, will continue to rise and when the dollar goes over the psychological barrier of $1.40, the European Central Bank will sound the alarm.

The only solution – assuming rejection by Germany of any relaxation – will be to promote a bankruptcy declaration of some kind, not only by Greece but also by two other European Union countries, so as to check the erratic course of the Euro as against the dollar, without this posing any threat to German supremacy.

The Germans will sacrifice the European periphery so as to secure sufficient removal of the spreads from the countries of the European periphery to put a brake on the revaluation of the euro against the dollar. This is why it is not enough just to look at Greece to find out what we are up against. Only a generalized crisis of confidence vis à vis the European periphery will send investors back to the dollar.

The more Bernanke keeps printing dollars, the more inclined the Germans will be to place in jeopardy the credibility and creditworthiness of the European periphery. The financial recklessness of the FED is unquestionably placing overt pressures not only on Germany but also on Japan, as well as pinning China into a mandatory and generalized rejection of any possible consideration of revaluing the Yuan. Bernanke's injections of money to safeguard the shallow and fragile American upturn and in the final analysis to stave off – desperately – the risk of a second recession or twofold bottoming-out make his policy destabilizing for the global economy and so extremely dangerous.

Germany will defend by all means its policy of strictness and discipline. There is no way that it will risk its own stability and prosperity for the sake of undisciplined never-do-well peripheral European economies. It is not the Fourth Reich perennially discussed by marginal publications and analysts but the stamp of its own historical memory on account of the fatal mistakes and tragic failures of the inter-war Weimar Republic[36][37][38]. The Germans

---

[7] Ludwig von Mises who anticipated the Great Depression, writes in the preface to the English edition of his book "The Theory of Money and Credit" (firstly published in 1912) in Vienna, "And the thing which is chiefly advocated as a remedy is nothing but another expansion of credit, such as certainly might lead to a transitory boom, but would be bound to end in a correspondingly severer crisis" and Mises adds in the last words of his preface, impressively earlier than what we are facing right now "Recurring crises are nothing but the consequence of attempts, despite all the teachings of experience and all the warnings of the economists, to stimulate economic activity by means of additional credit" [34].

[8] The problems that arise from Obama's administrative initiatives, directed by old-fashioned Keynesianism and voracious expansionism, reinforced by organized political groups and unions that contributed so much crucially to the Obama election, are deeply and brightly examined by Rowley and Smith (2009) [35]. The new research very fairly changes the roles of Keynes and Roosevelt into the faces and policies of G. W. Bush and Barack Obama. The paper explains how the laissez-faire capitalism developed the dynamism of the American economy. In our tough times, the book concludes, we can revive the American economy by keeping the principles and operations of market capitalism and applying a list of policies based on a public choice approach.

today, more than ever, base their democracy on stable long-term foundations, resolutely rejecting unsound expansionist policies and untenable iconoclastic approaches.

The more American laxness feeds German severity, the heavier will fall the shadow of this unequal relationship with Germany on the weaker members of the European periphery. The unorthodox and anti-conventional measures employed by Bernanke from the first Bush-Paulson package to the second mammoth Obama-Geithner package and up to the latest movement of 600 billion dollars represent one failure after another. It is all absorbed by the financial sector, with nothing going into the real economy.

Like the supernova that radiates its full brilliance just before its conversion into a black hole whose magnetic field absorbs everything around it, this is precisely the mode of operation of the US financial system. After the splendor of the 2003-2007 period with its dazzling profits and radiant unearned increments, it is as if it has been extinguished forever and is drawing everything into itself. It does not allow anything through into the real sector the US economy.

It is a fact that you will frequently hear certain individuals saying "Ben, print some more money!" The new money is invested in gold exchange-traded funds, in oil futures, in commodity derivatives, in the new speculative bubbles that are being prepared in the emerging countries. What little remains in the USA goes to Dow Jones, with almost nothing being invested in the hope of a dollar devaluation making American products cheaper.

But as Germany has shown, competitiveness is not to be achieved in this way. This is why America is staggering through a fragile upturn, accompanied by growing unemployment and the lurking great risk of a double dip. This situation has been brought about by the latest desperate, and riskier than ever, move by Ben Bernanke.

Republicans and especially the Tea Party is opposed to this unacceptable, uncontrolled and chaotic situation and wants to restore fiscal and monetary stability and above all the Classical American Constitutional Tradition[9] of the limited but stable state, dynamic private sector, hard work and initiative. Their proposals are simple and easily comprehensible. No to abolition of tax breaks, yes to smaller deficits and finally a balanced budget, smaller public debt and no more newly-printed dollars.

The reality is that the Tea Party's impressive victory in the last intermediate elections (November 2010), has humiliated and diminished Obama. But the effective result of this development could be the exercise of political pressure for supervising the Treasury and keeping the constitutional limit of public debt at a potential control level. If this idea is taken up both by the House of Representatives and by the Senate, notwithstanding the continuing Democratic majority there, strict control of, and immediate curbs on, public expenditures, if accompanied by retention and consolidation of the tax exemptions introduced by Bush and if Obama abandons his flirtation with the idea of abolishing them, it is quite probable that the foundations will be laid for fiscal rationalization of the American economy. Lower taxes will promote development and curtailment of public expenditures will impose stability.

Only such a world, with a stable America alongside a stable Germany will be in a position to exert significant and real pressure on China to revalue the Yuan so that the global economy can start to divest itself one by one of the disequilibria both in trade balances and in

---

[9] Douglass North showed that the rise and success of the western world historically was based on prevailing institutions of individual liberty, free enterprise and secure property rights. In his book (1981) page 188 he writes "The story of this chapter (14) is how the framers of the Constitution attempted to control the state and how ultimately those controls broke down." (see reference [17]).

finance. These are the prerequisites for a stable and reliable global upturn based on the performance of the real economy and on heightened competitiveness.

Such a global upturn, in an environment of fiscal and monetary stability, will be balanced and symmetrical over the whole scale of magnitudes, imposing a decisive and prohibitive check on movements of speculative capital, predatory exploitation of wealth which in its next phase will most certainly involve tapping of the tremendous potential of the emerging countries. If all of the developed countries can display stability, then the dynamism of the emerging countries will be the global economic system's most precious gift, offering the developed countries an exit from the crisis and the emerging countries consolidation and diffusion of wealth even to the most marginalized sections of their communities.

Otherwise, if America and Obama, in alliance with the legendary hero of freshly printed money Ben Bernanke, persist in their out-of-control policies then what will ensue will be a relentless global monetary war which will on the one hand provide tremendous opportunity for speculative profiteering and on the other will lead countries to bankruptcy.

The way of fiscal and monetary stability is the way of virtue, which is why it is thorny and difficult. The lure of fiscal packages and monetary injections is obvious to all, but their results, after a brief and fitful revival, will be disastrous.

The choice centres on the difference between the lure of the easy and a confrontation with the difficult. But societies and economies that are successful are not those that are attracted by the temptations of easy solutions, only to fall victim subsequently to stagnation and recession. They are those that face up to the difficulties and manage to survive and ultimately to prosper.

CONCLUSION: EMERGING GREECE FROM THE CRISIS. THE FREE MARKET LIBERAL SOLUTION

In a macro-economic environment where the global public debt crisis is Keynesian, the only tried and tested way to emerge from it is to follow the approach dictated by policies of promoting the free market. In other words limiting the size of the state and the extent of its intervention to bring it into complete conformity with the requirements of supply-side economics.

Faced with the impasse of social democratic politics both internationally and in Greece, the greatest and most welcome surprise in Greece's grey and gloomy political landscape was the announcement by the President of the New Democracy party, Antonis Samaras, of his comprehensive economic proposal entitled euphemistically Zappeio II[10], which brings to the fore the most dynamic mix of a well organized free market liberal economic policy upheld by the twin pillars of privatizations and low taxation. Zappeio II is in itself an economically free market liberal ideological manifesto which, in conjunction with the timeless conservative traditions, principles and values of the people of Greece: integrity, hard work and ingenuity, has the potential to make the greatest contribution to effective handling of the crisis and the construction of a new state, a private-oriented economy and a dynamic community that will turn away from lowest-common-denominator leveling and acknowledge the distinction, the

---

[10] Zappeio is the Athenian Classical Mansion where it usually takes place conferences of the Greek political leaders on major political issues.

leadership, of the intelligent and able, who provide the only competent and effective guide for promotion of both the public and the national interest.

The Political Economy of Zappeio is the all-out counter-offensive of the Centre-right against the sterile, ill-fated and - in a word - unsuccessful politics of the Memorandum[11]. The Political Economy of Zappeio is the most apt riposte to social democracy in its death throes which, following the demise of its lamentable cousin socialism, seeks through introduction of its disastrous economic architecture to sound the death knell of the Greek economy.

Essentially, in today's painful Greek economic reality, what are in conflict are two diametrically opposed economic strategies. On the one hand social-democratic procrastination and reluctance to make drastically urgent breaks and on the other the free market liberal economic dynamic which wants to, and is obliged to, impose them immediately. Worst of all is the fact that the social democrats (PASOK) are not only in the former camp but also the sophisticated leadership of it, is surrounded by hard-line palaeolithic socialists, who are in no way willing to see any reform or any structural change proceed. Thus the only economic policy tool remaining in the hands of the sophisticated leading social democrats is imposition of taxes on everything under the sun and the siphoning off of incomes. In brief the strangling of the totality of our economy.

The truth is that social democrats have traditionally relied on state intervention in the economy. Their policy and their economy philosophy has always been to accord the collectivity priority over the individual. Collective structures and centralized institutions have had preference over individual initiative, free entrepreneurial action and individual rights. In this way, whether via the socialist populism of Andreas Papandreou or via the more house-trained social democracy of George Papandreou, each – father and son – in his own way, PASOK led Greece into an indisputable and unprecedented impasse.

George Papandreou, who prior to his election advocated Keynesian reheating of the economy, increases in salary, income redistribution, with assurances that "the money is there", is today in a weakened position and is canvassing for fellow-travelers and proposing unholy alliances in support of ineffective policies. Unthinkable expectations. As I analyzed in Epikentra, as early as Autumn 1998, politics of this character spells the End for Social Democracy [39]. Today's politics of the Memorandum, Part I (2010) or Part II (2011), are simply the finale to the Last Great Regression to Keynesian and Social Democratic ideas.

In contrast, therefore, to what is being implemented through the dead-end social-democratic economic strategy, based on over-taxation and the gouging of incomes, that has been in force over the nearly two-year period since they assumed office, what Greece needs immediately if it is to recover from the grave economic crisis into which we have been plunged is implementation of a full-blooded free market leral economic programme based on immediate and drastic reduction of non-salary expenditures in the hard core of the public sector, on abolition of ineffective public sector instrumentalities, on an extensive programme of privatizations in the broader public sector, on genuine liberalization of professions, on

---

[11] Memorandum is the economic agreement between Greece and Troika. Troika is the three major institutional lenders, European Union, European Central bank, and International Monetary Fund, of the Greek economy. Memorandum is based on economic Draconian austerity that includes heavy taxation, public expending cuts, and free market oriented structural reforms. On the other hand Memorandum offers generous financial support at reasonable interest rate, remarkable lower than that of the market. Nevertheless the emphasis of the application of Memorandum on the heavy taxation and much less on the cuts of public expending with the non activation of the program of privatization and liberalization of the Greek economy, rendered Memorandum totally inappropriate and failed economic policy.

flexibilization and freeing of the labor market from government regulations and stifling bureaucratic controls, on disengagement of business operations from trade unionist and syndicalistic malpractices and of course on reductions in taxation. Only coherent, consistent and well organized application of these free market liberal policies can lead us to economic upturn with corresponding increase in tax receipts, and indeed from all sources.

The New Democracy economic proposal that was recently put forward at the Zappeio moves precisely, and most satisfactorily, in this direction. Zappeio Political Economy exemplifies Supply Side Economics, the famed Reaganomics: this is the first time that the Flat Tax has been adopted so clearly, unambiguously and firmly by the leader of a Centre Right party. In the New Democracy program privatizations and entrepreneurial drive have become the key developmental lever for the Greek economy generally. This is not a package of populist proposals but an example of rational and sober free market liberalism! No New Democracy leader in the past has ever put forward proposals so clearly free market liberal, and indeed from the august Zappeio Megaron. I make the comparison not only with the Karamanlis period where the key element was the inert and stagnant theory of the modest center, but also with the Mitsotakis period where outside a very narrow circle the Flat Tax appeared something incomprehensible to the well-meaning and something unacceptable to the malicious and ignorant. I reassert that the Flat Tax is a symbolic demonstration of how with Zappeio II Antonis Samaras has crossed the Rubicon. He has brought free market economic liberalism back to its birthplace in New Democracy.

The Flat Tax was supported passionately and explicitly by Antonis Samaras, above and beyond the symbolic dimension of its uncompromisingly free market liberal content, as an extremely effective economic measure, as succinctly illustrated by the Laffer curve [40]. The reason that the Flat Tax is so effective is that it possesses the quality of increasing production and productivity alike, of both labor and capital! It is the tax which, single-handed, represents the total taxation revolution Greece so badly needs! With reforms and schisms of this kind we can change our country, overcome the crisis and again place Greece on an upward trajectory of progress.

George Papandreou is entirely right when he says that instead of restructuring our debt we should first restructure our country! But to restructure the country we must first restructure the memorandum, and the only person to say this so powerfully and persuasively is Antonis Samaras, and he has said it from outset! This is the best way to overcome the crisis, not only in Greece but also internationally. With an economic policy of this kind that is comprehensive, sober and well-organized, so as to provide a framework for development of free markets, entrepreneurial dynamism and private initiative, within a context of low taxation and minimal state coercion.

The fact is that today's economic travails in Greece are the end product of perennial structural problems caused by the extensive statism, bureaucracy and socialistic management of the economy from 1974 onwards, both by centre-right and by centre-left governments. It is this situation that produced the present-day Gordian Knot of the Greek economy, which holds hostage the most productive and creative forces in Greece. The present-day Gordian Knot of the Greek economy cannot be undone through traditional Keynesian policies but must be cut through with the decisiveness and the power that was shown by an Alexander the Great. That is to say with the power of free markets and the rigor and precision of the economic rationality that is generated by them. Virtue and Daring are what the economy needs, and Freedom and Democracy.

Private sector, hard work and initiative. Their proposals are simple and easily comprehensible. No to abolition of tax breaks, yes to smaller deficits and finally a balanced budget, smaller public debt and no more newly-printed dollars.

The reality is that the Tea Party's impressive victory in the last intermediate elections (November 2010), has humiliated and diminished Obama. But the effective result of this development could be the exercise of political pressure for supervising the Treasury and keeping the constitutional limit of public debt at a potential control level. If this idea is taken up both by the House of Representatives and by the Senate, notwithstanding the continuing Democratic majority there, strict control of, and immediate curbs on, public expenditures, if accompanied by retention and consolidation of the tax exemptions introduced by Bush and if Obama abandons his flirtation with the idea of abolishing them, it is quite probable that the foundations will be laid for fiscal rationalization of the American economy. Lower taxes will promote development and curtailment of public expenditures will impose stability.

Only such a world, with a stable America alongside a stable Germany will be in a position to exert significant and real pressure on China to revalue the Yuan so that the global economy can start to divest itself one by one of the disequilibria both in trade balances and in finance. These are the prerequisites for a stable and reliable global upturn based on the performance of the real economy and on heightened competitiveness.

Such a global upturn, in an environment of fiscal and monetary stability, will be balanced and symmetrical over the whole scale of magnitudes, imposing a decisive and prohibitive check on movements of speculative capital, predatory exploitation of wealth which in its next phase will most certainly involve tapping of the tremendous potential of the emerging countries. If all of the developed countries can display stability, then the dynamism of the emerging countries will be the global economic system's most precious gift, offering the developed countries an exit from the crisis and the emerging countries consolidation and diffusion of wealth even to the most marginalized sections of their communities.

Otherwise, if America and Obama, in alliance with the legendary hero of freshly printed money Ben Bernanke, persist in their out-of-control policies then what will ensue will be a relentless global monetary war which will on the one hand provide tremendous opportunity for speculative profiteering and on the other will lead countries to bankruptcy.

The way of fiscal and monetary stability is the way of virtue, which is why it is thorny and difficult. The lure of fiscal packages and monetary injections is obvious to all, but their results, after a brief and fitful revival, will be disastrous.

The choice centres on the difference between the lure of the easy and a confrontation with the difficult. But societies and economies that are successful are not those that are attracted by the temptations of easy solutions, only to fall victim subsequently to stagnation and recession. They are those that face up to the difficulties and manage to survive and ultimately to prosper.

REFERENCES

[1] Ricardo David, "On the Principles of Political Economy and Taxation", in P.Sraffa and M.Dobb, eds*., The Works and Correspondence of David Ricardo,* Cambridge University Press: Cambridge (1953).

[2]   Mitsopoulos and Pelagidis, *Analysis of the Greek Economy: Rentiers and Reform* Papazisis [in Greek] (2006)

[3]   Mitsopoulos, M. and T. Pelagidis *The Cato Journal,* 29(3) 399-416 (2009)

[4]   Mitsopoulos, M. and T. Pelagidis, *Understanding the Crisis in Greece. From Boom to Bust,* Palgrave Macmillan (2011).

[5]   Smith Adam, *An Inquiry into the Nature and Causes of the Wealth of Nations*, Oxford University Press (1976).

[6]   Mises, L. von, *Liberalism: The Classical Tradition*, trans. Ralph Raico, ed. Bettina Bien Greaves, Indianapolis: Liberty Fund (2005).

[7]   Mises, L. von, *Human Action: A Treatise on Economics,* in 4 vols., ed. Bettina Bien Greaves, Indianapolis: Liberty Fund (2007)

[8]   Hayek Friedrich, *Studies in Philosophy, Politics and Economics*, Routledge (1978).

[9]   Buchanan, James M., *The Limits of Liberty. Between Anarchy and Leviathan*, The University of Chicago Press (1974).

[10] Buchanan, James M., *Constitutional Political Economy,* 4(1) (1993).

[11] Buchanan, James M. and Wagner, Richard E., *Fiscal Responsibility in Constitutional Democracy*, Martinus Nijhoff, Leiden (1978).

[12] Clausewitz Carl von, *Principles of War*, Dover Publications (2003).

[13] Evangelopoulos Panagiotis, Property and Market, Papazisis [In Greek] (2000).

[14] Evangelopoulos Panagiotis, *International Review of Economics*, 54(1), 13-34 (2007).

[15] Evangelopoulos Panagiotis, *Economic Affairs*, 29(4),72-77 (2009).

[16] Coase, Ronald H., *The Firm, the Market, and the Law*, The University of Chicago Press (1988).

[17] North Douglass C., *Structure and Change in Economic History*, New York: W.W. Norton and Co.(1981)

[18] North Douglass C., Institutions, Institutional Change and Economic Performance, Cambridge: Cambridge University Press (1990).

[19] North, D. C. and R. Thomas *The Rise of the Western World: A New Economic History,* Cambridge: Cambridge University Press (1973).

[20] Friedman, M., *Capitalism and Freedom*, Chicago: Chicago University Press (1962).

[21] Papandreou, A. *Economics as a Science*, Lippincott (1958).

[22] Papandreou, A. *Paternalistic Capitalism*, The University of Minnesota Press (1972).

[23] Papandreou, A. and J. T. Wheeler *Competition and its Regulation*, Prentice-Hall (1954).

[24] Papandreou, A. and U. Zohar *Project Selection for National Plans*, New York: Praeger Publishers (1974).

[25] Jackson, Mark, *Constitutional Political Economy*, 16, 277-284 (2005).

[26] Parente, S.L. and Prescott, E.C. *Barriers to Riches*, Cambridge MA: The MIT Press (2000).

[27] Bitros, G.K. and A. Karayiannis (2008) *Journal of Institutional Economics*, 4(2) 205–230 (2008).

[28] Bitros, G.K. and A. Karayiannis *European Journal of Political Economy*, 26, 68–81 (2010).

[29] Karayiannis, A. and A. Hatzis *European Journal of Law and Economics* (forthcoming).

[30] Hayek Friedrich, *The Road to Serfdom*, Routledge (2007).

[31] Buchanan, James M. and Wagner, Richard E., *Democracy in Deficit: the Political Legacy of Lord Keynes*, Academic Press, New York (1977).

[32] Akerlof G.A.and Shiller R.J., *Animal Spirits*, Princeton University Press, Princeton (2009).

[33] Evangelopoulos Panagiotis, *Economic Affairs*, 29(4), 80-82 (2009).

[34] Mises, L. von, *The Theory of Money and Credit*, trans. H.E. Batson, Indianapolis: Liberty Fund (1981).

[35] Rowley, C. K. and N. Smith, *Economic Contractions in the United States: A Failure of Government*, Fairfax, VA: The Locke Institute, and London: Institute of Economic Affairs (2009).

[36] Feuchtwanger, E. J., *From Weimar to Hitler: Germany,1918-33*, Basingstoke: Macmillan (1995).

[37] Kershaw Ian (ed) *Weimar: why did German democracy fail?,* New York : St. Martin's Press (1990).

[38] Peukert, Detlev, *The Weimar Republic: the Crisis of Classical Modernity*. New York: Hill and Wang (1992).

[39] Evangelopoulos Panagiotis, *Epikentra*,6 [in Greek] (1998).

[40] Laffer, Arthur B. *"The Laffer Curve: Past, Present, and Future" Executive Summary Backgrounder"*, Heritage Foundation, No 1765, June 2004.

In: Greece: Economics, Political and Social Issues
Editor: Panagiotis Liargovas

ISBN: 978-1-62100-944-3
© 2012 Nova Science Publishers, Inc.

Chapter 4

THE POLITICAL ECONOMY OF THE GREEK CRISIS REVISITED: ECONOMIC GROWTH VERSUS POLITICAL DEVELOPMENT?

Pantelis Sklias[*]
University of Peloponnese,
Department of Political Science and International Relations,
Korinthos, Greece

ABSTRACT

The assessment of current macroeconomic indicators of Greece justifies the critical situation of the country. However, the normative neoclassical framework of analysis does not provide an adequate insight and explanatory basis of this situation since it does not consider the historical context within which this phenomenon has been taking place. I argue that we are currently facing a unique paradox. On one hand, current reality is that of a state battling to avoid default. On the other hand, the economic performance of the past 30 years contrasts this reality.

In this chapter, the major principles of new institutional economics and international political economy are applied in a historical context in order to provide the necessary tools to capture contemporary economic and political reality in Greece.

The Greek crisis can be seen as the result of inadequate institutional building and poor political performance during the last 30 years. Europeanization and modernization of the 90's have not been supported by the necessary institutions. Incomplete measures of the EMU mechanism have exacerbated the situation. High economic performance did not coincide with the low level of political and institutional development in the country. It is shown empirically that the lack of political and institutional development is a causal factor of the Greek crisis which could have been prevented otherwise.

---

[*] E-mail address: psklias@hotmail.com

INTRODUCTION

A comprehensive reading of the Greek situation is more likely to unveil and subsequently debunk a number of economic development myths. These myths are, in essence, related to political and institutional development attributes. In other words it remains to be seen whether the broadly acknowledged positive economic performance of 1977-2007, was followed by the analogous political development, technological and institutional changes.

The Greek crisis should have been prevented. Although the widely held view is that, the Greek crisis was evident in the dim macroeconomic outlook and thus imminent and unavoidable, I suggest that the crisis was also unavoidable but for an entirely different set of reasons which escaped attention; namely the lack of consistent and coherent political and institutional development. This is also a key difference of Greece from its European counterparts or other countries with similar or even more unfavorable macroeconomic indicators.

Using Greece and its crisis as an illustrative example I seek to demonstrate how ignoring the holistic perspective may very well have been the global economy's Trojan horse for the Greeks, and a root cause for the crisis that should have been prevented. I will also show empirically that the political and institutional development attainment level is a critical component and a root cause in the Greek crisis. I also support the view that what at first instance appears to be bad public financial practices and policy making, it is in essence lack of real political and institutional development.

In this respect, at first this chapter will analyze the commonly known Greek economic vulnerabilities. It will then proceed with the analysis of how the weak European monetary context contributed to the Greek crisis. Thirdly, it will present that the aforementioned negative conditions had little effect on the Greek economic performance in its historical context. Fourthly, this chapter will analyze the political and institutional essence of the Greek crisis.

FRAMEWORK OF ANALYSIS

From the above perspective, the Greek economic crisis is important because its ripples were felt at the foundations of the European [Monetary] Union as well. A permanent economic support mechanism has been put into place in order to address related economic digressions at the member state level. All the same, many have debated extensively the issues of the Greek crisis, seeking the root causes of the problem and its consequences on national, EU and global level. In the majority of these analyses, a series of factors are highlighted as the key to understand the nature of the problem. Namely, high public deficit, irrational public spending, foreign debt, lack of exports, minimum competition basis, default functioning of the labor market, are among the profound variables that resulted to the final outcome that we are all aware of. While these factors are profound aspects of the Greek financial and economic failure, nevertheless, I argue that this is only part of the reality.

Thus, there are a series of equally important economic parameters which should have stirred Greece towards a radically different, and certainly more positive economic outcome in the present day. Some of the most prominent are the following:

- The infusion of increased EU funding towards Greece for the whole period of study; that is 30 consecutive years (1980-2010);
- The increased revenues of the two main heavy Greek industries, shipping and tourism during the same period of reference (1980-2010);
- The fact that in 2007 Greek economic performance was one of the most successful among the EU 27 member states; the satisfactory performance of the Greek economy is also indicated by the fact that in September 2009 Government bond spreads were at a reasonably favorable 121 basis points, which is surprising considering the turn of events only a few months later when they reached between seven to ten times higher.
- The often worse economic indicators of other developed states such as Japan in terms of public debt in relation to the GDP or other EU member states in terms of external debt; none of which are now in a similar debt crisis.

Although these facts do not negate the wrong actions of Greek economic policy makers, we are still in front of a unique paradox. On the one hand, today's reality is that of a state battling to avoid default. On the other hand, the economic performance of the past 30 years contrasts today's reality.

While the normative neoclassical economic interpretation is an inevitable reading of the Greek crisis, it is more so in the direction of providing a rationale and description of the economic outcome. The real requirement, however, is to pinpoint the root causes and, what I believe is the essence of the Greek problem; i.e. the underpinnings of the crisis beyond the success or failure of a mere fiscal exercise to reach the economic indicators [1]. In other words it remains to be seen whether the positive economic performance, was also followed by the necessary technological and institutional changes [2].

A comprehensive reading of the Greek situation is more likely to unveil and subsequently debunk a number of economic development myths, the following being the most prominent:

- Failed macroeconomic policies are the sole root cause of the Greek crisis;
- Political stability , policy continuity and sustainability has been prevailing in Greece and maintained by the Greek political leadership;
- A strategic vision for the country's development is being shared among the ruling parties.
- The Greek people's attitude and perceptions employ the top level shared vision and thus promote and practice economic and political development, averting interweaving and corruption.

These myths are, in essence, related to political and institutional development attributes such as political stability, long-term policy consistency and coherency and a shared strategic vision for the country. Significant attainment levels for these indicators are frequently taken for granted in developed economies, including the US, Japan, or the EU and most members in the Euro zone. However, these are also the attributes that differentiate Greece from its counterparts despite any other shared similarities in deficits, debts or other dim macroeconomic figures.

Institutional development may lead to a path-dependent pattern of development. The view that some of the institutions create stagnation instead of development was introduced by

North (1990) and has been further elaborated by Eggertsson (2005) and Drobak and Nye (1997) who assess why institutions that create relative economic backwardness emerge, persist and they also consider the possibilities and limits of institutional reform[3][4]. Further research evaluates the role of institutions in providing credibility to regulatory and other policies, thus providing an adequate explanatory framework to understand policy successes or failures, especially in countries which have been through financial and economic crisis such as Argentina or to provide alternative policy solutions to overcome development shortfalls in specific cases such as the African agricultural development (Spiller and Tommasi 2007, Kirsten et al. 2009) [5] [6].

GREEK ECONOMIC WEAKNESSES

Sklias and Galatsidas (2010) among others, have demonstrated the long run structural weaknesses of the Greek economy [7]. In this regard, many economic indicators can reveal these structural negative characteristics that contributed to the Greek crisis. In this section I will demonstrate that Greek economic indicators are not much worse than similar ones of other Eurozone members.

For example, Table 1 shows the aggregate debt for Spain, Portugal, and Greece. As it can be observed the Greek total debt is almost 300% of GDP but at the same time it is less than the similar figure in Spain and Portugal. If this is true why the Greek crisis is deeper and more aggressive than the crisis in Spain and Portugal?

Table 1. Aggregate Debt (end 2009)

	Spain		Portugal		Greece	
	EUR Bn	%	EUR Bn	%	EUR Bn	%
Total Debt						
EUR Bn	5,315		783		703	
% GDP	506 %		479 %		296 %	
by issuer						
General government	676	13 %	121	15 %	293	42 %
Financial corporations	1,669	31 %	238	30 %	120	17 %
Non-fin corporations	2,053	39 %	246	31 %	165	23 %
Households	918	17 %	178	23 %	123	17 %
		100 %		100 %		100 %
by instrument						
Short-term	1,586	30 %	271	35 %	189	27 %
Non-resident deposits	549				106	
Bonds	156		44		11	
Loans	258		49		72	
Trade credit	623		32			
Long-term	3,730	70 %	512	65 %	514	73 %
Bonds	1,472		173		301	
Loans	2,258		339		212	
		100 %		100 %		100 %

Source: Lapavitsas et al. (2010) [8].

Another important issue is the question of who holds the Greek debt. In this regard as Figure 1 shows the main holders of the Greek external securities are European countries such as France, Germany, Italy, Belgium and the Netherlands. The non-European countries hold only the 19% of the Greek debt securities. The conclusion is straightforward: Greece owes billion of Euros to the most powerful (core) European countries. Thus, it is not a cliché to say that the eurozone is an area that creates large amounts of surpluses (i.e. Germany) as well as large amounts of deficits (i.e. Greece, Spain, Portugal) at the same time. But if this is the case why the Greek crisis is so different? It seems that the idea of why the Greek crisis is so aggressive cannot be justified only by the structural vulnerabilities of the Greek economy.

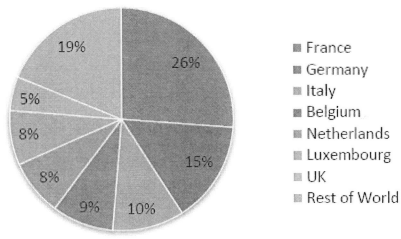

Source: Lapavitsas et al.(2010).

Figure 1. External Holders of Greek Debt Securities.

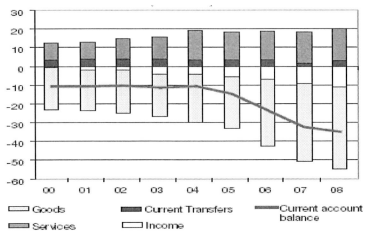

Source: Athanassiou (2009) [9].

Figure 2. Evolution on the Current Account Balance and its Components.

Another important issue is competitiveness. As Figure 2 shows the Greek current account balance in the last 10 years is not only negative but also less than 10%. However, if we analyze the current account not only for Greece but also for other European countries (figure 3) it can be argued that Greece is not the only European country that suffers from huge deficits. In this regard, neither the current account deficits nor competitiveness can be a rational exlanations of why the Greek case is so different.

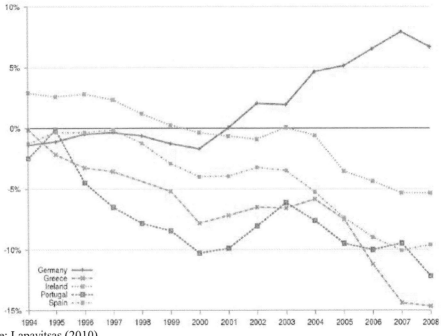

Source: Lapavitsas (2010).

Figure 3. Current Account Deficits.

Table 2. Real GDP Growth (1999-2005)

	Real GDP	Contributions from: Domestic Demand	Net Exports
Ireland	6.3	4.4	1.9
Greece	4.1	4.5	-0.4
Spain	3.6	4.6	-1.0
Finland	2.7	1.9	0.8
France	2.2	2.6	-0.4
Belgium	2.0	1.7	0.3
Austria	2.0	1.4	0.6
Netherlands	1.6	1.2	0.4
Portugal	1.5	1.8	-0.3
Italy	1.3	1.5	-0.2
Germany	1.2	0.4	0.8
Euro Area	1.9	1.8	0.1

Source: Ahearne and Pisani-Ferry (2006) [10]

The aforementioned analysis shows that the Greek case is not a unique case within the European area. A rational explanation based exclusively on structural economic vulnerabilities cannot justify the importance and the magnitude of the Greek crisis. This can be also observed from the real GDP growth (annual average 1999-2005). It is clear from Table 2 that Greece ranked second in terms of real GDP growth within the eurozone, with Ireland, being in the first place. Thus, the Greek crisis cannot be seen only from the point of view of the structural vulnerabilities of its economic sector.

GREECE WITHIN THE WEAK INSTITUTIONAL CONTEXT OF THE EUROPEAN MONETARY UNION

When considering the Greek crisis we usually ignore that it has taken place within a wider context, that of the EMU. Even though, the aforementioned analysis plays an important role for the explanation of the Greek crisis I claim that it is not the most important cause that has contributed to the crisis. Featherstone (2011) claimed that the Greek sovereign debt crisis has two main elements, the failing of the state and the skewed European regime [11]. Indeed, the EMU's political economic and institutional context seems to be a rather complicated framework for some of its member states like Greece, Portugal, Spain and Ireland, namely the "weak" economies. Amisano *et. al.* (2009) when proposing a possible approach to study the changes brought about by EMU to the intra-euro area adjustment to asymmetric shocks stated that the '*EMU has brought very little changes to the transmission mechanism of asymmetric demand and cost push shocks...EMU does not appear to have changed the structural factors that facilitate a smoother macroeconomic adjustment within EMU, for which structural reforms remain of paramount importance*' [12].

The Greek crisis not only revealed but also made evident that the EMU context is a complex political and economic environment in which many peripheral European economies remain vulnerable to the political and economic shocks that can happen in a regular basis mainly because of conflicted national interests and preferences in the European level [13]. As De Grauwe (2010e) argues '*large areas of economic policies remain in the hand of national governments creating asymmetric shocks that undermine the sustainability of the monetary union*' [14]. In this regard, the weak European politico-economic institutional context, in which the current Greek crisis was developed, has also contributed to the current crisis.

This context can be better analyzed in two different levels, firstly, on the application of the Optimal Currency Areas (OCA) criteria to the EMU [15]. Secondly, at the level of the evaluation of the main political and economic institutions and their vulnerabilities in the European level. Many European countries and especially Greece were unable to afford the vulnerable and one-sided, weak political and economic European context in which they lost important elements of their political and economic sovereignty. This context together with their own political and economic structural deficiencies (Sklias et al., 2010) creates an explosive mix of conditions that in the long run will spill over their negative impact, regionally and globally.

Bayoumi and Eichengreen (1992) had predicted that 'supply shocks are larger in magnitude and less correlated across regions in Europe than in the United States underscores that the European Community may find more difficult to operate a monetary union than the

United States' [16]. In this framework, it is obvious that the United States can overcome a shock faster than the EU. As Figure 4 shows within the EMU there is a great asymmetry of demand and supply shocks. As a result, Greece, as it was proved practically after the global crisis in 2008, was unable theoretically and empirically to manage and to cope with the exogenous/endogenous economic shocks within the EMU.

Despite of the above, existing major institutional, political and economic vulnerabilities within the EMU affected directly or indirectly the Greek performance. According to Hix (2005) *'Without an established reputation, public opinion in states that suffer asymmetric shocks is likely to turn against the ECB quicker than it would against a national central bank [...] without a binding commitment by and clear incentives for the governments to abide by these contracts, the credibility of these coordination efforts is questionable'* [17]. Moreover, the Stability and Growth Pact (SGP) that was adopted as the main institutional project for the stability and growth within the eurozone seems that it is a poor and unsustainable institutional foundation (De Grauwe, 2010e). As McNamara (2005) argues *'although the SGP has the word growth in its title, it is not likely to promote growth, but rather to be excessively restrictive'* [18]. Thus, one could argue that the rules of the game do not guarantee the same level of viability for all the participating parts.

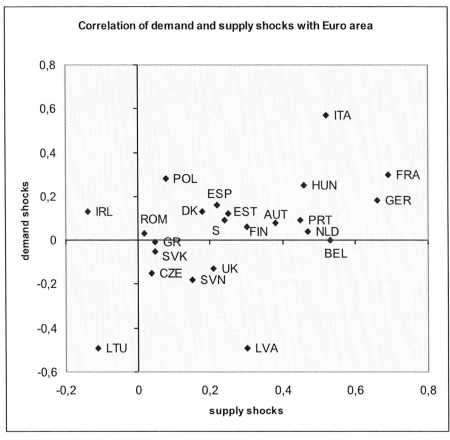

Source: Baldwin and Wyplosz (2006).

Figure 4. Asymmetry of Shocks.

Greece and the other peripheral countries with weak economies cannot afford to remain in a European context full of deficiencies, flaws and inequalities.

Even though, the aforementioned analysis of the skewed European regime has played an important role to the Greek crisis, the uniqueness and the importance of the Greek crisis cannot be justified only from the aforementioned conditions. The European regime alone cannot answer the question of why the Greek case is more severe and deeper than the crisis in Portugal, or in Spain.

GREEK ECONOMY ON THE MOVE: AN 'UNEXPECTED' RESULT

Though, there are many reasons to believe that the Greek crisis is a subsequent fact, this chapter argues that this is only a part of the reality. The Greek crisis is rather an unexpected result for many scholars. In this regard it can be argued that a normative macroeconomic analysis appears to be limited in scope, thus providing an analytical framework that may deflect from reality and lead to misunderstandings. In this respect, one can also observe that during the last thirty years, several positive economic characteristics, both internally and regionally, have been developed. They could generate a totally different economic and political result for Greece. According to this perspective some of the most prominent characteristics are the following:

First, the infusion of increased EU funding towards Greece for the whole period of study; that is 30 consecutive years (1980-2010); it is characteristic that 24 billion Euros have been earmarked for the period 2007-2013 which is the fourth package in a row since 1989. The same amount was also absorbed in the period 2000-2006 (the third package). In total, it is estimated that an amount of more than 50 billion euros has been transferred to the country from the EU, since 1985[1].

Second, the increased revenues of the two main heavy Greek industries, shipping and tourism during the same period of reference (1980-2010) were enormous. According to the Annual Report 2010-2011 of the Union of Greek Ship-owners (2011) [19]:

> 'Foreign exchange earnings in December 2010 amounted to €15,418 million, compared to € 13,552 million in 2009 i.e., an increase of 13.77% reaching 6.72% of the domestic product and covering 35.28% of the trade deficit. According to the Bank of Greece, earnings from shipping were exceptionally high compared to those of other EU Member States, calculated at 6% of Greece's GDP whilst in the other EU Member States they do not exceed on average 1%. Moreover, continuing a trend established since 2003, in 2010 foreign exchange earnings from shipping exceeded the ones from tourism (€ 9,614 million) and came second in the balance of payments after exports (€ 17,081 million). [...] In the decade 2000-2010, shipping contributed 140 bn € in foreign exchange earnings to the Greek economy. This is equivalent to half of the entire public debt of the country in 2009 amounting to 280 bn € or 3.5 times the receipts from the EU for the period 2000-2013 amounting to 46 bn €'.

Therefore, the sector of shipping made significant cash contributions to the Greek economy. It could be argued that Greece has two significant sectors whose performance could

---

[1] http://www.tovima.gr/finance/article/?aid=178063

contribute to moderate the effects of the crisis through income and employment generation as well as cash flow injections.

Third, the 2007 Greek economic performance was one of the most successful among the EU 27 member states and part of a similar long-term trend. In this respect, the September 2009 Government bond spreads were at a reasonably favorable 121 basis points, which is surprising considering the turn of events only a few months later when they reached between seven to ten times as much. When the Greek Prime Minister Giorgos Papandreou stated from the Kastelorizo (small Greek island in the Southeastern Aegean) that Greece is in severe financial turmoil then a huge wave of speculation affected almost any Greek financial and economic indicator. Figure 5 demonstrates that the Sovereign and Bank CDS increased by nearly 170 points and subsequently the Greek cost of borrowing exploded.

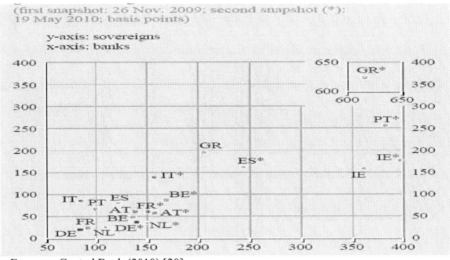

Source: European Central Bank (2010) [20].

Figure 5. Sovereign and Bank CDS.

Additionally, as we can see from Table 3 below there are many countries that from 2007 to 2010 failed to fulfill one of the most important Maastricht criteria, the public debt to GDP ratio. These countries were Portugal, Malta, Italy, France, Spain, Denmark, Greece, Belgium and many others. This is again a sign that the Greek debt ratio was an important factor, a necessary condition for the Greek crisis but not the sufficient one. Although these facts do not negate the wrong actions of the Greek economic policy makers, we are still in front of a unique paradox. On the one hand, current reality is that of a state battling to avoid default. On the other hand, the economic performance of the past 30 years contrasts this reality.

THE POLITICAL AND INSTITUTIONAL ESSENCE OF THE GREEK CRISIS

I argue that the Greek economic problem is not only an economic but also a political problem that can take many forms. Political and institutional (in)stability matters.

Table 3. Public Debt-to-GDP Ratios in the Euro area

Source: European Commission (2009) [21].

A lot of scholars have explained how the political and institutional variables affect public economic function and, eventually, the government performance [22], [23], [24], [25]. The outcome of the economic crisis in Greece has revealed the fact that political institutions in the country have been far from being mature and suitable to achieve specific sustainable development targets and objectives. It can be argued that the structural deficiencies of the Greek political system have been revealed as a result of the crisis. As Mitsopoulos and Pelagidis (2009) state *'the design of the Greek political system has led to rent seeking and the blockage of reforms'* [26].

Table 4. Reforms in euro-area countries

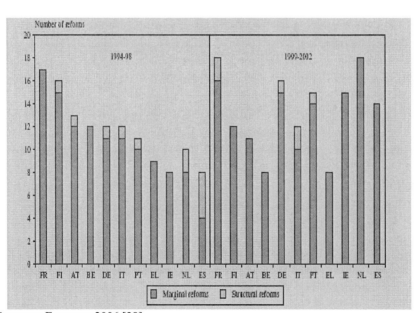

Source: European Economy 2006 [29].

Populism has also been addressed as one of the structural characteristics of the Greek national system. This may have been one of the root causes for mismanagement [27], [28]. In this framework, modernizing the Greek economy was very much connected with the function of a political system which was not ready to deal with a series of subsequent challenges.

Table 4 shows the number of marginal and structural reforms undertaken in the Euro zone area. It is demonstrated that reforms in Greece were the lowest in the Eurozone. At the same time no structural reforms can be identified.

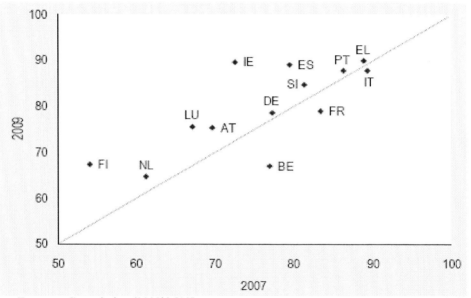

Source: European Commission (2009b) [30].

Figure 6. The perceived need for structural reforms in 2007 and 2009.

The same is the case when we try to perceive the needs for structural reforms (Figure 6). Greece is the first country in the row. In case we interconnect structural reforms with research activity and innovation we also come to the same conclusion (Figure 7). Economic growth in Greece has not been followed and/or supported by the necessary innovations and technological development.

Clientelism in the Greek political system the last thirty years led to a series of rational or irrational calculations [32]. The possibilities of political reforms were limited. Featherstone (2005), stresses that the problem of governance still remains, even though he considers 1996 as a turning point for the "Europeanization" of the country, coinciding with Premier Simitis' political agenda . This governance problem puts the nature of Greece's convergence with the EU in question. More precisely he points out that [11]:

> "Contemporary Greek politics are marked by tensions between pressures for reform and the structural constraints to their realisation. The pressures combine those emanating from processes of Europeanisation (European Union agendas on economic reform, for example) and the domestic demand for 'modernisation' (the agenda of former Premier Simitis). The two have been seen as synonymous in Greece. The resultant tensions have created a fundamental issue of governability: in a number of areas, Greece is 'une societe bloque' . There are systemic weaknesses deriving from the institutional capacity of the state, the regime of

'disjointed corporatism', and cultural practices of clientelism and 'rent-seeking'. These constrain agency and leadership strategies. The analysis places the recent Simitis project in an historical context and attempts to delineate patterns of change and continuity. The reform process has been asymmetrical and uncertain in character. The problem of governance remains and, in turn, it questions the nature of Greece's convergence with the EU."

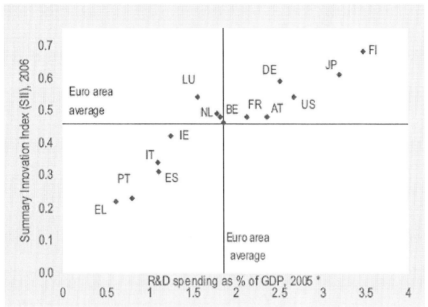

Source: European Commission (2007) [31].

Figure 7. Research and development and innovation performance.

Policy sustainability and continuity in the country can also be an issue to be argued. In my opinion the Simitis' government case is also one that demonstrates the lack of policy continuity among governments of the same party in Greece (in this case the socialists' government). Simitis' pro-European modernization project, managerial and technocratic style has had very little similarities with his predecessor's political approaches. Convergence with the EU would not be considered as an easy path to be undertaken as it was the case with A. Papandreou era. In Simitis era it would be the priority number one. As Featherstone (2005, p. 228) mentions:

> 'Economic and social reform was to be placed alongside a fresh start politically. Simitis and his supporters advocated a greater separation of the 'party' from the 'state': a break with the incestuous 'rousfetti' politics or bureaucratic clientelism of the recent past. This was a condemnation of the Andreas Papandreou years..'

The same inconsistency can also be observed as a result of numerous ministerial reshuffles of a given government, which limits the possibilities to achieve specific policy goals within a given timeframe, not to say about institution-building potential. The dominating figure of Andreas Papandreou is a typical example of this situation. It is characteristic that only during the first four years of his governance (1981-1985) he used 70 members to serve his governments. In 1984 only, the country experienced 5 ministerial reshuffles and in 6 cases we experienced individual changes of ministers or vice ministers. During the second period of his governance (1985-1989) 105 people have participated in government ministerial positions. In the first 1,5 years of his second term 4 government reshuffles took place. We can also notice examples of government members who have seen the entrance and the exit of the government 12 times. It is evident that policy consistency, efficiency and implementation is a task almost impossible to be realized, under the said circumstances.

The lack of adequate institutional – building in Greece has also led to a gap between "declarations" and "materialization". This has also been proven in the case of Simitis 'modernisation' process which was declared but not materialized since it was not supported by the necessary institutional structural changes. The gap between typical and real modernization has also been demonstrated in the case of Greek politics [33]. Open Method of Coordination (OMC) was not successfully applied by the Greek political authorities [34], [35]. This mismatch has also been successfully assessed in various cases especially when considering the relations between the state and specific social organised groups. One such case relates to the teachers' unions against modernisation policies as advocated by Simitis' policy priorities and guidelines [36].

Eventually, reforms were not followed and/or supported by an adequate institutional framework in order to materialise specific policies. There are 'cross-national factors rather than idiosyncratic characteristics that influence the inability and reluctance of a state to comply and conform respectively' [37]. Furthermore, low level of trust between the citizens and government policies has also increased the cost of applying those [38]. Applying rational policies has also been even more difficult due to informal privileges for specific labor groups in the public sector.

CONCLUSION

In the chapter I argued that the Greek crisis should be seen in a historical context rather than the result of failed recent economic policies. Restricting our analysis in the post 2004 economic policy performance leads us to misleading and incomplete conclusions as well as wrong policy recommendations for the future.

The same is the case when we attempt to assess the economic reality of the post 1980 era by adopting mere normative macroeconomic indicators and framework analysis. Restricting our analysis to such indicators we can wrongly anticipate the fact that Greece satisfied all the economic criteria to avoid the 2008 crisis. Nevertheless, this has not been the case and the country is under the EU-ECB-IMF supervision, although one can easily observe that some of the crucial economic indicators are in a much better stake comparing to the ones of other EU countries.

I claim that our analysis should make use of the main working tools and methods of new institutional economics and international political economy. I claim that the Greek crisis can be seen as the result of inadequate institutional building and poor political performance over the last 30 years. Europeanization and modernization of the 90's have not been supported by the necessary institutions. The gap between typical and real modernisation policies is more than evident. The political system of the 90's has very much been based on the clientelism and premature characteristics of the 80's without any notion of innovation and political development. The issue has also been exacerbated by the incomplete framework of the EMU mechanism which was constructed in such a way that could neither predict and retain institutionally weak countries (such as Greece) from distortive policies nor provide any kind of incentives or motivation for modernisation and political institution building.

Finally, high economic performance did not coincide with the low level of political and institutional development in the country which finally led to a crisis that could have been prevented.

REFERENCES

[1] European Commission, 'The Economic Adjustment Programme for Greece', Occasional Papers No. 61, European Economy, Directorate-General for Economic and Financial Affairs, European Commission. (2010), http://ec.europa.eu/economy finance/publications

[2] North, Douglass, *Institutions, Institutional Change and Economic Performance*, Cambridge University Press (1990).

[3] Eggertsson, Thrainn, *Imperfect Institutions: Possibilities and Limits of Reform*, University of Michigan Press (2005).

[4] Drobak, John and Nye, John *Frontiers of the New Institutional Economics*, Academic Press (1997).

[5] Spiller, Pablo and Tommasi, Mariano *The Institutional Foundations of Public Policy in Argentina: A Transaction Costs Approach*, (Political Economy of Institutions and Decisions), Cambridge University Press (2007).

[6] Kirsten, Johann, Dorward, Andrew, Poulton, Colin and Vink, Nick (eds.) *Institutional Economics Perspectives on African Agricultural Development*, International Food Policy Research Institute (2009).

[7] Sklias P., Galatsidas G., 7, *Middle Eastern Finance and Economics*, (2010).

[8] Lapavitsas, C., Kaltenbrunner, G., LAmbrinidis, G., Lindo, D., Meadway, J., Mitchell, J., Painceira, J.,P., Pires, E., Powell, J., Stenfors, A., and Teles, N., *The Eurozone Between Austerity and Default. Research on Money and Finance*, Occasional Report, September. (2010)

[9] Athanassiou, E, *Intereconomics*, 364-372 (2009)

[10] Ahearne, A., and Pisani-Ferry, J., *Bruegel Policy Brief*, 1, (2006).

[11] Featherstone, K. *West European Politics*, 28(2), 223-241(2005).

[12] Amisano G., Giammarioli N., Stracca L. 'EMU and the Adjustment to Asymmetric Shocks: the Case of Italy', European Central Bank: Working Paper Series, No.1128, p.20, (2009).

[13] Maris, G., *An Assessment of the Last Ten Years of the Eurozone: The Case of Greece*. Unpublished MA Dissertation, Kings College London, London (2010)

[14] De Grauwe, P., *Open Economies Review*, 21, 172, (2010e).

[15] Baldwin, R., and Wyplosz, C., *The Economics of European Integration*. McGraw-Hill Education, Berkshire (2006).

[16] Bayoumi, T., and Eichengreen, B.,'Shocking Aspects of European Monetary Unification'. *NBER Working Paper* No. 3949, p.35, (1992)

[17] Hix, S. *The Political System of the European Union*. Palgrave Macmillan, New York. p.330, (2005).

[18] McNamara, K., R., 'Economic and Monetary Union: Innovation and Challenges for the Euro', in Wallace, H., Wallace, W., and Pollack, M., 2005. *Policy-Making in the European Union*, Oxford University Press, Oxford p. 156, (2005).

[19] Union of Greek Ship-owners, Annual Report 2010-2011, Piraeus, p. 10 (2011).

[20] European Central Bank, Financial Stability Review, Eurosystem, June, (2010)

[21] European Commission,. Annual Report on the Euro Area. European Economy, 6, Luxemburg, (2009a).

[22] Roubini, N., and Sachs, J., *European Economic Review*, 33, 903-938 (1989)

[23] Grilli, V., Masciandaro, D., and Tabellini, G., *Economic Policy*, 13, 341-392, (1991).

[24] Corsetti, G., and Roubini, N.,'The Design of Optimal Fiscal Rules for Europe after 1992' in Torres, F., and Giavazzi, F., (eds) *Adjustment and Growth in the European Monetary System*, Cambridge University Press, Cambridge, (1993).

[25] Alesina, A., and Giavazzi, F., *The Future of Europe: Reform or Decline*. MIT Press, Cambridge, (2006).

[26] Mitsopoulos, M., and Pelagidis, T., *The CATO Journal*, 29(3), 406, (2009).

[27] De Grauwe, P.,*CEPS Policy Brief*, 204, 1, (2010c).

[28] Tsakalotos, E., *Oxford Review of Economic Policy*, 14(1), 114-138, (1998).

[29] European Economy, The EU Economy: 2006 Review. European Commission, Directorate-General for Economic and Financial Affairs, No. 6, Brussels, (200)

[30] European Commission, Quarterly Report on the Euro Area. 8(4) (2009b).

[31] European Commission, Annual Report on the Euro Area 2007. European Economy, No. 5, Luxemburg, (2007).

[32] Caplan, B., *The Myth of the Rational Voter: Why Democracies Choose Bad Policies*. Princeton University Press, Princeton (2007).

[33] Kazakos P. *From incomplete modernization to crisis: reforms, depts and inertia in Greece1993-2010 (Από τον Ατελή Εκσυγχρονισμό στην Κρίση: Μεταρρυθμίσεις, Χρέη και Αδράνειες στην Ελλάδα 1993-2010)*. Patakis publisher, Athens (2010).

[34] Angelaki, M., *Social Cohesion and Development*, 2(2), 129-138 (2007).

[35] Sotiropoulos, D., *Journal of European Social Policy*, 14(3), 267-284 (2004).

[36] Athanasiadies H. and Patramanis A., *The Sociological Review*, 50(4) 610-639, (2002).

[37] Mbaye, H., *European Union Politics*, 2(3), 259-281, (2001).

[38] Boix, C., and Posner, D., *British Journal of Political Science*, 4, 686-693, (1998).

In: Greece: Economics, Political and Social Issues
Editor: Panagiotis Liargovas

ISBN: 978-1-62100-944-3
© 2012 Nova Science Publishers, Inc.

Chapter 5

EURO AND THE TWIN DEFICITS: THE GREEK CASE

Nikolina E. Kosteletou[*]
University of Athens,
Department of Economics, Athens, Greece

ABSTRACT

Since the beginning of 2010 and as a result of the debt crisis in the eurozone and specifically in Greece, fiscal imbalances have been at the center of interest. Related to these imbalances are imbalances of the external sector, which are equally important, as they need financing by net inflows from abroad. Financial integration and the euro have been blamed for the sharp deterioration of the Greek Current Account deficit, during the last two decades. In this chapter, we show that the increase in external deficit is related to the expansionary fiscal policy. The twin deficit hypothesis is empirically verified for the period 1991-2010. The relationship has distinct characteristics for the period after the country became a member of the eurozone. In the context of a portfolio model it is shown that the fiscal budget, but also interest rate fluctuations, growth and competitiveness have an important role for the determination of the Current Account. Empirical investigation is realized with panel data from Southern eurozone countries. All of them have Current Account deficits. It is found that not only fiscal policy of these countries affects their Current Account deficits, but also fiscal policy of the eurozone surplus countries of the North has a role to play. Interdependence among the countries of the eurozone suggests that fiscal policy can be used for the elimination of external disequilibrium within the eurozone.

Fiscal policy should be coordinated but not uniformly applied. Consequently for the case of Greece as well as for the other eurozone countries with deficits, the improvement in their fiscal situation will have a beneficial influence on their CA deficit, if accompanied by a combination of favorable changes in the net private savings, competitiveness, interest rates and also fiscal adjustments in eurozone countries with surpluses.

---

[*]E-mail: nkost@econ.uoa.gr

INTRODUCTION

This chapter aims at investigating the relation between government budget balance and the Current Account (CA) balance for the case of Greece. These two balances have been crucial for recent developments that brought the country at the brink of default. Budget balances have accumulated to a public debt amounting to 127.10 % of GDP in 2009, the year that the global financial crisis hit the Greek economy in the form of a debt crisis. CA deficits piled up to a net external debt equal to 88% of GDP in 2009. Rising public debt and net external debt, as percentages of GDP, reflect structural rigidities of the Greek economy. Their rise in recent decades was also the result of financial integration and the adoption of common currency.

Analysis of the relationship between the CA and fiscal policy has attracted theoretical as well as empirical attention. There are two major competing theories: the positive association of CA deficit and the government budget deficit, known as the twin deficit hypothesis, derives from the Keynesian tradition. According to this view an expansionary fiscal policy stimulates output and demand which has a deteriorating influence on the CA. At the other extreme, the two deficits have no connection according to the Ricardian Equivalence Hypothesis. Any fiscal expansion, or contraction induces intertemporal reallocation of savings, leaving the CA balance unaltered. In line to this approach, an increase in the budget deficit, increases private saving and has no effect on the CA. Whether or not the two deficits are positively related, has important policy implications. If the twin deficit hypothesis is valid, a government can improve the country's CA through a fiscal contraction and vice versa.

Empirical research for individual countries or group of countries has provided unclear results. Evidence in support to the twin deficit hypothesis primarily comes from the US experience in the 1980s and 2000s [1], [2], [3], [4]. In Edwards [5] and Blanchard [6] it is claimed that CA deficits of the US and other rich countries have their origins in private saving and investment decisions and that fiscal deficits often play a marginal role. For the US there are other empirical studies verifying a negative relation between the two deficits. When fiscal account worsens, the CA improves, as in Roubini [7], Kim and Roubini [8]. There are numerous other studies that confirm the twin deficit hypothesis for other countries, such as Baharumshah [9] for the case of Thailand. Daly and Siddiki [10] test the hypothesis for OECD countries, with cointegration analysis. In 13 out of 23 OECD countries for the period 1960-2000, the twin deficit hypothesis is accepted. Empirical studies dealing with the impact of budget deficits on CA deficits, for Greece, are inconclusive. Evidence from Vamvoukas [11] and also from Pantelis et al. [12] for the period 1960-2007 confirm the twin deficit hypothesis. On the other hand Papadogonas and Stournaras [13] provide support to the Ricardian equivalence hypothesis for the EU member states (Greece is included in their sample). According to them, CA developments in Greece are explained by factors related to financial and economic integration. Kaufmann, Scharler and Winckler [14] reject the twin deficit hypothesis for Austria. Vasarthani et al. [15], estimate a model for the determination of the CA for the EU countries with panel data, over the period 1980-2008. Their results provide a weak support to the twin deficit hypothesis.

This chapter is structured as follows. Section 2 presents some basic historical properties of the data that help us to understand the co-movements occurring between the two deficits for the case of Greece. First a brief overview of their relation for the period 1960-2010 is described. Then the Greek case is compared with other eurozone countries of the South. Section 3 offers the theoretical background of the relation between the two deficits. In this section a portfolio model is used to explain developments in the CA and budget balances. Factors related to financial and economic integration such as interest rates and growth differentials are essential characteristics of this model. Section 4 provides empirical evidence based on panel data from Southern eurozone countries. Finally, section 5 concludes with a summary of our results.

FACTS

The Greek Deficits: A 50 Year Perspective

This section analyzes the behavior of the Greek general government budget balance and the CA balance since 1960. The discussion of these two variables is divided into six distinct time periods. A brief historical review helps us to place the recent experience of the Greek economy in proper context. Emphasis is then given to the analysis of the most recent developments covering the period immediately preceding and after the introduction of euro into the economy.

Figure 1 depicts annual data for the two deficits as percentages of GDP for the period 1960-2010. All over this period the CA balance has been in deficit, ranging from 1.94% of GDP in 1981 to 13.35% in 2003.The budget balance was in moderate surplus during the early years of our sample. It turned into a deficit for the first time in 1967 and reversed back to surplus until 1973. The budget deficit became increasingly large over 1973-1991 and 1999 - 2010, although it clearly followed a political cycle throughout the period. It received its highest value15.35% of GDP in 2009. It was also over 10% in 1988 through 1990, 1992 and 1993. In Figure 1 a loose positive relationship between the two variables with their correlation coefficient equal to 0.84 is observed. This could support the twin deficit hypothesis. But in the mid 1990s the relation is reversed for a few years; that is, the two deficits follow opposite trend. Then their movement again synchronized through the end of our sample with the exception of 2010, the fist year under the Economic Adjustment Program. Between 1990 and 1999 the fiscal balance dramatically improved from a deficit of 14.03% of GDP to 3.10%.

For the twin deficit hypothesis and variations in the CA balance, the role of private savings relative to private investment is important as implied by the basic macroeconomic identity according to which the CA is equal to the difference between national savings, S and investment, I:

$$CA = S-I \tag{1}$$

Breaking down S and I into its public and private sector components, (1) becomes:

$$CA = (Sp-Ip) + (Sg-Ig) \tag{2}$$

where subscript p denotes private sector and subscript g denotes and public sector.

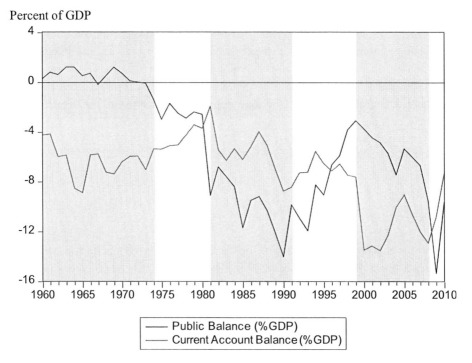

Figure 1. General Government Budget balance and Current Account Balance, 1960-2010.

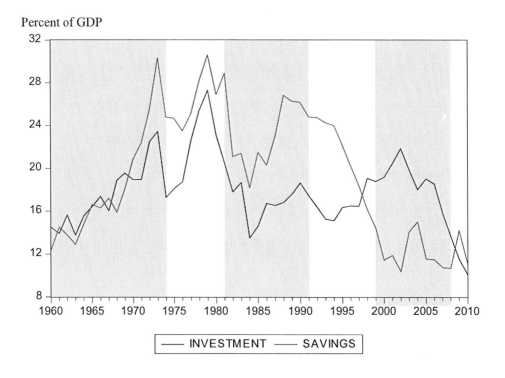

Figure 2. Private Investment and Private Saving, 1960-2010.

From (2), the CA is related to the excess public saving (Sg-Ig), which corresponds to the budget balance. Hence equation (2) is used as a basis for discussing the twin deficit hypothesis. A positive relation between CA and excess government savings holds only under the condition that the difference between Sp and Ip remains constant. The evolution of (Sp-Ip) is very important for the twin deficit hypothesis. Figure 2 shows the data for Sp and Ip over 1960-2010. It can be observed that for a long period preceding the 1990s, private saving and investment move together, verifying the Feldstein Horioka 1980 puzzle. During 1970-1997, the difference between Sp and Ip is positive. Private saving has followed a downward trend since 1988. Falling private savings and negative public savings, have put a downward pressure on the CA balance. The increase in private investment from 1993 to 2003 indicates that for this period the driving forces of the widening CA deficit come from reduced saving as well as higher investment demand. Table 1 summarizes average values of the two deficits, the public debt, growth, inflation, relative unit labor cost and unemployment rate, for each of the six phases and also their values for the more recent years 2007-2010.

Table 1. Current Account Balance, General Government Budget balance and Other Indicators, 1960-2010 (period averages)

	%of GDP			GDP growth[4] (%)	Inflation[5] (%)	Change in Relative Unit Labor Cost[6] (%)	Un-employment rate[7]
	Current Account[1]	Budget Balance[2]	Public Debt[3]				
1960-1974	-6.30	0.41	14.87	7.51	5.04	-3.08	4.31
1975-1981	-4.12	-3.46	21.08	3.69	17.11	1.38	2.33
1982-1991	-6.17	-9.96	52.83	1.18	18.56	-0.36	6.74
1992-1999	-6.92	-7.45	94.31	2.00	8.90	0.57	9.60
2000-2007	-11.78	-5.57	102.12	4.27	3.28	0.24	9.94
2007	-12.02	-6.67	105.41	4.28	2.90	1.25	8.3
2008	-12.91	-9.55	110.72	1.02	4.15	1.46	7.7
2009	-10.82	-15.36	127.10	-2.04	1.21	0.41	9.5
2010	-7.33	-9.63	142.76	-4.47	4.71	-2.18	12.6

1. net exports of goods and services.
2. general government.
3. debt of the general government, for the years 1970-2010. Debt of the central government, for the years 1960-1970.
4. GDP growth of real output (2000=100).
5. from the national consumer price index (2000=100).
6. annual change in relative real labor cost (-) sigh denotes gains in competitiveness, (-) loss. Performance relative to the rest of the former EU15, (unit labor cost in real terms 2000=100).
7. % of civilian labor force (break in series, 2001).
Source: European Commission, Economic and Financial Affairs and own calculations. Data on the 1960-1970 debt come from the Greek Ministry of National Economy, Administration of Economic Policy.

Next, we describe the main features and events related to the six phases of the CA and the public deficit behavior.

Phase 1, 1960 -1974: These were years of stable exchange rates, moderate inflation, low debt to GDP ratios and high growth rates. Also it was a period of political unrest, including the imposition of the dictatorship which lasted from 1967 to 1974. Public sector surplus, averaging 0.41% of GDP became negative in 1973 and remained increasingly negative from then onwards. Phase 1 was marked by the 1961 Association Agreement between Greece and the European Economic Community (EEC).[1] The Government was obliged to gradually reduce tariffs as well as other forms of trade barriers. The CA deficit which averaged 6.3% of GDP reached an unprecedented high level, 7.0% of GDP, in 1973. This coincided with the year of the first oil shock. GDP grew at an average rate of 7.51% which was greater than its growth in the following consecutive years.

Phase 2, 1975 – 1981: A democratically elected[2] conservative government ruled the country throughout this period. It allowed small but steady increases of the public sector deficit, which climbed from 0.1% of GDP in 1973, to 9.1% in 1981. The CA deficit, relative to the previous phase decreased to an average of 4.12% of GDP. This was to a large extent the result the Greek drachmae depreciation policy which started in 1975. From Table 1 it can be observed that the country's relative unit labor cost declined. Remarkably, competitiveness improved from 115.68 units in the previous phase to 96.31 during phase 2. The end of this phase coincides with the accession in1981 of Greece as a full member in the EEC.

Phase 3, 1982 – 1991: The socialist party was in power and governed the country from November 1981 through 1989. The public sector deficit climbed from 6.8% in 1982 to 12.14% of GDP in 1991, while the CA deficit worsened by 12% on the average, relative to the previous period. More specifically the average budget deficit/GDP ratio almost tripled, while the public debt/GDP ratio more than doubled relative to the previous period. The average CA deficit amounted to 6.17% of the GDP despite two devaluations of the currency in 1983 and 1985. The second devaluation accompanied by a stability program improved the CA balance only temporarily. This is the usual case with devaluations. The benefits lasted for 3 years as free trade with EEC countries inflated imports without a corresponding rise in exports. Trade barriers were abolished with other EEC member countries and therefore the CA deficit as a percentage of GDP rose from 1.95% to 8.45% in ten years from1981 to 1991. As a consequence of the increase in the oil price and expansionary fiscal and monetary policies implemented by the government, inflation rose to an average of 18.56%. Greece lost in terms of competitiveness. The increase in the public sector debt and deficit were justified as a relief to the lower and middle income classes that had been deprived during the previous periods.

Phase 4, 1992 – 1999. These have been years of austerity and structural adjustments as the country's economic performance was dominated by the convergence program that would lead to the Economic and Monetary Union (EMU). EMU was realized in three stages, starting in July 1990 as described initially in the Delors Report. The details of the unification process including the convergence criteria about the public debt and budget deficit, inflation and the long run interest rates were specified in the Maastricht Treaty which has been in effect since

---

[1] The Association for Entry Agreement was put into action in 1962 but was suspended during the dictatorship period.

[2] November 1974.

November 2003.[3] The necessary changes referred mainly to the banking sector and the conduct of monetary policy in general. For the Greek economy the adjustment process included, among others, the complete freedom of transactions, the end of the Central Bank granting credit to the public sector, the independence of the Central Bank, the loss of monetary policy tool and finally the irrevocable fixing of conversion rates. Based on statistical data of 1999, it was decided in 2000, that Greece would join the EMU in 2001. Hence, the year 1999 marked the end of an era. Table 2 shows the values of the Maastricht criteria for the Greek economy in 1992, when the effort of convergence practically started and their values in 1999.

The CA deficit increased by 0.75% on average relative to the previous period, amounting to 6.92% of GDP (the average of this phase). However, if we look at Figure 2 we draw two important conclusions: the private investment and saving change their behaviour relative to the past and follow divergent paths. From 1993 private investment increased while saving continued a declining path that had already started in 1988. The falling real and nominal interest rates, as well as positive expectations about the country joining EMU, induced people to save less and consume more. Also declining real and nominal interest rates and the liberalization of financial markets made borrowing easy and pushed up demand for investment, especially for construction. These combined with the introduction of euro in 2001 contributed to the doubling of CA deficit as a percentage of GDP.

Phase 5, 2000-2007: In 2000 the EU Council decided that Greece satisfied the conditions for entry as determined by the Maastricht Treaty, so at the beginning of 2001 the country became a member of the EMU. Since then fiscal balance has never been below 3% of GDP despite a stability program submitted in 2000. Fiscal austerity was gradually relaxed. The stability growth pact criteria aimed at ensuring budgetary discipline were repeatedly violated not only in Greece but also in other countries of the eurozone. In 2004, government budget deficit climbed to 7.4% of GDP in support of financing the organization of the Olympic Games. Easy access to borrowing, for the government as well as for the private sector, from the eurozone financial markets contributed to high growth rates, averaging 4.27%. This was the second highest growth rate behind Ireland in the eurozone for the years preceding the economic crisis.

Table 2. Maastricht Criteria and relevant values for Greece

Criteria		1992	1999
Budget deficit (% of GDP)	Not higher than 3%	-10.92	-3.09
Public Debt (% of GDP)	not more than 60%	78.37	93.99
Inflation (%)	not more than 1.5 percentage points above the rate of the three best performing Member States	15.88	2.64
Interest Rate (%)	Not more than 2 percentage points above the rate of the three best performing Member States in terms of price stability	24.13	6.3

High growth free mobility of capital, goods, services and labor, the adoption of a strong currency and positive expectations resulted in the widening of the CA deficit. The average

---

[3] signed in 1991 by the Head of the EEC countries.

CA deficit/GDP equal to 11.39% almost doubled when compared with the previous period. Throughout this period, the percent of CA/GDP had been the highest among the OECD countries. In 2009 when the crisis hit the Greek economy with some delay, GDP growth became negative. The budget deficit, public debt and CA were among the worse in the euro area. As the new year 2010 arrived, the possibility of sovereign default became evident.

Phase 6, 2008-to present: The financial and economic crisis of 2007, transformed to a public debt crisis arrived in Greece a year later in 2008. Output growth declined to 1.02% that year and became negative in 2009, inducing the Government to expand its spending. In addition, as 2009 had been an election year, the budget deficit reached 15.36% of GDP and the public debt 127% of the GDP. In 2008, the % of CA/GDP peaked at 13%.This was the highest among the OECD countries as the external debt was piling up. The reason for this was easy borrowing, increased spending and deterioration in competitiveness, which according to EU Commission services' calculations, was equal to 10-20% in 2009.[4] As a consequence of all these in 2010 borrowing from the markets became too expensive for the Greek Government. In May 2010, the first rescue package of 110 billion euros was prepared for Greece by EU and the IMF. The rescue plan also included the Economic Adjustment Program that aimed at restoring confidence and financial stability. The Program's objectives had been to introduce structural reforms in the public sector and also to reform the institutional framework of the private sector. Return to the free market was planned for 2013. A year later in mid 2011 it had become clear that the austerity measures had failed in almost all of the program's objectives and this despite the sacrifices of the middle and low class people. Additionally, the economy had turned into deep recession as output shrank by 4.47%, in 2010 and unemployment rate peaked at 12.6%. The only macro variable that improved was the CA deficit which was reduced to 7.33% of GDP. Under these circumstances in July 2011a new austerity package was prepared. This was the prerequisite for a second rescue package from the Eurozone countries and the IMF. In November 2011 the Eurozone leaders decided a 50% write down on Greek bonds, enabling a 100 billion euro cut in the country's sovereign debt. Also they decided a second rescue package of 100 billion euros.

Comparison with Other Countries

In this section, we compare the CA and government fiscal balance situation between Greece and a group of eurozone countries, during 1991-2010. 1991[5] marks the beginning of the convergence period for the first group of the 11 EU countries that joined the EMU in 1999 and Greece that joined in 2001.The aim is to examine the Greek case in relation to a group of countries that - at least before the economic crisis- had similar developments in their basic macro variables of our concern.

In this group we have included the Southern EU countries, that is, Spain, Portugal, Italy, France, and also Cyprus and Slovenia. A weak and deteriorating external sector is a common feature of these countries, with Greece and Portugal being in the worst position. This can be observed from Figure 3 that shows the course of the CA as a percentage of GDP. Italy's and France's CA surpluses have turned into deficits since 2004 and Cyprus after 2001.

---

[4] Adjustment Program for Greece, April 2010.
[5] The first stage of convergence as determined in the Delors report starts in mid 1990.

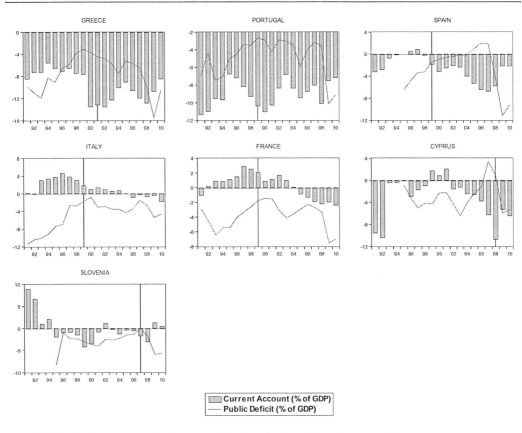

Vertical line in diagrams marks the year of the introduction of euro in respective economy.
Data Source: European Commission, Economic and Financial Affairs.

Figure 3. Current Account and Government Budget Balances, 1991-2010 (% of GDP).

We notice a temporary improvement in CA deficits lasting for two or three years after the introduction of Euro and also for the years 2009-2010, as a consequence of the economic crisis. CA deficits have piled up to a rising external debt over the years.

With respect to the net external debt position, measured by the Net International Investment Position[6](NIIP) as a percentage of GDP, Greece Portugal and Spain are in the worst situation. Figure 5 shows public debt and the Net International Investment Position as percentages of GDP of the countries of our group. By looking at the charts of Figure 5, it is concluded that some countries suffer from a dual problem: high public debt ratios matched with high or even higher external debt ratios. These countries are Greece, Portugal and Spain and to a much lesser extent Italy and Slovenia. Cyprus has a positive NIIP as a percentage of GDP, for all the years under consideration, while France's NIIP is characterized by moderate positive as well as negative positions.

The question that can be raised is about the sources of financing the net external debt of Greece, Portugal, Spain and Italy, since mid -1990s. The answer is related to the financial

---

[6] Net International Investment Position as published by the IFS of the IMF.

integration of EU and the creation of euro that has eased borrowing conditions for both the public and private sector.

Interest rates were falling rapidly during the convergence period in all countries of our sample. Figure 6 show the downward path followed by long run interest rates vis a vis the German rate. After euro was introduced and before the bursting of economic crisis long run interest rates of all countries of our sample almost coincided, with the exception of Slovenia and Cyprus. However, after 2008, the difference between the long run interest rate of each individual country and Germany's increases reflecting default risk that these countries face to a smaller or larger degree. Figure 7 depicts the path followed by real short run and long run interest rates. Real interest rates follow a downward trend. Leaving aside Cyprus and Slovenia, in all other cases these rates have started increasing moderately, since 2004. These rates have declined since 2008, in accordance to the ECB base rate, while real long interest rates go up following the path of nominal interest rates.

The countries of our group share an additional characteristic of their external sector that is worth noting: their trade balance with respect to other EU countries has been in deficit since 2000. The annual sum of the trade deficits has been increasing since then and is matched by a widening surplus of a different group of eurozone countries (Figure 8).

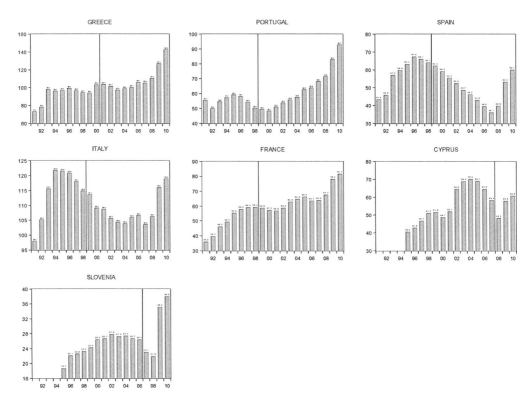

Vertical line in diagrams marks the year of the introduction of euro in respective economy.
Data Source: European Commission, Economic and Financial Affairs.

Figure 4. Public Debt, 1991-2010 (% of GDP).

Euro and the Twin Deficits 97

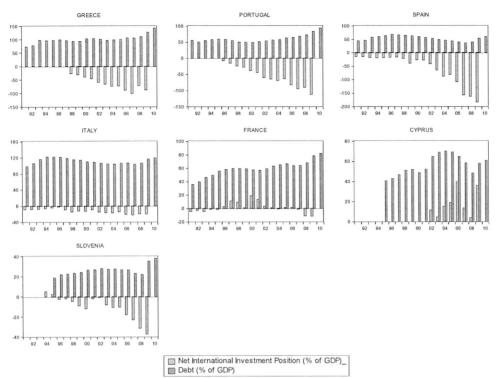

Data Source: European Commission, Economic and Financial Affairs, and IFS of IMF.

Figure 5. Public Debt and the International Investment Position (% of GDP).

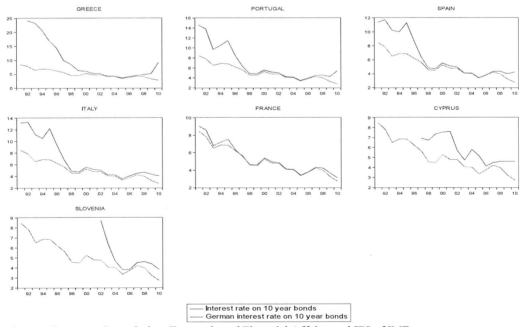

Data Source: European Commission, Economic and Financial Affairs, and IFS of IMF.

Figure 6. Long Run Interest Rates (interest rate on 10 year bonds)

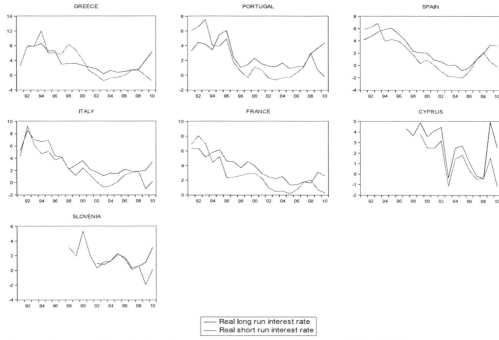

Data Source: European Commission, Economic and Financial Affairs, and IFS of IMF.

Figure 7: Real Short Run and Long Run Interest Rate (1991-2010)

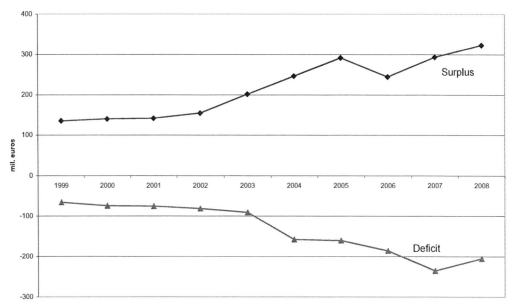

Note: *Deficit* includes: trade deficits of Austria, France, Italy, Spain, Portugal, Greece, Luxemburg, Cyprus, Malta and Slovenia with other eurozone countries..

Surplus includes: Trade surpluses of Germany, Belgium, Ireland, Holland and Slovakia, with other eurozone countries.

Figure 8. Intra-eurozone trade balances.

This second group is comprised by surplus[7] eurozone countries. These are Germany, Belgium, Ireland, Holland and Slovakia. The widening disequilibrium between the two groups reveals a severe loss in competitiveness for the deficit countries, after the introduction of the euro.[8] That is why we are going to refer to the group of Southern EU countries as the deficit group, or, countries and to the other group as the surplus group.

Regarding the government budget balance, we observe from Figure 3 that it has been in deficit for all countries of our group for all years under consideration. Budget deficits as a percentage of GDP have improved during the 1990s although loosening fiscal policies after attaining the accession to EMU criteria have increased fiscal deficits in all countries of our group with the exception of Spain. Public debt as a percent of GDP has been under control in all countries until before the economic crisis. Figure 4 shows the stock of public debt as a percentage of GDP. We can observe the performance of the public debt/GDP for the case of Italy and Spain. In Italy, the public debt as a percentage of GDP fell from a high of 121.84 in 1994 to103.62 in 2007 and in Spain it fell from a high of 67.45 in 1996 to 36.13 in 2007. In 2010 as a consequence of the economic crisis, public debt climbed to unprecedented levels. It reached 142.75% of GDP in Greece, 119% in Italy, 93% in Portugal, 81.70% in France, 60.11% in Spain, 60.80% in Cyprus and 38.00% in Slovenia.

As an indication of how different or how close to Greece, the economies of the other countries in the deficit group are with respect to variables related to the twin deficits, we estimate the correlation coefficients between data on variables from Greece and data coming from the rest of deficit countries. The closer to unity is the coefficient the closer are the variations in corresponding variables. Further, we take for granted that the relevant series follow similar paths, if estimated correlation coefficients are greater than 0.7. Otherwise, we assume there is no relation between the two series. Table 3 reports the relevant estimated coefficients.

From Table 3 it is concluded that a) the CA/GDP of Greece does not correlate with CA ratios of any other country of our sample. As expected, correlation with the German CA/GDP ratio is negative.

Table 3. Correlation coefficients (Greece with other deficit countries)

	Portugal	Spain	France	Italy	Cyprus	Slovenia	Germany
CA/GDP	0.05	0.6	0.3	0.55	0.04	0.25	-0.57
Budget Deficit/GDP	0.79*	0.77*	0.88*	0.53	0.08	0.48	0.25
Public debt/GDP	0.91*	-0.10	0.89*	0.20	0.16	0.82*	
Net International Investment Position/GDP	0.74*	0.72*	0.27	0.86*	-0.52	0.61	
Long run Interest rate	0.84*	0.33	-0.43	0.04	-0.15	-0.10	
Private Savings/GDP	0.43	0.73*	.061	0.56	-0.00	0.55	
Private investment/GDP	0.88*	0.95*	0.86*	0.95*	0.81*	0.81*	
Relative unit labour cost	0.95*	0.77*	0.97*	0.79*	0.93*	0.98*	0.95*

Note: the * denotes correlation coefficients with values greater than 0.70.

---

[7] It is reminded that here we are referring to intra - EU trade deficits.
[8] Slovenia joined EMU in 2007 and Cyprus in 2007 but for two years before their economics were functioning with fixed exchange rates, under the Exchange Rate Mechanism (ERM II).

Also, negative –not shown here- are the correlation coefficients of the German CA/GDP with corresponding ratios of the other countries of the deficit group. b) Greek budget deficit/GDP is closely correlated to that of Portugal, Spain and France. c) On the basis of correlation coefficients greater than 0.70, Greece is closer to Portugal and Spain[9] and then to France. It is very loosely, if at all, related to Italy, Cyprus and Slovenia, which is a reasonable outcome, since for Cyprus and Slovenia joined EMU later than Greece, Slovenia in 2007 and Cyprus in 2008. As for Italy, it is a huge economy compared to Greece, with very different structure, performance and history. Hence, their corresponding economic variables follow different trends.

THEORETICAL BACKGROUND

Channels through which the Budget Balance Influences the Current Account and *Vice Versa*

The two balances influence each other through various channels. Theoretical support to the twin deficit hypothesis and causality running from the public deficit to the external deficit derives mainly from the conventional Keynesian and Mundell - Fleming approach.

First, according to the Keynesian tradition, an expansionary fiscal policy stimulates income and spending through the multiplier mechanism. Part of increased spending falls on imports, hence the CA deteriorates and the twin deficit hypothesis is verified. This is true irrespective of exchange rate regime, capital mobility situation or phase of the business cycle of the economy.

Second, in a Mundell-Fleming framework [16], [17] with perfect capital mobility and negligible transaction costs, fiscal expansion increases real interest rates that in turn trigger capital inflows. As a result real exchange rate appreciates, deteriorating the CA. Whatever the exchange rate regime is, even in a common currency area, such as the eurozone, this mechanism is effective. However, uncoordinated fiscal policy in a currency union may lead to divergent inflation, real interest rates, real exchange rates finally to widening external imbalances.Causality running from the CA balance to the budget balance is supported by other views. Financial integration and easier access to borrowing for member countries causes deterioration of their CA balances, raising questions of sustainability by financial markets. Gourinchas [18], among others, argue that governments should protect their economies from such a potential by lowering public deficits. If such a policy is implemented, the two deficits are inversely related and the twin deficit hypothesis does not exist.

An inverse relation between the two deficits is found for the US, for the period 1973-2004, by Kim and Roubini. The observed "twin divergence" as they call it is in effect when the main driver of the two balances is an output shock. They claim that because during economic recessions unemployment is high and output falls, fiscal policy is expansionary to stimulate economic activity and the budget balance worsens. At the same time, as spending falls, the CA improves. On the contrary during the booms, when the economic activity is high

---

[9] Six out of eight cases of estimated correlation coefficients have values >0.70 for Portugal, 5 for Spain, 4 for France, 3 for Italy and Slovenia, 2 for Cyprus. In the case of Germany, Finland and Holland, there is one, at most, respective correlation coefficient with a value > 0.70.

fiscal balance improves implying coexistence of deteriorating CA balances and improving budget balances. So, according to their explanation, there is no causal effect between the two deficits but there exists an inverse association.

Stiglitz [19] supports the twin deficit hypothesis, with causality running from the CA to the budget balance. He argues that countries with persistent or expanding CA deficits are often obliged to run fiscal deficits to maintain aggregate demand. "Without the fiscal deficit, they will have high unemployment."[10]

The synchronized variation in private sector's saving and investment, known as the Feldstein-Horioka puzzle [20], supports the twin deficit hypothesis, as can be inferred from equation (2).(Marinheiro [21], Blancahrd-Giavazzi [22]). More recent empirical work has proved that the Feldstein-Horioka puzzle is not more valid neither is the twin deficit hypothesis.

An alternative approach known as the Ricardian Equivalence Hypothesis suggests no relation between the two deficits (Barro [23], [24]). The Ricardian Equivalence predicts that a fiscal expansion has a positive effect of the same size on private savings, while real interest rates, investment and CA balance remain unaffected. Rational individuals know that if public expenses increase this year, next year or sometime in the near future, taxes will be raised. Therefore, they save today to pay increased taxes in the future. Papadogonas - Stournaras [13] findings support this view.

A Portfolio Model

Whatever the underlying forces behind the two deficits are, widening imbalances in the euro area countries cannot be explained without considering the effect of financial and economic integration and the common currency. In what follows we construct a portfolio model in the context of which the relation between CA and budget balances can be discussed. Under the condition of financial integration and a single currency, it is assumed that short run interest rates are common for all countries, while long run interest rates may differ. Therefore, financial assets bearing different rates of return are not perfect substitutes, in the portfolios of investors. Assume for simplicity that prices are constant and that the Union we are referring to is comprised of two countries representing two groups with distinct characteristics. The first is the surplus countries group comprised by countries of the core of the currency union. Deficit countries are included in the second group. The difference between the two groups is that all indicators of real variables, such as income per capita, distribution of income, adjustment productivity of labour, competitiveness of the economy, as well as the structure of production and institutional framework are superior in the surplus relative to the deficit group. Also, the financial sector of the surplus group is more developed and efficient. Deficit countries benefit from the formation of the currency union with the surplus group, in terms of lower nominal and real interest rates and easier access to borrowing in general. This situation induces widening deficits in both public and CA balances.

It is also assumed that the external sector of the union as a whole is in balance. So CA surplus of the first group equals the deficit of the second. At this stage, for simplicity of analysis, the two country groups will be referred as the home and the foreign country: the

---

[10] Stiglitz (2010), p 326.

deficit countries group will be the "home" country while the surplus group the "foreign" country. The CA balance is equal to the change in the net holdings of foreign assets held by domestic residents. If it is positive it corresponds to the country's net lending abroad, if negative, to net borrowing from abroad:

$$CA = \Delta(F-B) \tag{3}$$

where, Δ, denotes first difference. F is the holdings of foreign assets by domestic residents and B is the holdings of domestic assets by foreign residents. It is assumed that foreign assets, F, are comprised by bonds issued by the government or the private sector of the foreign country, with an average rate of return Rf, whereas, B, domestic assets are bonds issued by the government or the private sector of the home country, with an average rate of return Rb. Residents of the union can hold their financial wealth in the form of money, M, or bonds F, or B. Money, M, has also a rate of return equal to Rm. The rate of return of each form of asset is its interest rate. Hence demand for each asset[11] depends positively on its own interest rate, negatively on the other assets' interest rates and it also depends on income, Y. Subsequently, demand for foreign assets Fd by domestic residents is a function of Rf, Rb, Rm and Y, home country's income:

$$Fd = f_d(\overset{(+)}{R_f}, \overset{(-)}{R_b}, \overset{(-)}{R_m}, \overset{(+)}{Y}) \tag{4}$$

Signs of (+) or (-) denote the sign of partial derivative of the demand for F with respect to corresponding variables in (4). Similarly, demand for domestic bonds Bd, is described in equation (5):

$$Bd = b_d(\overset{(-)}{R_f}, \overset{(+)}{R_b}, \overset{(-)}{R_m}, \overset{(+)}{Y*}) \tag{5}$$

The star (*) refers to foreign country variables.

To determine the factors affecting the asset supply side we argue that B and F are issued by the corresponding country's government or private sector, to finance their borrowing requirements. The higher is the stock of public debt, PDebt, the higher is the stock of bonds that have been issued. Also, the lower is the interest rate the higher is the supply of bonds. Therefore, supply of foreign bonds,[12] Fs, depends positively on the foreign country' stock of public debt, PDebt* and negatively on Rf. Supply of domestic bonds, depends positively on PDebt and negatively on Rb.

$$Fs = f_s(\overset{(+)}{P\,Debt*}, \overset{(-)}{R_f}) \tag{6}$$

$$Bs = b_s(\overset{(+)}{P\,Debt}, \overset{(-)}{R_b}) \tag{7}$$

---

[11] Demand for F corresponds to the (supply of) lending by domestic residents to foreigners. Similarly, demand for B corresponds to the (supply of) lending to domestic residents by foreigners.

[12] Supply of F corresponds to the demand for borrowing by foreigners, while supply of B corresponds to the demand for borrowing by domestic residents.

Consequently, when demand for each asset is equal to its supply, the actual stock of F and B depends on all forces included in corresponding demand and supply functions:

$$F = f(\overset{(?)}{R_f}, \overset{(-)}{R_b}, \overset{(-)}{R_m}, \overset{(+)}{Y}, \overset{(+)}{PDebt^*}) \tag{8}$$

$$B = b(\overset{(-)}{R_f}, \overset{(?)}{R_b}, \overset{(-)}{R_m}, \overset{(+)}{Y^*}, \overset{(+)}{PDebt^*}) \tag{9}$$

In (8) the direction of influence of R_f on F depends on whether the effect originates from the demand for foreign bonds, F (supply of lending) or the effect originating from the supply of F (demand for borrowing). The same holds for the ambiguous effect of R_b on the stock of bonds, B, in (9). By substituting the equilibrium equations (8) and (9) in (3) we end up with the CA balance as a function of variables coming from the asset market:

$$F - B = \phi(\overset{(?)}{R_f}, \overset{(?)}{R_b}, \overset{(-)}{R_m}, \overset{(+)}{Y}, \overset{(-)}{Y^*}, \overset{(-)}{PDebt}, \overset{(+)}{PDebt^*}) \text{ and}$$

$$CA = \Delta(F - B) = \Delta(\phi(\overset{(?)}{R_f}, \overset{(?)}{R_b}, \overset{(?)}{R_m}, \overset{(+)}{Y}, \overset{(-)}{Y^*}, \overset{(-)}{PDebt}, \overset{(+)}{PDebt^*})) \tag{10}$$

If additionally we assume that a change in the stock of public debt corresponds to that year's budget balance, BB, with the opposite sign, we can rewrite (10) as

$$CA = \zeta(\overset{(?)}{\Delta R_f}, \overset{(?)}{\Delta R_b}, \overset{(-)}{\Delta R_m}, \overset{(+)}{\Delta Y}, \overset{(-)}{\Delta Y^*}, \overset{(+)}{BB}, \overset{(-)}{BB^*}) \tag{11}$$

Again, the effect of a change in Rf or Rb on the CA balance is subject to the dominance of the effect from the demand or the supply side of the relevant bonds market. It is noted that the CA is influenced by the change in interest rates and not by their levels.

Next we shall discuss the effect of financial integration on the CA balance and its relation with the budget balance. Within our framework of analysis financial integration causes stronger adjustments in the home country[13] than in the foreign country. The government of the home country takes the opportunity to increase its borrowing to finance its requirements, by increasing the supply of government bonds, B. In turn, this inflates public debt, as well as the budget deficit by the same amount, ceteris paribus. The increase in the supply of B, given the fact that there exists sufficient demand for domestic bonds, increases the stock of bonds, B, in the home country. From (3) (CA=Δ(F-B)), it is implied that the CA balance deteriorates. Besides, unless other adjustments take place, the worsening of the CA, is matched by a worsening of the budget balance. Therefore, the twin deficit hypothesis holds under the hypothesis of the Government and private sector unlimited capacity to borrow from financial markets. In fact, what we will estimate is a linear specification of (11) that has the following form:

---

[13] Representing the weaker economies.

$$CA_{ti} = a_0 + a_1 \Delta R_{fti} + a_2 \Delta R_{bti} + a_3 \Delta R_{mti} + a_4 \Delta Y_{ti} + a_5 \Delta Y_{ti}^* + a_6 BB_{ti} + a_7 BB_{ti}^* + u_{ti} \quad (12)$$

Coefficients α_1, α_2, α_3 can be either positive or negative:

$\alpha_1 > 0$, if the effect coming from the demand side prevails over the effect coming from the supply side of the market for F. It implies that as ΔRf increases, CA improves. In words, the higher is the increase in foreign interest rates, the greater is the demand for foreign bonds, by domestic residents.

As F increases, our country's CA improves.

$\alpha_1 < 0$, if the effect coming from the supply side of the F market prevails. Similarly,
$\alpha_2 > 0$, if effect coming from the supply side of the market for B prevails.
$\alpha_2 < 0$, if effect coming from the demand side of the B market prevails.
$\alpha_4 > 0$, $\alpha_5 < 0$, $\alpha_6 > 0$, $\alpha_7 < 0$. u_{ti} is the disturbance term.

In any case it is the variation in interest rate that matters for the determination of the CA balance, not their level.

RESULTS OF THE EMPIRICAL RESEARCH

Our intention has been to test empirically the twin deficit hypothesis for Greece over the period 1991-2010 that covers the convergence process, the adoption of euro as well as the economic crisis. However the number of annual observations of our time series is quite restricted for the derivation of reliable conclusions. For this reason we have increased their number by using panel data. These come from our sample of Southern euro area countries, that is, apart from Greece, Portugal, Spain, Italy, France, Cyprus and Slovenia. As discussed in the previous section, Greece has more similarities with these countries than with northern euro area countries. Consequently, estimated results apply to all countries of our sample and to Greece as well.

Saving – Investment

Before proceeding with the empirical investigation of the two deficits it is important to examine the savings-investment behavior. The reason is that financial integration that lead to the reduction in nominal and real interest rates as well as the optimism about the future of the EMU, influenced savings as well as investment interfering in the relation of the two deficits. The identity CA=(Sg-Ig) +(Sp-Ip) suggests that our preliminary investigation should involve the following relations:

1) private savings Sp and private investment Ip. If these two variables are positively correlated with correlation coefficient equal to one then the Feldstein-Horiaka puzzle is verified, as well as the twin deficit hypothesis. For any other value of the correlation coefficient, the twin deficit hypothesis should be further investigated. So, we should test

$$Sp=\beta_o + \beta_1 Ip \qquad (13).$$

$$\text{If } \beta_0=0 \text{ and } \beta_1=1 \qquad (13)'$$

then the Feldstein-Horioka Puzzle is valid and the twin deficit hypothesis is accepted.

2) If the Feldstein-Horioka puzzle doesn't hold, the relation between net public savings, (Sg-Ig), and net private savings, (Sp-Ip), should be investigated. In case net public and private savings are positively correlated, the twin deficit hypothesis is verified. In case of negative correlation, or, of no correlation at all, twin deficit hypothesis should be further examined. We should test

$$(Sg-Ig)= \gamma_0+\gamma_1(Sp-Ig) \qquad (14)$$
$$\text{If } \gamma o>0 \text{ and } \gamma_1>0 \qquad (14)'$$

then, the twin deficit hypothesis holds, otherwise it should be further checked.

$$\text{In the special case where } \gamma o= 0 \text{ and } \gamma_1= -1 \qquad (14)''$$

the Ricardian Equivalence hypothesis is valid and the twin deficit hypothesis is rejected.

Testing the above relations involves the following steps:

Fist, we check for unit roots, with the standard tests. Second, if all or some of these variables are not stationary, we test for cointegration and finally we examine whether the long run coefficients satisfy conditions (13)' or (14)'. Tables 4, 5 and 6 summarize the estimated results.

From Table 4 it is inferred that whereas the variable Sp can be considered as stationary, Ip, (Sg-Ig) and (Sp-Ip) cannot. Therefore we proceed by testing for cointegration. Most of the tests[14] for the existence of contegrating vector suggest that private investment and private savings are cointegrated (Table 5).The same is true for net government savings (Sg-Ig) and net private savings, (Sp-Ip). Table 6 demonstrates the estimated coefficients for the long run relationships. As can be observed, conditions (13)'and (14)' are not satisfied. Their rejection does not imply the rejection of the twin deficit hypothesis, which should be further investigated.

Table 4. Unit root tests (panel data for deficit eurozone countries, 1991-2010)

Variables	Hadri z	Levin, Lin and	Im, Pesaran and	ADF-Fisher Chi-

---

[14] There exist other tests, not reported here, available from the econometric package Eviews 7. If all these tests are taken into account, our conclusions will not be altered.

	statistic	Chu t*	shin W-statistic	square
Sp	5.66*	-2.26*	-1.57**	22.89***
Ip	2.62*	-0.76	-1.21	18.18
(Sg-Ig)		0.91*	1.35	9.72
(Sp-Ip)		2.31	-0.67	18.65

Note: the asterisks *, **, *** correspond to statistics according to which, the
Ho hypothesis of a unit root, cannot be rejected at the 1%, 5% and 10% level of significance.

Table 5. Cointegration tests (panel data for deficit eurozone countries, 1991-2010)

Variables	Kao test	Panel pp statistic	Panel ADF statistic	Group ADPstatistic
Ip, Sp	4.55	-3.56 *	-3.39*	-1.68**
(Sg-Ig), (Sp-Ip)	-1.61**	-1.14	-2.06**	-1.23***

Note: the asterisks *, **, *** correspond to statistics according to which, the
Ho hypothesis of no cointegration cannot be rejected at the 1%, 5% and 10% level of significance.

Table 6. Estimated coefficients of cointegration equations (panel data for deficit eurozone countries, 1991-2010)

equation	β_0	β_1	γ_0	γ_1
$Sp = \beta_0 + \beta_1 Ip$	27.72*	-0.49*		
$(Sg-Ig) = \gamma_0 + \gamma_1 (Sp-Ig)$			-3.72*	-0.40*

Note: The asterisk, *, denotes statistical significance of relevant coefficients at the 1% level of significance.

It is interesting to comment that Ip and Sp are inversely related, as expected from the visual inspection of the individual country figures of these time series (Figure 9) Also, the excess government savings,(Sg-Ig) and the excess private savings, (Sp-Ip) are inversely related. This could support a weak Ricardian Equivalence Hypothesis.The inverse association between the two deficits suggests that the expansion of the government excess savings in the eurozone deficit countries leads to the crowding out of the private sector excess savings. And of course, the opposite holds. Figure 10 shows the path of net private and public savings for the countries of our sample. Their inverse relation is indeed noticeable. Therefore, as there is no certainly about whether the twin deficit hypothesis is rejected, we proceed by estimating the portfolio model, in order to draw further information about the two deficits.

Estimation of the Portfolio Model

The purpose of this section is to estimate equation (12) with panel data from the deficit eurozone countries and from Germany, representing the "foreign" surplus country of our theoretical framework.

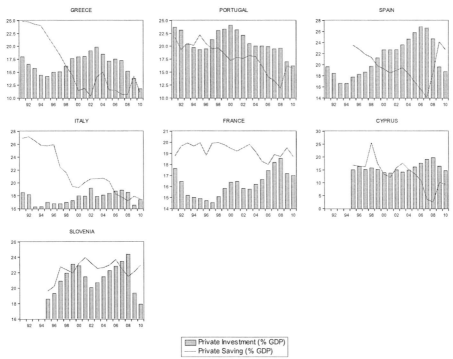

Data Source: European Commission, Economic and Financial Affairs.

Figure 9. Private Saving and Investment (%GDP).

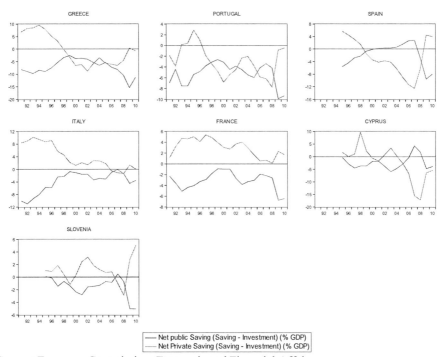

Data Source: European Commission, Economic and Financial Affairs.

Figure 10. Net Private and Public Saving (% GDP).

With the intention to make data from different countries more comparable and also correct for inflation, data on the CA and budget balances are expressed as percentages of GDP. In place of ΔY we have tried GDP growth, y, for deficit eurozone countries and in place of ΔY^*, Germany's GDP growth y^*. Initially, we have tested for stationarity of our variables.Table 7 reports unit root tests. According to the majority of those tests, stationarity of the variables cannot be rejected at the 1% or 5% level of significance. So, we proceed with the estimation of (12).

Empirical results for equation (12) estimated with cross section fixed effects panel data are reported in Table 8, column (1). Because estimated coefficients of GDP growth, for the deficit countries as well as for Germany, are insignificant at the 10% level, we proceed with a new estimation in column (2), where output growth has been substituted with unit labor cost of the deficit countries with respect to Germany's, RULC, under the assumption that $\alpha_4 = \alpha_5$.

In columns (3) and (4) coefficients of ΔRb and ΔRf are constrained to be equal, but with opposite signs. So, the change in the interest rate spread $\Delta(Rb-Rf)$ appears as an independent variable. The difference between column (3) and (4) is that (3) includes relative output growth, $(y-y^*)$ whereas (4) includes relative unit labor cost, RULC.

Table 7. Unit root tests (Panel data for deficit eurozone countries, 1991-2010)

Variable (level)	Test statistics			
	Hadri z statistic	Levin, Lin and Chu t*	Im, Pesaran and shin W-statistic	ADF-Fisher Chi-square
CA/Y (CA balance/GDP)	2.35*	-0.96	-1.80**	27.13*
ΔLR (long run interest rate)	5.54*	-.98*	-2.07*	26.06*
ΔGLR (Germany' long run interest rates)	7.79*	-3.04*	-0.12	10.13
ΔSR (short run interest rate)	5.52*	-3.36*	0.82	16.53
BB/Y (budget balance/GDP)	0.97	-.59**	21.73***	23.11**
GBB/GY (Germany's Budget balance/GDP)	7.47*	-3.21*	-2.85*	29.88*
y (output growth)	1.70**	-2.21*	-2.39*	28.17*
gy (Germany's output growth)	3.39*	-5.73*	-4.49*	45.35*
ULC Unit labour cost	7.02*	-2.39*	0.04	14.95
GULC (Germany's unit labour cost)	7.39*	-4.04*	-1.17	16.55
RULC (Relative unit labour cost ULC/GULC)	4.95*	-0.20	0.81	8.19

Note: The asterisks *, **, *** correspond to statistics according to which, the Ho hypothesis of a unit root cannot be rejected at the 1%, 5% and 10% level of significance.

Euro and the Twin Deficits

**Table 8. Estimation of the portfolio model for the deficit Eurozone Countries
1991-2010**

Dependent Variable: CA/GDP (%)				
Independent variables	(1)	(2)	(3)	(4)
ΔRb (change in the long run interest rate)	-0.56*	-0.56*		
ΔRf (change in Germany's long run interest rates)	0.55*	0.43*		
Δ(Rb-Rf)			-0.54*	-0.54*
ΔRm (short run interest rate)	-0.14*	-0.17*	-0.18*	-0.18*
BB/GDP (Public balance as a % of GDP))	0.14*	0.15*	0.12*	0.15*
BB*/GDP*(Germany's Public balance/as a % of Germany's GDP)	-0.16*	-0.15*	-0.16*	-0.15*
y (output growth)	-1.83			
y*(Germany's output growth)	-4.03			
(y-y*)			0.52	
RULC (Relative unit labour cost: Deficit countries unit labour cost with respect to Germany's)		0.17*		0.17**
(CA/GDP)(-1)	0.75*	0.71*	0.74*	0.71*
Constant	-0.65	1.34	-0.97*	1.28*
Adjusted R-squared	0.957	0.957	0.956	0.957
Total panel observations(unbalanced)	103	103	103	103

Note: The asterisks *, **, denote statistical significance of relevant coefficients at the 1% and 5% level of significance, respectively.

Our preferred estimations are those of columns (2), (3) and (4), on the basis of significance of the estimated coefficients. Estimated values of coefficients of interest rates and budget deficits are very similar for all 4 equations of Table 8.

Finally, before proceeding with the evaluation of our results, we should note that the lagged dependent variable has been also included in all estimations as it improves their general performance and also reduces autocorrelation. Subsequently, from Table 8, we observe the following:

First, concerning the effect of fiscal policies: the budget balance and the CA as percentages of GDP are positively related as implied by the positive and significant, at the 1% level, coefficients on BB/GDP in columns (1)-(4). This is consistent with the prediction of our model, as α_6 coefficient is expected to be positive, verifying the twin deficit hypothesis. It is reminded that according to our approach, the channel of influence is through the bonds market: an expansionary fiscal policy is financed through the issue of government bonds. If increased supply of bonds is met by higher demand, then the change in B, ΔB is positive and exerts a deteriorating effect on the CA balance, through equation (3), which is CA=Δ(F-B). If ΔB>0 andΔF=0, then the CA is negative.

It is interesting that Germany's budget balance as a percentage of its GDP is inversely related to the CA balance of the deficit countries, as percentage of GDP. This is expected from our model which predicts α_6, the coefficient on BB*, to be negative. Moreover it must be noted that the budget balance effect of the Southern countries and of Germany (as percentages of their GDP) on the CA/GDP ratio, is of almost equal but opposite value. In terms of equation (12) this implies that α_6 coefficient is equal to α_7. This suggests that domestic as well as foreign fiscal policies are equally important in affecting external imbalances in the eurozone. So, an expansionary fiscal policy in Germany reduces the CA deficits of Southern eurozone countries. And of course the opposite is true, that is a tightening fiscal policy in Germany, widens the deficits of the Southern eurozone countries. If this is true, an underlying hypothesis about twin deficits for Germany must hold. But this must be empirically investigated.

Second, about the effect of interest rates: in columns (1) and (2) of Table 8, specific coefficients are estimated for the variation in the long run interest rates, ΔRb and ΔRf.

The negative sign on ΔRb can be explained as follows. Increasing reductions in Rb causes the deterioration in the CA balance (as a percentage of GDP). According to our theoretical approach, the worsening of the CA is the outcome of a positive effect on the supply of B, which deteriorates the CA. Hence, for periods of declining interest rates, increasing negative changes in the long run interest rate is matched with wider CA deficits. This happens because governments as well as the private sector can benefit by increasing their borrowing (issuing bonds) under the condition of fast falling interest rates. Therefore, widening CA deficits of the Southern eurozone countries over 1991-2000 have been, to a certain extent, the result of sharp reductions in long run interest rates (Figure 6). We could therefore claim that deteriorating CA balances of the deficit eurozone countries has been, to a certain degree the result of financial integration and deregulation of the capital markets. The opposite effect is true, that is decreasing variations in the interest rates –as in the period after 2000- are related with improving CA balances as a percentage of GDP. Converge of interest rates among the EMU countries should, in part, explain an improvement in CA balances after the introduction of the Euro. The same interpretation can be given for the negative sign of the estimated coefficient of the variation in short run interest rate, ΔRm. It should be noted that the estimated effect of ΔRm is much smaller (less than half) than the effect of ΔRb, indicating the importance of long term borrowing in relation to the CA/GDP ratio.

Similarly, we can explain the positive sign on ΔRf. Decreasing (increasing) variations in Rf, Germany's long run interest rate, result in widening (narrowing) CA deficits of the eurozone peripheral countries. The channel of influence is again the bonds market, but this time Germany' bonds market: as ΔRf falls, demand for F bonds issued by the German Government, decreases. As supply of F adjusts, ΔF becomes negative and the CA balance worsens, from $CA=\Delta(F-B)$.

Third, about the GDP growth: The coefficient of relative GDP growth (y-y^*) in Column (3), is positive implying that higher GDP growth in deficit eurozone countries relative to Germany's GDP growth, contributes to the improvement in the CA Balances, as a % of GDP, of Southern eurozone countries. The coefficient on relative unit labour cost, in column (2) and (4) also indicate positive effect on the CA, as a % of GDP. This is in accordance to the predictions of our model, if $\alpha_4=\alpha_5$ in (12) and if relative unit labour cost takes the place of relative growth rates. Furthermore, relative unit labour cost is an indicator of a country's competitivess. So, the positive effect implied by our estimation indicates that a loss in competitiveness (increase in relative unit labour cost) for the deficit eurozone countries worsens further their CA deficits. It could be claimed that the effect of relative unit labour cost, or competitiveness, originates from the traditional CA approach, according to which CA is determined by competitiveness, relative income and other variables related to the demand side of the economy.

Implications for the Greek Economy

The results of our empirical investigation for the deficit eurozone countries hold for Greece as well. Hence, the deterioration of the Greek CA during the last two decades can be attributed to some extent to the financial integration and the introduction of Euro. Sharp decline of the interest rates in the 1990s, made borrowing easier for the public as well as for the private sector. Also, we found that fiscal policies matter and most surprisingly, German fiscal policy, representing the policies of the EU core euro countries, matters for the Greek Current Account. The twin deficit hypothesis therefore holds for the case of Greece. The Greek CA can improve through policies promoting the improvement of the country's competitiveness, that is, the Greek relative unit cost must decline. This can be achieved not just by introducing horizontal cuts in incomes of public and private sector wage earners[15]. There are alternative policies that can be realized, such as promoting investment, technologies and innovations in exporting sectors, cutting taxes on selected products or industries. Unfortunately, the economic and political developments that have brought the country to the brink of default have created insecurity about the future and adverse expectations. These together with severe and repeated wage cuts have lead domestic spending and investment to a nadir level. Given the economic environment of insecurity and instability, the country's competitiveness has declined, despite the decrease in the relative unit labour cost. The importance of the German Budget Balance in affecting the Greek CA indicates the crucial role that policy factors in the core countries of the EU can play. Unlimited lending to the Greek government to pay its debts will not help the country to recover from recession. On the contrary, a better synchronization of fiscal and monetary policy program for the eurozone as a whole, but not applied with uniformity could be more successful. It must be noted that the criteria of the Stability Growth Pact were repeatedly violated in the past by many countries for various reasons.

CONCLUSION

In this chapter we have examined the effect of the government deficit on the CA balance with special emphasis on the case of Greece. First, we studied the statistical data of the two deficits placed in a historical context and compared them with data coming from other Southern eurozone counties. During recent years the CAs of these countries have been in deficit. This contrasts with Northern or core eurozone countries that have CA surpluses. Then we constructed a portfolio model incorporating the effect from financial integration and the creation of the euro. According to this the channel of influence from fiscal policy to the CA balance is the bonds market, where governments and the private sector can borrow. Finally we have tested our portfolio model with panel data coming from the countries of Southern

---

[15] As the 2010 and 2011adjustment programs of the EU and IMF dictate.

euro area and Germany, representing the surplus countries of Northern eurozone for the period 1991-2010. The conclusions we have drawn can be summarized as follows:

First, the twin deficit hypothesis is confirmed. An expansionary fiscal policy worsens the CA and the opposite of course, holds. This is true for the eurozone countries with CA deficits. The sample of deficit countries includes Greece, Portugal, Spain, Italy, France, Cyprus and Slovenia.

Second, fiscal policy of the surplus eurozone countries represented in our empirical investigation with Germany, influences CA balances of countries of Southern eurozone. We found that expansionary (contractionary) fiscal policy of the German government improves (deteriorates) the CA deficits of countries of the South.

Third, fluctuations in the long run as well in short run interest rates affect the CA. A sharp decline in long run and short run interest rates, as during the 1991-1999 period has a deteriorating effect on the CA. Variations in the German long run interest rates also influence CA deficits of the South with an opposite sign.

Forth, competitiveness, measured as the relative unit labour cost is important. An improvement in competitiveness reduces the CA deficit.

As a final remark, the interdependence between South eurozone and core eurozone countries is crucial in determining CA imbalances within the EMU. For the elimination of these imbalances fiscal coordination, but not uniformity is important. Unilateral decisions such as reductions in the government budget balance are inadequate for the elimination of external distortions.

REFERENCES

[1] Abell, J.D., *Journal of Macroeconomics,* 12(1), 81-96 (1990a).

[2] Abell, J.D., *Southern Economic Journal*, 57, 66-74 (1990b).

[3] Frankel, Jeffrey, *Journal of Policy Modelling*, 28(6), *653-663* (2006).

[4] Ghazi Shukur and Abdulnasser Hatemi, *Journal of Applied Statistics*, 29(6),817-824 (2002).

[5] Edwards S., *Brookings Papers on Economic Activity*, 1, 211-288 (2005).

[6] Blanchard, O., *IMF Staff Papers,* 54(2) 191-219 (2007).

[7] Roubini, Nouriel, *Cato Journal*, 26(2) (2006).

[8] Kim, S. and Roubini, N., *Journal of International Economics,* 74(2), 362-383 (2008).

[9] Baharumshah, A.Z. and Lau, E., *Journal of Economic Studies,* 34(5-6), 454-475 (2007).

[10] Daly, V. and Siddiki, J.U., *Applied Economics Letters,* 16(10-12), 1155-1164 (2009).

[11] Vamvoukas, G.A., *Applied Economics,* 31(9), 1093-1100 (1999).

[12] Pantelidis, P.,E Trachanas, A. Athanasenas and C. Katrakilidis , *International Journal of Economic Sciences and Applied Research* 2 (2), 9-32 (2009).

[13] Papadogonas, T. and Stournaras, Y., *Journal of Policy Modeling,* 28(5), 595-602 (2006).

[14] Kaufmann, S., Scharler, J. and Winckler, G., *Empirical Economics,* 27(3), 529-542 (2002).

[15] Vasarthani M., Brissimis S., Papazoglou Ch., Tsaveas N. and Chondroyiannis G., "Factors Determining the Eurozone Current Account Imbalances: estimation with panel

data" in The Current Account of Greece, Causes of Disequilibrium and Policy Implications, Bank of Greece, (in Greek) (2010).

[16] Mundell R., *International Economics*, Macmillan, N.Y (1968).

[17] Fleming M.J, *Working Paper* 9, IMF (1967).

[18] Gourinchas, P.O. *Brooking Papers on Economic Activity*, 2, 147-209 (2002).

[19] Stiglitz J. E., Freefall: America, *Free Markets, and the Sinking of the World Economy*, W.W. Norton and Company, N.Y., London, (2010).

[20] Feldstein, M. and Horioka C., *Economic Journal*, 90, 314-29 (1980).

[21] Marinheiro, C.F., *Journal of Policy Modelling*, 30(6), 1041-1056 (2008).

[22] Blanchard, O. and Giavazzi F., "CA Deficits in the EuroArea, The end of the Feldstein horioka Puzzle?" MIT Department of Economics, W.P. no 03-05, 2002.

[23] Barro R.J., *Journal of Political Economy* 82 1095-1117 (1974).

[24] Barro R.J., *Journal of Economic Perspectives* 1, 37-542 (1989).

In: Greece: Economics, Political and Social Issues
Editor: Panagiotis Liargovas

ISBN: 978-1-62100-944-3
© 2012 Nova Science Publishers, Inc.

Chapter 6

IS A "BAD BANK" SOLUTION FOR A POSSIBLE FUTURE GREEK BANKING CRISIS?

Panagiotis Liargovas and *Spyridon Repousis*[†]
University of Peloponnese, Department of Economics, Greece

ABSTRACT

This chapter examines the "bad bank" solution for a possible future Greek banking crisis which might originate by the accumulation of non-performing loans in banks' loan portfolios. "Bad bank" solution in Greece is apart from all a funding problem and it is not the best solution to be implied because the Greek economy and the Greek banking sector are in a very weak fiscal position. Greek enhancement programme of €28 billion was not enough to stabilize the Greek banking sector and offer sufficient funding in the Greek economy. In order to prevent possible future liquidity crisis, there is need to improve liquidity buffer (safe assets) of the Greek banking sector which means higher capital adequacy standards to limit liquidity risk and implement better risk management. A combination of mergers and acquisitions would be the best solution.

INTRODUCTION

Many developed countries have had significant banking crisis and bank failures during the past thirty years. Central bankers feared widespread bank failures because they exacerbated cyclical recessions, large enough to trigger a financial crisis. In addressing the problems, the central banks or governments stepped in early to supply liquidity which in most cases helped to avert a panic by investors.

The development of financial markets has increased, not reduced, the demand for funding liquidity [1]. Liquidity crises are the endogenous result of the built-up in risk-taking and associated over-extension in balance-sheets in a prolonged period. The easing of funding liquidity constraints during expansion phase supports risk-taking and increased exposure,

---

[*] E-mail address: liargova@uop.gr
[†] E-mail address: spyrep@otenet.gr

improving liquidity and boosting asset prices. Volatility and risk premiums fall, over-extending balance sheets. The subsequent turnaround is sudden.

Most governments protected depositors, in whole or in part, up to the statutory minimum. Liquidators were used occasionally and only for smaller institutions. When large commercial banks were in trouble, problems were resolved usually through mergers and a mix of capital injection and increased government control. Failure episodes have resulted in numerous legal and regulatory changes.

The current financial crisis was rapidly developed and was spread into a global economic shock, resulting in a number of bank failures, declines in various stock indexes and large reductions in the market value of stocks and commodities.

Large scale interruptions in bank lending activities can cause negative shocks to the real sector. Greenspan (1999) suggests that countries most susceptible to banking shocks are those that lack developed capital markets [2]. Countries with well-developed capital markets insulate borrowers by providing good substitutes when banks stop lending.

According to the International Monetary Fund (2009, pp. xiii), three issues are of particular relevance: (1) access to liquidity, (2) dealing with distressed assets and (3) recapitalizing weak but viable institutions and resolving failed institutions.

Banks are the primary if not the only source of funds to about all companies in Greece. During January 2009, there were talks about implementing a "bad bank" solution in Greece. The Hellenic Bank Association in a press release February 17, 2009, stressed that Greek banks do not hold toxic assets to their balance sheets. This was confirmed by the Bank of Greece (Central Bank of Greece) [3]. Up to now no "bad bank" has been established.

According to Bank of Greece Governor's Act 2471/10 April 2001, the minimum initial capital required by the Bank of Greece (Central Bank of Greece) to authorize credit institutions is € 18 million. The cost of buying bad assets may be many billion of Euros causing a funding problem. Financial sector is Greece accounts to about 16.17% to 17.74% of Gross Domestic Product, as shown in Table 1.

Table 1. Gross Added Value for Greek financial sector

(current prices in million Euros)	2006	2007	2008	2009
Financial sector	34,535	37,484	38,680	42,128
Gross Domestic Product	210,459	226,437	239,141	237,494
Percentage of Financial sector to Gross Domestic Product	16.41%	16.55%	16.17%	17.74%

Source: Hellenic Statistical Authority.

LITERATURE REVIEW:
BAD BANK SOLUTION AND HISTORICAL EXAMPLES

The deregulation of financial markets has frequently been accused of creating an excessively risky lending and investing (in new financial products) environment, especially after the repeal of the Glass-Steagall Act in 1999 which had separated commercial and investment banking.

"Bad Bank" is a term for a financial institution or an asset management company created to hold nonperforming assets owned by a state guaranteed bank. "Bad banks" are created to address challenges arising during an economic credit crunch where private banks are allowed to take troubled assets off their books.

"Toxic" or "bad" assets are assets for which there are no buyers, and as a result, no clear value. Mortgage backed securities and subprime loans are two examples of toxic assets. In the global economic crisis of the early 2000s, bad assets became an issue of major concern, especially in the United States. Such assets precipitated a radical freefall of the American economy as the financial industry attempted to cope with them.

"Bad bank" institutions have been created to address challenges arising during an economic credit crunch wherein private banks are allowed to take problem assets off their books. Securum, a Swedish bank founded to take on bad assets during the Swedish banking rescue of 1991 and 1992, is an example of such a bank.

If a bank becomes overloaded with toxic assets, it may be unable to respond to changes in the market, or to serve its customers. This can create concerns among customers of the bank, who may panic in response to the bank's instability and finally make the bank more unstable. In these cases, the bank's best move is to try and get rid of the toxic assets, but it may have a difficult time in doing so, because of the inability to find buyers.

These assets had a value at some point in time, and many believe that they still have, even if no one will buy them. When a bank acquires large numbers of toxic assets, these assets inflate the value of the bank's books, but contribute nothing real to the bank's financial position. In other words, the bank has a lot of money on paper, but it cannot actually sell its toxic assets, and as a result it has minimal liquidity.

Some investors may volunteer to take on toxic assets at a fraction of their face value, bargaining on the fact that the assets will become saleable again at some point in the future, but banks are often reluctant to accept such deals.

By segregating assets, the bank tries to keep away the bad assets from contaminating the good ones. Contagion risk of a bank failure is very high. Runs and contagion resulting from failure or near-failure of firms are widely feared in banking more than in other industries because of their perceived greater speed and wider adverse impact beyond banking to other financial sectors and the macro economy [4].

An economic reason for the implementation of a good/bad bank strategy derives from investors' reaction to the segregation of assets. Monitoring is better when assets are separated and buyers are better informed because sellers have superior knowledge of assets' quality. As Akerlof (1970) described, sellers of bad quality goods ("lemons") can be dishonest. By extending Gresham's Law, the bad assets tend to drive out good assets due to quality heterogeneity and asymmetric information [5].

Several governments have used bad banks to address credit crises before they get worse. To be effective, this technique must satisfy several criteria. Firstly, the bank is run by the government, or by a government agency which insures bank deposits, and it is usually set up as a self-liquidating trust, which means that after the mission of the bank is accomplished, it is dissolved.

At the end of the 1980s, more than 1,000 Saving and Loans institutions in the United States were threatened by insolvency due to financing with divergent maturity dates in connection with high interest rates for depositors but comparatively low rates on mortgage lending. In 1989, the Resolution Trust Corporation (RTC), a bad bank, was founded with government funding and to a limited extent with money from private investors. Bailout reached a total of 153 billion dollars to US taxpayers as of December 31, 1999 [6]. Costs of intervention were generally larger than anticipated.

Bad banks are only one of many potential solutions to an economic crisis, and they must be weighed carefully, along with other options. The panic of government officials when faced with financial crises can contribute to some very bad decisions which may have long-lasting repercussions.

Hall (2009) analyzed the UK second comprehensive bank bailout plan on 19 January 2009 to reinvigorate lending to the domestic economy [7]. There were serious doubts surrounding the likely efficacy of the rescue package and widespread market concerns about its likely impact on public finances.

Calomiris (1998) showed that the practice of bailing out banks has encouraged financial structures to keep profits private while losses are borne by the public [8]. He also showed that ninety episodes of banking collapse have occurred from 1983-1998. Twenty of them have produced bailout costs for governments in excess of 10% of their country's GDP.

Scandinavian financial crisis of the early 1990s followed a period of financial liberalization in the 1980s. Liberalization caused a rapid expansion in the volume of bank loans for speculative investment and banks became more sensitive to creditor default rates. After a big drop in the world oil price in 1986, Norway, an oil-exporting country, experienced a shift in its current account balance of payment from a surplus to a deficit and a devaluation of the Norwegian krone in 1986. A recession began in 1988 and followed a financial crisis among savings banks and real estate market.

The value of Krona was fixed to a basket of currencies and it was both significantly and increasingly overvalued relative to this basket. The government sought to protect its value by maintaining high interest rates. Commercial and retail borrowers sought foreign currency denominated credits at lower rates. Swedish banks facilitated borrowing and lending in foreign currencies. With the exchange rate fixed, the foreign exchange risk was not managed. In 1992, the rapid deflation of the real estate bubble led to fall of stocks. Loss on non-performing loans and declining collateral values had to be recognized which adversely impacted bank capital. Banks were neither safe nor sound. Loan losses were accumulating in the banking system, the Krona was devalued and unemployment was increasing.

The first to be affected were finance companies that had provided loans against the upper range of the value of assets pledged as collateral. Banks provided part of the financing of the finance companies. By lending through finance companies, banks could circumvent exposure limits. The crisis mainly developed a credit risk and a concentration risk, but it became acute due to the manifestation of liquidity risk [9].

The government funded the failed banks through its new Government Bank Insurance Fund (GBIF) in January 1991. The GBIF was an independent legal entity with the aim to provide liquidity to two private guarantee funds. It also imposed conditions such as hiring and firing key personnel, board composition and investment decisions.

Large losses were reported by three banks with about half of the total assets in the banking sector. The GBIF poured liquidity into insolvent banks and began to purchase securities (preferred securities) floated by relatively healthy banks. Norwegian parliament allowed government, by law, to write down a bank's common stock to zero against its losses. The economy started to recover in 1993 and banking crisis was over and by the end of the 1990s the government sold most of its banking stocks to private investors.

The crisis in Sweden started with heavy losses reported by the country's largest saving bank, Forsta Sparbanken, in 1991. Then, commercial bank, Nordbanken, owned 71% of common stocks by Swedish government, also reported big losses. The government purchased a new stock issue and bought out the private stockholders at the equity issue price, in contrast to Norway where private equity was written down to zero before government intervention. Government took full control of Nordbanken and splited the bank's assets into two parts: the "good" assets were still within the bank while the "bad" assets were spun off into a separate legal entity, an asset holding company, called Securum, created in 1992 [10]. Securum financed the purchase with a loan from Nordbanken and a government equity infusion.

A second "bad bank" was also created for Gota Bank when it failed in early 1992 and bad assets were transferred to the asset management company, called Retriva. The remaining "good" assets of Gota Bank were auctioned off and purchased by Nordbanken in 1993 with no payment to Gota Bank's stockholders. Securum's basic aim was to liquidate the troubled or "bad" assets.

Sweden also issued a blanket guarantee of all bank loans in the banking system, until July 1996 and benefited existing bank stockholders. Also Swedish Central Bank provided liquidity by depositing large foreign currency reserves in troubled banks and by borrowing freely at no risk the Swedish currency. Government's cash infusion limited to these two banks.

Jonung (2009), presented that the Swedish approach for resolving the banking crisis of 1991-1993 was successful for seven reasons: (1) the importance of political unity behind the resolution policy, (2) a government blanket guarantee of the financial obligations of the banking system, (3) swift policy action where acting early was more important than acting in exactly the right manner, (4) an adequate legal and institutional framework for resolution procedures including open-ended public funding, (5) full disclosure of information by the parties involved, (6) a differentiated resolution policy minimizing moral hazard, (7) proper design of macroeconomic policies to simultaneously end the crisis in both the real economy and the financial sector [11].

Bonin and Huang (2001), exhibited that China and Chinese banks also suffered from serious financial fragility manifested by high proportions of non-performing loans and low capital adequacy ratios [12]. Chinese government to reduce financial risks established four asset management companies for dealing with bad loans. They argued that the original asset management company design will not be successful in resolving the existing non-performing loans nor will it prevent the creation of new bad loans. They recommended redefining the relationship between parent banks and asset management companies by transferring the deposits of problematic enterprises along with their non-performing loans from parent banks to asset management companies.

By late September 2008, USA Treasury's original idea for getting money into the banks was referred to by its critics such as Joseph Stiglitz "cash for trash" and nationalization or socialization of losses while privatizing gains. The government would buy the toxic assets, under the Troubled Asset Relief Program (TARP), injecting liquidity and cleaning up the banks' balance sheets at the same time. Also access of USA banks to the Fed funds borrowing at almost a zero interest rate protected them by a new safety net.

Many analysts in the UK and the US proposed that governments should nationalize banks and follow the 'Swedish model' [13], [14]. According to this, the Swedish government nationalized banks, cleaned them up, and put them back on the market in competitive shape and in private ownership [15].

Mitchell (2001), developed a framework for analyzing tradeoffs between policies for cleaning banks' balance sheets under asymmetric information between banks and regulators regarding the amount of bad debt [16]. Hidden information and moral hazard are present. Two types of effects are identified: a direct effect on a bank's willingness to reveal its bad loans versus hiding them via loan rollovers and an indirect effect on firm behavior as a function of the bank's response.

IMPLEMENTING THE GOOD BANK/BAD BANK STRATEGY IN GREEK BANKING SECTOR

Will setting up a "bad bank" be a good move for a possible future crisis of the Greek banking sector? Can the Swedish model be adopted in Greece? These are questions that need answers and decisions. Always the actual decisions need to reflect the particular circumstances of each economy and the particular economic and financial conditions of the time.

For Greek bank deposits there is a safety net through a guarantee fund. The Hellenic (or Greek) Deposit and Investment Guarantee Fund was established by virtue of Law 3746/2009 in order to implement in Greece the deposit guarantee and investors compensation scheme in the event that institutions fail to return deposits. It is successor to the Hellenic Deposit Guarantee Fund, established under Law 2324/1995.

The coverage for the aggregate deposits of each depositor held by a Hellenic Deposit and Investment Guarantee Fund amounts to a maximum of 100,000 Euros. In calculating the amount of compensation payable to depositors, the credit balance on their account(s) is set off against any counterclaims filed by the credit institution against the beneficiary-depositor. From its establishment up to now, Hellenic Deposit and Investment Guarantee Fund paid compensation to the depositors of the Arab-Hellenic Bank; total accumulated resources came to 80.664 million Greek Drachmas (or about 237,000 Euros) at the end 1999.

The safety net offered by such schemes may provide incentives for Greek banks to assume excessive risks. This could take the form of excessive lending to borrowers who are not creditworthy or more generally, a tendency toward imprudent management of their depositors' money ("moral hazard" problem). Also, depositors reassured by the existence of guarantee schemes, may neglect to check the solvency of the credit institutions with which they place their deposits. According to the Annual Financial Reports of the Hellenic Deposit and Investment Guarantee Fund, total assets were 1,582,392,677.35 Euros in 2008.

Deposit guarantee schemes are not the only and best solution to prevent crises in the case of bank failures. They may weaken market discipline. The core factor of the crisis nowadays is the disruption to the wholesale interbank markets and mainly institutional investors in money market funds.

There are both similarities and differences between Greece today and Sweden of early 1990s. Swedish and Greek crisis were supported by lax monetary and fiscal policies, financial liberalization and financial innovations. Boom turned into bust with declining volume of credit, deleveraging, failing asset prices, distress of the financial system and government intervention to support the banking system. Financial crisis impacted on the real economy. Also the Swedish system had a few major banks to deal with, as the Greek banking system.

Greek banking system liquidity was supported by issuance of preferred stocks acquired by the Greek government as part of the liquidity enhancement plan of 28 billion Euros (Law 3723/2008) or 11.7% of Gross Domestic Product in 2008. Until October 2009, Greek banks had used part of the enhancement plan up to €11.3 billion Euros accepting Greek government bonds in exchange of preferred stocks with annual return of 10% (Bank of Greece, press release 20 October 2010). Now Greek banks issue covered bank bonds to increase their liquidity.

There have been discussions about establishing a Greek "bad bank". Also, the nationalization of banks has been proposed. Generally, the main purposes of bank nationalization are: a) to avoid "throwing good (taxpayers') money after bad", b) to transfer control of operations away from management of banks that have lost credibility and have a high risk of insolvency, c) to save taxpayers' money by forcing losses to shareholders and creditors, d) to recover taxpayers' money by capturing the "upside" potential from a bank revival, e) to avoid future moral hazard and punish managers of banks that took excessive or stupid risks and f) to redirect bank policies towards socially desirable goals and away from bad practices [17].

But nationalization does not mean that government can run banks better than the private sector. The government has no comparative advantage in garbage disposal. Political pressures for uneconomic activities and large losses for taxpayers will be a real matter. Nationalization of a bank may prove necessary as a last resort but it is not a real long term solution. Banks who need additional capital would be required to raise it privately in the short term. Failing that, government would buy preferred stocks, converting into common stocks, unless paid down by new private capital and future profits. Smaller or weaker banks could sell out to stronger or merge with them.

The adverse conditions prevailing in the global money and capital markets had a negative impact on the Greek banking sector. Fundamentals reflected Greek banks' very limited exposure to the toxic assets associated with the US subprime mortgage market. Liquidity problems and most important non-performing loans are the greatest problems of Greek banking sector. A non-performing loan is a loan when payments of interest and principal are past due by 90 days or more.[1]According to Basel II and Basel Capital Accord July 1988, updated in April 1998, non-performing loans consist of: a) other real estate owned assets which are taken by foreclosure, b) loans that are 90 days or more past due and still accruing interest and c) loans which have been placed on non-accrual.

Non-performing loans of Greek banks have increased substantially and accounted to 7.7% in 2009, compared to 5% in 2008. At the same time profits before taxes were €66million in 2009, in comparison with €1.047 billion in 2008 (Bank of Greece, Annual Report 2009, p.197). Most of them were revenues from financial portfolio. Capital adequacy ratios of Greek banks have improved from 10.7% in 2008 to 13.2% in 2009. Table 2, shows financial accounts of four major Greek Group of Banks and as can be seen, capital adequacy ratios are above minimum requirements. Non-performing loans at end of 2009 have increased by €4.8 billion in comparison with end of 2008.

---

[1] Or at least 90 days of interest payments have been capitalized, refinanced or delayed by agreement, or payments are less than 90 days overdue but there are good reasons to doubt that they will be made in full.

Table 2. Major Group of Banks (consolidated amounts)

	Piraeus Bank		Alpha Bank		Eurobank EFG		National Bank of Greece	
(Thousand of Euros)	31/12/2009	31/12/2008	31/12/2009	31/12/2008	31/12/2009	31/12/2008	31/12/2009	31/12/2008
Loans to customers	38,683,228	39,015,655	51,399,939	50,704,702	55,837,000	55,878,000	74,752,545	69,897,602
NPLs > 90 days (%)	5.10%	3.60%	5.70%	3.90%	6.70%	3.90%	5.40%	3.30%
NPLs > 90 days (Amount)	1,972,845	1,404,564	2,929,797	1,977,483	3,741,079	2,179,242	4,036,637	2,306,621
Total Assets	54,279,791	54,889,856	69,596,047	65,269,954	84,269,000	82,202,000	113,394,183	101,323,242
% of loans to customers to total assets	71.27%	71.08%	73.85%	77.68%	66.26%	67.98%	65.92%	68.98%
Revenues from financial (commercial and investment) portfolio	174,863	-13,348	171,522	-6,848	171,000	219,000	428,415	427,289
Profits before taxes	286,615	385,788	501,817	625,633	398,000	818,000	1,252,065	1,937,014
Capital Adequacy Ratio	9.80%	9.90%	13.30%	9.80%	12.70%	10.40%	11.30%	10.30%
Tier I	9.10%	8.00%	11.70%	8.00%	10.90%	8.50%	11.30%	10.00%

Source: Financial Statements of Group of Banks.

A further decline in loan quality is expected. A rising ratio of non-performing loans to total loans implies that banks' health worsen and will have to increase deposit interest rates. However, it is also of some concern that revenues from financial portfolio and especially trading income, represented a considerable large chunk of profits before taxes. The increase of trading income was attributable mainly to the increase in the price of Greek government bonds and stock prices in the second and third quarters of 2009. These trends have currently reversed.

Looking again at the "bad bank" strategy, the purpose of a "bad bank" is to help resolve a financial crisis caused by an abundance of non-performing assets on the books of major banks. Trying to work-out all the non-performing loans inside the bank is not successful. It only prolongs the healing process in the organization and reduces the ability of the bank to lend more to the public and businesses. Once the bank risks are materialized, banks react by tightening their lending standards, thereby reducing the supply of bank loans to the private sector for investment and consumption.

A Greek "bad bank" plan could consist of the following key elements in order to address the challenges of "bad bank" strategy, as Schafer and Zimmermann (2009) have supported [18]:

- Non-performing assets should be valued based on current market prices prior to their takeover by the bad bank. Bad assets for which there is no market should be transferred to the bad bank at a zero price and therefore at zero cost for the government as the bad bank's sponsor.
- The government should recapitalise the rescued bank (the remaining good bank) through the acquisition of a stockholder stake; in extreme cases, the remaining good bank should be taken over by the government.
- The bad bank should be funded by the government. External experts should be entrusted with the management and future sale of the bad assets at the government's expense. If a profit remains after the proceeds from holding the troubled assets until expiration date (or selling those assets to the market have materialised and operating costs have been deducted), these profits should be distributed to the former stockholders.
- The government should announce its commitment to the future re-privatisation of its stake in the rescued bank. When establishing a bad bank, the government should make a binding commitment to how long it has to sell its stocks in the good bank following the closure of the bad bank.
- All "systemically relevant" banks should be identified and required to participate in the plan.

According to Schafer and Zimmermann (2009), the takeover of toxic assets by the government at zero cost and the corresponding write-down of assets will create transparency, avoid the high expense of pricing distressed assets, and insure that stockholders are the first ones to bear the cost of failure. The risk of moral hazard will also be effectively limited. A zero-cost acquisition is also justified based on the fact that the active management of the bad assets is impaired by their complex structure. This approach will also keep the bad bank's initial capital requirements at a minimum. Furthermore, Greek government must dismiss upper management employees for non-performing loans and corruption.

Finally, there will be a need for weekly or monthly 'stress tests' (to avoid worsening value of collaterals) and credit ratings of borrowers and auditing banks.

The Greek government would buy bad loans without knowing how to value them because they are illiquid. Pacing too law a value would force Greek banks and other assets to register big losses that could reduce their capital and make it harder for them to start again or increase lending. But inflated values would bailout Greek banks, their stockholders and executives at the expense of taxpayers.

Greek banks would try to get too high price for their assets. It's a valuation problem of bank assets. There are no current market prices for bad assets because although they can be valued and can be traded, trading has slowed as sellers and buyers will disagree about what the price should be. The value is based on future cash flows and assumptions about bad assets. Bad loans are weighting down the financial system because private sector experts can't determine their worth. Greek government would pay more for the bad assets than their current market price, assuming that values will eventually rebound. It would be a gift for bank stockholders and debt holders but taxpayers would be the great losers.

Repairing the balance sheet of the banks is only one important element to get the banks back to normal lending activities. The other major element is organizational efficiency.

A bad bank solution to a possible future Greek banking crisis would not eliminate the toughest choices that need to be made as to decide which banks are insolvent or need to be closed or partly nationalized or completely taken over.

If a Greek bank is found to be insolvent, the troubled assets could be taken by the government. Its stockholders and debt holders would partially or fully wiped out.

But it may be better to boost the banking system by increasing its capital rather than by reducing its loans. Given a fatter capital cushion, banks would have more time to dispose of the bad loans. The Greek government already asked banks to cancel all dividend payments. Otherwise, if Greek banks on their own, cancell dividend payments, it would signal weakness. Even healthy Greek banks will want to sell assets because almost all assets will have become more risky and switch into safer assets. Bebchuk (2008) has proposed that it is crucial to separate the buying of distressed assets from bank capital injections [19]. These should be separate policy initiatives. The current disruption of credit markets and credit flows from Greek banks to Greek real economy will surely have a negative impact on jobs, capital spending and housing prices. Now it is very costly for Greek banks to foreclose. Banks do not want to force a sale in current economic environment because foreclosure firesales will have a negative effect on the values of houses and properties and will reduce the value of collateral in the bank portfolio. If one or a few Greek banks will be forced to sell assets at low or discounted values (firesale), they will make the crises worse. So firesale must remain at low and necessary levels.

A critical factor in a possible establishment of a Greek bad bank is a cooperation agreement involving multiple banks. If Banks A, B, and C agree to sell their non-performing assets to the nationalized bank, and Bank D doesn't go along with the plan, the market will continue to be unstable. Finally, non-performing assets must be written down before they are sold to the bad bank. In other words, banks cannot demand "fair market value" or the paper value of their toxic assets. They must agree to write down the total debt and pay a loss to get the asset off their books.

Greek government could force private sector participants to absorb losses before government financial intervention (minimizing moral hazard). It is very difficult to design a plan to provide such private parties with incentives aligned with those of taxpayers. Divergence between the interests of the private side and those of taxpayers is very possible because bad assets may be overpaid. The government must set the extent to which the private side will enjoy favorable terms. It is difficult to avoid or to ensure that private parties do not make excessive gains at taxpayers' expense. Private side can be kept at a minimum level.

By not adopting the 'good' and 'bad' bank solution, the system remains as corrupted as before. The bad assets will continue to need resources out of the economic system. Even if a huge bank becomes insolvent, in the end the virtue of the bad bank is that it makes the situation painfully clear.

Bailouts instead of enforcing appropriate discipline on the banks, rewarding those who have been prudent and letting fail those that had an extraordinary risk, help banks that did the worst in risk management.

Another view of good/bad bank strategy is that in Sweden the role played by government ownership of the failed banks was politically acceptable since government has a long history of partnering with the private business sector. Also nepotism and outright corruption is a minimal problem in the case of Sweden. These are absolutely different in Greece where there is no good history of partnering government with private sector. Public and private sectors are characterized by high levels corruption.

The financial crisis hit Sweden in September 1992 – less than a year after the election (in October 1991) but crisis for Greece was near national parliamentary elections and politicians of two major parties could not cooperate.

Bank of Greece by providing liquidity acted as a buffer or lender of last resort but at the same time it increased risk-taking and created "moral hazard" problem. On the other hand, it has been supported that when the lender of last resort does not charge penalty rates, the bank chooses the same level of risk and a smaller liquidity buffer than in the absence of a lender of last resort [20].

Also, private sector buffers mean higher level of capital which is costlier than other forms of financing. In boom times, market requires low levels of capital to increase expected returns and there are incentives to shift activity to Special Investment Vehicles and Conduits. In bad times when capital will be really needed, it will be difficult to have it.

So, capital and money are needed to create a bad bank in very large amounts. An apparently straightforward solution to the non-performing loans is Greek authorities to infuse capital when there is problem of solvency. But the Greek government has not this ability to infuse capital because of its bad fiscal position. Greece is experiencing the first domestic recession since early 1990s, with a very low private sector credit expansion and a public sector trying to address fiscal imbalances. Therefore, funding of a bad bank is difficult. The main features of Greek crisis are the large fiscal deficit, the huge debt and the continuous erosion of the country's competitive position. Greek large fiscal deficits and debt can not be financed from domestic saving. Greece's gross national saving, public and private combined, were just above 5% of GDP in 2009 (Bank of Greece, Annual Report 2009). This shortfall is due to Greece's large fiscal deficits but also to the fast increase in private consumption over the past few years. The current account deficit reached 14.6% of GDP in 2008 and the large trade deficit is directly attributable to the loss in competitiveness.

When it became clear that the budget deficit for 2009 would be significantly higher than expected, rating agencies downgraded Greece's government debt. This was followed by downgrading in a number of Greek banks. Budget deficits and government debts have followed an upward trend since 2006, as can be seen from Table 3.

Table 3. Greek fiscal statistical data

(Million Euros)	2006	2007	2008	2009
Budget deficit	7,496	11,478	18,303	32,342
Government Debt in nominal prices, end of year	205,738	216,731	237,252	273,407
Gross Domestic Product (GDP) in current prices	210,459	226,437	239,141	237,494
Budget deficit as percentage of GDP	3.6%	5.1%	7.7%	13.6%
Government debt as percentage of GDP	97.8%	95.7%	99.2%	115.1%

Source: Hellenic Statistical Authority.

In the aftermath of severe financial crisis, the value of government debt tends to explode [21]. A set of 30-year projections of public debt for a dozen of major industrial economies (Austria, France, Germany, Greece, Ireland, Italy, Japan, the Netherlands, Portugal, Spain, the United Kingdom and the United States) lead us to conclude that fiscal problems are bigger than suggested by official debt figures. Greek public debt ratio in the next decade will exceed 150%. Furthermore, a greater danger arises from a rapidly ageing population [22].

The European Union, the European Central Bank and the International Monetary Fund acting as an international lender of last resort announced a €110 billion financing package in order to safeguard financial stability in the euro area. Among key elements of the package is setting up a Financial Stability Fund, of about €10 billion, to ensure a sound level of bank equity.

CONCLUSION

This paper showed that the Swedish model cannot be replicated in the case of Greece under the current crisis. The Swedish model was designed for a relatively stable macroeconomic and financial environment. The Swedish crisis of the early 1900s was a local problem in a small open economy with a pegged exchange rate. Abandoning the pegged rate in November 1992, and depreciating its currency, Sweden followed an export-oriented strategy to recover, relying on the rest of the world to maintain aggregate demand for its exports.

Greece has a very low competiveness and cannot depreciate its currency which is the Euro. Also the current crisis is global and there is a more globalized, less transparent and more sophisticated financial system than that in the early 1990s.

Bad bank solution in the case of Greece is apart from all a funding problem and it is not the best solution to be implied because the Greek economy and the Greek banking sector are in a very weak fiscal position.

In order to prevent possible future liquidity crisis, there is a need to improve liquidity buffer (safe assets) of the Greek banking sector. This means higher capital adequacy standards to limit liquidity risk and better risk management. The introduction of the leverage ratio and the short-term liquidity coverage ratio of "Basel III" draft proposals will help Greek banks to improve their strength. But regulatory reform although necessary, is not a sufficient condition for a safer financial system. In a possible future Greek banking sector crisis a combination of mergers and acquisitions would be the most appropriate solution.

REFERENCES

[1] Borio, C., Market distress and vanishing liquidity: anatomy and policy options, Working Papers No.158, *Bank for International Settlements*, Monetary and Economic Department (2003).

[2] Greenspan,A. http://www.federalreserve.gov/boarddocs/speeches/1999/199909272.htm

[3] Bank of Greece, *Annual Report* (2009) *(In Greek language)*.

[4] Kaufman, G., *Journal of Financial Services Research*, 8, 123-150, (1994).

[5] Akerlof, G., *The Quarterly Journal of Economics*, 84(3), 488-500 (1970).

[6] Curry,T.,andShibut,L.,
http://*www.fdic.gov/bank/analytical/banking/2000dec/brv13n2_2.pdf*.

[7] Hall, M., *Journal of Banking Regulation*, 10, 215-220, (2009).

[8] Calomiris, C., *Harmful bailouts*, American Enterprise Institute for Public Policy Research, On the Issues, (1998).

[9] Bank for International Settlements, Bank failures in mature economies, *Basel Committee on Banking Supervision Working Paper No.13.*, (2004).

[10] Eckbo, B.E., Scandinavia: Failed banks, state control and a rapid recovery, in *Managing in a downturn: Leading business thinkers on how to grow when markets don't*, Financial Times Prentice Hall, Great Britain, (2009).

[11] Jonung, L., *The Swedish model for resolving the banking crisis of 1991-93: Seven reasons why it was successful*, Economic Papers 360, Economic and Financial Affairs, European Commission (2009).

[12] Bonin, J., and Huang, Y., *Journal of Asian Economics*, 12, 197-214, (2001).

[13] Krugman, P., *The New York Times*, 22 February, (2009).

[14] Richardson, M., and Roubini, N., *The Washington Post*, 15 February, (2009).

[15] Erixon, F., *World Economics*, 10(1), 1-12, (2009).

[16] Mitchell, J., *Journal of Financial Intermediation*, 10, 1-27, (2001).

[17] Elliot, D., *Bank nationalization: What is it? Should we it? , Initiative on Business and Public Policy*, The Brookings Institution, February, 26, (2009).

[18] Schafer, D., and Zimmermann, K., *Intereconomics,* July/August, 215-225 (2009).

[19] Bebchuk, L., *A plan for addressing the financial crisis*, Harvard Law School, Discussion Paper No.620, 9, (2008).

[20] Repullo, R., Liquidity, *International Journal of Central Banking*, 1, 47-80, (2005)

[21] Reinhart, C., and Rogoff, K., *This Time is Different: Eight centuries of Financial Folly*, Princeton University Press, USA, (2009).

[22] Cecchetti, S., Mohanty, M., and Zampolli, F., *The future of public debt: prospects and implications*, Working Papers No.300, Bank for International Settlements, Monetary and Economic Department (2010).

In: Greece: Economics, Political and Social Issues
Editor: Panagiotis Liargovas

ISBN: 978-1-62100-944-3
© 2012 Nova Science Publishers, Inc.

Chapter 7

AN ASSESSMENT OF BUSINESS AND SME GROWTH POLICIES APPLIED IN GREECE IN THE 1994-2002 PERIOD

Constantinos Ikonomou[*]
University of Athens,
Department of Economics, Athens, Greece

ABSTRACT

This chapter synthesizes the picture of Greek state, regional and local policies supporting business and SME growth between 1995 and 2002, incorporated within the broader EU Cohesion and Regional Policy framework. Then, it introduces a new microeconomic methodology to assess their national-level impact. Synthesizing the picture of policies for business and SME growth is a difficult task for any state, as they have to be contextualized first. Hence, a more general introductory discussion is held on main useful points for evaluating business and SME state-support policies: their different origin, focus and targets, what is often seen as a policy fragmentation, the policy interaction and timing, the need to distinguish between recipient and non-recipient firms and other issues that are discussed and taken into account in policy assesment studies (as from [1] to [12]). Assessing the effects of state-level policies on business growth should investigate their particular association, by focusing especially on policy recipients. If policies target at the broader change of local and regional environments, a focus should be given on the role of these environments, by taking into account at the same time that firms receive influence from their more specific rather than the more general, external environment, as discussed in organization theory ([13],[14],[15]). A large representative sample of SMEs is used, surviving between 1995 and 2002. Data are collected from different sources. Business level data are drawn from the Greek VAT database. Information on the local and regional environment is collected from the respective local and regional accounts. Policy status information is drawn from the Greek Integrated Information System. Business growth is measured as cross-sectional change between the final and initial year. After removing growth outliers, the means and medians of assisted and non-assisted firms are compared. By matching these results with those found in the

---

[*] E-mail address: ikonomcos@gmail.com

OLS and ANOVA models produced that make use of dummies, a conclusion is reached on the positive policy impact on business and SME growth. The models highlight the significance of capital and labour variables, as suggested in neoclassical theory and expected from various readings in literature. As several of the local and regional level variables are not found to significantly associate with business growth variables, the overall success of policies in delivering business growth is put under question. More intense changes at the local and regional environment are needed or changes focusing more upon business and SME growth outcomes. Furthermore, more study is needed to shed light on the causes of limited success. The use of new assesment methods and tools (as those found in [2] to [12]) could reveal the needs in institutional building, in developing and using local and regional instruments and mechanisms, emphasizing the delivery of more successful business and SME growth outcomes.

INTRODUCTION

The internal growth of businesses is influenced by their environment, specific to each firm or more general ([13],[14],[15],[16]). Studying environmental influence on firms is a complex task, subject to various analytical perspectives and views on how businesses grow, as those held by Coase [18], Penrose [19] or the microeconomic theory. During the last century, more than one hundred of theories attempted to explain better how businesses grow in size (see for example their various categorisations in [20], [21], [22], [23]), often in a conflicting or complementary perception or relation.

Their combination is a difficult task to undertake, but a necessary one when conclusions should be reached on the influence exercised from an environment or the internal to businesses causes upon their growth. A good way (but not necessarily the most reliable from an epistemological point of view) to analyse and combine these theories or views is by differentiating between growth causes, especially between the factors derived from the external and the internal to firms environment. Creating such lines of distinction among business growth causes could help to provide more complete insights, even though the borders of such lines in practice may be actually blurred ([24], [25], [26]) and the creation of integrative explanatory models (as in [27]) a difficult task to undertake.

A hypothesis-testing approach is often used to test some pre-existing hypotheses on the particular influence of factors affecting business and SME growth, internal or external to firms ([24]). External to firms factors, their possible interaction and that with internal, can be grouped in some more general groups of factors hypothesized to bring growth, as already filtered in mainstreamed economic growth literature. Such factors are extensively discussed for example in neoclassical theory, endogenous growth theory, location theory, cluster theory, industrial organisation theory, legal studies, urban growth and land studies.

Even though economic growth and development theory has associated growth with factors such as the role of industry, sector of activity, manufacturing industry, the legal environment, region, distance from national centres, infrastructure development, land values, capital and human capital availability, their influence on business and SME growth, though hypothesized to bring growth, would not necessarily have a single direction. Further investigation is needed in testing their influence upon firms, given that the environment for each firm is different from the broader economic environment. For example firms in some particular regions may never take advantage of capital or human resource availability surrounding them or may not benefit from their legal environment ([28] to [34]). Besides, a central role attributed to policy making is exactly the turning of such general growth enhancing factors to positive influence for the majority of firms.

The hypothesis-testing method helps to better integrate and bridge the gap between industrial, legal, regional or other more general economic policies that seek to change such factors and enhance their effects in the private sector and the general reception of policies from businesses or SMEs.

In that respect, many studies in business and SME growth literature testing the associations between firm growth and business finance, human capital, education, industrial organisation, the role of particular industries such as manufacturing, or that of size, economies of scale and distance from centres (as for example found in [35], [36], [37], [38], [39], [40]), attempt to filter more carefully the respective long-standing debates held in economic growth and development theory, in various environments (as those in [41], [42], [43], [44], [45]).

A growing empirical evidence on SME and general business growth in local and regional environments attempts to integrate existing knowledge on how various factors influence business growth, by focusing on the importance of particular environments for business growth (see for example in [40], [47]). Such studies test simultaneously the validity of general growth theories in the particular business environments studied or at least what is often called "expectations" from theory. In this way, they highlight a principal disciplinary value of economic geography that suggests economic phenomena and their expression in space to differ ([46]). It is by definition in geographical theory that business or SME growth is expected to associate with different factors, in different local and regional environments. New evidence, provided from different national environments, may shed more light on some aspects of firm growth and some particular factors influencing it. Thus, the value of studies that create more general pictures on the influence exercised on business growth in national environments by focusing at the variety of their local and regional factors is important (as in [47] or [48]).

From a geographical point of view therefore, it does not seem to be valid to synthesize a single, uniform picture on the impact of local and regional environment on business growth. Some geographical factors would influence more the growth of firms than others, at least at a certain historical period or point in time. But this does not mean that the rest of the factors are negligible. For example if education is not found to be significant in a model, this does not mean that it does not play a role, even indirect. This could relate to the choice of other technical aspects of modelling. A uniform picture would also mean that such environments influence in a particular way the growth of firms and SMEs and, as a result, that knowledge on the variety and characteristics of economic factors in a state or region and their interaction is of secondary importance. The geographical perspective further contributes to an understanding of how particular economic environments are likely to direct business growth towards particular paths, as discussed for example in [40] for the influence exercised on growth-oriented firms in "unfavourable regional environments" or in [49] that refer to the influence on mature manufacturing firms in "remote rural areas".

In practice, using hypothesis-testing helps to distinguish between a certain -hypothetical-understanding on how businesses are influenced from environmental factors and what is actually achieved in such particular environments. For example, it is generally expected that education affects positively and improves business growth. But if this is not found in peripheral national or European regions, this is an interesting conclusion that could also relate to the inadequacy of this particular environmental factor (for example other types or degrees of education may be needed), to the more general interaction of environmental factors with businesses (through the creation of links of universities with industries) or even to businesses themselves (as recipients of education). Seen from this perspective, the presence of "determinants" or "patterns" on business and SME growth in space (as discussed for example in [50]) does not mean that business growth trajectories are predefined. Business growth patterns will not necessarily be repeated in other geographical or national environments or even in another time period.

By way of deduction, we could conclude on the necessity to study business growth and its causes in different geographical environments, local, regional or national. Enriching evidence on business growth with what appears to take place in different national environments could be of a more general perspective and value for the study of business growth. Even though a certain degree of abstraction is always needed when studying the causes of business growth and is, in practice, implemented by focusing on some particular growth-factors, understanding the pluralism and complexity of factors influencing business growth from a geographical perspective (at the local, regional, national or international level) could be a valuable contribution to theory. Another way to put this is by clarifying that any theoretical conclusions reached from a single geographical environment on business and SME growth may be biased, inaccurate and limited by time and spatial conditions.

For this purpose, an emphasis should be given on the role of policies implemented in different environments. This point has been well raised by Hart and McGuiness [51] who claimed that the causes of unexpected findings on SME growth, such as those found in unfavourable regional environments (in [40]) may relate to public policy. Hence, SME growth studies should take into account implemented policies, otherwise conclusions on the primary causes of business and SME growth cannot be finalised.

By taking into account these points, there is also a need to provide evidence from peripheral European states -like Greece- that, while being far from European centres, have businesses forced to operate in an "unfavourable" -in European competition terms- economic environment. Peripheral European states implement various policies on business and SME growth. As a country receiving support from EU Regional and Cohesion policy, Greece has followed policies that targeted at firm growth either directly or indirectly, through the general European Regional and Cohesion Policy framework for local and regional growth. The country, as other Cohesion countries, is a policy lab, implementing a policy direction for regional growth and competitiveness pursued at the EU level and the more general improvement of growth conditions at the local and regional environment. The most recent de-stabilisation of the Greek economy raises further a question whether policies on business growth were not successful or that successful, for example for the possible reasons discussed in [52]. Assessing simultaneously the direct and indirect policy influence on business growth is a difficult and complicated task to consider.

ON THE EVALUATION OF POLICIES AIMING AT BUSINESS AND SME GROWTH

A growing number of studies focus on the evaluation of state policies seeking to support businesses and SMEs (see in [1] to [12] and [50] to [59]). Many of these studies provide evidence of success or failure of policy supports, using a variety of case-studies drawn from different countries, regions and industries/sectors and suggesting how policies ought to be, to achieve successful outcomes. The selected case studies differ, given the differences in the national, regional or industrial environments, the nature of policies and the different focus attributed to various policy aspects.

Policies may not always state explicitly business growth as their target. Policy documents may only imply that or include it within a broader range of targets and policy makers may not consider it as a priority [56], [61]. For example policies may prioritise monetary stability and other general economic growth targets, indirectly reducing decline, business and SME failure. Furthermore, not all businesses receive support, due to limitations in funding, lack of, or failure in targeting support or due to different policy priorities and perceptions on how to prioritise support.

Business and SME support policies may have an impact of firm growth or not, considered as successful or non-successful respectively (see for example in [5], [10], [12]). They can also have a negative impact, in which case they could be even considered as harmful. The degree of policy success is not the same. Policies differentiate in several respects and their influence upon businesses is rather complex. Even though they are exercised from an environment external to businesses, they may act from inside the firm, depending on the policy. For example a regional policy supporting innovation in start-up firms acts internally to these particular firms-recipients as similarly does an ad-hoc institution seeking to support firms internally ([5], [6], [8]). Furthermore, policies act primarily on firms receiving support. Therefore a fundamental distinction can be made for analytical purposes between recipients and non-recipients. The focus on firms-recipients is given in studies focusing on the role of particular support institutions ([5], [6], [8]]. In such cases, recipients may be compared against firms-recipients of support from other institutions ([11]). The growth of non-recipients is attributed to other, additional factors rather than policy (or the enhanced competition from policy-supported firms). From this perspective, studying the differences in growth causes between these two groups, policy recipients and non-recipients, should introduce the policy factor and attempt to explain its growth influence on recipients. Other factors introduced in business growth analyses can be studied for their impact on or association with both policy recipients and non-recipients.

In general, there is a large typology of policies targeting directly or indirectly to business and SME growth, not necessarily having or seeking the same outcomes. They can be categorised in terms of (i) their character ("soft" or "hard", directly or indirectly targeting businesses, involving innovation, training or personal development etc) (see in [55]), (ii) their level of application -at the level of industry, sector, national or other spatial- (see in [57]), (iii) specific characteristics of recipients or subjects of policies, for example their size (such as the SMEs or larger firms), their particular ownership structure (such as self or family-owned), or their potential growth-orientation (such as those targeting extreme growers or the so-called "gazelles"). Policies can also be analysed in terms of (iv) which institutions or intermediaries apply them, for example incubators, industrial parks, regionally-based institutions or other, (v) in terms of the policy instruments used (see in [55, 58]) or (vi) their thematic nature, for example education and knowledge policies (see in [58]). Different states have different policies and use their own range of policy mechanisms, institutions and regulations. Many countries incorporate similar to each other policies, such as those emphasising national competitiveness agendas nowadays, influenced by the contemporary debates on national competitiveness or those on entrepreneurship and SMEs [32]. Other types and categories of policies may also exist, depending on the categorisation criterion or criteria. This abundance of typologies can create confusions in assessment efforts, but is valuable to understand various aspects of policy making and success.

Another distinction is made for the period covered by various policies (e.g. for the "generations" of policies) and between policies used in the past (such as protectionist policies) and more modern policies. For example industrial policies in European states have changed over the years their rationale and spectrum of incorporated instruments and targets.

During the previous decade they were derived from various needs but more recently were enriched and discussed to relate to numerous targets, such as reducing market failures, the promotion of strategic trade and infant-industry, the spread of network externalities and standardisation, the need to avoid various disruptions in dynamic business development, to receive and transfer codified or tacit knowledge, to create and spread technological or non-technological innovation, the organisation of systems of innovation and clusters and the provision of conditions for competitiveness more generally [60].

It is also likely that policies may replace each other. For example, competition policy in the U.S.A. is suggested to substitute entrepreneurship and small business policies [53]. Similarly, in contemporary Europe, industrial and manufacturing policies are bypassed or considered to have a secondary value in comparison to small business, entrepreneurship and regional development and Cohesion policies. The EU Regional and Cohesion Policy, when applied, acts as a more general framework that incorporates various aspects of business support policies, including policies on competitiveness and SME support.

Table 1 shows the different application of state policies between a more multi-faceted case study such as that applied in Britain and the case study of countries applying EU Regional and Cohesion Policy. Replacements can create difficulties or differences in assessing policy targets and their effects, for example when policy evaluations focus on various policy levels or advanced policy themes.

Apart from the variety of policies, policy-mixing and policy interaction are also important to consider. States, regions or industries follow different policy-mixes rather than simply different policies. For example, during the last twenty years in Europe many European countries have followed a combination of regional and industrial policies, mixed with elements of small business policies and related to their mainstreamed competitiveness agenda.

At the same time, other states -usually the most advanced- have larger, long-term agendas on small businesses, with special institutions set up for the small and medium enterprise support and development, not necessarily related to regional development agendas ([2], [61]). Clearly, policy-mixes differ from state to state. It is therefore important to understand the applied policy-mixes in the case study of a state and/or that of its regions/industries and to create the more general picture of policies and how these are structured at the state or other geographical level. The interaction between policies further complicates the study of policy impact on business and SME growth, as it is often difficult to isolate the interacting effects of policies. Hence the focus should be placed on the overall policy results, derived from the combination of policies, which may be difficult to draw in some particular cases studied.

Table 1: State, regional and local policies for business and SME growth

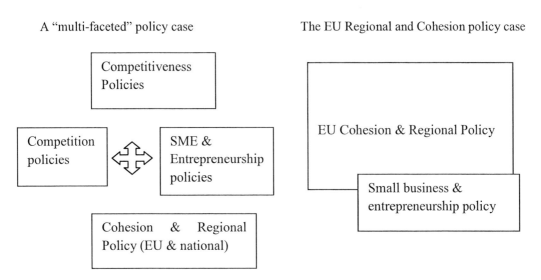

Assessment is also made complex because policy effects may cover relatively long periods. Previous policy periods may have an effect upon a present period currently assessed. If assessment exercises are not made at the completion of a policy period, then policy effects may not be fully considered. This time-lag element is difficult to be taken into account and could be a source of bias for the analysis of effects of a certain policy period, despite the robustness of analyses used. Usually, there is a period elapsing after the official deadlines of policy application that the completion of a scheduled policy takes place. Evaluation can extend and include policy effects on that period. Changes in policies occur over a study period, which are not easy to evaluate and sometimes even to find out and record. Such reasons impede the accurate assessment of policy effects.

Various other limitations exist in assessing business and SME growth policies. These relate to data issues, their availability for limited or specific periods, various restrictions in obtaining and using policy information (for example in accessing policy databases for businesses), the lack of agreement(s) on which policy-assessment tools to select[1] and often the representativeness of business and of policy-supported samples. They may differ also if viewed from a subjective angle, as in the case of various assessments by SME owners, managers and businessmen on the business environment that may differ from established views on policy effects held by planning or guiding authorities, for example in particular regions and localities (e.g. in [8]).

Additional issues raised in studies assessing the impact of policies on business or SME growth are: (i) the use of control groups for comparison purposes, among different samples or groups of businesses [40]; (ii) the choice of a segmented or a holistic view of business growth policies and (iii) the focus on particular groups of supported firms, for example the start-ups,

---

[1] Emphasizing on modelling as an assessment method is also subject to the appropriate selection of models

surviving firms or specific firms favoured by policies, such as the "industrial champions", the "winners" or other (see for example in [54]).

The counter-factual question of what would have happened in the absence of a particular policy is also raised with regard to business growth and has also been termed as the "additionality" issue [55][2]. The absence of policy can be due either to a total lack of any applied type of policy or to the absence of particular policy elements. For example, a regional level policy may focus less on business growth and more on social aspects of development. Similarly, policies can focus on start-ups rather than survivors or on both. Hence, it is important to realise when assessing policies which are the policy elements contained and which not. Other factors affecting SME growth need to be incorporated in the study, especially in the absence of an explicitly-stated business support policy.

FOCUSING ON THE RELATIONSHIP BETWEEN POLICY AND BUSINESS GROWTH

The necessity for the distinction between policy and non-policy environments and for their association to business growth or non-growth is emphasized in Table 2. Policy-supported firms can be seen as a separate stratum in the business population. In general, four are the scenarios for business growth: (i) for growth to take place in policy environments, (ii) for growth to take place in non-policy environments, (iii) for non-growth in policy environments, and (iv) for non-growth in non-policy environments. These four scenarios can be used to separate a business population/sample, by distinguishing both in terms of policy factor and the business growth performance (Table 2).

Even if appropriately incorporated in the analysis as a factor, policy is not necessarily associated with business growth. Besides, as stated above, business growth may not be a policy target, for some policy types.

The distinction between scenarios (i) and (ii), i.e. between business growth happening in supported and non-supported environments is important for realising the necessity of business growth policies. In answering the counter-factual question of what would have happened in the absence of policy we compare the scenarios (i) and (iii) with the possible scenarios (ii) with (iv).

In other words we compare across situations where there is and there is not a policy environment. If policy brings business growth and the lack of policy does not (scenarios (i) and (iv)), this finding highlights the significance of policy. If policy does not bring growth (as in (iii)) and non-policy does bring growth (as in (ii)) then this highlights policy failures to deliver business growth.

The scenarios developed in Table 2 are static and do not incorporate the element of the degree of policy success or other aspects, such as a distinction between policies setting explicitly or not business growth targets. It also takes no account of policy interaction or policy-mix. However, it is indicative of the role that business support policies can have and is of special importance when business growth is an explicitly stated target. The differential impact of policy on business growth or decline is emphasized in Table 3. Extreme business

---

[2] Additionality should not be confused with the concept of policy "added value".

growth, stagnation, decline or failure may occur, in environments where policy is applied or not.

The question of policy success relates to a concise answer on whether the case studied belongs exclusively to scenario (i), in Table 2. In such case an answer is provided on the positive effect of policies on business growth. If however the answer from studying business or SME growth lies within the scenario (iii), then further research is needed to clarify the picture of business and SME growth, by revealing for example the special groups of firms (e.g. firms of particular sizes, industries or regions) for which there might be evidence of success.

Table 2. The crossroad between policy status and the different business growth outcomes

Policy status / Conditions	Policy support	No policy support
Business Growth	(i) +	(ii) +
Business non-Growth	(iii) -	(iv) -

Table 3. A more detailed account of the crossroad between policy status and business growth outcomes

Policy status /Conditions	Policy	Non-policy
Extreme Business Growth	+	+
Business Growth	+	+
Business Stagnation	-	-
Business Decline or Failure	-	-

THE CASE STUDY OF THE GREEK ECONOMY IN THE PERIOD 1994-2002

The present work investigates the effects of Greek policies targeting at business and SME growth implemented under the EU Regional and Cohesion Policy framework, in the 1994-2002 period. It uses for this purpose a sample of Greek small and medium sized enterprises (SMEs) surviving over the period. The Greek economy is an interesting international case-study for a number of reasons. It has recently arrived at the epicentre of international interest, due to the dramatic increases of its debts and its overburdening at the aftermath of the international crisis. However Greece, one of the EU member-states and member of the Euro-zone, was one of the first EC members that benefited from EU Regional and Cohesion Policy and had followed its application. Hence, a question is raised whether EU policies have achieved their outcome in Greece and to what extent such policies had focused on substantial growth targets, such as that of the growth of businesses and SMEs.

The Greek economy was achieving high growth rates for several decades before entering the EC. In the 1970s it had faced the two oil shocks and suffered from the first signs of de-industrialisation, as in the rest of economies in Europe. The 1980s have witnessed a shift towards state-centred policies that attempted to resolve problems derived from these two main causes and other international or domestic, such as the overburdening of debts in several large private firms that were transferred to a state control, in order to control the explosive state of unemployment[3].

The study period selected presents a particular interest, as a more concrete effort is put in operation to resolve structural problems, as those relating to private sector activity and to maximise the effects of policies targeting at the growth of businesses and the private sector more generally. These efforts were based on the "New Industrial Strategy" launched, which laid the emphasis upon competitiveness and the broadening of policy making to a wider spectrum of policies and new forms of support. Several of these were softer than those used before, for example those under the Greek Law of Development. The new strategy highlighted the need to create consensus-based policies among social and economic partners, emphasized on industrial peace and the synthesis needed among contradicting actors and their views on policy making, often inspired from ideological roots and an intense political atmosphere. It was reflected in the 1997 Report on the New Industrial Strategy, a guiding strategic document for industrial growth that appeared for the first time in Greece's modern economic history. Even though published in the middle of 1994-1999 programming period and while the operational program for "Industry and Services" was under operation, it influenced its preparation, scheduling and overall operation.

As most of the EU state economies at the period, the Greek economy implemented a national-level program for its competitiveness, theoretically informed at this stage by the views on the "new competition" (as in [62], crystallised for Greece in [56]) and the need to create new institutions and expand the range of implemented policies. The structure of the operational program is seen in Table 4.

It focused on private sector support (by the use of the specific Greek Development Law at the period), business modernisation, private investments in various industries, financial support through various hard or soft instruments and the necessary provisions for human capital in the private sector. This period is associated with the creation of financial institutions and instruments, a mutual guarantee fund, a first effort to promote venture capitals, factoring and leasing, to introduce modernisation techniques and instruments for business and SME growth and enhance more generally growth conditions, for example through policies on quality and certification of the Greek productions (that introduce various forms of ISO), on human resource development and training and on new firm formation.

From a financial point of view, it can be argued that more emphasis is attributed to infrastructure for business growth, private business investments and business modernisation, since the larger share of funds is devoted on the first three axes of the program (Table 5).

---

[3] As in many local areas it exceeded 35%.

Table 4. The structuring of the 1994-1999 Operational Program for Industry and Services

Axis 1	Axis 2	Axis 3	Axis 4	Axis 5
Infrastructure	Private Investments	Business Modernisation	Financial SME support	Human Capital
Policies for the promotion of certification	Large industrial investments	Investments for International Competitiveness	Financial Institutions and Instruments	Special categories of intra-business training for employees
Private or mixed industrial infrastructure	Investments through the Greek Development Law	Technological modernisation,	Mutual Guarantee fund	Training of employees and executives for international competitiveness (in Axis 3)
Private or mixed industrial infrastructure in Northern Greece	Large manufacturing investments	Quality	Venture Capitals	Training for technological equipment issues
Restructuring of declining regions	Specific Industrial/ manufacturing investments	Innovation	Support of credit Associations	Management of the Programme
Support in exports		Manufacturing flexibility	Interest rate support	Training of public sector employees engaged in the programme
		Promotion of ecology-friendly methods in production	Promotion of factoring	Studies for the support of management of Industrial programme
		Technological transfer	Promotion of leasing	Special training actions for special measures of the programme
		Job security and Hygiene	Improving SME competitiveness	
			Technical supports to Chambers and industrial associations	
			Improvements in the function of existing industrial institutions and promotion of necessary changes at the institutional and proprietary framework	
			Creation of Register – (network) for SMEs, SME institutions, Consulting Businesses and intermediate institutions that participate in the management of SME programmes	
			Promotion of partnerships and association (private-public partnerships, associations, mergers, constant subcontracting relationships, mixed enterprises)	
			Subcontracting promotion	
			New firm formation support (cases that are not supported by the Greek Development Law)	
			Support for purchasing consulting services	
			Manufacturing support	

Note: The program included a sixth axis focusing on its implementation.
Source: [63].

Table 5. Programming and implementation (until 31/12/2001) of the 1994-1999 Operational Program for Industry and Services

			Axis 1	Axis 2	Axis 3	Axis 4	Axis 5	Axis 6	TOTAL
Programming		TOTAL EXPENDITURE	345,812.8	860,400.0	1,359,730	270,623	17,202	26,991	2,880,758.8
	PUBLIC EXPENDITURE	E.U.	187,078	238,000	330,106	125,891	12,901	16,176	910,152
		National	85,190	116,800	196,774	17,219	4,301	10,815	431,099
		TOTAL	272,268	354,800	526,880	143,110	17,202	26,991	1,341,251
	PRIVATE EXPENDITURE		73,544.8	505,600.0	832,850.0	127,513	0	0	1,539,507.8
Implementation	Structural Funds Participation	TOTAL of ERCP support	171,145.907	227,936.7	334,598.9	103,507.9	12,243.509	15,718.2	865,151.1
		ERDF	171,145.907	227,936.7	334,598.9	103,507.9	0	15,718.2	852,907.6
		ESF	0	0	0	0	12,243.509	0	12,243.5
		National Public Participation	83,398.439	111,008.3	178,624.1	15,328.5	4,196.198	10,478.8	402,944.4
		Private Participation	59,744.833	455,245.8	830,031.7	89,536.7	0	86,673	1,434,645.7
	Payments	TOTAL	323,443.087	834,628.9	1,383,359.4	213,483.9	16,597.902	27,087.4	2,798,591.6
		PUBLIC	264,088.533	355,352.9	528,228.9	122,160.8	16,597.902	27,087.4	1,313,507.5
		PRIVATE	59,354.555	479,276	855,130.5	91,323.1	0	0	1,485,084.2

Notes:

1. Amounts in thousands of Euros.

2. The axes are described in Table 4.

Source: [64].

Table 6. The initially programmed expenditure for each one of the 1994-1999 Regional Operational Programs and their respective sub-programs (schemes) for SME and business support and investment

Regional Operation Programs	Total budget EL(94) 176	Total Cost for the program	Total Cost for the sub-program	Description of sub-program on industrial, productive and manufacturing (from the R.O.P.)	Total Public expenditure for the sub-program	Private sector participation at the sub-program
Anatoliki Makedonia and Thrace	823,5	688,964	181,744	Special program for manufacturing development	167,932	13,780
Kentriki Makedonia	977,4	816,918	72,861	Promotion of business competitiveness	62,811	10,080
Dytiki Makedonia	347,9	304,959	28,133	Support of productive investments	16,236	11,897
Notio Aigaio	430,0	380,000	94,547	Support of productive sectors	90,346	4,200
Voreio Aigaio	366,5	327,949	16,986	Support of selected industrial sectors and advantages	6,985	10,000
Attiki	1098,1	938,470	375,617	Productive investments	352,137	23,480
Dytiki Ellada	501,6	501,600	116,858	Regeneration of manufacturing production zones	22,201	99,600
Sterea Ellada	623,0	623,029	196,538	Productive Sectors	106,052	90,486
Peloponissos	440,2	440,200	56,455	2nd Sector support	10,640	45,815
Krete	558,3	435,300	56,500	Centre for economy and research in South-East Mediterranean	45,600	10,900
Thessalia	609,9	560,895	83,763	Manufacturing	38,425	9,771
Ionia Nisia	274,4	274,150	17,743	Productive tissue and rural development	17,170	573
Ipiros	376,1	346,946	55,298	Improvements in business competitiveness	35,303	19.995

Source: [66].

Note: Amounts in million of ECUs.

These policies emphasized the national component of business support policies rather than the industrial or spatial, in a top-down direction. Policies on competitiveness are combined with a more general policy framework at the 1994-1999 period to structurally adjust the economy, improve macroeconomic national-level indicators and prepare for entering at the Euro-zone, in 2002 [65].

Within the general framework of the EU Regional and Cohesion policy applied at the period, a number of additional policies are implemented offering financial support to businesses. As the vast majority of Greek businesses have low sizes, these policies can be viewed to be SME supportive policies more generally.

The EU Cohesion and Regional Policy at the period was broken down into various programs, particular for each Greek region, the Regional Operational Programs (R.O.P.s). These programs contained a special scheme of industrial and productive investments and support, specific to each region and implemented via the regional authorities. Table 6 comprises information on all these Regional Operation Programs and the related SME support and investment schemes. Information is also provided on the expenditure, public, EU, national or private.

Finally it must be argued that at the local level (municipality or department) very few examples of policies appear supporting SMEs and businesses.

Two main sources of business and SME support policies targeting at business growth can be argued to exist: (i) those directly targeting at business and SME growth, through the New Industrial Strategy and the various schemes of business support from each regional operation program and (ii) those indirectly focusing on growth, at the more general level of the EU Regional and Cohesion Policy implemented at the period. The direct policies are mostly applied at the firm level, while indirect policies focus at the local and regional level, seeking to contribute more generally to local and regional growth.

Hence, in assessing the effects of policies on business and SME growth, a methodological approach should be followed that relates these different levels of policy implementation. Given that Greece becomes a general policy lab at the period, where policies for business growth hitherto unknown are implemented, both directly and indirectly, the focus is given on the more general question whether policy support finally achieved a business growth outcome or not. This question refers to scenarios (i) or (iii) in Table 2. Conclusions are drawn from evidence provided for the Greek economy overall.

DATA, METHODOLOGY AND THE VARIABLES USED

The sample was selected from the Greek VAT business register. V.A.T. data are widely used in studies assessing the impact of various factors on SME growth [50]. Firms were initially selected from four regions and five industries of the Greek economy. Using a simple random sampling method, a sample of 1,089 firms surviving between 1995 and 2002 was selected. Given that policies continue after the official end of a programming period, extending the final year of study after 1999 was decided to provide a better assessment of policies implemented in the 1994-1999 period. The 1995-2002 period covers the full period of implementation of the 1994-1999 programming.

Stratification was made for the employment variable, by the use of employment bands. Specific quotas were applied for the regions and industries selected, to ensure that the number of firms/observations in each combination of region, industry and employment band would not be less than 50. The selection of regions was based on an index of peripherality, ranking the regions in different levels of centrality/ peripherality at the study period. Firms were selected from the two more central regions in Greece (Attiki and Kentriki Makedonia), one middle-peripheral (Thessalia) and one very peripheral Greek region (Ipiros)[1].

The study focuses on some of the most peripheral EU regions, some of which suffer form a double-peripherality, both at the EU level and inside Greece. Even though, as discussed businesses may achieve higher levels of growth in peripheral regions [40], such an outcome depends on various national, regional and local growth conditions.

All firms selected in the sample had an initial size (for 1995) of more than 5 and less than 199 employees. Smaller in size firms were excluded from the study for a number of reasons: data in lower size levels are usually less reliable; the overall population of such firms in business databases may be inaccurate; non-official economic activity is found in such firms and it is difficult to capture the official activity. By following the current at the period EU definition on SMEs, the firm sizes used comprised the initial micro, small or medium sizes[2]. This was expected to enhance representativeness at the business population that is composed in Greece mainly from these three firm sizes. Tested successfully against the overall Greek business population by the use of non-parametric tests, the sample's representativeness makes the present study interesting for inference purposes for the Greek economy overall. Given that firms at the EU level have larger sizes, the focus upon SMEs of relatively larger sizes makes the present study interesting also from a European perspective. A similar study could take place for German Landers or the British regions, comparing the effects of state, regional and local policies on business growth policies, across regions and in different administrative and policy environments. Although firm sizes used are the initial firm sizes for the year 1995, small and medium-sized enterprises may grow to different sizes over the study period, from micro to very large.

Data provided for the initial (1995) and final (2002) year of the implementation of the specific policy programming period were turned to a number of variables at the business level, for both the initial and the final year. Categorical variables were turned to dummies, to study each dummy (each category) separately. Variables at the business-level were brought together with variables at the local and regional environment, which are first collected and then created from the Greek local and regional accounts. An additional source was used for information at the municipal (local) level through the Hellenic Statistical Authority. These variables were selected in order to study the general impact of the European Cohesion and Regional Policy in changing the local and regional environment and affecting upon SME and business growth. The choice for this set of variables was based on their frequency in related studies on business growth, survival, formation rates and death. The logic put forward is similar to that found in [48], which claims that variables affecting firm formation rates are likely to affect firm growth, both in numbers and sizes, as well as firm deaths.

---

[1] Greece is composed of 13 NUTSII-level regions, four of which are island regions. More recently, the implementation of the Greek part of Egnatia road is progressively removing the character of extreme peripherality for the region of Ipiros, which remains however one of the most peripheral European.

[2] An additional initial size was necessary to introduce small and medium sizes as dummies and use a third group, that of micro, as one control or test group.

Local and regional variables are standardized divided by their respective population, while the rates of employment and turnover variables are also introduced. Business growth was measured as the 1995-2002 change in business employment and turnover respectively. Turnover was first deflated, to avoid potential misinterpretations of turnover changes, in a period of significant reduction of inflation for Greece.

The policy factor was introduced by using information on which firms received financial support at the period, drawn from the Greek Integrated Information System. This is a policy database used for assessment and monitoring purposes by national and EU authorities implementing EU Cohesion and Regional Policy. Overall 315 firms out of 1089 were found to receive policy support from the various Operational Programs applied by the EU Cohesion and Regional Policy at the particular programming period. These included firms supported from the program for Industry and Services[3]. After identifying the policy recipient firms, a dummy variable for the policy status at the firm level (POLSTAT) was created, taking a zero value (0) for non-supported firms and the value of one (1) for supported firms. This dummy was used to test the effect of EU Cohesion and Regional Policy at the firm level. The more general impact of policies was tested through the rest of the regional and local variables introduced.

All variables contained in the finally constructed data panel (cross-sections for two different years, initial and final), are given in Table 7, distinguished in dependent and independent. For analytical purposes, these variables-proxies were grouped into several categories from general economic growth and development theory, some of which are found in the variety of similar groupings in studies on business growth, birth, survival and death ([48], [50], [51], [67]). Information on the local and regional economic environment is further enriched by numerous local and regional variables grouped in several categories of economic growth factors. Though these are not macroeconomic national-level variables, their use allows testing a number of hypotheses put forward in related SME and business growth studies on the importance of economic environment and the role of capital, human capital, education, land, physical capital and infrastructure and other conditions.

Regional savings and deposits were selected to test the neoclassical hypotheses on the role of regional capital on regional growth ([67]; [68]). Similarly that is applied with the variable of regionally declared income. The taxes, direct and indirect, reveal limitations in the regional income and act as its stabilizers (a general role for taxes). The role of taxes is also seen at the regional level through the variable of the number of taxpayers, and at the local level through the municipal fees and income. The local grants and expenses are also considered as a factor that can associate with business growth, because of the local accountability.

Changes in the population density are used as variables representing labour to test hypothesis in neo-classical literature ([68]) and also do reflect changes in the size of regional and local markets that are considered as important in readings from location literature and those on how clusters are formed and sustained. Population density can be considered also as a proxy for the availability of labour and human capital.

---

[3] Further efforts were made to relate the sample with additional policy information on the programs implemented by the Ministry of Industry and the Regional Operational Programs in Attiki and Kentriki Makedonia, collected directly from the authorities in charge of these Programs. Overall these three Programs represented the major programming efforts for SME and business support implemented at the study period. This task did not give fruitful results. Hence, the policy information was based only on the single policy database.

Table 7. The variables used in the study, their description and source of data

Variable	General Category	Definition/description	Level, type, relation to firm	Source of data
Dependent variables				
EMPLGR	Business Growth, 1994-2002	Employment change, from 1994 to 2002	Business level, numerical, internal	Business Census
TURNGR	Business Growth, 1994-2002	Turnover change, from 1994 to 2002	Business level, numerical, internal	Business Census
EMPL95[8]	Initial Employment value, 1995	Number of employees in the firm, in 1995	Business level, numerical, internal	Business Census
TURN95	Initial Turnover value, 1995	Turnover amount, in MEuros, in 2002	Business level, numerical, internal	Business Census
EMPL02	Final Employment value, 2002	Number of employees in the firm, in 1995	Business level, numerical, internal	Business Census
TURN02	Final Turnover value, 2002	Turnover amount, in MEuros, in 2002	Business level, numerical, internal	Business Census
EMPLGR_RL	Relative Business Growth, 1994-2002	Employment change from 1994 to 2002 divided by initial employment	Business level, numerical, internal	Business Census
TURNGR_RL	Relative Business Growth, 1994-2002	Turnover change from divided by initial turnover	Business level, numerical, internal	Business Census
EMPLGR_RLAV	Relative Business Growth, 1994-2002	Employment change from 1994 to 2002 divided by average employment change from 1994 to 2002	Business level, numerical, internal	Business Census
TURNGR_RLAV	Relative Business Growth, 1994-2002	Turnover change from 1994 to 2002 divided by average turnover change from 1994 to 2002	Business level, numerical, internal	Business Census
LogEMPLGR	Logarithmic Employment Growth,	Logarithmic Employment change, from 1994 to 2002	Business level, numerical, internal	Business Census
LogTURNGR	Logarithmic Turnover Growth,	Logarithmic Turnover change, from 1994 to 2002	Business level, numerical, internal	Business Census
Independent variables				
REG1_95	Region, 1995, level of peripherality	Attiki, central	Business level, Dummy, external	Business Census
REG2_95	Region, 1995, level of peripherality	Kentriki Makedonia, central	Business level, Dummy, external	Business Census
REG3_95	Region, 1995, level of peripherality	Thessalia, middle-peripheral	Business level, Dummy, external	Business Census
REG4_95	Region, 1995, level of peripherality	Ipiros, peripheral	Business level, Dummy, external	Business Census
IND1_95	Industry, 1995	Construction	Business level, Dummy, external	Business Census
IND2_95	Industry, 1995	Manufacturing	Business level, Dummy, external & internal	Business Census
IND3_95	Industry, 1995	Services	Business level, Dummy, external & internal	Business Census

Table 7. (Continued)

Variable	General Category	Definition/description	Level, type, relation to firm	Source of data
IND4_95	Industry, 1995	Tourism	Business level, Dummy, external & internal	Business Census
IND5_95	Industry, 1995	Trade	Business level, Dummy, external & internal	Business Census
LGST1_95	Legal status, 1995	Unlimited liability firms	Business level, Dummy, internal	Business Census
LGST2_95	Legal status, 1995	Mixed liability firms	Business level, Dummy, internal	Business Census
LGST3_95	Legal status, 1995	Limited liability firms	Business level, Dummy, internal	Business Census
LGST4_95	Legal status, 1995	Sole traders	Business level, Dummy, internal	Business Census
LGST5_95	Legal status, 1995	Other legal statuses	Business level, Dummy, internal	Business Census
MICRO95	Economies of scale, 1995	Initial micro firm size	Business level, Dummy, internal	Business Census
SMALL95	Economies of scale, 1995	Initial small firm size	Business level, Dummy, internal	Business Census
MEDIUM95	Economies of scale, 1995	initial medium firm size	Business level, Dummy, internal	Business Census
HTE	Education	Changes in Higher technical education 1991-2001	Regional level, numerical, external	Regional accounts
HVcE	Education	Changes in higher vocational education 1991-2001	Regional level, numerical, external	Regional accounts
UnE	Education	Changes in university-level education 1991-2001	Regional level, numerical, external	Regional accounts
SE	Education	Changes in secondary-level education 1991-2001	Regional level, numerical, external	Regional accounts
CmplSE	Education	Changes in Compulsory secondary Education, 1991-2001	Regional level, numerical, external	Regional accounts
IL	Education	Change of Illiteracy, 1991-2001	Regional level, numerical, external	Regional accounts
FINACT	Human capital	Change of financial activity, 1991-2001	Regional level, numerical, external	Regional accounts
ACTIVE	Human capital	Change of Activity rates, 1991-2001	Regional level, numerical, external	Regional accounts
SelfEMPL	Human capital	Change of self-employment per 100 inhabitants, 1991 - 2001	Regional level, numerical, external	Regional accounts
SalEMPL	Human capital	Change of salaried employment, 1991-2001	Regional level, numerical, external	Regional accounts
SelfEMPLMNF	Human capital	Change of self-employment in manufacturing 1991-2001	Regional level, numerical, external	Regional accounts
UNEMPL	Human capital	Change in unemployment, 1991-2001	Regional level, numerical, external	Regional accounts
POPDENS_9401	Human capital	Change in Population density, 1994 - 2001	Local level, numerical, external	Local accounts
PRHSINV_9401	Land values	Change in private investment in housing, 1994 - 2001	Local level, numerical, external	Local accounts
NEWHS100_9401	Land values	Number of new houses per 100 inhabitants, 1994 - 2001	Local level, numerical, external	Local accounts
TELLINES_9400	Infrastructure	Change of telephone lines per 100 inhabitants, 1994 - 2000	Local level, numerical, external	Local accounts
TELLINES_9401	Infrastructure	Change of telephone lines, 1994 - 2001	Local level, numerical, external	Local accounts
HOTELBED_9400	Infrastructure	Change in hotel beds, 1994 - 2000	Local level, numerical, external	Local accounts
HOTELBED_9401	Infrastructure	Change in hotel beds, 1994 - 2001	Local level, numerical, external	Local accounts

Variable	General Category	Definition/description	Level, type, relation to firm	Source of data
DEPOSITS_9400	Capital	Change in deposits, 1994 - 2000	Local level, numerical, external	Local accounts
SAVINGS_9400	Capital	Change in savings, 1994 - 2000	Local level, numerical, external	Local accounts
INCDECL_9401	Capital	Change in declared Income, 1994 - 2001	Local level, numerical, external	Local accounts
INDTAX_9401	Capital	Change in indirect taxes, 1994 - 2001	Local level, numerical, external	Local accounts
DIRTAX_9401	Capital	Change in direct taxes, 1994 - 2001	Local level, numerical, external	Local accounts
TAXPAY_9401	Capital	Change in the numbers of tax payers, 1994 - 2001	Local level, numerical, external	Local accounts
MANFSML_9401	Manufacturing surrogate	Change in the number of manufacturing SMEs and large firms (>10 employees), 1994 - 2001	Local level, numerical, external	Local accounts
MANFSMLINV_9401	Manufacturing surrogate	Change in the investments made by manufacturing SME and large firms, 1994 - 2001	Local level, numerical, external	Local accounts
MANFSMLVA_9401	Manufacturing surrogate	Change in the value added of manufacturing SMEs and large firms 1994 - 2001	Local level, numerical, external	Local accounts
MANFSMLSAL_9401	Manufacturing surrogate	Change in the sales of manufacturing SMEs and large firms, 1994 - 2001	Local level, numerical, external	Local accounts
MUNCF	Municipal Fees	Levels of Municipal Fees in 1997	Local level, numerical, external	Local/munic. accounts
MUNCIN	Municipal Income	Levels of Municipal Income in 1997	Local level, numerical, external	Local/munic. accounts
DIST	Distance	Distance from the centre of Athens	Business level, numerical, external	Michelin guide
POLSTAT	Policy support status	Policy status for recipient firms throughout	Business level, dummy, external & internal	Integrated Information System

The education, which has been given special attention for its effects on growth in the endogenous growth theory, the discussion on the role of knowledge and that of local and regional clusters, is studied across a number of proxies.

The study of different educational levels is not considered uniform and the full range of educational levels at the region are selected, from illiteracy, compulsory and secondary education, to higher technical, university-level, as well as vocational education.

Infrastructure is mainly presented through the number of telephone lines. Though they are many types of infrastructure, the focus is given on the telecommunications, due to their necessity in the growth of businesses, the significant changes and a breakthrough of telecommunication markets in Greece at the study period and given several problems that could be presented with interpretation of other variables. Furthermore, a proxy on a tourist infrastructure is introduced, the number of hotel beds, given the importance of tourism in the Greek economy and the subsidiary role that it plays on the local and regional economies for developing business activities across a range of industries.

The characteristics of the labour market and the human capital were also introduced through a number of proxies. These are the activity rates, the levels of unemployment, self-employment, salaried employment and the self-employment in manufacturing. These relate to discussions on the role of labour markets and human capital on local and regional for growth.

The private investments in housing and the number of new houses in 100 inhabitants are two proxies used to test the effects of land prices on business growth, given the increases in house values in Greece at the period.

Specific surrogates are introduced for the manufacturing industry, to test the evidence on manufacturing and its association with the growth of SMEs.

For all these variables, it is the impact of their change over time that is studied rather than their initial conditions. The underlying assumption is that changes in the local and regional economic environment will bring firm size changes. For example the increase in the number of telephones or other types of infrastructure and the increase in the amounts of saving will affect SME growth. Human capital proxies (education and labour variables) have become available from the census of population (taking place every ten years) and were used to estimate longer changes in the economic environment (between 1991 and 2001), given that the final year of the census coincides with the end of the selected policy programming period[1].

Several variables are introduced as dummies in the models and other as numerical. All dummy variables are introduced for the initial years only to test initial influence exercised on business growth. A number of problems such as the relocation from one region to another or the change in legal status or industry are overcome in this way. It is assumed that the initial region and initial regional environment of firms influence their growth and related growth decisions, such as those on location. Similarly this assumption is made for the use of industry and legal status dummies, which reflect the initial industrial environment and legal status of the firm.

The role of geography is further introduced by using the variable of distance from Athens (DIST). This is a business-level variable, used as a surrogate for distance from the main economic, institutional and market centres. The underlying assumption being that distance acts as a barrier for SME and business growth, given the representative selection of SMEs

---

[1] 1994-1999 or 2002 for all projects and before the implementation of the new programming period starts

from more peripheral regions in the sample. The incorporation of the very peripheral region of Ipiros in the sample is expected to influence towards that direction. The mountainous area that divides the country geographically has been a significant obstacle at the period for businesses and the transportation of goods from Ipiros, a region naturally disadvantaged to reach larger and central domestic and European markets. Business growth problems and barriers are expected to be revealed through a significant association of the variable of distance with business growth measures, in the models created.

An extensive use of dummies is made, reflecting initial environmental firm conditions. The latter are distinguished in the regional economic environment, the industrial environment and that of firms as legal entities.

Based on the firm growth performance, a distinction is made in the sample between growth outliers, positive or negative, and firms growing or reducing size more steadily. Even though various techniques are suggested in literature, outliers were identified by using a simple ranking method of the two growth variables, employment and turnover growth. The structuring of different study-groups in the sample is summarized in Table 8. The Table presents also the groups of SMEs, by removing micro firms, when necessary.

Overall 283 firms received policy support out of the 1,023 firms in the sample, after removing the outliers. This is a large proportion of firms, representing 27.6% of the sub-sample of steadily growing firms.

Table 8. Breaking up the sample into several sub-samples

In Table 9 the sample without outliers (of 1,023 firms) is further broken down by policy status and initial size. The proportion of firms receiving policy supports increases with size (as seen from observing the percentages in the parentheses). As the sample was randomly selected and as in general, the demographic pattern of distribution of firm sizes in business populations is such that more firms are found in lower sizes, this finding appears to highlight an emphasis attributed in Greece on the support of firms of larger initial sizes, especially those of medium-sizes.

Employment and turnover growth is found to distribute normally for the sample of 1,089 and the sample of 1,023 firms growing more steadily. This is found for policy supported, non-supported and for all firms, by bringing the diagrams together (Appendix Figures 1-1, 1-2, 1-

150 Constantinos Ikonomou

3 and 1-4). This is a good indication of the valid use of parametric statistics in the following analysis.

Table 9. Distinguishing the sample without outliers (1023), its policy sub-sample (283) and the sub-sample of non-supported firms (740) by firm size (percentage of policy supported or non-supported firms for the particular size in parentheses)

	Sample without outliers (1023)	Policy Supported (283)	Non-supported firms (740)
Micro	178	9 (5.1%)	169 (94.4%)
Small	505	102 (20.2%)	403 (79.8%)
Medium	340	172 (50.6%)	168 (49.4%)
Total	1023	283 (27.7%)	740 (72.3%)

The models developed provide evidence on the effect of business support policies, by focusing on the significance of the POLSTAT variable. However indicative conclusions can also be drawn from a prior analysis of the means and medians of supported and non-supported firms and SMEs. Their use can help to indicate the direction of causality, a delicate issue that cannot be inferred from the models developed, in the case that much enhanced means and medians are found for policy supported firms.

A number of conclusions can also be reached on the overall success of EU Cohesion and Regional Policy by testing whether changes in the local and regional environment (measured through numerous variables-proxies for the local and regional environment) are associated with SME growth.

ANALYSIS OF MEANS AND MEDIANS OF POLICY RECIPIENT FIRMS

The study of the means and medians for employment and turnover growth (EMPLGR and TURNGR), as well as for employment and turnover growth rate (EMPLGR_RL and TURNGR_RL) can contribute to reach some preliminary conclusions on what is the impact of policy on business and SME growth and on its importance.

It is worth mentioning that the means may be influenced by extreme values that could bias their levels. This general problem is much less reflected at the sub-sample of 1,023 steady-growth performers, after the removal of outliers. Table 10 presents the values of means and medians for the full sample of 1089 firms and the policy sub-sample of 315 firms that is contained on it. It also presents the same variables for the sub-sample of 1023 steady growth performers (that contained 845 SMEs) and the subsample of 274 policy-assisted SMEs. A first observation is that the means and medians of employment and turnover growth in the two policy sub-samples of 315 firms and 274 SMEs are enhanced in comparison to the means and medians in the sample of 1089 firms and 845 SMEs, respectively.

This indicates that policies increase the medians of employment and turnover growth and hence firm size. Even after removing outliers and the micro firms and by focusing only on SMEs, the means and medians of employment and turnover growth remain higher in the policy sample. In particular mean employment is much higher in the policy sub-samples than in the respective full samples. The employment mean for the sample of policy assisted SMEs is 6.65 in comparison to 3.78 for the non-assisted SMEs. The means for the policy sample of 315 firms are even more enhanced, reaching significantly increased levels of 28.59 for employment growth instead of 19.88 in the full sample of 1089 firms. These are significant differences, given that growth outliers have already been removed.

Table 10. Means and medians for different samples

MEANS	Sub-sample, number of firms	EMPLGR	TURNGR	EMPLGR_RL	TURNGR_RL
Policy Sample for 1089 firms	ALL firms, 315	28.59	10.9	55.3%	233.1%
1089 Sample	ALL firms, 1089	19.88	5.98	49%	248.2%
Policy Sample for 1023 firms	SME only, 274	6.65	4.52	26.8%	157.9%
1023 Sample	SME only, 845	3.78	3.05	21.8%	171.6%
MEDIANS	Sub-sample, number of firms	EMPLGR	TURNGR	EMPLGR_RL	TURNGR_RL
Policy Sample for 1089 firms	ALL firms, 315	6	2.31	14.3%	123.5%
1089 Sample	ALL firms, 1089	1	0.89	5.3%	113.6%
Policy Sample for 1023 firms	SME only, 274	4	2.16	7.3%	114.2%
1023 Sample	SME only, 845	0	1.11	0%	104.5%

Note: Employment is measured in number of employees and turnover in M€.

Evidence from the study of the medians is also indicative of the positive effects of policy on employment and turnover growth. Although the employment median for the full sample of 1089 and that of 845 SMEs is 1 and 0 respectively, for the policy assisted firms is 6 and for the policy assisted SMEs 4 employees, respectively. Similarly the turnover growth median in the full sample of 1089 firms and that of SMEs are lower than those found in the policy sample of 315 firms and the respective of 274 SMEs.

Overall differences between the full and the policy samples in the levels of employment and turnover growth are more evident for the policy samples, especially for the sample of 315 that includes micro firms and those firms that have grown very fast. This is also reflected in the annual means and medians of the same samples, in Table 11.

Annual employment and turnover growth rates are higher for the policy sub-samples than for the full samples. Every year, all policy assisted firms increase employment size by 3.57, while policy assisted SMEs more particularly increase their sizes only by 0.83 employees. In other words, it takes less than three years for all policy assisted firms -taken together- to increase their average sizes by more than 10 employees, while for the policy-assisted SMEs it takes more than ten years. This difference is however due to those firms that grow extremely fast. Therefore we can draw a more general conclusion that policy succeeds in increasing employment and turnover growth, after removing extreme growth outliers.

Table 11. Annual means and medians for different samples

ANNUAL MEANS	Sub-sample, number of firms	EMPLGR	TURNGR	EMPLGR_RL	TURNGR_RL
Policy Sample	ALL firms, 315	3.57	1.37	6.9%	29.1%
Full Sample	ALL firms, 1089	2.48	0.75	6.1%	31.0%
Policy Sample	SMEs, 274	0.83	0.57	3.4%	19.7%
Full Sample	SMEs, 845	0.47	0.38	2.7%	21.5%
ANNUAL MEDIANS	Sub-sample, number of firms	EMPLGR	TURNGR	EMPLGR_RL	TURNGR_RL
Policy Sample	ALL firms, 315	0.75	0.29	1.8%	15.4%
Full Sample	ALL firms, 1089	0.125	0.11	0.07%	14.2%
Policy Sample	SMEs, 274	0.50	0.27	0.09%	14.3%
Full Sample	SMEs, 845	0	0.14	0%	13.1%

Note: Employment is measured in number of employees and turnover in M€.

ANALYSIS OF MODELS THAT INCLUDE THE POLICY STATUS VARIABLE

Using the econometric software STATA, two types of models are created, OLS and ANOVA, both incorporating the independent POLSTAT variable and calculated for the sample of 1023 without outliers. ANOVA models include only the dummy among the independent variables.

Apart from employment growth (EMPLGR) and turnover growth (TURNGR), the variables of logarithmic transformations of the cross-sectional employment change and turnover change (LogEMPLGR and LogTURNGR) are also used as dependent, although they do not include negative changes or size decreases. This is due to the fact that logarithms, by definition, do not include positive numbers. Therefore it can be argued that they regard only the analysis for firms and SMEs increasing sizes and only these. These models have however higher levels of R-square and an enhanced predictive value.

The relative expressions of employment and turnover cross-sectional changes are distinguished in two ways: a) those where cross-sectional size change is divided by initial size, which are the relative employment and relative turnover growth (EMPLGR_RL and TURNGR_RL) and b) those where cross-sectional size change is divided by the average size change over the period, which are the relative average employment and turnover growth (EMPLGR_RLAV and TURNGR_RLAV). The list of all dependent variables is found in Table 7.

The results from these models are presented in Tables 12a, 12b, 13a, 13b that includes all significant variables in levels of significance above 90%, the respective levels of significance and the F-values for each variable. A parsimonious approach is followed to build the OLS models which is that of sequential modeling for all different factors found significant, until only few significant factors are built in the model (as in [49]). The levels of R-square (and adjusted R-square), the number of observations (N) and the necessary information about the degrees of freedom also appear in the Tables.

An Assessment of Business and SME Growth Policies Applied in Greece ...   153

With the single exception of models for relative turnover growth, all other ANOVA and OLS models reveal a significant association of the POLSTAT dummy with employment and turnover growth (Tables 12a, 12b, 13a and 13b).

The OLS associations with POLSTAT are positive, highlighting that the policy status variable follows the same direction with business growth variables. Hence, the first and important conclusion from the evidence provided in the models in Tables 12a-13b is that policy is significantly associated with business and SME growth, in almost all cases, irrespective of whether it is measured in absolute or relative terms. This finding, if combined with previous evidence from the analysis on enhanced means and especially medians, leads to a conclusion that confirms the positive impact of policies on business and SME growth in Greece, in the study period. In terms of Table 2, we fall in the case of scenario (i), hence no additional study is necessary.

By focusing on the logarithmic ANOVA models that include only positive increases in business growth, it appears that the variables of central regions (REG1 and REG2 for Attiki and Kentriki Makedonia respectively) significantly and positively associate with turnover growth. This model has the highest level of R-square. Hence, it is likely turnover (rather than employment) size increases are achieved in central regions, while peripheral may benefit more from relative size increases (as seen in the association of REG3 with TURNGR_RL), i.e. from increases in comparison to their initial sizes.

Table 12a. ANOVA models including policy variable (POLSTAT) for 1023 firms (F-values and levels of significance for each independent variable)

	EMPLGR	TURNGR	LogEMPLGR	LogTURNGR
Model F-value	8.12****	33.22****	24.62****	55.42****
POLSTAT	16.07****	4.36**	3.71*	17.75****
REG1				6.30**
REG2				6.87***
IND1	15.11***		3.26*	
IND3				17.34***
IND4		9.90**		25.84***
LGST1_95	9.83***		13.89***	51.85***
LGST2_95	3.59*		7.01***	
MICRO95	8.45***	56.43***	63.03***	88.90***
SMALL95	19.14***	66.28***	33.93***	61.90***
N	1023	1023	509	873
Degrees of Freedom (df)				
Model df	6	4	6	8
Residual df	1016	1018	502	864
Total df	1022	1022	508	872
R-square	0.0457	0.1155	0.2274	0.3391
Adj. R-square	0.0401	0.1120	0.2181	0.3330

Note: asterisks for levels of significance.

*, ** and *** indicate significance at the 90%, 95% and 99% level.

**** indicates extremely high significance ($P < 0.001$) and is used to emphasize results only for the POLSTAT and the overall model.

Table 12b. ANOVA models including policy variable (POLSTAT) for 1023 firms (F-values and levels of significance for each independent variable)

Note:

	EMPLGR_RL	EMPLGR_RLAV	TURNGR_RLAV
Model F-value	13.97****	10.50****	3.97***
POLSTAT	15.43****	17.49***	6.54**
IND1	18.98***	8.70***	
LGST4		19.34***	
MICRO95	25.70***	20.16***	4.37**
SMALL95	20.50***	16.08***	8.92***
N	1023	1023	1023
Degrees of Freedom (df)			
Model df	4	5	3
Residual df	1018	1017	1019
Total df	1022	1023	1022
R-square /	0.052	0.0491	0.0116
Adj. R-square	0.0483	0.0444	0.0086

asterisks for levels of significance.

*, ** and *** indicate significance at the 90%, 95% and 99% level.

**** indicates extremely high significance ($P < 0.001$) and is used to emphasize results only for the POLSTAT and the overall model.

It was not possible to create the TURNGR_RL model

Table 13a. OLS models with policy variable (POLSTAT) for 1023 firms (F-values and levels of significance for each independent variable)

	EMPLGR	TURNGR	LogEMPLGR	LogTURNGR
POLSTAT	9.6217****	0.9629****	0.2756**	0.5456****
IND1	-9.9384****		-0.2382**	-0.4327****
IND4		1.4351***		-0.9287****
LGST1				0.7346****
LGST3	-6.2682**		-0.4598***	
LGST4	-8.8466**			
LGST5	-12.6490**		-0.7736***	
MICRO95	9.3604***	-3.8266****	-1.4229****	
SMALL95	10.1858****	-3.1089****	-0.7388****	0.6147****
MEDIUM95				1.5535****
HTE				0.1517**
POPDENS_9401	-0.0337**			
DIST	-0.0195**	-0.0013*		
Constant	9.8247**	5.1212****	3.2947****	-1.2530****
N	1015	1023	509	873
F	5.56****	27.22****	24.53****	68.83****
df model	9	5	6	7
df residual	1005	1017	502	865
R-square/	0.0474	0.1180	0.2267	0.3390
Adj. R-square	0.0389	0.1137	0.2175	0.3337

Note: asterisks for levels of significance.

*, ** and *** indicate significance at the 90%, 95% and 99% level.

**** indicates extremely high significance ($P < 0.001$).

Table 13b. OLS models with policy variable (POLSTAT) for 1023 firms

(F-values and levels of significance for each independent variable)

	EMPLGR_RL	TURNGR_RL	EMPLGR_RLAV	TURNGR_RLAV
POLSTAT	0.2996***		0.2313****	0.1272**
REG3		0.5010		
IND1	-0.3334****		-0.1686****	
IND4				
LGST1				
LGST3	-0.4033****			
LGST4	-0.5509****		-0.3925****	
MICRO95	0.8107****		0.3221****	0.1374**
SMALL95	0.4802****	0.4264*	0.2089****	0.1473***
MEDIUM95				
ACTIVE	1.9921*		1.5793**	
SAVINGS_9400		-0.0044**		
DEPOSITS_9400		-0.0029**		
Constant	0.0679	3.0074****	-0.1842****	0.4325****
N	1023	1015	1023	1023
F	12.20	2.32	9.65****	3.87****
df model	7	4	6	3
df residual	1015	1010	1023	1019
R-square	0.0776	0.0091	0.0539	0.0113
Adj. R-square	0.0712	0.0052	0.0483	0.0083

Note: asterisks for levels of significance.
*, ** and *** indicate significance at the 90%, 95% and 99% level.
**** indicates extremely high significance ($P < 0.001$).
If there is no asterisk, the significance levels are close to 90%.

In the OLS models, the importance of centrality is captured indirectly through the significance of the variable of distance from Athens (DIST) and its negative association with both employment and turnover growth (EMPLGR and TURNGR). This association could highlight that the further away is a business located from Athens, the less is likely to increase absolute employment and turnover sizes, when growth outliers are removed.

Several other variables from the local and regional environment are found to significantly associate with business growth variables, in the OLS models that include all numerical variables. For example higher technical education in the regions significantly associates with logarithmic turnover growth, for the Greek SMEs increasing sizes. However, no other surrogate variable for education is found to significantly associate with business and SME growth. This point makes it difficult to reach more solid conclusions on the role of regional educational institutions on regional growth, as the proxies selected refer generally to the levels of education available at the region but not necessarily on those provided by the domestic regional educational institutions. Changes in population density also associate with absolute employment growth (EMPLGR). The OLS models for firm growth rates provide additional evidence on the role of human capital and labour markets, through the proxy of activity rates (ACTIVE), even though at a lower level of significance. These models also have low predictive capacity (due to low levels of R-square). However, it is worth mentioning that proxies for capital (for savings and deposits) are found to significantly associate with turnover growth rates (TURNGR_RL). Local levels in savings and deposits should relate with capital availability. Their significance with turnover growth rates appears to relate to the discussion held in literature on the role of capital, at the local level for investment, for supporting demand or other purposes. It can be argued that Greek firms and SMEs are influenced by local and regional capital and human capital changes over the study period, given the positive association of capital and human capital variables with some of the business growth variables.

There is evidence on the significance of the industrial activity and that of legal status that significantly associate with various measures of business growth, absolute, relative or logarithmic. However the OLS model shows an inverse association between business growth on the one hand and industrial or legal status dummies on the other. For example the construction industry (IND1) is found to negatively associate at a high level of significance with EMPLGR, LogEMPLGR, EMPLGR_RL and EMPLGR_RLAV. This wouldn't have happened if construction was bringing significant employment increases over the period. Hence, this could evidence the limited effects of the industry on employment generation.

All models provide evidence on the highly significant association of firm sizes, especially for micro and small firms, with various measures of business growth. In the OLS models, firms of micro sizes significantly associate at a high level of significance with all measures of employment growth used (EMPLGR, LogEMPLGR, EMPLGR_RL and EMPLGR_RLAV). The negative association of micro size with logarithmic employment growth (LogEMPLGR) refers to surviving micro firms increasing sizes (only) and does not necessarily reveal a positive net job impact. But as seen in Table 9, very few micro firms obtained policy support in the sample, while it is also reminded that growth outliers were removed (some of these were micro firms). A more accurate conclusion can be drawn from the association of logarithmic employment growth with small size that is also negative and significantly associated, given that a larger proportion of small firms obtain support. On the contrary the highly significant association of logarithmic turnover growth with initial small and medium sizes is positive, highlighting the role of SMEs for turnover increases. The association of the micro and small size with the relative measures of employment and turnover growth in the OLS models is high and positive, revealing the association of sizes with achieving higher growth rates. Overall this evidence seems to confirm the importance of the SME sector in Greece and its contribution for achieving growth rates and turnover growth in absolute terms, while their significance in employment change is also found, especially for smaller sizes. Finally, it is noteworthy that from the rich pool of local and regional variables selected to be studied only a limited number were found to be significant. For example municipal-level variables, educational, infrastructure or industrial variables are scarcely (if not totally) found to have any significance in their association with business growth.

CONCLUSIONS

The present chapter assessed the impact of state-derived policies on SME and business growth, implemented in Greece in the period between 1995 and 2002. Using a large sample of 1089 firms, it calculated enhanced means and medians in the case of policy supported firms when compared against those of the non-supported. Policy status was found to significantly and positively associate with business and SME growth in almost all models of business growth containing the policy-status dummy. The significance of some particular factors-proxies for SME and business growth and survival is highlighted. Not all local and regional level variables are found to be significant, in both models and for all different business growth measures used. Even though a uniform picture of significance of local and regional factors should not have been expected, the variety of findings helps to reflect upon the need for more intense changes or changes focusing upon business and SME growth at the local and regional environment. Such changes could enhance the levels of significance and of coefficients in the association of such factors with business growth.

Furthermore, even though business and SME growth is found to associate with changes in capital and human capital, it is likely that its concentration in central areas pronounces domestic geographical imbalances. This prospect is enhanced by the previous finding on the importance of central areas for employment and turnover growth, for example through the negative association of the variable of distance (DIST) in Table 13a or the possible location of growth outliers in central areas.

Hence, even though the picture of policies directly targeting at SME and business support was found to be successful and to have a positive impact, the overall success of EU Cohesion and Regional Policy in delivering business and SME growth should rather be recorded as problematic and deserves more scrutiny. More study is needed to understand the absence of significance in the associations of business growth variables, absolute or relative, with some particular factors and the possible causes of limited success or even failure of implemented changes at the local and regional environment that have a limited association with business and SME growth. Such study could take effect by using a broader range of assessment tools (such as those extensively explored in [2]-[12]), which could reveal the need to support local and regional instruments, the process of institutional building, the creation of new mechanisms and the delivery of more successful policy outcome at the local, regional and, as a result, at the national level.

APPENDIX

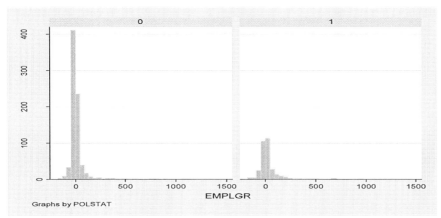

Note: The policy status variable (POLSTAT) is a dummy, taking the 0 value for the absence of policy status and 1 for the firms having policy status.

Figure 1.1. The distribution of employment growth by policy status (of policy-supported and non-supported firms) in the full sample (1089 firms).

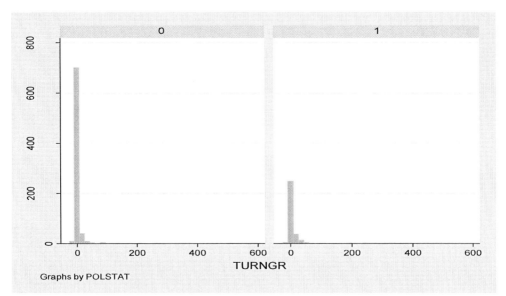

Note: The policy status variable (POLSTAT) is a dummy, taking the 0 value for the absence of policy status and 1 for the firms having policy status.

Figure 1.2. The distribution of turnover growth, by policy status (for policy-supported and non-supported firms) in the full sample (1089 firms).

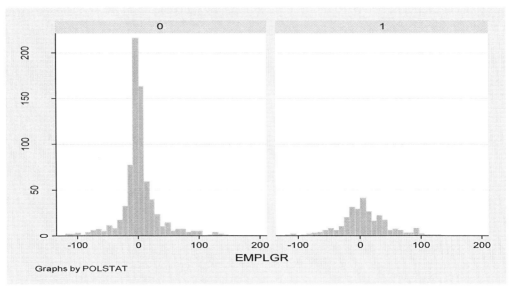

Note: The policy status variable (POLSTAT) is a dummy, taking the 0 value for the absence of policy status and 1 for the firms having policy status.

Figure 1.3. The distribution of employment growth by policy status (of policy-supported and non-supported firms) in the full sample (1023 firms).

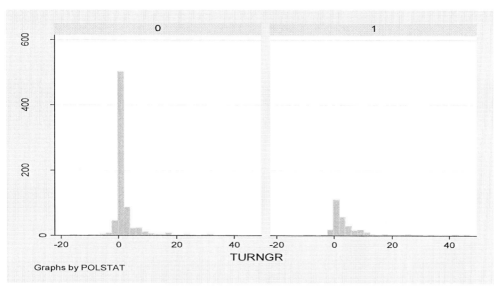

Note: The policy status variable (POLSTAT) is a dummy, taking the 0 value for the absence of policy status and 1 for the firms having policy status.

Figure 1.4. The distribution of turnover growth, by policy status (for policy-supported and non-supported firms) in the full sample (1023 firms).

REFERENCES

[1] A. Cosh, and A. Hughes, (Eds) *Enterprise Challenged: Policy and Performance in the British SME Sector 1999-2002*, ESRC Centre for Business Research, University of Cambridge, Cambridge, (2003).
[2] R.J. Bennett, *Environment and Planning C: Government and Policy,* 26(2), 375-397 (2008).
[3] R.J. Bennett and P.J.A. Robson, *Small Business Economics,* 25, 255-271 (2005).
[4] R.J. Bennett and P.J.A. Robson, *Journal of Small Business and Enterprise Development*, 11, 1, 95 - 112 (2004).
[5] R.J. Bennett and P.J.A. Robson, *Regional Studies,* 37(8), 795-811 (2003).
[6] R.J. Bennett and P.J.A. Robson, *Policy Studies,* 24(4), 163-186 (2003).
[7] R.J. Bennett, P.J.A. Robson and W.J.A. Bratton, *Applied Economics,* 33, 871-885 (2001).
[8] P.J.A. Robson and R.J. Bennett, *Small Business Economics*, 15, 193-208 (2000).
[9] R.J. Bennett and P.J.A. Robson *ESRC Centre for Business Research, University of Cambridge,* WP 181, September 2000 (2000a).
[10] R.J. Bennett and P.J.A. Robson, *Policy Studies,* 21(3), 173-190 (2000b).
[11] R.J. Bennett and P.J.A. Robson, *Policy Studies,* 20(2), 107-131 (1999).
[12] R.J. Bennett and P.J.A. Robson, *Entrepreneurship and Regional Development,* 11, 155-180 (1999).
[13] M.J. Hatch, *Organization Theory: Modern, Symbolic and Postmodern Perspectives*, Oxford University Press, Oxford (1997).

[14] J. Pfeffer, and G. Salancik, *The External Control of Organisations: A Resource Dependence Perspective,* Harper and Row, New York (1978).

[15] H.E. Aldrich, and J. Pfeffer, *Annual Review of Sociology*, 2, 79-105 (1976).

[16] J.G. Covin, and D.P. Slevin, *Strategic Management Journal*, 10(1), 75-87 (1989).

[17] D.J. Storey, *Understanding the Small Business Sector*, Thompson Learning, London (1994).

[18] R. Coase, *Economica*, 4, 386-405 (1937).

[19] E. Penrose, *The Theory of the Growth of the Firm*, Oxford University Press, Oxford (1959).

[20] J.-Il You, *Cambridge Journal of Economics*, 19, 441-462 (1995).

[21] F. Trau, Why do Firms Grow? ESRC Centre for Business Research, University of Cambridge, WP 26, March 1996.

[22] P. Milgrom, and J. Roberts, *Canadian Journal of Economics*, 21(3), 444-458 (1998).

[23] P.E. Hart, *Review of Industrial Organization,* 17, 229-248 (2000).

[24] F. Janssen, L' impact de l' environnement sur la croissance de l' emploi: une etude empirique des P.M.E. Belges, accessed at http://web.hec.ca/airepme/images/File/agadir/Janssen%20D.pdf (2011).

[25] Liao, J., Welsch, H.P., Pistrui, D., Internal and External Predictors of Entrepreneurial Growth: An Empirical Investigation of the Moderating Effects of Infrastructure Elements, (1999), accessed at http://usasbe.org/knowledge/proceedings/proceedingsDocs/USASBE1999proceedings-liao.pdf (2011).

[26] B. Hillebrand and W.G. Biemans, *Journal of Business Venturing,* 56, 735-743 (2003).

[27] J. Wiklund, H. Patzelt, and D.A. Shepherd, *Small Business Economics,* 32, 351-374 (2009).

[28] M.R. Binks, and C.T. Ennew, *Small Business Economics,* 8(1), 17-25 (1996).

[29] T. Beck, A. Demirguc-Kunt, and V. Maksimovic, *The Journal of Finance*, 60(1), 137-177 (2005).

[30] N.J. Foss, (Eds) Resources, Firms and Strategies: A Resource-Based Perspective, Oxford University Press, Oxford (1997).

[31] A. Cosh, A. Hughes, and M. Weeks, *The Relationship Between Training and Employment Growth in Small and Medium-Sized Enterprises*, ESRC Centre for Business Research, University of Cambridge, WP 188, Cambridge (2000).

[32] S. Fagernas, P. Sarkar, and A. Singh, Legal Origin, Shareholder Protection and the Stock Market: New Challenges from Time Series Analysis, ESRC Centre for Business Research, University of Cambridge, WP 343, Cambridge, June 2007.

[33] R. La Porta, F. Lopez-de-Silanes, A. F. Shleifer and R.W. Vishny, *Journal of Financial Economics*, 58, 13-27, (2000).

[34] R. La Porta, F. Lopez-de-Silanes, A. F. Shleifer, and R.W. Vishny, *Journal of Financial Economics*, 57, 1147-1170 (2002).

[35] L. Becchetti, and G. Trovato, *Small Business Economics*, 19, 291-306 (2002).

[36] T. Bates, *The Review of Economics and Statistics,* LXXII, 4, 551-559 (1990).

[37] J.E. Kwoka, and L.J. White, *Small Business Economics,* 16, 21-30 (2001).

[38] Y. Ijiri, and H.A. Simon, *The American Economic Review*, 54(2), 77-89 (1964).

[39] H. Dietmar, S. Konrad, and M. Woywode, *The Journal of Industrial Economics,* 46(4), 453-488 (1998).

[40] P. Vaessen, and D. Keeble, *Regional Studies*, 29(6), 489-505 (1995).

[41] R.M. Solow, *Quarterly Journal of Economics,* 70, 65-94 (1956).

[42] M.W. Reder, *The Journal of Human Resources,* 2(1), 97-104, (1967).

[43] P.M. Romer, *Journal of Political Economy*, 94(5), 1002-1037 (1986).

[44] D.A. Aschauer, *Journal of Monetary Economics*, 23(2), 177-200, (1989).

[45] J. Tirole, *The Theory of the Industrial Organisation*, M.I.T. Press, Cambridge, Mass (1997).

[46] R.J. Johnson, *Multivariate Statistical Analysis in Geography*, Longman, New York (1978).

[47] P. Westhead, and T. Moyes, *Entrepreneurship and Regional Development,* 4, 21-56 (1992).

[48] A. Moyes, and P. Westhead, *Regional Studies*, 24(2), 123-136 (1989).

[49] D. North, and D. Smallbone, *Journal of Rural Studies,* 12(2), 151-167 (1996).

[50] D. Keeble, and S. Walker, *Regional Studies*, 28(4), 411-427 (1993).

[51] M. Hart, and S. McGuiness, *Regional Studies*, 37(2), 109-122, (2003).

[52] P. Liargovas, *Small Business Economics,* 11(3), 201-214 (1997).

[53] W. Dennis, Research Mimicking Policy: Entrepreneurship/Small Business Policy Research in the United States, 64-82 in D.L. Sexton and H. Landstrom, (Eds) *The Blackwell Handbook of Entrepreneurship*, Blackwell, Oxford (2000).

[54] M.S. Freel, *Journal of Small Business and Enterprise Development*, 5(1), 19-32, (1998).

[55] D.J. Storey, Six Steps to Heaven: Evaluating the Impact of the Public Policies to Support Small Businesses in Developed Economies, 176-193 in D.L. Sexton, and H. Landstrom, (Eds) *The Blackwell Handbook of Entrepreneurship*, Blackwell, Oxford (2000).

[56] C. Pitelis, *Report for the Competitiveness and Industrial Strategy in Greece*, Ministry of Development, Hellenic Republic, October 1997 (in Greek) (1997).

[57] R.J. Bennett, Government and Small Business, 49-75 in S. Carter, and D. Jones-Evans (Eds) *Enterprise and Small Business: Principles, Practice and Policy*, Pearson, Essex (2006).

[58] S. Carter, and D. Jones-Evans (Eds) *Enterprise and Small Business: Principles*, Practice and Policy, Pearson, Essex (2006).

[59] Confederation of Business Industry, Encouraging Small Business Growth; Enabling the Enterprise Revolution, Enterprise Brief, 7, September 2006.

[60] European Commission, Industrial Policy in the Economic Literature; Recent Theoretical Developments and Implications for EU Policy, Enterprise Papers, no 12, Enterprise Directorate-General, European Commission, Report prepared by L. Navarro, (2003).

[61] Small Business Service, A Government Action Plan for Small Business: Making the UK the Best Place in the World to Start and Grow a Business, Department of Trade and Industry, January 2004.

[62] M., Best, *The New Competition; Institutions of Industrial Restructuring,* Polity Press, Cambridge (1991).

[63] E (94) 1833/2, No ERDF: 94.08.09.021, No ARINCO: 94 EL.16.020, 29 July 1994.

[64] Ministry of Development, Program for Manufacturing and Services, Final Implementation Report, Hellenic Republic, Ministry of Development, General

Secretary for Manufacturing, Office for the Management of EU Programs, Athens, June 2002.

[65] O.E.C.D., *Economic Survey of Greece 2007*, Policy Brief, Paris, 30 May 2007.

[66] E (94) 1832/8, No ERDF 94.08.09.008, No ARINCO 94. EL.16.008.

[67] R. Reynolds, D.J. Storey, and P. Westhead, *Regional Studies,* 28(4), 443-456 (1994).

[68] A. Pike, A. Rodriguez-Pose and J. Tomaney, Local and Regional Development, Routledge, Taylor and Francis, London (2006).

[69] H. Armstrong, and J. Taylor, *Regional Economics and Policy*, Harvester Wheatseaf, London (1993).

In: Greece: Economics, Political and Social Issues
Editor: Panagiotis Liargovas

ISBN: 978-1-62100-944-3
© 2012 Nova Science Publishers, Inc.

Chapter 8

THE COMMON AGRICULTURAL POLICY'S EFFECTS ON THE AGRICULTURAL SECTOR IN GREECE AND ITS ENVIRONMENTAL IMPACTS

Antonios A. Vorloou[*] *and Joanna Castritsi-Catharios*[†]
Hellenic Ministry of Labor and Social Security, Athens, Greece
University of Thessaly, Department of Ichthyology and
Aquatic Environment, Volos, Greece

ABSTRACT

The Common Agricultural Policy (CAP) has been many times quoted as one of the most important drivers for the agricultural sector in the European countries and its adverse effects on the environment. Various approaches have been used to investigate the actual links between the two. In this research effort the use of datamining techniques have been used in order to determine what are the links, if any, between the funding provided by the CAP to Greece during the 2nd Programming Period (1994-1999) and the changes in the agricultural sector during that period and in particular the environmental effects of the programs. The results indicate that the three larger financial programs were having some impact to agricultural production. These programs were the Less Favored Areas program, the Farming Investment Plans program and the New Farmers' program. All this programs were funded in Greece by Measure 1.1 of the 2nd Community Support Framework (CSF) for Greece. The main field of environmental investment for the Farming Investment Plans was drop irrigation but this amounted only to 2% of the total investment plans for the whole of the country. On the other hand, no direct linkage with the agricultural production of the three Accompanying Measures of the EU CAP was observed. These Measures were the Organic production program, the Rare Animal Breeds Preservation program and the Reduction of Nitrates Pollution program. Although these programs are more directed towards environmental protection, their limited impact is hardly surprising since these three programs have a narrow scope with regard to areas affected as well as funds provided. The results confirm that the link between the CAP and

---

[*] E-mail address: avorloou.katseli@gmail.com
[†] E-mail address: cathario@biol.uoa.gr

the agricultural sector size exists but the actual impact of the environmental reform of the CAP during the 90s had hardly any effect in Greece since it was largely underfunded.

INTRODUCTION

Agriculture is still an important sector of the European Union's (EU) economy in terms of its share to the Gross Domestic Product (GDP) and the labor force employed more so in Southern European countries. Various reports by the European Environmental Agency (EEA) note that the extent and causes of the environmental impact of agricultural practices vary significantly across Europe, notably by farm and crop type [1], [2] and [3] and that such anthropogenic activities in Greece affect inland waters [4]. While agriculture can exert significant pressure on the environment, it is also itself influenced by Member State or EU programs, which have a significant influence on the development of agricultural production capacity and intensity. A particular example is the large-scale public programs to aid the farming sector through the management of water regimes (river regulation, wetland drainage and irrigation schemes), as well as the subsidies given for agricultural production.

The total numbers of cattle, pigs, sheep and goats in the EU have been nearly stable since 1990. High livestock population densities are associated with excessive concentrations of manure, leading to an increased risk of water pollution.

In the EU, legislation and national programs seek to minimize this problem with some success. Livestock production in the EU has become more specialized and intensive. Overstocking can be attributed partly to the provision of production incentives, including payments per head of livestock under the Common Agricultural Policy (CAP), although socio-economic drivers have also encouraged some regionalization of livestock production and localized overgrazing.

MATERIALS AND METHODS

In order to assess the effects of agriculture on the environment, dynamic quantitative models can be of great use. The EEA has developed a modeling framework first introduced by the OECD, which is called "Driving forces-Pressure-State-Impact-Response" (DPSIR), [5]. The modeling framework has been shown to be an important tool to trace cause and effects linkages within identified indicators and to find data gaps.

Machine learning methods, have an inherent ability to discover patterns in ecological datasets that are not possible to detect using conventional linear-regression models. The aim of this research was to identify the links between the agricultural sector and the E.U. financial tools of the Common Agricultural Policy using data mining technics. For the application of the DPSIR framework the following definitions have been used:

- Agricultural pressures are the sector's parameters which affect the environment;
- Driving Forces are the financial tools used by the E.U. in order to influence the agricultural sector;

The data were compiled into a database and a software tool was used for implementing data mining decision tree techniques which was based on an improved version of the C4.5 algorithm and it is called See5. In order to process, better understand and illustrate the data introduced into the database, a Geographical Information Systems (GIS) software has also been used. Pressure data involve either the production of agricultural products measured in tones or in production area measured in stremata (1,000 meters squared) or finally in animal units. The types of data which were included in this category were obtained from three separate sources, namely:

1. Eurostat data aggregated at the Country or Regional level;
2. The Food and Agriculture Organization of the United Nations (FAO) data aggregated at the country level and
3. The National Statistical Office of Greece (NSOG) data were aggregated at prefecture level (NUTS 3).

This type of data where used because in a research effort encompassing the whole Driving Force – Pressure – State – Impact – Response cycle, from which this research has been an integral part, it has been shown that environmental "State" data were linked to agricultural 'Pressures" data in regards to the size of cultivated areas as well as to the volume of production of agricultural products [6]. At the same time data regarding nitrogen surpluses were examined in order to determine agricultural sector trends. Driving Force data were financial data from European Union funds for the agricultural sector. Table 1 describes the E.U. Funded programs which were used in the research as Driving Forces to the agricultural sector.

Financial data fall into two main categories according to the source of the funding. The first type is the one funded from the European Agricultural Fund Guidance sector and the second type from the European Agricultural Fund Support sector. From the Guidance sector the 2nd and the 3rd Community Support Frameworks (CSF) are funded and from the support sector the Common Market Organizations and the Accompanying Measures of the Common Agricultural Policy such as the Biological Production and Reduction of Nitrate Pollution are funded.

A sensitivity analysis carried out by [7] showed that the use of CORINE Land cover[1] provides unbiased and robust results that show the diversity of the local surpluses, even when the data set relating to agricultural statistics is deteriorated by aggregation on wider administrative entities. This result is particularly important insofar as surplus calculations on large territories can be carried out, covering several countries in which the level of resolution of agricultural statistics is notably different.

These conclusions strongly suggest that it is possible to carry out relevant and comparable assessments on a large area, despite the high heterogeneities of the statistics available according to the territories. Knowing, in addition, that aggregated statistics are quite often available for inter-census years, follow-ups over time become possible.

Thus the data collected were annual and aggregated at the level of prefecture. Because of the different nature of each financial program different types of data were collected.

---

[1] COoRdination of INformation on the Environment (CORINE) is a program of the European Commission.

It should be pointed out that Measure 1.1 of the 2nd CSF, which included the actions of support to New Farmers (NF), the Farming Investment Plans (FIP) and the Less Favored Areas (LFA) was the largest measure of the Operational Program regarding Agriculture in the 2nd CSF in payment amounts (60.76%).

Table 1. Financial Driving forces data used in this research

	Financial Measure	Description
1	2nd CSF Measure 1.1 - New Farmers (NF)	Applications for funding
		NF Funded
		NF according to age (3 categories)
		NF according to size cultivation (5 categories)
		NF according to type of cultivation (10 categories)
		Funds according to type of investment (26 categories)
		Funds according to character of investment (8 cat.)
2	2nd CSF Measure 1.1 - Farming Investment Plans (FIP)	Applications for funding
		FIP Funded
		FIP according to age (3 categories)
		FIP according to size cultivation (5 categories)
		FIP according to type of cultivation (10 categories)
		FIP Funds according to type of investment (26 categories)
		FIP Funds according to character of investment (8 cat.)
3	2nd CSF Measure 1.1 - Less Favoured Areas (LFA)	Applications for funding
		LFA Funded
		LFA Size of farms in hectares
		LFA Size of farms in Animal Units
4	CAP Accompanying Measure – Rare Animal Breeds Preservation	Payments
		Number of Animals
		Animal Units
5	CAP Accompanying Measure – Biological Production	Payments
		Area of production
		Products cultivated in size of cultivation (25 categories)
		New Persons entering in the Programme (5 year plans)
6	CAP Accompanying Measure – Reduction of Nitrate Pollution	Payments

RESULTS

First we shall examine each of the components of the research separately in order to better understand their trends. From the Driving Forces data the most representative programs from the 1st pillar and two programs of the 2nd pillar of the CAP were selected. From the 1st pillar which is the Guarantee section of the European Agricultural Guarantee and Guidance Fund (EAGGF) two agro-environmental measures were selected, namely the Biological Production and the Nitrates Reduction programs, and from 2nd pillar which is the Guarantee section of the EAGGF, the Farm Investment Plans and the New Farmers programs were selected.

The Farming Investment Plans program was aimed at assisting farmers at improving their holding through investments in machinery, buildings, animals etc. Figure 1 shows the funds allocated per Prefecture (NUTS 3) for the years 1994 and 1999. It is seen that the overall picture is that the program had an increasing absorption of funds between the years 1994 and 1999 especially in the northern regions of Central Macedonia, Western Macedonia and Eastern Macedonia – Thrace, in the region of Peloponnese and in the eastern prefectures of the Aegean islands.

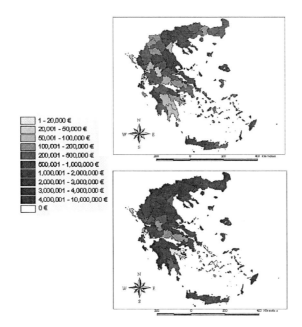

Figure 1. Funds allocated for Farming Investment Plans in 1994 (top) and in 1999 (bottom) in the Greek prefectures (NUTS 3).

Concerning the types of investments, Table 2 below shows the percentage distribution of investments in the Farming Investment Plans by type of investment separately for each one of the 13 main geographical regions of the country as well as in total. As can be seen from the Table, about one third (32%) of total investment goes to investment aiming at reducing production cost, whereas about one sixth (17%) goes to investment aiming at improving the quality of agricultural products. With a few exceptions this pattern is followed by all main regions of Greece.

Table 2. Percentage distribution of the type of investments in the Farming Investment Plans of Measure 1.1 of the 2nd Community Support Framework (CSF) for Greece by main geographical region

Region	Quality production improvements	Adjustment to the market needs	New activities development	Production cost reduction	Energy saving	Improvement of work conditions	Improvement of feeding health conditions	Environmental improvement	Total
Eastern Macedonia – Thrace	26	14	4	35	0	18	3	0	100
Central Macedonia	17	15	0	41	4	17	5	1	100
Western Macedonia	9	4	0	58	1	10	10	8	100
Thessaly	6	8	3	34	6	35	6	2	100
Ipiros	8	4	17	39	0	18	14	0	100
Ionian Islands	1	8	24	38	0	29	0	0	100
Western Greece	13	3	22	20	0	30	12	0	100
Sterea Ellada	7	5	9	48	4	16	11	0	100
Peloponissos.	32	20	3	18	0	13	12	2	100
Attica	40	33	6	21	0	0	0	0	100
Northern Aegean	17	5	31	8	4	13	17	5	100
Southern Aegean	20	20	16	30	0	11	2	1	100
Crete	19	3	16	36	6	13	5	2	100
Country Total	17	11	12	32	2	17	7	2	100

Out of the 13 regions four noticeable exceptions are the following:

- Attica where improvement in quality seems to be an absolute priority, absorbing 40% of investment of the region;
- Peloponnese where, like Attica, improvement in quality absorb the largest proportion of the investments of the region, namely 32%;
- Northern Aegean where priority is given to new activities which absorb the 31% of investment of the region and
- Thessaly where 35% of investment is committed to improvement of work conditions.

The New Farmers program was aiming at assisting new young farmers at establishing a new holding through a fixed amount of money as well as specific investments in machinery, buildings, animals etc. Figure 2 illustrates the number of beneficiaries per Prefecture for the years 1994 and 1999.

We notice that the program had an increasing numbers of beneficiaries all over Greece, but especially the prefecture of Aitoloakarnania in the region of Eastern Greece stands out as the prefecture with the largest number of beneficiaries in 1999.

The Biological Production program which was one of the agro-environmental measures of the CAP, was assisting farmers to make the transition from conventional agricultural production methods to Biological production for an initial period of 5 years. The program was active from the years 1996 until 2002. In Figure 3 the funds allocated per prefecture for 1996 as the starting year, the year 1999 an interim year can be seen.

The Common Agricultural Policy's Effects on the Agricultural Sector ...

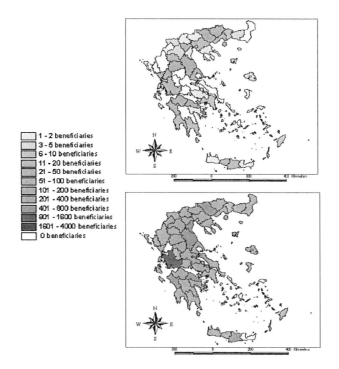

Figure 2. Number of beneficiaries for the New Farmers Programme in 1994 (top) and in 1999 (bottom) in the Greek prefectures (NUTS 3).

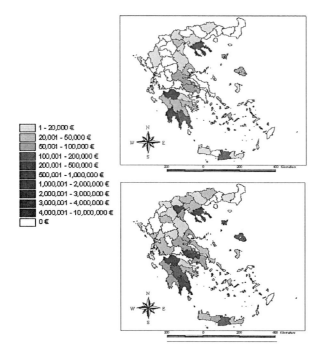

Figure 3. Funds allocated for the Biological Production Program in 1994 (top) and in 1999 (bottom) in the Greek prefectures (NUTS 3).

The overall picture is that the program had a steady pace of absorption of funds between these two years and it was especially active in the regions of Peloponnese and Central Macedonia, regions with large agricultural sector.

The Reduction of Nitrate Pollution program which was also part of the CAP agro-environmental measures, was applied in Greece initially in the Region of Thessaly as a pilot program. This region was selected due to the large amount of Nitrates pollution caused by large scale agricultural production. The program started in 1996 and ended in 1998. In Figure 4 we can see the funds allocated for the prefectures in the region of Thessaly in the years 1996 and 1997. We notice that the program did not start to absorb funds in all the prefectures of the region from the first year but the next year it was active in all the prefectures and especially in the prefecture of Larissa where intensive use of fertilizers is more profound.

When one examines the agricultural sector data, such as the nitrogen surpluses created by agricultural practices there seem to be a decreasing trend and combined with the general trend of higher ratio of organic to chemical fertilizer, the agricultural sector is showing an improving environmental attitude.

In Figure 5 we can observe that the Nitrogen surplus applied on agricultural land in the years 1990 and 1997 in the 13 regions of Greece. From the figures we notice that in general the surpluses were decreasing between these two years. More specifically we observe that the reductions are more important in the regions of Northern Greece (Western Macedonia, Central Macedonia and Eastern Macedonia –Thrace) and the islands (Ionian Islands, Northern Aegean and Southern Aegean).

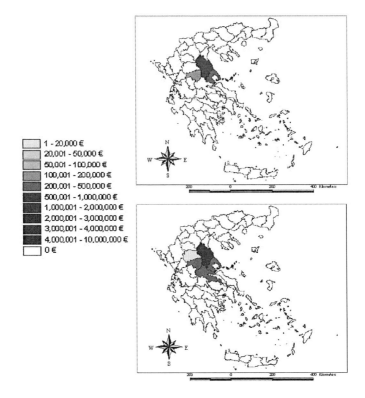

Figure 4. Funds allocated for the Reduction of Nitrates Pollution Program in 1996 (top) and in 1997 (bottom) in the Greek prefectures (NUTS 3).

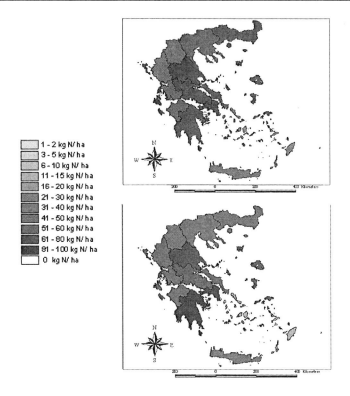

Figure 5. The Nitrogen surplus applied on agricultural land in 1993 (top) and in 1997 (bottom) in the 13 regions of Greece.

On the other hand Nitrogen surpluses remain relative stable in the regions of Thessaly, Attica and Peloponnese. In the region of Thessaly in particular, where agricultural production is very intensive, the absence of reduction of Nitrogen surpluses has led to the implementation of the Reduction of Nitrates Pollution program which started from 3 prefectures of the Region in 1996. According to a report of the EEA mentioned earlier [3] total nitrogen (N) mineral fertilizer consumption in EU-15 decreased by 12 % from 1990 to 2001 (3-year averages). During this period, consumption decreased in most of the EU-15 Member States, except in Spain and Ireland. The biggest decreases (more than 30 %) occurred in Denmark and Greece.

Examining the agricultural pressures data in Figure 6 we observe that the agricultural area in the years 1990 and 1997 has decreased in most regions of Greece. This trend is more noticeable in the central regions (Sterea Ellada) as well as the southern regions (Peloponnese, Crete). The same trend has been observed with agricultural sector production. The decrease corresponds with the diminishing significance of the agricultural sector on the GDP and the Greek economy during the resent years.

The results of the data mining exercise showed that the 3 larger financial programs were linked to agricultural production. These programs were the following:

- The Less Favoured Areas program;
- The Farming Investment Plans program and
- The New Farmers' program.

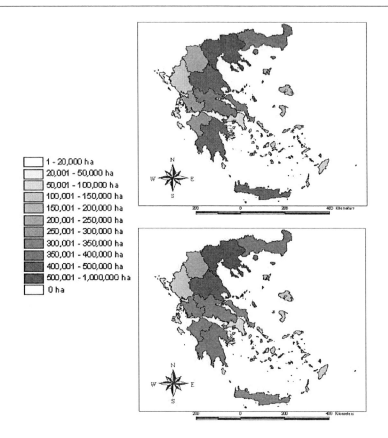

Figure 6. The Agricultural area in 1990 (top) and in 1997 (bottom) in the 13 regions of Greece.

All of the above programmes were funded in Greece by Measure 1.1 of the 2nd Community Support Framework (CSF) for Greece. The main field of environmental investment for the Farming Investment Plans was drop irrigation but this amounted only to 2% of the total investment plans for the whole of the country, as can be seen in Table 2.

On the other hand, no direct linkage with the agricultural production of the 3 Accompanying Measures of the EU Common Agricultural Policy (CAP) was observed. These Measures were the following:

- The Biological production program;
- The Rare Animal Breeds Preservation program and
- The Reduction of Nitrates Pollution program

CONCLUSION

The results indicate that the programs which were more directed towards environmental protection had a very limited impact on the agricultural sector. This is hardly surprising since the three environmental programs studied were designed with a very narrow scope regarding the size of the areas affected as well as funds provided.

As far as the accompanying measures of the CAP are concerned, for the biological production program it is noteworthy that although the program was applied in all the prefectures there is a disparity with regard to the funds allocated. Some prefectures such as Achaia, Halkidiki, Lakonia, Messinia and Iraklion seem to be absorbing most of the money from the beginning of the program in 1996 until 2002, other prefectures such as Aitoloakarnania and Viotia after a slow start in 1996 increase the pace over the years and some other prefectures especially in the regions of Eastern Macedonia –Thrace and Ipiros do not get off the ground at all.

As far as Biological production is concerned according to a report of the EEA already mentioned [3], in 2001 organic production accounted for 2 % of EU-15 total production of milk and beef, but less than 1 % of total production of cereals and potatoes. Organic food products accounted for 1–2 % of total EU-15 consumption, with organic beef and cereals having a higher share than milk and potatoes. According to the same report [3], farm incomes will be the decisive factor for farmers to convert to or remain in organic farming. In 2001 organic farms generated incomes comparable to those of conventional farms. In particular, returns to family and employed labor are similar, which is significant given the labor intensive character of organic farming. Therefore in order for a program like Biological production to have a significant impact on the environment other factors apart from the subsidies given must be improved, such as specialized market outlets and higher market prices for the products.

With regard to the Reduction of Nitrates Pollution program it had a highly localized application in the region of Thessali starting from 3 prefectures in 1996 extending to 5 in 1997 and slowing down in 1998. Finally the Rare Animal Breeds Preservation program was unevenly distributed mainly focused in the region of Thessaly.

As for the non-environmental programs of the CAP and in particular the Farm Investment Plans and the New Farmers programs although the results of the research indicate that they have a significant impact on the agricultural sector, the initially slow pace of their uptake in 1994 can be attributed to the difficulties involving the procedures needed for a applicant to enter the program. This could show a poor initial design of the programs which has been improved over time demonstrating increasing absorption of funds steadily until 1999.

Since the non-environmentally friendly programs were significantly larger in size and geographical scope, the important conclusion was, not surprisingly, that the dominant factors in regards to the impact of financial programs were the amounts of funds used and the scope of the program therefore in order to have some impact the environmentally friendly programs have to be large in size and geographical scope.

REFERENCES

[1]   EEA, *Environment in the European Union at the turn of the century*, Copenhagen (1999a).

[2]   EEA, *Environmental indicators: Typology and overview*, Copenhagen (1999b).

[3]   EEA, Agriculture and environment in EU-15− the IRENA indicator report, Copenhagen (2005).

[4] Ilias F. I., Ch. Lakis and A. Z. Papazafeiriou, *Journal of Biological Sciences* 11(6), 862-868 (2008).

[5] EEA, *Europe's water: An indicator-based assessment*, Topic report 1, Copenhagen (2003)

[6] Vorloou A.A., *Effects of the agricultural sector on the physico-chemistry and the ecosystem quality of inland waters* , PhD thesis, Ghent University, Belgium, 293 (2006).

[7] EEA, Calculation of nutrient surpluses from agricultural sources, Statistics spatialisation by means of CORINE land cover Application to the case of nitrogen, Copenhagen (2000)

PART II: POLITICAL ISSUES

In: Greece: Economics, Political and Social Issues
Editor: Panagiotis Liargovas

ISBN: 978-1-62100-944-3
© 2012 Nova Science Publishers, Inc.

Chapter 9

THE POLITICAL ECONOMY OF THE GREEK CRISIS: COLLECTIVE ACTION PERSPECTIVES

Panagiota Manoli[1]
University of the Aegean,
Department of Mediterranean Studies, Rhodes, Greece

ABSTRACT

This chapter looks at the political economy of the Greek crisis arguing that it exemplifies a collective action problem. Emphasis is placed on the domestic and European levels of policy as they have become increasingly interlinked especially since Greece's eurozone membership. Long before the outbreak of the 2008 global financial turmoil it was argued that the international financial architecture needed strengthening and better regulation. The 'domino' effect of the American mortgage crisis displayed the uncertainty over how the global financial market runs and the vulnerability of exposed deeply indebted, economies. As for Greece, at least three decades of undermining public interest and reckless borrowing led the country to an explosive combination of alarming levels of budget and current account deficit. The country's political system proved unable to implement much needed stabilization programs bringing the country's economy in a near collapse in spring 2010. The Greek crisis is definitely an economic and sovereign debt crisis in its expression but it has deeply intertwined political and social ingredients. At the European level, the crisis tested the EU's ability to take swift and efficient action to prevent contagion and hold the eurozone together.

INTRODUCTION

Economic liberalization and interdependence have changed the fundamentals of world's markets and finance undermining autonomous national economic and fiscal policy. Not only has the number of players increased but non-state, private actors have gained authoritative power over governments. Crisis management and collective action today is a qualitatively

---

[1] E-mail address: manoli@rhodes.aegean.gr

new game. This new era of global economy is best manifested by the catalyst role of credit rating agencies in the management of the current crisis. By their decisions credit rating agencies exerted power over states: constituting 'governance without government' raising issues of legality and sovereignty [1].

Global interdependencies and the fear of a 'domino effect' of the Greek crisis brought a large scale financial rescue package (the largest one ever offered to a national economy) organized by the International Monetary Fund (IMF), the European Central Bank (ECB) and the European Commission (EC), the so called troika, bringing Greece's affairs into sharp focus.

The still unfolding, while writing this article, Greek sovereign debt crisis has attracted a level of global attention[2] that seems disproportionate to the small size of the country and its economy which accounts for about 2 percent of European Union's gross domestic product (GDP). The reasons are not hard to see. The existence of huge budget and current account deficits coupled with high levels of government and external debt brought the Greek economy close to collapse and presented the eurozone with its first serious test bringing numerous broader policy implications due to its spill-over effects to other European economies in recession, including Portugal, Ireland, Spain and Italy. At the level of European governance, it has raised questions about imbalances within the eurozone which has a common monetary policy but diverse national fiscal policies. Trade, financial and monetary integration in Europe has made Greece a member of the eurozone[3] deeply interconnected with major economies and has probably given it a disproportional weight in the stability of a global currency; the Euro. Moreover, it carries a transatlantic effect which was presented in a Report for the US Congress drafted already in the outbreak of the crisis [3]. First, falling investor confidence in the Eurozone could further weaken the euro and, in turn, widen the US trade deficit. Second, given the strong economic ties between the United States and the EU, financial instability in the EU could impact the US economy. Third, 14.1 billion USD of Greece's debt is held by US creditors, and a Greek default would likely have ramifications for these creditors. Fourth, there are similarities between the financial situation in Greece and the United States, implying that Greece's current crisis foreshadows what the United States could face in the future (others argue that the analogy is weak, because the United States, unlike Greece, has a floating exchange rate and the dollar is a reserve currency). Fifth, the debate about imbalances within the Eurozone reiterates how, in a globalized economy, the economic policies of one country impact other countries' economies.

The Greek crisis, one that has been long anticipated but was actually triggered by the financial turmoil caused by the American mortgage crisis of 2008, has developed from a peripheral incident to a systemic one calling into question the stability of the euro area and the success of a decades old European integration project. It is indicative of the high interdependencies in modern economy; a mortgage crisis in the world's largest economy (US) turns into a global financial and economic crisis which pushes a small eurozone economy

---

[2] Between 5 October 2009 and 31 December 2010, The Wall Street Journal published 5504 articles on the Greek crisis, the Financial Times published 5467 articles and the German Handelsblatt published 2471 articles (see reference [2]).

[3] Euro membership was popular in Greece in late 1990s with polls suggesting that nearly two-thirds of the population were in favor of the move. Greece had hoped to join the euro with the first wave of member countries in January 1999, but failed to meet the so called Maastricht criteria of low inflation and government debt and deficits.

The Political Economy of the Greek Crisis 179

(Greece) close to default and this feeds back into the European financial system threatening a systemic crisis of the euro.

In an interdependent world where markets have been deregulated, a response to crisis would depend on the ability of actors to get their act together. Collective action is proven difficult not only due to the increase in the number of type of actors but also due to the new context (political, technological) in which it is embedded; this is manifested in the building up of a crisis and its subsequent management. This chapter is an attempt to look at the political economy of the Greek crisis and its collective action aspects. Emphasis is placed on the domestic and European levels of policy as they have become increasingly interlinked especially since Greece's eurozone membership.

THE UNFOLDING OF THE CRISIS: A SNAPSHOT

Capital flows masked the extent of the fiscal problem in Greece for several years. Greece had pulled itself together to hold a successful Olympic games in 2004, it was modernizing and, and was a member of the club of advanced European economies. The Greek merchant marine was a strong force internationally. Greek banks were in strong position, having expanded in Southeast Europe and earning large profits. Recent experience with large capital flows would continue to underpin the country's modernization. Successive governments pointed to the relatively high (4.3 percent average) growth rate during 1993-1998 to refute those who worried about the sustainability of the Greek public finances. Greece's growth performance would continue into the future, automatically lowering a debt ratio that hovered between 90 and 100 percent of GDP. Joining the core of Europe, it was expected that, corruption, low tax bases and other structural weaknesses would gradually be sorted out. History, however, did not take this turn. Instead, the global financial crisis exposed the vulnerabilities of Greece's public finances and the weaknesses of the eurozone. Strong growth performance had hidden an equally strong accumulation of debt.

The outbreak of the global financial crisis in fall 2008 led to a liquidity crisis for many countries, including several European countries, but the Greek government initially weathered the crisis relatively well and had been able to continue accessing new funds from international markets. Soon, however, the global recession resulting from the financial crisis put strain on Greece's government budget as spending continued to increase but tax revenues weakened.

An important revision of deficit and debt data was first undertaken in 2004 when Greece confessed to having been in breach of European Union budget deficit rules since 2000, leading to suggestions that it may not have been entitled to join the common currency after all. The Commission also noted that Greece's debt had been above 100 percent of GDP since before Greece joined the euro, and that the statistical revisions had pushed the debt number up as well.[4] The then finance minister George Alogoskoufis (conservative Nea Democratia party) blamed the previous government, referring to what he termed 'creative accounting', for systematically misleading EU statisticians saying that 'the problem would not be so serious if it had happened only one year' [5]. Later on in October 2009, and following parliamentary elections, the announcement by the newly elected socialist government that the projected

---

[4] It has been reported that Greek governments with the help of financial institutions including Goldman Sachs used complex financial instruments to conceal the true level of Greece's debt (see reference [4]).

budget deficit for 2009 was 12.7 percent of GDP (rather than the 6.7 percent projection) alarmed Brussels. Although one can have doubts about how truly unexpected were the revelations of the Greek authorities for the EU officials, the key issue is that 'the systemic implications of the revelations were ignored – the fears of contagion were underplayed and the prevailing feeling was that the correct way to deal with the situation was to let Greece "swing in the wind" . These large differences between the first releases and the actual budget deficits critically compromised the credibility of Greece as a reliable partner in European financial affairs. The Greek prime minister George Papandreou referred to the National Statistical Service of Greece as a 'joke' [6] and a condition of the Greek bail out was that the national statistical service should be made fully independent as it happened.

In April 2010, Eurostat estimated Greece's deficit to be even higher at 13.6 percent of GDP. Increasingly investors were concerned about Greece's ability to repay its maturing debt obligations, estimated at 54 billion Euro (72.1 billion USD) for 2010. Further revelations regarding the country's fiscal health led the three ratings agencies (Moody's, Standard and Poor's and Fitch) to downgrade Greek debt to 'junk' status. Consequently, the spread on long-term government interest rates with Germany which had started rising more than in the rest of the euroarea since end 2008 reached record high. On 23 April 2010 the Greek government formally submitted a request for financial assistance from other European countries and the IMF to help cover its debt obligations. A massive bailout mechanism of 110 billion Euro to rescue Greece was approved on 11 May 2010 followed by austerity measures —amidst domestic protests —aiming at bringing down the country's budget deficit to less than 3 percent by 2012 and avoiding a sovereign default. By 2011 government debt was 327 billion Euro constituting close to 140 percent of the economy and estimated to rise to 340 billion Euro in 2012 constituting 159 percent of the economy. George Papandreou and several EU leaders indicated they would have favored a Europe only solution, but Germany wanted IMF participation, fearing it would end up footing the whole bill. The IMF's presence had also a political rationale, namely, to diffuse responsibility and deflect some blame for the impending pain away from Europe's 'benevolent' governments to the Washington-based 'villain' [7]. Arghyrou and Tsoukalas [8] however argue that the involvement of an external institution like the IMF in EU affairs could most probably widen market uncertainty over possible coordination failures between the EU and the IMF policy-makers and could fail to stabilize market expectations on a credible resolution of the Greek crisis.

The failure, however, of the agreed consolidation plan with the 'troika' due to among others its slow or partial implementation led at the beginning of 2011 to a persistent discussion about the renegotiation of the terms of the loan and a new midterm austerity program was approved by the Greek parliament in June 2011. Previously, the European leaders had approved a three-year extension of Greece's current bail-out loan to 2021, as well as an interest-rate cut of one percentage point. Continued sovereign debt crisis in several European countries and speculation on the debt serving led to a eurozone agreement on a new system for capital assess from the EFSF and a new program for Greece in July 2011 as presented in the next section.

The root cause of Greece's problems is a long period of fiscal indiscipline that started in the 1980s. Much of the increase in public debt (and the general government deficit) is attributed to a growing but inefficient public sector, industrial subsidies, social benefits, and increasing debt service payments. By 2009, approximately 850,000 people were employed in the public sector in a country of hardly 11 million. Most of Greece's biggest companies are either state run or state managed. According to figures available annually in the *Factbook* of the Organization for Economic Cooperation and Development (OECD), the budget deficit increased from less than 3 percent in 1981, the year Greece joined the European Community, to 11 percent in 1991. While public debt rose from roughly 30 percent of gross domestic product (GDP) to 82.2 percent in 1991. Since Greece joined the euro in 2001, its budget deficit has averaged 6 percent of GDP annually, double the supposed ceiling set down by the Maastricht Treaty and the primary budget balance moved from a surplus of 1.5 percent of GDP in 2001 to a deficit of over 8 percent of GDP in 2009. Greece's reliance on external financing for funding its double deficits (budget and current account deficits) left its economy vulnerable to shifts in investor confidence and with a chronically high external debt (115 percent of GDP in 2009). During periods in which borrowing was perceived to be cheap, especially after Greece's entry into the European Monetary Union (EMU), there was no mechanism to stop debt from accumulating; it was during such periods that the culture of 'soft budget constraints' was legitimized as 'rational' response to the new opportunities offered by the low interest rates and high growth environment [9].

WHY A COLLECTIVE ACTION PROBLEM?

The political economy of the Greek public debt crisis is largely a story of collective action problems resulting from powerful special interest groups and governance failure. A collective action problem is defined as a 'choice' problem where everyone who is part of a given group has a choice between two alternatives; if everyone involved chooses the alternative act that is individualistically rational (IR), the outcome will be worse for everyone involved, in their own estimation, than it would be if they were all to choose the other alternative (i.e., than it would be if they were all to choose the alternative that is not IR). Collective action problems emerge when strategic actors do not fully internalize the effects of their actions on others. These individual and policy externalities cause politico-economic outcomes to be inefficient from the domestic and the international community's points of view. According to Mancur Olson [10] individuals in any group attempting collective action will have incentives to 'free ride' on the efforts of others if the group is working to provide public goods. He also argues that some (smaller) actors are able to have a larger influence on policy than others as large groups are less able to act in their common interest than small ones. Poorer actors will usually have little choice but to opt for the free rider strategy, i.e. they will attempt to benefit from the public good without contributing to its provision. These actors and policy externalities cause politico-economic outcomes to be inefficient from the domestic and the international community's points of view. Yet, trust and expectations of others' attitude play a critical role in the choices made by agents in dilemmas of collective action [11]. For cooperation, it is necessary not only to trust others, but also to believe that one is trusted by others [12]. The logic of reciprocity suggests that it makes sense to nourish trust than alter material payoffs [13].

The Greek crisis can be viewed as a collective action problem in three respects. First, as the outcome of powerful interest groups pursuing their narrow (private) interests whose interlink to party elites and infiltration to public administration has undermined the provision of public goods and held up stabilization programs. Second, the inability of the political system to reach a minimum of consensus for much needed reforms to overcome the crisis is another expression of the failure of collective action at the domestic level. Third, the delayed European response and the lack of a coordinated management of the euro crisis for a long period since its eruption pointed to the differences among Europeans over Europe's economic governance, raised issues of trust, credibility and national sovereignty inflating problems of common stand.

Greece's most significant domestic collective action problem is undoubtedly the failure of the political system to stem the accumulation of public debt. Now far-sighted leadership ensured that Greece's politics and economics were bound to the European project since the early 1980s. Despite this, the Greek political system failed to ensure sustainability of public debt.

The impressive accumulation of Greek public debt reflects the failure of economic policy reform under the pressure of powerful interest groups (especially trade unionists in publicly owned enterprises) pursuing their narrow interests. Their political relationship with successive incumbents – the well known clientelistic model of political relationships — trumped concern over the general public's interest and caused a spending, deficit, and debt biases.

The unwillingness of the Greek policy makers to undertake expenditure cuts, even amidst the crisis, reflects the lower political cost of raising tax revenue compared to expenditure cuts.

Another impediment to collective action is weak norms of trust and reciprocity in modern Greek economy and society. This makes the success of economic reforms a much more complicated matter. Social capital and trust (the latter being the most important element of social capital) are highly relevant to public policy due to their effects on resolving problems of collective action such as the provision of various forms of public goods [14]. They are linked to the volatility and hence uncertainty of modern economic and institutional settings and are seen as the crucial conceptual mechanism to resolve this uncertainty by shaping the relations between partners and facilitating collective action: 'trust, the mutual confidence that no party to an exchange will exploit the others' vulnerability, is today widely regarded as a precondition for competitive success' as well as, for better public policy outcomes through improving the level of institutional performance.

At the European level, common institutions and agreements (such as the European Stability Pact) designed to ensure that free riding is punished and provide incentives to weak states to follow sound policies did not prove adequate to the task as discussed later on in the text. During and after the eruption of the crisis, negotiations among Eurozone members (especially in the first quarter 2010) regarding actions to contain the crisis revealed a clear split and fear of cost of policy choice as well as lack of mutual trust among European partners.

The same is true of international institutions, such as the IMF, that provide multilateral and bilateral economic surveillance. Despite the many warnings, these institutions did not prove effective in fending the crisis and alleviating its effects. Long before the outbreak of the 2008 global financial crisis, there has been a steady stream of proposals for strengthening the international financial architecture as a precondition for a more efficient prevention and handling of financial crises. Susan Strange in Casino Capitalism[15] was warning that '[m]ismanagement of money and credit was more dangerous that protectionism in trade policy'.

WHY REFORMS FAIL? THE DOMESTIC POLITICAL ECONOMY

It has been empirically supported that powerful special interest groups impede growth and reforms [16]. In Greek politics and economics alike, collective action problems manifested themselves in vigorous interest group (ranging from, lawyers, and truckers to loaders and unloaders in ports and public markets as well as trade unionists in publicly owned enterprises) competition for budget resources. Successive Greek governments have failed to reign and reverse the process of debt accumulation while public interest has been captured by party-political and private interests.

As Lyberaki and Tsakalotos [17] have shown in their research concerning two reform initiatives in Greece in the 1980s and 1990s, state officials and sectional interest groups create such distortion and uncertainty with regards to the allocation of the costs and benefits of a certain reform policy, that a majority can oppose it even if it will benefit all. The first reform effort promoted by the Greek socialist party, PASOK, in the 1980s was crucially undermined by the role of clientelistic practices in the appointment of personnel and in the use of the new institutions to consolidate its social and electoral base, thus reproducing the practices of the existing public administration. The second reform effort by the conservative Nea Democratia in the early 1990s was hardly any more effective, as it failed to gain support, not only from public sector employees (segments of which might be considered extensions of the prior protectionist regime), but also from the Federation of Greek Industries, which although could have been regarded as a natural ally of pro-market reform, it never became a major pro-privatization lobby. Powerful economic interests against reform included public sector suppliers and smaller private companies that feared competition.

Why are interest groups so powerful (in a democracy)? This is well known a story of imperfect information and underdeveloped good interest groups and other institutions that are unable to provide the checks and balances. In the Greek case, the failure of the political system 'which allocates both legislative and executive power to a mandate holder who essentially governs unchecked until the next election', does not allow voters to express their preferences [18]. Mandate holders (unofficially controlled by interest groups) favor the status quo, while having the power to promote any legislative and executive initiative without any checks and balances [19]. Media play a crucial role in the game of imperfect information, collaborating with interest groups and politicians and operating in an opaque and unchecked legal and institutional framework. The systematic removal of accountability and transparency from the activities of the legislature, executive, and judiciary strengthen the ability of the media to an unprecedented extent.

Experts on Greek politics and society have long referred to the 'free rider' individualism described as 'anomie' that transcends society and political system which is opposed to 'normative collective rationalities of the West' [20]. Sotiropoulos and others have argued that Greece (like Italy) has excelled in 'partitocrazia' or 'bureaucratic clientelism' whereas its European partners like France and Germany have their states run by bureaucracies strong enough to resist party intervention [21]. Consequently, political culture in modern Greece especially in the post-authoritarianism period, i.e. since 1974 has shown deep-rooted mistrust of public institutions and the state especially with regard to the latter's regulatory and distributive roles ([22][23][24]) alongside rent-seeking behavior with sectoral interests competing for favors, resources and subsidies [25]. Public policy has thus been undermined by relatively small but strong interest groups based on a variety of selective incentives whose rent-seeking behavior puts important limitations to the 'exit' and 'voice' options of the actors, thus inhibiting learning and policy change in public policy areas [26]. The country's membership in the European Union (EU) in 1981 and its subsequent Europeanization has spurred a literature on the rationality and alignment of public sphere and institutions in Greece with the European ones [27][28]. Analysts saw a window of opportunity for Greece to gradually become a more 'consensual partner' [29] and build a 'stabilization state' at home (see reference [25]). EMU membership was anticipated to coerce Greece's public finance the immediate entry into the European monetary system would bring external disciple and would alter Greek public and private behaviors in the direction of macroeconomic balance [30]. This however did not happen.

The most straightforward and simple answer to why reforms have failed in Greece is due to the 'partitocrazia' rather than a party based democracy which has drained the country from any aspects of institutional autonomy and has generated clientelistic acquired rights ('kektimena'). Mouzelis [31] points to three ways in which reform is obstructed: i) through 'targets transfer' which might be an endemic feature of parliamentary democracies but becomes dangerous in 'partitocrazia' systems, ii) discontinuity in administration whereas each ministerial reshuffling brings fundamental changes in the administration (including new bureaucracy and legislation) obstructing any continuity, and iii) absence of any extra-parliamentary control whereas political elites object any control or limitation on party authoritative power. Describing the lack of reforms in Greece, Kollintzas [32] has eloquently argued that:

> '... the interests of those within the system and those outside the system are contradictory. In the inevitable battle between the two, those within the system, almost always, win. The main reason for this is that even if the rent seeking behavior of the "insiders" is apparent to the "outsiders", the latter do not react to it, as their behavior is based on the logic of "Whatever is done will be done without me. So, why take the cost of opposing any given rent seeking?" Thus, it is those forces of "inertia of status quo" that prevail and not realized the useful reforms. Even more important ... is the opposite where a government tries to carry out a useful reform to those outside the system and the community as a whole, afflicting the interests of those within the system (e.g. privatization or change in a public utility).'

Indicative is the case of pension reform in Greece. As Featherston [33] has argued the reform efforts were incremental, rather than radical, following a path dependence, with pension regimes creating their own blocking constituencies. Corporatist politics were proved more relevant than the electoral arena per se and support (tacit or otherwise) coalitions were crucial to the feasibility of reform. Government's ability to choose the social model has been widely constrained by entrenched privileges domestically than market pressures (from the EU). The constraints on the reform process identified by Featherston questioned the nature of authority, legitimacy and participation in the Greek system:

> '...the EU stimulus to reform complemented a set of domestic pressures. However, the domestic system of interest mediation has largely thwarted reform. The reform process is marked by a strong configuration of institutional conditions undermining the will and capability to adapt. Negotiation reflects a game of "non-cooperation", with those currently

privileged fearing zero-sum outcomes and constituting powerful veto-players. Strategies of concertation have proved unsustainable, whilst unilateral approaches by government have failed to build coalitions and offer sufficient incentives. An acute problem of governance prevails, threatening Greek interests in the EU and the Union's ability to co-ordinate economic reform across an increasingly diverse membership'.

The excessive regulation of markets, administrative burdens and vague rules in Greece, paired with lack of accountability and enforcement, has meant that the bureaucracy is easily penetrated by various interest groups contributing to the creation of rents. Bureaucrats typically have a strong bargaining position taking advantage of the information they have regarding the implementation of public policies. EMU accession did not halt rent-seeking, rather the marked growth of the prior to the crisis years made the extraction of rents even more lucrative on the face on weak domestic institutions, credit growth and EU inflows financing consumption. From the point of view of each group, it is rational to lobby for budget transfers to its members. A euro of transfers obtained by the interest group is financed by taxes or borrowing spread over the entire country—current and future generations of tax payers bear the burden. Rational groups will spare no effort, money, and other resources (including strikes, closing highways and ports, and other actions costly to other groups in society) to secure such transfers. The resulting Nash equilibrium (i.e. a set of strategy choices where no player benefits by changing his/her strategy while the other players keep their own strategy unchanged) will be inefficient.

There is a second and related aspect of the domestic collective action problem. Taxpayers, who fund the government, do not internalize the connection between taxes paid and government services received, which strengthens incentives to not pay taxes and leads to narrow tax bases and high tax rates for those unlucky enough to be under the tax net. While, because the average Greek voter does not pay any income tax, (s)he regards the expansion of government as a "free good" (see reference [18]). According to OECD [34], the efficiency of tax collection in Greece in 2006 was the lowest among the eurozone countries. Analysts [35] have pointed out that taxes evasion is part of a broader culture of bribery and corruption that is rooted to the historical mistrust between the Greek state and its citizens. While recent steps to improve tax collection through the strengthening of tax administration are welcome, tax evasion remains widespread, especially among the self-employed. This reflects weak collection procedures, a large informal sector, frequent tax amnesties and a complex tax system . Various studies, including a recent one by the Federation of Greek Industries, have estimated that the government may be losing as much as 30 billion USD a year to tax evasion — a figure that would have gone a long way to solving its debt problems [36]. That accounts for close to 14.6 percent of the GDP and indicates that approximately 30 percent of revenues go uncollected. A European Union report on Greece's tax shortfalls [37] found that between 2000 and 2007, the country's average growth in nominal gross domestic product was 8.25 percent. Its taxes however grew at just 7 per cent. This is in contrast with other euro area members with similar economic growth, which recorded tax bonuses well beyond what standard elasticities justified over the same period. According to the same EU Report on Greece's tax revenues, their shortfalls in Greece is not due to cyclical factors but appears to be due to the negative effect of factors included in the residual of the decomposition, in particular, the performance of tax administration and enforcement .Today, Greece's extended recession has refueled tax evasion, with a sharp rise in fuel smuggling and fraudulent accounting by companies that under-report exports and fake transfers of funds to subsidiaries abroad. Yet the government lacks broad-based political support for modernizing the tax system. George Papaconstantinou, former finance minister, had to withdraw an EU and IMF backed measure of setting up special courts to handle tax disputes because of fierce opposition from members of the governing (socialist) party. As a result of poor tax collection, revenues rose only 5.5 percent last year against an initial target of 13.8 percent, in spite of two increases in value added tax [38]. Moutos and Tsitsikas (see reference [9]) referring to the problem of tax evasion claim that:

> ... [A] crucial factor in this respect, and which has been steadily eroding the foundations of Greek society and will impact on the resolution of the current fiscal crisis, is the interdependence between the tax burden, public good provision, tax compliance, and sectoral allocation of economic activity. The rise of budget deficits during the last three decades reflect, in addition to outright corruption, the increasing inability of the public sector to deliver on the public goods and services which higher-taxed citizens (i.e., the law-abiding ones who do not evade on their taxes and thus face tax burdens significantly higher than the economy-wide average) have every right to expect in return. This has created a further "legitimization" of tax evasion as more citizens consider that there has been a "breach of contract" with the state.

One of the most important challenges that Greek tax system confronts is widespread corruption that has shuttered the social and political life. In March 2011, Transparency International - Greece (TI-Greece) published its 2010 Annual Survey on Corruption in Greece covering the period between July and December 2010. It estimated that bribery cost Greece 632 million Euro in 2010 (837 million USD). Although down from a high of 787 million Euro (1.09 billion USD) in 2009, this was mainly due to a reflection of the effects of the financial crisis and the shrinking size of the Greek economy, as well as government efforts to reduce opportunities for corruption. The overall picture, taken over the four years since the survey started in 2007, is more troubling: on average more than one in ten people report having to pay a bribe for some kind of service, predominantly to public sector institutions. Lengthy proceedings and short statutes of limitations pose significant problems for prosecuting corruption in Greece. It is particularly striking that statutes of limitations for parliamentarians and ministers are shorter than for regular citizens. Greeks named political parties as the institution they perceived to be the most corrupt.

The Greek system for many years, if not decades, failed to prosecute corruption and tax avoidance. The absence of institutions to detect and punish cheating has led to non compliance with law and the explicit or implicit social contract. The rule of law in Greece has been associated with the rule of powerful politicians, wealthy industrialists and their promoters in the media.

As Guardian put it '[i]f "anomie" exists in Greece today, it is found in the separation between law and democracy and the destruction of any sense of the common good. Disobedience is a moral and civic response to governmental "anomie". It is what preserves democracy' [39]. The last expression of this disobedience is the 'won't pay' movement.

The result of this infiltration by private (and party) interests has been a gradual loss of bureaucratic autonomy to pursue the public interest. The web of relationships developed between private interests and the dominant political parties (PASOK and Nea Democratia) has eroded both the efficacy of public administration and the dynamism of the private sector as incumbent firms and public sector functionaries have been using their power to prevent fair competition and reform. Taken together, the high demand for transfers by interest groups and low capacity to tax led to large budget deficits which have in turn driven Greece's foreign indebtedness to alarming levels, necessitating the current bailout by the EU, ECB, and IMF.

Although the elites, and most of the Greek population are in favor of the bailout (though not of the austerity measures), it would not be a surprise if the elites switched in favor of default later, in case they thought that their power to shape policy in Greece could be compromised by policy proposals of the outside actors which went beyond the usual austerity measures. Actually (the lack of) political consensus, not to mention of social consensus, has become a central issue for the success of the reform program. Of course, as anticipated, the austerity measures that followed the bailout of March 2010 were particularly unpopular with the trade unions. Even though the public sector is the most serious patient, Spyros Papaspyros, the head of the country's union of public sector employees (ADEDY), proclaimed that 'We are not going to become sacrificial victims, regardless of the struggle to save the country' [40]. Though at the initial stage of the crisis there was some support for reform among ordinary Greeks, this has not been strong among party leaders. Leaders from all political spectrum have characterized as a mistake the agreed memorandum with the EU-IMF, demanding renegotiation of its terms despite the persistent demand by the 'troika' and the EU in particular for consensus among major political parties for the success of the reform and austerity measures. The German Chancellor, Angela Merkel, has urged the Greek opposition to 'live up to its historic responsibility', stressing that cross-party support had been achieved in the two other bailed-out eurozone members, Portugal and Ireland. '[I] couldn't participate in the discussions [at the EPP]. Mr Samaras should be happy about that, because I would have otherwise vehemently called on him to abandon his negative stance,' said Luxembourg Prime Minister Jean-Claude Juncker, who chairs the Eurogroup panel of eurozone finance ministers. Especially, the government's plan to raise 50 billion Euro from privatization sales in order to write down part of the country's large public debt triggered fierce opposition with both conservative and leftwing parties accusing the government of yielding to pressure from its creditors to 'sell the family silver' [41].

EUROPEAN COLLECTIVE ACTION PROBLEMS

Collective action problems at the European and global levels complete the picture. Theoretically, EMU prequalification requirements and EU treaty safety mechanisms ought to have ruled out the emergence of unsustainable debts in Greece and other euro area countries. The convergence criteria and strict limits on debts and deficits embodied in the Maastricht treaty (1992) are one such mechanism. The Maastricht treaty created the institutional framework for policy coordination consisting of a triad; an independent European Central Bank (ECB), the Excessive Deficit Procedure (EDP) and multilateral surveillance through the Broad Economic Policy Guidelines (BEPG). The institutional developments in economic policy-making reflected the recognition that 'a proper functioning of EMU requires a well developed coordination framework' while [42]:

> '... the rationale for economic policy co-ordination rests on the following grounds. Co-ordination is needed to take account of direct cross-border spillovers of national policies on

neighbouring countries. In addition, euro-area participants can also be affected indirectly by national policy actions. The average inflation rate and the exchange rate have become common goods. Thus, a national policy action that affects these variables can in turn impact the ECB policy decision on interest rates or the ECOFIN Council's judgment on exchange rates. Moreover, co-ordination should help countering temptation to resort to free-rider behaviour on the part of the Member States. Finally, besides economic arguments, co-ordination can also play a useful role from a political-economy viewpoint by helping to implement unpopular but necessary policy actions at national level'.

Nevertheless, the various coordination mechanisms and schemes that evolved did not prove sufficient for the tasks they were meant to accomplish. The Stability and Growth Pact (SGP) which was designed to coordinate national fiscal policies was another mechanism created but it was based on the supposition that the main threat to the EMU is irresponsible behavior by member state governments only; the consequences of private excessive borrowing and lending, and accompanying moral hazard and deficient corporate governance, were ignored. The annual national economic convergence programs and peer review mechanisms of the EU were to serve as warning signals and prompt corrective action but failed to do so. International surveillance of national economic policies by the IMF ought to have played a similar role.

Free rider problems have long existed at the European level. Forbearance to members of the club was extensive. Despite protestations to the contrary, many members of the euro club employed accounting and statistical gimmicks at critical moments. Questionable valuation of national gold reserves and booking as revenues of debts backed by future streams of revenues—which were allowed by Eurostat—are but two examples. Sanctions of members who violated fiscal rules were not always strictly enforced. Other weaknesses can be found in vague language—no strict timetable for lowering debt levels to 60 percent of GDP existed. Of the 27 EU member states, 20 currently exceed the deficit ceiling set out in the Stability and Growth Pact. Since 2003, more than thirty excessive deficit procedures have been undertaken but the EU has never imposed a financial sanction against any member state for violating the deficit limit. Capital markets however stepped in to 'impose' the necessary hard budget constraints on exposed governments. Such violations or ambiguities are much more than technical curiosa, especially when they are employed by the dominant members of the club. They weaken the peer review mechanism and signal to weak states that they can follow suit. Even as extensive forbearance was exercised, there was a sense that moral suasion would be a good enough substitute for rigorous monitoring of member states' public finances. The complacency was generalized. The international conjuncture also helped. The decade before the crisis was an era of low global interest rates, the result of a savings glut in developing countries attempting to build cushions of international reserves after their own crisis in the late 1990s, and ample levels of global liquidity supplied by central banks. Cheap capital flowed to supposedly safe peripheral European countries, leading to consumption and investment booms. The sense of complacency was such that led most European politicians and economists to discount the birth defects of the euro expounded by many economists. These economists (Feldstein, Krugman) pointed out that the euro area did not satisfy the criteria of a classical optimum currency area (OCA). Labor outflows—the safety valves for regions of an OCA buffeted by asymmetric real shocks—are not extensive in the euro area. A single European Treasury does not either exist to provide fiscal transfers to regions hit by shocks.

The reduction in transaction costs facilitated by a common currency in Europe would be large enough to spur trade and growth and facilitate real convergence. Given the belief in the inevitability of the political union in Europe, large external imbalances reflecting current account deficits in European periphery and surpluses in the European north, would be as meaningless as the discussion of such imbalances between states in a real federation. This vision, however, to turn into reality will require hard work and time to complete the European architecture.

The financial crisis has laid bare three basic flaws in Europe's single currency project [43]. First, it is the weakness in the enforcement mechanisms for fiscal discipline among eurozone members. As early as 2003, France and Germany, themselves transgressors, agreed that the pact's strictures need not apply to them undermining fiscal credibility and eurozone governance and pointing to a two-tier Europe with one law applying to the big countries and another for the small. Second, the conceit that there could be no bail-out mechanism for fiscal delinquents was made obsolete by events. A collective rescue had to be mounted or else a Greek default would put the euro at risk. After a fierce bargaining in April and May 2010 it ended in a new EU borrowing facility as well as bilateral financial aid to complement the IMF package. Still however, the mechanism had to be reinforced in July 2011. Third, it revealed the lack of effectiveness of the much-vaunted peer review process and collective surveillance by the European Commission.

THE EUROPEAN ACT AND POLICY REFORM

The response to the Greek crisis took time to advance and it was a Brussels design. Policy reform and stabilization of the Greek economy seemed to be unattainable without external enforcement mechanisms. How policy reform was tunneled?

It has been argued [44] that the process leading to stabilization can be described as a war of attrition between different socioeconomic groups with conflicting distributional objectives; stabilizations occur when a political consolidation leads to a resolution of the distributional conflict. When socioeconomic groups perceive the possibility of shifting the burden of fiscal change, elsewhere, each group may attempt to wait the others out. This war of attrition ends when certain groups 'concede', via legislative agreement, electoral outcomes, or ceding power of decree to policymakers, and allow their political opponents to decide on the allocation of the burden of the fiscal adjustment. Foreign interventions or rescue agreements act as game changers that they may alter agents' behavior and lead to rapid concession by one side. That has been the role played by Berlin in the eurozone context as well as of other European institutions and the IMF. European urge was a catalyst for the Greek government to pass a five-year austerity bill — a precondition of additional loans from the EU and IMF — in parliament in the end of June 2011 against a backdrop of massive public opposition. The parliament passed the austerity package by a slim majority, with 155 members of parliament voting in favour, 138 against and five abstentions. Prime Minister Papandreou had previously attempted to form a government of 'national unity' or 'national salvation' which failed, meeting high demands by the main opposition party, Nea Democratia, and it was undermined by lack of support within his own ruling party. Papandreou proceeded to a largely cosmetic cabinet reshuffle, strengthening the position of his internal party rivals by including them in the government and 'sacrificing' his previous finance minister, the unpopular technocrat George Papaconstantinou, in a bid to smooth the passage of the austerity plan.

The EU's response to the financial crisis took time to advance. Since the fall of 2008, the EU has moved to address the long-term needs of the financial system, however, deep differences among EU members were exposed over the most effective policy course to pursue to address the causes and effects of the financial and economic crises. European governments have acted both independently and in concert through the EU, reflecting the dual nature of the EU system.

On May 9, 2010, the Economic and Financial Affairs Council (ECOFIN) of the European Union, in response to the financial crisis unfolding in Greece and worrying over the financial stability in the eurozone, endorsed a comprehensive set of temporary, emergency measures. The rescue plan created over the weekend of 8 – 9 May included both the EFSM and EFSF and the ECB's securities market program. A key measure was the establishment of a European Financial Stabilization Mechanism (EFSM), with a volume of 60 billion euro, composed of loan guarantees and euro bonds, to protect euro zone members from market speculation and rescue them in future crises. The mechanism is part of a comprehensive package of measures to redress the financial situation in Europe. According to the regulation, member states in difficulties caused by exceptional circumstances — e.g. a serious deterioration in the international economic and financial environment — beyond their control may ask for financial assistance from the mechanism. Its activation will be subject to strong conditionality to preserve the sustainability of public finances of the beneficiary member state and enable it to regain its capacity to finance itself on the financial markets. Loans will be managed by the European Central Bank. The European Financial Stability Facility (EFSF) was also established as a special purpose vehicle set up to make loans to euro area countries, other than Greece, up to an amount of 440 billion euro, supplemented with a 250 billion euro IMF commitment. These support measures will be replaced by the permanent European Stability Mechanism (ESM) in 2013. In an effort to reinforce supranational monetary stability and promote monitoring, and transparency, the European Commission [45] released its proposals in May 2010 envisaging a budgetary and macroeconomic surveillance framework and fines for those partners that do not comply with the regulations. A complementary agenda with additional reforms (called the Euro Plus Pact) was endorsed in March 2011 among euro area Member States, as well as six non eurozone countries that have chosen to sign up: Bulgaria, Denmark, Latvia, Lithuania, Poland and Romania. It focuses on four areas: competitiveness, employment, sustainability of public finances and reinforcing financial stability.

Continued speculation against the euro and continuing sovereign debt crisis in several European countries was the catalyst for the EU to introduce a new support mechanism for vulnerable economies as a way to shield the eurozone from similar crises in the future leading to the adoption of a new bailout programme worth of 109 billion Euro for Greece in July 2011. On a eurozone Summit on 21 July, the eurozone heads of government agreed upon a new system for access to capital from the EFSF without having to go back repeatedly to the EU Council of Ministers. The maturity on all EFSF credit has been increased from 7.5 years to as much as 40 years, while the cost of that credit will be cut to about 3.5 per cent. All outstanding debts, including the previous EFSF programs, can be reworked under the new rules. The EFSF has been granted the ability to participate directly in the bond market by buying the government debt of states that cannot find anyone else interested, or even act preemptively should future crises threaten, without needing to first negotiate a bailout program. The EFSF can even extend credit to states that were considering internal bailouts of their banking systems. It is a massive debt consolidation program for both private and public sectors. The decision-making occurs within the fund, not at the EU institutional level. Essentially, this agreement removes any potential cap on the amount of money that the EFSF can raise, eliminating concerns that the fund is insufficiently stocked. Technically, the fund is still operating with a 440 billion euro ceiling, but now that the Germans have fully committed themselves, that number is a mere technicality [46].

The crisis has struck Europe especially hard because it has coincided with a period of weak political leadership which has made crisis management even harder. The European leaders are faced with what Dani Rodrik [47] has described as the 'political trilemma' of the world economy. The three nodes of this trilemma are international economic integration, the nation-state, and mass politics. He uses the term 'nation-state' to refer to territorial-jurisdictional entities with independent powers of making and administering the law. The term 'mass politics' refers to political systems where: a) the franchise is unrestricted; b) there is a high degree of political mobilization; and c) political institutions are responsive to mobilized groups. In the handling of the current crisis, worries about legitimacy (of a Eurozone rescue of Greece, in the context of the so-called 'no bailout clause' of the Maastricht Treaty) have given way to concerns over national sovereignty. The debates brought back two competing visions of Europe. The first vision of an intergovernmental EU sees Europe as a community of sovereign states, with diverse preferences, domestic priorities, and international constraints. In such a community being bound together by a common currency reduces the transaction costs of cooperation. The second vision born by neo-functionalists sees the EU as transcending monetary union, calling for closer political union and a European economic governance to safeguard also monetary stability. Solidarity and further institutionalization of the European economic governance are given priority to narrowly defined, national preferences. The actual EU response to the crisis reflects elements from both visions. Differences between the two centers of gravity in the EU, namely France and Germany on Europe's vision were also exposed during the crisis management. France has traditionally supported European Union institutions and currently advocates a form of "European economic governance," while federal Germany has become much less willing to subordinate national interests to European ones and has been a strong defender of national sovereignty, especially over budgets. In a recent speech in Bruges, Merkel spoke of the need to move away from 'the community method,' led by the European Union's Commission, to what she called 'the union method,' in which the nation-states effectively take the lead in cooperating with the Commission and other EU institutions [48].

Analysts have highlighted the prolonged stand-off over a rescue plan for Greece and the corresponding risk of a sovereign default spreading to Portugal, Spain, Ireland and even to Italy. This in turn exposed profound weaknesses in the governance of the eurozone and sharp divisions between France and Germany reflecting ideological differences and domestic concerns questioning fiscal solidarity. German demands focused on enforcing fiscal discipline, even through automatic fines to member states. Guido Westerwelle, Germany's foreign minister argued that it would be intolerable to 'throw German and EU money out of the window and thereby reduce the pressure on Greece to reform' [49] raising the fear of moral hazard and an ethical dilemma; helping member countries in need encourages the same profligate behavior that one is trying to discourage, while, declining to help exacerbates the magnitude of the problem, raising the rescue cost, creating political conflict. Accordingly, because it is a 'no transfers' community of sovereign states, transferring public funds from those who obeyed the rules to those who did not 'would create hostility toward Brussels and between euro area countries'[50]. Politicians in Germany have been reluctant to rescue Greece, partly because such a move would be deeply unpopular after Germans have undergone reforms in recent years to keep their budget deficit under control. Angela Merkel has opposed any notion of creating eurobonds — that would link different countries together and would make borrowing cheaper for countries with shaky finances but more expensive for those with a top rating such as Germany while it would spread debt. Local elections in May 2010 in the state of North Rhine-Westphalia played significant role in German Chancellor Angela Merkel's resistance to emergency loans. But German reluctance is not solely to blame for the delay of the European response to the crisis; the length and bitterness of the negotiations has shed light on differing national interests within the EU block European leaders have been at odds with one another and with the ECB over demands by Germany and Finland that private investors bear some of the burden of a new Greek bailout, over banks' taxation (French proposal), over fiscal discipline and the necessity of sanctions, over the issuing of eurobonds and many other aspects of Europe's financial reconstructing.

The EU's indecisiveness in dealing with the crisis reveals the underlying problem of individual, national preferences and institutional adolescence. Zachariadis claims that the latter is very important today because 'treaty-fatigue precludes institutional innovation when it is needed the most' (see reference [7]).

CONCLUSION

The problems of supervision, governance and collective action are not confined only to the Greek case and the Eurozone. Some sort of governance of global financial markets was proposed in the last G-20 meeting in London on 2 April 2009 where German Chancellor Merkel spoke on behalf of all of the leaders in favor of adopting global regulations for financial markets and hedge funds, saying that'[a]ll financial markets, products, and participants, including hedge funds and other private pools of capital which may pose a systemic risk must be subjected to appropriate oversight or regulation' [51]. Such statements signify the new context within which crises erupt and are managed and the magnitude of the disorder in global finance. In the Greek case, though the crisis was triggered externally (by the global financial turmoil), its grounds were to be found in a failing domestic governance while it was further exaggerated by the inability of Europe to respond promptly.

This chapter looked at the political economy of the Greek crisis using insights from the discussion on collective action problems to shed light on the (domestic) forces that contributed to this gigantic policy failure. It also examined European collective action issues that contributed to a slow policy response, which failed to provide sufficient incentives to Greece to stem its fiscal profligacy. As argued, the Greek crisis is definitely an economic and sovereign debt crisis in its expression but it has deeply intertwined political and social ingredients [52] embedded in interest games and power politics, transcending the domestic,

European and global policy domains. In this regard understanding the escalation of the crisis as well as the parameters of crisis resolution and subsequent reform and is a complex task. The crisis which has been described as 'a grueling war of attrition' (Stournaras quoted in Beesley) has caused huge political tensions inside the country and throughout Europe, as wealthy donor countries confront the consequences of sharing a common currency with weaker economies and partners [53].

How have collective action problems been resolved in the Greek case? Given the domestic context in Greek political economy where successive governments have been entrapped in a bargaining process that succumbs to stalemate, unable to build effective alliances and to offer incentives to reform, EU has acted as a game changer in the unfolding crisis, pushing for political concession and enforcing reform. The long-term ineffectiveness of the Greek political system and its inability to reform necessitated external mechanisms such as the Memorandum agreed with the troika, the ECB and the EFSF, that would restrict rent seeking behavior, limit the power of 'partitocratia', and forge a minimum of consensus for reform and the provision of public goods. In essence, as Kollintzas argues 'the Memorandum is nothing else but the application of traditional economics to the problems presented above (see reference [32]). Thus, the Memorandum is intended to impose policy makers to eliminate budget deficits, reduce the national debt, improve the country's competitiveness by reducing the waste of the public, enhancing competitiveness for goods and services ... and, releasing the labor market from the devastating collective bargaining and institutional protectionism ...'. For the Greek administration, nevertheless, restoring credibility (towards the Greek constituency, the global markets and its European partners) is a prerequisite to increase the chances of success that the stabilization programs will bear. What exaggerates collective action problems is the long period of required adjustment and the questionable commitment of the political elite to reform amidst high political cost and domestic protest.

On the European front, the piecemeal approach of the EU which took it almost two years to come up with a long term plan for debt consolidation and management of external imbalances of Eurozone members, revealed the complex structural context within which European leaders had to take action but it also became part of the problem. Europe's policy makers had to find a way to balance the prerequisite of European solidarity, appeasing investors fears and pandering to their constituencies which were angry for different reasons (i.e. angry anti-bailout constituency in Germany and other northern countries on the one hand, and angry anti-memorandum, constituency, 'indignados' in the southern periphery on the other hand).

The crisis underlined the doubts concerning legitimacy and solidarity raised after Maastricht. As Dyson observed, a new sense of solidarity that would support "burden-sharing" within EMU' was likely to prove elusive, as 'EMU's Achilles' heel was the prospect of people being asked to make sacrifices for others with whom there was a weak sense of identity' [54]

There is a new structural context within which collective action takes place. With so many players (national governments, European institutions, the ECB, credit rating agencies, interest groups and so on) and diverse interests and preferences it is not all surprising that the initial response to the Greek crisis (a solution orchestrated by Brussels) was a sub-optimal one. Still, the management of the financial crisis points to the role of politics, or the lack of it. This chapter did not look into important parameters set by the globalization of finance, the role of private authority and international financial institutions in eliciting strategies and tactics. It rather focused on two interrelated aspects; the domestic and European context of the Greek crisis.

ACKNOWLEDGMENTS

I would like to thank Alekos Mourmouras for his thoughtful comments and input while drafting this paper.

REFERENCES

[1]   Sinclair T.J., *Review of International Political Economy*, 1(1), pp. 133–59 (1994).
[2]   Tzogopoulos G. Η Ελληνική Κρίση στα Διεθνή ΜΜΕ, [The Greek Crisis in International Media], Working Paper 16, ELIAMEP, Athens (2011).
[3]   Nelson, R. M., Belkin P. and D. E. Mix, Greece's Debt Crisis: Overview, Policy Responses, and Implications, CRS Report for Congress, R41167, Congressional Research Service, 27 April (2010).
[4]   Story, L., Landon T. Jr. and N. D. Schwartz , '*Wall St. Helped to Mask Debt Fueling Europe's Crisis*', New York Times, 13 February (2010).
[5]   Carassava A. 'Greece admits it cheated to join euro zone,' *International Herald Tribune*, 23 September (2004).
[6]   Papandreou, G.A. (2010) Ομιλία Πρωθυπουργού Γεωργίου Α. Παπανδρέου στη Βουλή [Speech of the Prime Minister George A. Papandreou at the Parliament], 21 May. Available at: http://www.primeminister.gr/2010/05/21/1983, [Assessed: 5 May 2011].
[7]   Zachariadis N. *Mediterranean Quarterly*, 21(4), 42 (2010).
[8]   Arghyrou M. G. and J. D. Tsoukalas *The World Economy*, 34(2),174, (2011).
[9]   Moutos Th. and Tsitsikas Ch.,Whither Public Interest: The Case of Greece's Public Finances, CESifo Working Paper Series No. 3098, p.3-4 (2010).
[10] Manur, Olson, *The Logic of Collective Action: Public Goods and the Theory of Groups*, Harvard University Press, 2nd ed. (1971).
[11] Rothstein B. 'Social Capital in the Social Democratic State' in *Democracies in flux: The evolution of social capital in contemporary societies*, edited by R. Putnam, Oxford University Press, New York, 290 (2002).
[12] Gambetta, D. 'Can We Trust Trust?' in D. Gambetta (ed.) *Trust: Making and Breaking Cooperative Relations*, Oxford: Blackwell, 216 (1988).
[13] Kahan Dan M., *Michigan Law Review*, 102, 98 (2003).
[14] Paraskevopoulos C., Social Capital and Sustainable Development in Greece, LSE/European Institute, 4 (2004).
[15] Strange S., *Casino Capitalism*, Manchester University Press (1997).
[16] McCallum J. and A. Blais, *Public Choice*, 54(1), 3-18,(1987).
[17] Lyberaki, A. and E. Tsakalotos, *New Political Economy* 7(1), 93-114 (2002).
[18] Mitsopoulos M. and Th. Pelagidis, *Cato Journal*, 29(2) 399 (2009).
[19] Mitsopoulos, M. "Majority Rule, Minority Rights and Corruption." SSRN Working Paper No. 1018827, (2007).

[20] Tsoucalas, C. 'Greek National Identity in an Integrated Europe and a Changing World Order', *Greece, the New Europe, and the Changing International Order* edited by Harry J. Psomiades and Stavros B. Thomadakis, Pella Publishing Company, Inc., New York, pp. 57-78 (1993).

[21] Sotiropoulos D.A. 'A Colossus with Feet of Clay: The State in Post-Authoritarian Greece', *in Greece, the New Europe, and the Changing International Order* edited by Harry J. Psomiades and Stavros B. Thomadakis, Pella Publishing Company, Inc., New York, pp. 43-56, (1993).

[22] Demertzis N. ed. *Η Ελληνική Κουλτούρα Σήμερα [The Greek Culture Today]*, Odysseas, Athens (1994).

[23] Diamandouros, N., *Cultural Dualism and Political Change in Post Authoritarian Greece*, Estudios Working Papers Centro de Estudios Avanzados en Ciencias Socials, Madrid (1994).

[24] Sotiropoulos, D.A., *Formal Weakness and Informal Strength: Civil Society in Contemporary Greece,* Hellenic Observatory Discussion Paper no.16, Hellenic Observatory, LSE/European Institute (2004).

[25] Pagoulatos G., *Greece's New Political Economy: State, Finance and Growth from Postwar to EMU*, Palgrave, London (2003).

[26] Pelagidis Th., *Η Εμπλοκή των Μεταρρυθμίσεων στην Ελλάδα: μια αποτίμηση του εκσυγχρονισμού [The Blocking of Reforms in Greece: an assessment of modernization]*, Papazissis, Athens (2005).

[27] Lyberaki A. 1993, *Η Σύγκλιση που δεν έγινε: συγκριτική οικονομική επίδοση Ελλάδας Ευρωπαϊκής Ένωσης 1980-1988 [The Convergence that never happened: comparative economic performance of Greece and the European Union 1980-1988]*, Athens, Papazisis (1993).

[28] Ioakimidis P., 'The Europeanization of Greece: An Overall Assessment' in *Europeanization and the Southern Periphery*, edited by K. Featherstone and G. Kazamias, Frank Cass, Portland, pp. 73-94 (2001).

[29] Featherstone K. ed., *Politics and Policy in Greece: The Challenge of 'Modernisation'*, Routledge, London (2006)

[30] Alogoskoufis G. 'Greece and the Monerary Unification', *in Greece, the New Europe, and the Changing International Order* edited by H. J. Psomiades and S. B. Thomadakis, Pella Publishing Company, Inc., New York, pp.163-178 (1993).

[31] Mouzelis, N. Γιατί αποτυγχάνουν οι μεταρρυθμίσεις, [Why Reforms Fail], To Vima tis Kyriakis, 29 June (2003).

[32] Kollintzas T. 'Οι "εντός" και οι "εκτός" του συστήματος' [The "insiders" and "outsiders" of the system], Euro2Day, 23 February. Available at: http://www.euro2day.gr/specials/opinions/132/articles/627731/Article.aspx, [Accessed: 26 July 2011].

[33] Featherstone K., *Journal of European Public Policy* 12(4), 733 (2005).

[34] OECD Economic Surveys: Greece, OECD, Paris, p.12 (2009).

[35] Ballas, A. and H. Tsoukas 'Consequences of distrust: The vicious circle of tax evasion in Greece' in *The Ethics of Tax Evasion*, edited by R.W. McGee, South Orange, NJ: The Dumont Institute for Public Policy Research, pp. 284-305 (1998).

[36] Daley S.,'Greek Wealth is Everywhere but Tax Forms', *New York Times*, 1 May (2010).

[37] Servera M. C. and G. Moschovis (2008), Tax Shortfalls in Greece, ECFIN Country Focus, vol. 5 issue 5, 14 March. http://ec.europa.eu/economy_finance/publications/publication12298_en.pdf. (Accessed: 5 May 2011).

[38] Hope K. (2011b), 'Greece plans tough tax evasion laws', Financial Times, 21 February.

[39] Douzinas C. (2011), 'Greek protests show democracy in action', Guardian, 7 February.

[40] Hope K. (2010), 'Papandreou Walks Tightrope as Endgame Approaches', *Financial Times,* 4 March.

[41] Hope K. (2011a), 'Greek PM calls for consensus on privatisation', *Financial Times*, 14 March.

[42] European Commission , Co-ordination of economic policies in the EU: a presentation of key features of the main procedures, Euro Papers, Number 45, Directorate-General for Economic and Financial Affairs, Brussels, July (2002).

[43] Barber L., 'Can the Euro survive?', *Financial Times*, 29 October (2010).

[44] Alesina A. and Drazen A., *The American Economic Review*, 81(5) pp. 1170-1188 (1991).

[45] European Commission, Reinforcing economic policy coordination, Brussels, COM(2010) 250 final, 12 May (2010).

[46] Zeihan P. and M. Papic (2011), Germany's Choice Part 2, Stratfor, 26 July. Available at: http://www.stratfor.com/weekly/20110725-germanys-choice-part-2, [Accessed: 27 July 2011]

[47] Rodrik D, *Journal of Economic Perspectives*, 14(1), pp. 177–186 (2000).

[48] Erlanger S., 'Europe's Odd Couple', New York Times, 13 January (2011)

[49] Evans-Pritchard A., 'Greece Accuses Germany of "Squalid Game" in Debt Crisis,' *The Telegraph,* 22 March (2010).

[50] Issing O., 'A Greek Bail-out Would Be a Disaster for Europe', *Financial Time*s, 16 February (2010).

[51] Bryant C., 'EU Leaders Push Sweeping Regulations', *Financial Times*, 22 February (2009).

[52] Lyrintzis Ch. (2011), Greek Politics in the Era of Economic Crisis: Reassessing Causes and Effects, GreeSE Paper no 45, Hellenic Observatory Papers on Greece and Southeast Europe, Available at: http://eprints.lse.ac.uk/33826/1/GreeSE_No45.pdf , [Accessed: 20 July 2011].

[53] Beesley A. (2011), 'Greece: Ireland's partner in crisis', *The Irish Times*, 4 June 4.

[54] Featherstone K., *Journal of Common Market Studies*, 49(2) pp. 193–217 (2011).

In: Greece: Economics, Political and Social Issues
Editor: Panagiotis Liargovas

ISBN: 978-1-62100-944-3
© 2012 Nova Science Publishers, Inc.

Chapter 10

THE GREEK ECONOMIC CRISIS: A TRIGGER FOR PUBLIC ADMINISTRATION REFORMS?

Stella Ladi[1]
Panteion University, Department of Political Science
and History, Athens, Greece

ABSTRACT

Greece initially signed a Memorandum with the European Commission (EC) and the European Central Bank (ECB) that was followed by further agreements in order to get financial assistance and to avoid a total collapse of its economy following the severe international economic crisis. The Memorandum and the subsequent agreements, apart from its suggestions for the economy, offer detailed steps for structural reforms that affect all public services in Greece. One of the most important aspects of the structural reforms is the reduction of the size of the state. This chapter applies Hall's framework of policy change and claims that Greece is facing the possibility of a paradigm shift in its administrative structure. Empirical data from current public administration reforms such as the local government reform 'Kallikratis' and the transparency reform 'Cl@rity' are discussed in order to evaluate the process up to now and whether a new coherent model exists.

INTRODUCTION

A wave of public administration reforms has been under way in Greece since it was hit by the international economic crisis that broke out in 2009. A combination of factors has made Southern Europe, Ireland and especially Greece more vulnerable to speculative attacks and thus more gravely affected by the crisis. Greece was the first country to seek financial assistance from the European Union (EU) and as a result in March 2010 the leaders of the

---

[1] E-mail address: stellaladi@gmail.com

Eurozone created a financial aid mechanism which involves the participation of the International Monetary Fund (IMF) and of the Euro countries through bilateral agreements. The European Commission and the European Central Bank (ECB) were made responsible for overseeing the implementation of the agreement and a Memorandum of economic and financial policies was signed in May of 2010. The Memorandum sets out public administration reforms that have started to be adopted at a rapid pace. It is claimed that Greece has become a unique case-study of radical public administration reform. No matter if the current policy choices are eventually evaluated as a failure or success, they will definitely have a lasting effect on the country and it is possible that they will affect administrative reform elsewhere in Europe.

In order to evaluate the depth and width of the administrative reforms that are currently under way in Greece, Hall's classic distinction between incremental first and second order change and paradigm shift will be employed [1]. Hall's distinction is a useful framework for organizing our information about administrative change in Greece given that we are still at the beginning of the reform period and that there is a need to schematize change before moving to macro-level analysis. Pollitt and Bouchaert (2009) have rightly pointed out that any classification of change as first, second or third order change is to a great extent subjective [2]. In response to their fair criticism, our methodology includes primary material in the form of legislation, EU reports and official statements as well as in-depth interviews with some of the key actors (i.e. government officials, trade union and academics) in the reform process. It is argued that the Greek case demonstrates that special emphasis should be laid upon the role of exogenous actors such as the EU and the IMF in the design of the reforms but increasingly so in their implementation. The unique blend of exogenous and domestic actors and pressures for change within an EU member-state offers the opportunity of re-evaluating Hall's well-established theoretical framework and developing new theoretical and methodological tools for its advancement.

The chapter is organized into three sections. In the first section the theoretical framework of the chapter is presented and three propositions are put forward. The second section outlines Greece's dominant administrative paradigm and its key problems and failures. The third section discusses the current public services reform process and classifies them as first, second or third order change. Some claims are made about the overall direction and degree of the current administrative reform. The chapter concludes with some general conclusions about policy change and Hall's framework as well as about Greece's administrative model after the crisis.

FRAMEWORK OF ANALYSIS

Analyzing change while it happens is a difficult but fascinating task. On the one hand the richness of the available data and perspectives is vast, but on the other hand events unfold at a very fast pace and the conclusions reached cannot be final. In this chapter, the attempt is to summarize and categorize the main administrative reforms that have been implemented or announced as a result of the economic crisis. Hall's discussion of policy paradigm shift [3] is particularly interesting for the case of Greece and is applied in this chapter. What follows is a summary of Hall's framework and the design of a set of theoretical hypotheses derived from his theoretical assumptions which are useful for the better understanding of the Greek case but also for the elaboration of Hall's model itself.

Hall developed his theoretical framework in order to explain Britain's macroeconomic policy shift from Keynesianism to monetarism in the late 70s under the administration of Margaret Thatcher. His model is chosen because it was meant to explain radical change - which is the type of change that Greece is expected to achieve as far as its administrative structures are concerned. There are two aspects of Hall's work that are particularly useful for our argument here. The first is his distinction between simple change and radical transformation and the second is his discussion about the conditions of paradigm shift. As far as change is concerned Hall distinguishes between three different types of policy change:

a) first order change, which refers to instrument settings change, while overall goals and policy instruments remain the same. For example, the unemployment benefit is increased without changing its allocation rules and procedures;

b) second order change, when both policy instruments and their settings change but policy goals remain the same. The example in this case, would involve both a change in the amount spent on unemployment benefits as well as in the rules and procedures involved in its allocation;

c) third order change (or policy paradigm change), which occurs rarely but when it happens is radical and involves a change in the "framework of ideas and standards that specifies not only the goals of policy and the kind of instruments that can be used to attain them, but also the very nature of the problems they are meant to be addressing" [4]. In this third type, the whole logic of the unemployment policy would change and it would involve a new definition of what unemployment policy should be addressing including a change in its goals (i.e. which part of the unemployed population should be targeted) and instruments (i.e. the unemployment benefit *per se*).

First and second order change are incremental, which means that they take place at a slower pace and build upon existing processes and institutions. Paradigm shift, as Hall (1993) argues, does not necessarily follow first and second order change and it is not incremental in nature. Thus more modeling is needed in order to explain it. This takes us to the second important aspect of his work, which describes the conditions of a paradigmatic shift.

The parameters of a paradigmatic shift that Hall describes are particularly helpful for the development of our research propositions. In his study of macroeconomic paradigm shift he picked up three important conditions that made the shift possible. First, the change from one paradigm to another is not just the result of changing views of experts but a much more political action. Experts always have conflicting views and some of them will contribute to the discourse behind the change and some will not. The process of change itself is political and involves internal and external factors that empower one new direction over another. Second, the authority of policy is of particular importance. During a paradigmatic shift, there will be changes "in the locus of authority over policy" [5]. We would add that not only will the authority usually be new but also the clearer and the stronger the new authority is, the most likely it is for the paradigmatic shift to take place. Third, policy experimentation and policy failure are central in the movement from one paradigm to another. A common process is the introduction of reforms aiming to adjust the previous paradigm to a new situation. Such adjustments often lack intellectual and policy coherence and the result is policy failure. Nevertheless, policy failure and policy experimentation feeds into the process of paradigm shift.

Following Hall's parameters of paradigm shift, the theoretical propositions that are put forward in this chapter in order to evaluate the Greek case, but also in order to further elaborate the theoretical framework applied here, are as follows:

- The administrative reform currently taking place in Greece is characterized by first, second and occasionally third order changes. There is a tendency for paradigm shift to take place.
- A new intellectual and political authority is steering the reform. This new locus of authority is international and not domestic and thus legitimization and implementation problems have multiplied.
- Intellectual and policy coherence are necessary for the success of the reform, but in reality coherence is limited. Policy experimentation and policy failure are the most likely outcomes of the current process given the time pressure.

We now turn to the description of the dominant administrative paradigm in Greece in order to understand the target of the reform.

DOMINANT ADMINISTRATIVE MODEL IN GREECE

The contemporary administrative model in Greece was established in the 1970s in light of Greece's transition to democracy but also in light of the economic stringency of the period. The conservative party of New Democracy (ND) under the leadership of Konstantinos Karamanlis stayed in power until 1981 which was the year that Greece became a full member of the European Community (EC). In 1981, the Panhellenic Socialist Movement (PASOK) took office, with Andreas Papandreou as the Prime Minister, and basically stayed in power until 2000 with the exception of 1989-90 when a short-lived coalition government came to power and the period 1990-93 when ND governed. By the 1980s the democratic institutions and political parties had been consolidated and the new socialist government invested in the establishment of welfare state institutions and the empowerment of disadvantaged social groups. As a result the size of the state grew. Pagoulatos [6], notes that in the 1980's the state model in place can be described as developmental and it was the 1990's when it was succeeded by the stabilization model because of the necessity for Greece to prepare for entering the European Monetary Union (EMU). Although this was a very important shift for the liberalization of the economy, the size of the state did not decrease. Quite the opposite, it continued growing and with it the public debt also increased.

Greek public administration has traditionally been hierarchical and centralized as far as its institutions and control mechanisms are concerned. Its administrative system is dominated by the party in government which means that continuity in governance cannot be guaranteed [7]. Two of the most common allegations against public administration in Greece are lack of effectiveness and widespread corruption. Interestingly, Sotiropoulos [8] in his book about the state and reform processes in southern Europe shows that Greece (and the rest of southern

Europe) are lacking in effectiveness but not dramatically more than western Europe and Scandinavia. Nevertheless, corruption levels of the administration are particularly high, although further comparative research is necessary in order to evaluate its exact level and degree. Patronage, which is caused by the dominance of the party in office, is possibly the most important reason for the failure of Greek public administration. It undermines the technical and personnel capacity of public administration by violating the values of meritocracy in the selection and development of personnel. Patronage has a great impact on public procurement and the choice of contractors. In a way, patronage is in many instances the cause of both corruption and of ineffectiveness. Another aspect of the dominant model in Greece is legalism and formalism which is not followed by profound controls and strict sanctions of law-breakers. Quite the opposite, respect for formal rule is fragmented and informal practices often oppose and ignore formal rules [9]. The large number of often conflicting regulations is frequently the result of client-patron relations and of attempts to deviate from the general rule in order to offer benefits to specific social groups [10]. Similarly to the Italian case, the existence of a strong policy community of constitutional and public law experts has further strengthened legalism [11].

Two characteristics of the state-economy relationship have been mostly blamed for the weakness of the Greek economy and for its incapacity to deal with the international financial crisis. Firstly, tax evasion by individuals and also by businesses is common. Irregular payments by businesses are widespread and as a result significant amounts that the government budget relies upon never enter the government coffers. Secondly, state spending on social protection is high while the results, to say the least, are unequal. Public expenditure on social provision has increased over the years due to the expansion of the welfare state and welfare institutions but its coverage is skewed. For example, spending on family and unemployment benefits is low, while the cost of pensions is high [12].

Because of the above characteristics of the public administration, the implementation of reforms has been very problematic up to now - which means that the odds are against the success of the current attempt at reform. Processes of Europeanization were expected to facilitate public administration reforms but the literature on Europeanization and Greece shows that although there is a tendency to convergence, a large number of cases of inertia also exists [13]. For example, long before the current crisis Featherstone [14] had shown that Greece managed to achieve the Maastricht criteria and to participate in the EMU but there was no evidence of long term economic convergence especially if we looked at areas such as pension system reform. Inertia is clearly observed in other policy areas such as administrative reform [15] and environmental policy change [16]. Examples of all kinds of domestic mediating factors obstructing the Europeanization of Greek policies can be found in the literature. The most usual factors are political institutional capacity, policy legacies and policy preferences. Instances of resilience to change can be found in all sectors and normally all three mediating factors seem to be at work. For example, the EU cohesion policy had to confront a centralised government, lack of coordination, strong political parties and a lack of political will for change. The result has been that although some institutional changes have been introduced, the regions have remained weak and the absorption of structural funds has been limited. Change could only be observed in policy objectives, styles and practices [17], [18] which are what we have described as first and second order change. In the next section, the public administration reforms that have been put in place since the economic crisis that

CURRENT PUBLIC ADMINISTRATION REFORMS

Greece – owing to the severe economic crisis that it has been facing - was the first EMU country to seek financial assistance from the EU in February 2010. European leaders, alarmed at the possibility of a Greek default, which could cause instability in the Eurozone, promised to take determined and coordinated action to help Greece. As a result, in March 2010, a financial aid mechanism which involved the participation of the IMF and of the Euro countries through bilateral agreements was agreed. The European Commission and the ECB would overview the implementation of the agreement and a Memorandum of economic and financial policies, as well as a Memorandum of Understanding on specific economic policy conditions were signed in May of 2010. The Memorandums included public administration reforms that started to be adopted at a fast pace and where enhanced by further agreements (July 2011, October 2011). In this section the key changes are discussed and they are categorized as first, second or third order changes according to Hall's model. Further, we attempt to make an assessment of the overall situation up to now.

The Memorandum of economic and financial policies (2010) outlines three areas of reform: fiscal policies, financial sector policies and structural policies. Public administration reforms are mainly included in the structural policies section, which is the focus of the chapter and has proven to be the most difficult to implement. A brief discussion of the fiscal and financial sector policies is necessary in order to demonstrate the breadth of the reform process that is currently taking place in Greece. As far as fiscal policies are concerned, the initial agreement was that the general government deficit will be reduced below 3% of GDP by 2014. At the same time, expenditure would be cut by 7% of GDP and revenue would be increased by 4% of GDP. In order to achieve these targets, major structural fiscal reforms including pension reform, health sector reform, tax reform, public financial management, fiscal framework and debt management framework modernization have been planned and have already started being implemented. Concerning the financial sector policies, the challenge noted by the Memorandum was the management by the banks of the tight liquidity conditions, and thus the primary concern was to preserve the financial sector's soundness and its capacity to support the Greek economy.

The structural policies directly target the dominant paradigm and include modernization of public administration, restructuring labor markets and income policies, improving the business environment and competitiveness, rationalization of public enterprises and improving the take-up of EU structural and cohesion funds.

The main features of the dominant administrative model are challenged by most of the structural reforms (e.g. health system reform, rationalization of public enterprises) but the focus of this chapter is on the reforms directly targeting public administration.

The Memorandum [19] clearly sets the public administration reforms and their time frame as conditions for the payment of the loan that has been agreed. What follows, is a brief presentation of these reforms and an evaluation of their current level of implementation as well as of the order of change they introduce.

1. *Changing the remuneration system for public sector employees:* the aim is to adopt a unified remuneration system that covers basic wages and allowances of all public sector employees and centralizes their payment. Additionally, remuneration should reflect productivity and tasks. In order to achieve that, as requested, legislation has been passed for a Single Payment Authority and the full implementation of the new remuneration system is planned for January of 2012 [20]. Not much has happened in adjusting wages to reflect productivity and tasks, although the time frame required action by September 2010. The centralization and rationalization of the public sector employees remuneration system can be characterized as second order change, because with the introduction of a new Authority both the instruments and the settings have been changed. The change that concerns productivity and tasks could be described as third order change because the goals (i.e. the rationale behind payment) would have to change but also the whole concept of the role of public sector employees and the way they should work would be reconsidered. This is probably the reason why this second part of the reform has been even more delayed than the first part. In October of 2011 a law specifying the new remuneration system but also introducing labor reserve in the public sector was passed [21]. It is the first time labor reserve is employed in Greek public administration and it will signify an important reduction in the numbers of public sector employees. This development can also be characterized as third order change because for the first time the state will stop being perceived by Greeks as a secure employer with endless employment capabilities.

2. *Public procurement:* e-procurement for all sectors and levels of governments was initially planned for the end of 2010, but in February 2011 the contract for the provision of the IT platform had still not been signed [22]. The consultation process for the establishment of an independent authority overseeing public procurement was concluded in February 2011 but the vote on the relevant legislation is still pending [23]. This is second-order change because it concerns policy instruments and their settings but the goals of public procurement remain the same. Nevertheless, if successful, this reform would affect the nature of public procurement because it will create a great obstacle to the corrupt practices of the past.

3. *Transparency of public spending:* the government agreed to ensure transparency of public spending by publishing all its decisions online. Indeed, via the 'Cl@rity' programme all public entities decisions should be published online and they cannot be implemented unless they are uploaded on the Cl@rity website [24]. Progress in this field was acknowledged by the Interim report [25]. Cl@rity is an interesting reform because it went further than was required by the Memorandum and included not only public spending documents but all government acts. It is safe to define it as a second-order change because it affects the policy instruments used in order to enhance transparency.

4. *Local administration reform:* the requirement was to adopt legislation reforming local government by June 2010. In fact, as of 1st of January 2011, a law incorporating prefectures into regions and thus reducing their number from 76 to 13 and at the same time reducing municipalities from 1034 to 325 and municipal corporations from 6000 to 1500 has started to be implemented. This reform was named 'Kallikratis' and has already led to important budgetary savings [26]. It remains to be

seen if the provision of public services at the local level will become more efficient. To say the least, the challenge ahead will be huge, until the transfer of responsibilities and resources has been completed. 'Kallikratis' can be best described as second-order change because it changes both the policy instruments and their settings. It is an incremental change because it follows and deepens 'Kapodistrias' which was a previous reform of local authorities introduced in 1997 [27].

5. *Review of central government:* the agreement was to perform an independent review of the organization and functioning of the central administration in order to adopt measures for the rationalization of the use of resources, the organization of public administration and the effectiveness of social programmes by June of 2011. It was decided to have two separate reviews: one on central government (overseen by the Ministry of the Interior) and one on social programmes (overseen by the Ministry of Labor). The last review of the Economic Adjustment Programme for Greece [28] observes delays in the agreement of the terms of reference between the Greek government and the OECD that has been chosen as the contractor for the two reviews. Nevertheless, the reviews do not constitute change in themselves and in order to make an assessment of their significance, we have to wait for the decisions that will follow their publication.

6. *Better Regulation:* the aim is to implement the Better Regulation Agenda and to ensure the reduction of administrative burdens for citizens and enterprises. This is work in progress and the cooperation with the OECD is expected to play a role in this reform. It is not possible to assess the level of the reform at this stage because of the limited level of implementation up to now.

This brief discussion of the administrative reforms agreed by the Greek government and the EC demonstrates that it is mainly second order change that is currently taking place. Common international trends such as decentralization, e-governance, more flexible human resource management and a struggle to achieve economy, efficiency and effectiveness are all present in the reform process. If we add to that pension reform, health care reform, the plan to reduce numbers of schools and eventually universities, the 'recovery plan' for the railway sector and for public transport as well as the ambitious privatization programme that the government has announced, it can be argued that all these changes add up to a major reform that has the potential of becoming a new policy paradigm for Greece. In the next and final section we return to our three theoretical propositions in order to discuss the theoretical and empirical implications of these observations.

ANALYSIS AND CONCLUSION

The 2008 financial crisis showed the extent of globalization by the way it quickly spread and transformed itself according to the weaknesses of each country. A common revelation for most countries was that governments cannot sustain their large budget deficits and thus the discussion about public spending cuts, efficiency of the state and rationalization of public administration intensified. Greece is one of the most interesting cases because although it is a member of the EMU, and possibly because of that, it has found itself at the heart of the

European crisis. Its economy came near to collapse and a loan from the IMF and from EMU members was the only realistic solution. The Memorandum set out clear public administration reforms that are currently being adopted. Additionally, a wave of privatizations is under way and reforms in social security, health, transport and education sectors are being introduced. The volume of changes that are currently taking place make Greece a strong candidate for a paradigmatic shift. The success and the sustainability of this shift are still open questions and it won't be possible to evaluate them until some time has passed. We now turn to the three theoretical propositions outlined at the beginning of this chapter.

The first proposition concerns the order of change that can be observed in Greece following Hall's framework. In light of the discussion about the reforms introduced or announced as a result of the Memorandum, it can be argued that the majority of the changes can be described as second-order changes. Most of the time they involve changes in policy instruments and their settings but policy goals remain the same. This can be said for the majority of the changes introduced. For example, 'Kallikratis' changed the structure and competencies of local government but did not change local governments' key goals. The same applies to 'Cl@rity', which improved the instruments that can guarantee transparency, but it cannot be claimed that transparency is a new value for the Greek administrative system. Changes which are underway such as the Single Payment Authority or e-procurement are also best described as second-order changes because they mainly involve changes in the instruments and not in the goals or values. Nevertheless, if we consider that one of the main weaknesses of Greek public administration up to now has been the implementation of legislation, a change in the policy instruments can prove to be as important as a change in goals and values. In other words, although the goals and values of meritocracy, transparency, economy, efficiency and effectiveness existed, they were not put into practice to the extent that they are now, at least as far as legislation is concerned, and this is a major change in itself. We can thus argue, that in addition to Hall's observation, the Greek case shows that if changes are cumulative, even if they mainly concern policy instruments, they can lead to third-order change which is best described as paradigm shift. Additionally, even if the nature of the problem has not been re-defined in Greece, what has happened is that the severity of the outcomes of the problem, have been reconsidered due to the experience of the crises. We can therefore argue that even a redefinition of the outcomes of the problem can lead to paradigm shift.

The second proposition concerns the intellectual and political authority that is steering the reform. According to Hall, a new intellectual and political authority steering the reform is one of the conditions for successful paradigm shift to take place. As for the new political authority steering the reform in Greece, it is true that a new socialist government was elected in autumn 2009 and it is this new government that is now managing the reform process. Yet, although the government is new, it is still the 'product of a dysfunctional system' [29] which means that it is not as fresh as a paradigmatic change would call for. Giorgos Papandreou brought with him his own national consultants and organized a small group of international experts to help him with the reform process [30]. However, this group of national and international experts is not vocal enough and thus it is difficult to characterize it as the new intellectual authority that is steering the reform. In addition, what is argued here is that the new locus of authority behind change in Greece is more international than domestic. This means that apart from the domestic actors, it includes official and experts in the EU, in the ECB, in the IMF and in other European countries such as Germany and France. Their participation concentrates mainly on the design and evaluation of the Economic Adjustment Programme for Greece and the implementation is left to the domestic actors, although with the latest agreement (October 2011) it has been agreed that their presence in the ministries will become permanent. This indeed is causing legitimization and implementation problems, which takes us to the third and last proposition.

Based on Hall's second condition for successful paradigmatic shift, it is claimed that although intellectual and policy coherence are necessary for the success of the reform, in Greece they are limited. This is why policy experimentation and policy failure are the most likely outcomes of the current process, especially when time pressure is taken into account. It is indicative that all interviewees [31] said that the reform does not follow a concrete model such as New Public Management. This does not come as a surprise because models are usually intellectual creations and a lot of the time governments do not follow them consciously. In the case of Greece though, incoherence is also evident in other aspects of the current administration. In fact, the government is in the difficult position of having social values and roots (the governing party PASOK is the socialist party of Greece), and at the same time pushing for quite liberal reforms as far as public services are concerned. Moreover, the government came into power with a discourse about green development and open governance [32] and it has found itself in a situation of limited resources and different priorities dictated by its international donors. It is argued that this internal incoherence is likely to lead to policy experimentation and policy failure that nevertheless, are central in the movement from one paradigm to another. The question is if this incoherence will also lead to political instability and a very long time frame for the reforms –something which, given the international financial pressure, the Greek economy will not be able to sustain.

ACKNOWLEDGMENTS

I would like to thank the audience of the seminar organized by the Cyprus Center for European and International Affairs, Nicosia University, 3rd December 2010 for their comments on an early draft of this paper. I would also like to thank the staff of the Center for their help with the transcripts of the interviews conducted for this research. Finally, I would like to thank P. Liargovas, the editor of the book for including my chapter in this interesting volume.

REFERENCES

[1]   P. Hall, *Comparative Politics*. 25, 275 (1993).
[2]   Ch. Pollitt and G. Bouckaert, *Continuity and Change in Public Policy and Management*, Cheltenham: Edward Elgar (2009).
[3]   P. Hall, *Comparative Politics*. 25, 275 (1993).
[4]   P. Hall, *Comparative Politics*. 25, 275 (1993) p 279.
[5]   P. Hall, *Comparative Politics*. 25, 275 (1993) p 280.
[6]   G. Pagoulatos, *Greece's New Political Economy*. Hampshire: Palgrave (2003).
[7]   C. Spanou, *Journal of European Public Policy*. 5, 467 (1998).

[8]   D. Sotiropoulos, *Κράτος και Μεταρρύθμιση στη Σύγχρονη Νότια Ευρώπη* [State and Reform in Contemporary South Europe]. Athens: Potamos (2007) pp 48-61.

[9]   C. Spanou, 1996, *International Review of Administrative Sciences*. 62, 219 (1996).

[10] D. Sotiropoulos, *Κράτος και Μεταρρύθμιση στη Σύγχρονη Νότια Ευρώπη* [State and Reform in Contemporary South Europe]. Athens: Potamos (2007).

[11] G. Capano, *Public Administration*. 81, 781 (2003).

[12] K. Featherstone and D. Papadimitriou, *The Limits of Europeanization*. Basingstoke: Palgrave Macmillan (2008) pp 57-60.

[13] S. Ladi, *Public Administration* (accepted and forthcoming) (2011).

[14] K. Featherstone, *Journal of Common Market Studies*. 41, 923 (2003).

[15] C. Spanou, *Ελληνική Διοίκηση και Ευρωπαϊκή Ολοκλήρωση* [Greek Administration and European Integration]. Athens: Papazisis (2001).

[16] S. Ladi, *Ελληνική Επιθεώρηση Πολιτικής Επιστήμης* [Greek Political Science Review]. 29, 40 (2007).

[17] Ch. Paraskevopoulos, *Government and Opposition*. 36, 253 (2001).

[18] G. Andreou, *South European Society and Politics*. 11,241 (2006).

[19] Memorandum of Economic and Financial Policies, 78 (2010).

[20] Law Gazette no.784, Hellenic Republic.

[21] Law 4024/2011, Hellenic Republic.

[22] European Commission, *The Economic Adjustment Programme for Greece, Third Review*. Occasional Papers 77, 58 (2011).

[23] http://www.opengov.gr/ypoian/ (visited 21/6/11).

[24] http://diavgeia.gov.gr/en (visited 22/1/11).

[25] European Commission, *The Economic Adjustment Programme for Greece, Interim Review*, Athens (14-17 June 2010).

[26] http://kallikratis.ypes.gr/ (visited 22/1/11).

[27] Law 2539/1997, Hellenic Republic.

[28] European Commission, *The Economic Adjustment Programme for Greece, Fourth Review*. Occasional Papers, 82 (2011).

[29] I. Grigoriadis, *World Policy Journal*. Summer, 101 (2011).

[30] A. Kovaios, *To Vima* (14/8/10).

[31] Five interviews with policy officials, academics and trade union leaders where conducted in Athens between 1st and 21st of April 2011.

[32] PASOK, *PASOK Election Programme*. Athens (2009).

In: Greece: Economics, Political and Social Issues
Editor: Panagiotis Liargovas

ISBN: 978-1-62100-944-3
© 2012 Nova Science Publishers, Inc.

Chapter 11

ANTI-MONEY LAUNDERING AND ANTI-FRAUD METHODS TO DETECT AND PREVENT OCCUPATIONAL FRAUD IN THE GREEK PUBLIC SECTOR

Panagiotis Liargovas[*] and Spyridon Repousis[†]
University of Peloponnese,
Department of Economics, Tripolis, Greece

ABSTRACT

According to the General Inspector of Greek Public Administration, only one per cent of corruption in the Greek public sector is detected and Greek state fraud losses from corrupted public servants are estimated to 20 billion Euros annually. This is a great amount if we bear in mind that since May 2010, the European Union, the European Central Bank and the International Monetary Fund, approved a joint, 110 billion Euros financing package to help Greece ride out its debt crisis, revive growth and modernize the economy. This chapter examines occupational fraud in the Greek Public Sector and suggests the steps that can be taken to avoid and combat it. It has become clear in the anti - money laundering field that having co-equal programs "to know your customer" and "to know your employee" are essential. Implementing a Know Your Employee program and methods from anti - money laundering and anti - fraud field, relevant with fictitious payments to employees, administration of Greek public sector can detect and prevent occupational fraud. Using direct and indirect methods such as behavior profile of employees, Benford's Law, job rotation, segregation of duties and others, administration of Greek public sector can restore a climate of mistrust and reduce occupational fraud. Our proposals offer important solutions for political analysts, politicians and society as a whole.

---

[*] E-mail address: liargova@uop.gr
[†] E-mail address: spyrep@otenet.gr

INTRODUCTION

According to the General Inspector of Greek Public Administration, only one percent of corruption in the Greek public sector is detected and Greek state fraud losses from corrupted public servants are estimated to 20 billion Euros annually [1]. Also delays in judicial processes are a common feature. In the Annual Report of the General Inspector of Greek Public Administration for 2008, 888 cases of occupational fraud were examined and 46.8% of them, were initially detected by complaints of employees, citizens and vendors [2]. At the same time, most occupational fraud cases (31.5% of the whole fraud cases) come from accounting and financial management departments and they are relevant with employee fraud such as bribery, corruption, fictitious payments and overbilling. According to 2007 Transparency International Corruption Perceptions Index (CPI), Greece had 4.6 CPI score which indicates medium to high degree of public sector corruption as perceived by business people and country analysts. CPI score ranges between 10 (highly clean) and 0 (highly corrupt) [3]. Greece faces a dual challenge. It has a severe fiscal problem with deficits and public debt that are too high and it has a competitiveness problem. Greek budget deficit for 2009 was significantly higher than expected (15.4%), but as shown in Table 1, budget deficit and government debt during the last years are increasing continuously. Also, since May 2010 a rescue package of 110 billion Euros was approved jointly by the European Union, the European Central Bank and the International Monetary Fund, to help Greece ride out its debt crisis, revive growth and modernize the economy. So, fraud-loss amount of 20 billion Euros annually from corrupted public servants is significant. Corruption thrives on misinformation and secrecy. When economic and business decisions are taken on the basis of the size of a kickback rather than quality, then a climate of mistrust is working against the interests of employees and shareholders in the market economy and against the interests of a developing world [4].

The next section of the chapter reviews previous literature about occupational fraud, while section 3 presents solutions for the Greek Public Sector. Section 4 offers some concluding remarks.

Table 1. Greek fiscal statistical data

(Million Euros)	2006	2007	2008	2009
Budget deficit	12,109	14,465	22,363	36,150
Government Debt in nominal prices, end of year	224,204	238,581	261,396	298,032
Gross Domestic Product (GDP) in current prices	211,314	227,134	236,936	235,035
Budget deficit as percentage of GDP	5.7%	6.4%	9.4%	15.4%
Government debt as percentage of GDP	106.1%	105.0%	110.3%	126.8%

Source: Hellenic Statistical Authority, Press Release 15 November 2010.

LITERATURE REVIEW

Corruption and Occupational Fraud are much more than an isolated criminal phenomenon. Corruption in public sector is a worldwide problem. Corruption is the abuse of public power for private gain. Occupational Fraud is linked with White-Collar Crime. White-Collar crime, according to Sutherland (1949), may be defined approximately as a crime committed by a person of respectability and high social status in the course of his or her occupation.

In the 1950s, criminologist Donald R. Cressey developed a theory to explain why people commit fraud [5]. He decided to interview fraudsters who were convicted of embezzlement. Cressey's final hypothesis published in *Other People's Money: A Study in the Social Psychology of Embezzlement*, was: "*Trusted Persons become trust violators when they conceive of themselves as having a financial problem which is non-shareable, are aware this problem can be secretly resolved by violation of the position of financial trust, and are able to apply to their own conduct in that situation verbalizations which enable them to adjust their conceptions of themselves as trusted persons with their conceptions of themselves as trusted persons with their conceptions of themselves as users entrusted funds or property.*"

Over the years, the hypothesis has become better known as the Fraud Triangle. His premise was that there are three components – incentive/motivation/pressure, opportunity and rationalization. Pressure refers to something that has happened in the fraudster's personal life that creates a stressful need for funds, and thus motivates to steal. Opportunity reflects the knowledge and opportunity to commit the fraud. Finally many excuses could serve as a rationalization, including some benevolent ones where the fraudster does not actually keep the stolen funds or assets but uses them for social purposes [6]. The Fraud Triangle illustrates some of the fundamental concepts of fraud deterrence and detection.

Since Sutherland (1949), there were several influential attempts by criminologists to expand the definition beyond a narrower focus on the high-status criminals or fraudsters [7]. The most influential attempt to distinguish among different forms of white-collar crime has been that of Clinard and Quinney (1973) [8]. They divided white-collar crime into two types: occupational crime and corporate crime. Occupational crime or fraud consists of offences committed by individuals for themselves in the course of their occupations and offences of employees against their employers. Corporate crime, on the other hand, is defined as the offences committed by corporate officials for their corporation and the offences of the corporation itself.

According to the ACFE's *2010 Report to the Nations on Occupational Fraud and Abuse*, occupational fraud is a global problem and estimated that the typical organization looses 5% of its annual revenue to fraud. Applied to the estimated 2009 Gross World Product, this figure translates to a potential global fraud loss of more than $2.9 trillion. The fraud cases of ACFE's Report came from 106 nations, with more than 40% of cases occurring in countries outside the United States. In their study, more than 85% of fraudsters had never been previously charged or convicted for a fraud-related offense. The most common behavioral warning of fraud, displayed by the perpetrators were living beyond their means and experiencing financial difficulties.

Among the 1,021 U.S. cases in the ACFE's study, who investigated cases between January 2008 and December 2009, the median fraud loss was $105,000. Billing schemes were present in 27.6% of these cases, while corruption was reported in 21.9% of cases. In a trend reflected worldwide, the impact of anonymous fraud hotlines is clear, as 37.8% of the U.S. frauds in the study were detected by tip, followed by management review (17.1%) and internal audit (13.7%).

Private and public companies can be defrauded by insiders (employees, directors) and outsiders, or a combination of both through collusion. Although there are countless crime schemes the principal categories are: a) skimming: diversion of funds belonging to a company, prior to the recording of such funds in the company's accounts, b) embezzlement: diversion of funds, assets or stock from the organization either in the form of cash or cheques or by bank accounts, c) false invoicing and overbilling: the most common type of insider fraud is illegal activities consisting of an arrangement of excessive payments for goods or services purchased for the company in return for kickbacks from cooperative suppliers, d) payroll fraud: the fraudster is trying to get the company pay for work that has not been performed such as ghost pay-rolling, falsified time worked, commission schemes, e)expense schemes: the fraudster misclassifies, overstates, duplicates or claims fictitious expenses, f)bribery and corruption: collusion between vendors and employees either by inflated invoicing by the vendor in return for kickbacks to the conspiring.

The struggle against fraud is not an area where any state has had a sufficiently high success rate to become complacent, particularly when bearing in mind the evidence of the scale on which such crimes are being committed. Occupational fraud continues to destroy trust in the public sector. It is, therefore, a systemic problem.

OCCUPATIONAL FRAUD: SOLUTIONS FOR THE GREEK PUBLIC SECTOR

Asking employees how they feel about the Greek public sector, is an excellent way to assess employee satisfaction and uncover possible opportunities for fraud. When used correctly, employee surveys can improve morale and help employees feel involved and in control of what happens to them in the workplace. Public sector fraud examiners can use employee surveys to help government to improve their policies, procedures and processes, and to assess opportunities for fraud. So, questions can be designed to assess the probability of a fraudulent event occurring within the organization based on internal controls, internal control environment and resources available to prevent, detect and deter fraud.

Implementing a Know Your Employee (KYE) program means that the Greek public sector has a program in place that makes it possible to understand an employee's background and conflicts of interest. Policies, procedures, internal controls, job descriptions, code of conduct/ethics, levels of authority, compliance with personnel laws and regulations, accountability, dual control and other deterrents should be firmly in place. KYE is a basic tool in detecting suspicious activity of employees. Suspicious or unusual employee activity and red flags can include: a) employee lives a lavish lifestyle that could not be supported by his or her salary, b) employee frequently overrides internal controls or established approval authority or circumvents policy, c) employee uses resources of Greek public sector to further private interest, d) employee avoids taking vacations, e) employee assists transactions where the identity of the ultimate beneficiary or counter party is undisclosed.

Two methods can also used to detect and prevent occupational fraud in the Greek public sector: direct method and indirect method. The direct method identifies assets through specific financial transactions whereas the indirect method infers that there are assets through financial analysis. Using the direct method, assets can be traced through the point of payment or the point of receipt. The asset hider might want to hide funds through on book schemes or off book scheme, depending on whether the activity runs on the books of the business or not.

Corrupted employees are using the Greek public sector money to gain through fictitious payments to vendors and employees and overbilling or overstatement of reported expenses or inflated invoices. These are on-book fraud schemes and are illicit funds drawn from the Greek state.

In a fictitious payable scheme, a payable is created for a debt that is not owned. Through the establishment of fictitious vendors payments can be made to entities or individuals that do not exist. A good starting point to detect fictitious payable scheme in the Greek public sector is to analyze cash receipts and disbursement journals as well as ledger accounts for unusual activity. Purchase orders, invoices and bank accounts should be examined closely by looking at monthly statements.

An internal auditor should follow any payments on accounts identified to be suspicious based on financial analysis and review accounts for which there are no tangible products attached to the payable. Accounts such as consulting fees, commissions and advertising are good places to check.

Fictitious payments to employees are used to disguise income by having salary payments go to no-existent or fictitious ("ghost employee") or former employees. To search for payroll schemes, the following records should be checked: i) payroll lists of attendance, ii) printouts of current and former employees which lists their start and termination dates along with their Social Security Numbers, iii) personnel files, employment applications, tax withholding forms, and authorized deductions.

To identify payroll fraud schemes, a Greek public sector internal auditor should compare the list of all current and former employees from the personnel office to the current payroll list. Things to take into account include unexplained or unusual increases in wages expense and employees that never take a vacation or never take sick leave. Job rotation is a strong measure to prevent occupational fraud.

The red flags of employee fraud schemes are: use of a common name, e.g., Papadopoulos, no physical address, missing employee information, invalid social security numbers, no evidence of work performance [10].

Ghost employee schemes can be uncovered by having personnel (other than the payroll department) distribute and deposit payroll to a bank and requiring identification of the payee. Duties should be segregated for payroll preparation, payroll disbursement (into payroll and withholding tax accounts), payroll distribution, payroll bank reconciliations and human resources departmental functions [11]. A list of duplicate addresses or deposit accounts may reveal ghost employees or duplicate payments. Payroll preparation, distribution and reconciliation should be strictly segregated. In addition, the transfer of funds to payroll bank accounts should be handled independently of the other functions. Finally, establishing a Greek public sector central and unified internal supervisory agency and a central and unified unit of employees' payments would strongly help to decrease occupational fraud.

Overbilling schemes are on-book schemes which require the assistance of a third party contractor or supplier. The major categories of billing schemes are shell company schemes (fictitious entity who do not produce goods or services and are created for the sole purpose of committing fraud), overbilling involving existing vendors and personal purchases with company funds.

In an overbilling, the payer adds an illegal payment to a legitimate business expense or trade payable. The cooperative third party then forwards the excess payment either directly to the intended recipient or even to employees. To uncover overbilling schemes, the auditor should look on invoices or other billing documents for "extra" or "special" charges, particularly those which do not require a delivery of goods for payments and also, for discrepancies between the purchase order or invoice amount and the actual amount of payment. The auditor should pay particular attention on invoices that appear changed or photocopied as well as on unusually large bills or bills which break a consistent pattern of amounts, schedule or purpose.

Also there must be established a separation of duties among authorization, purchasing, receiving, shipping and accounting and should compare and analyze purchases and inventory levels. A few more suggestions for detecting and preventing false billing and overbilling are:

a) Greek state must monitor trends of purchase approval by employee.
b) Generate reports sorting purchases by type.
c) Shell companies typically bill for services rather than goods in order to avoid detection at the receiving stage. Look for employees who approve an unusually high level of services based on their job function.
d) Rotate purchase authority among supervisors and monitor trends in expenditures based on who approves invoices.
e) Conduct surprise audits at the purchasing function.
f) Compare the signature of those who received goods or services to the individuals who approved the purchases.
g) Be alert for erasures, white-outs with support documents.
h) Payment coding should be analyzed for abnormal descriptions.

Fraud relevant with overbilling invoices and invoicing procedures in the Greek public sector can be detected by using Benford's Law [12]. The theory behind Benford's Law was first proposed by Simon Newcomb, an astronomer and mathematician. In 1881, Newcomb noted that the first few pages of his logarithm book were used more and were more worn and dirtier than the other pages. Since the first pages of a logarithm book lists multi-digit logs beginning with the digits 1, 2, and 3, Newcomb theorized that scientists spent more time dealing with logs that began with 1, 2, or 3. He also found that for each succeeding number the amount of time decreases. He devised a formula to explain the observation: the probability of a number beginning with digit X is equal to $\log10(1+(1/X))$.

During the 1920s, Frank Benford, a physicist employed by General Electric Co. in New York, attempted to test Newcomb's theory. In testing the frequency in which certain digits randomly appear, he calculated the frequencies in which each of the digits appeared in a data set and his analysis was published in a paper titled *The Law of Anomalous Numbers*. But, he also calculated the probability of the second digit of multi-digit number being "N" (any number). He calculated these percentages by using the following formula:

$$\sum_{d_1=1}^{9} \log(1+(1/d_1 d_2))$$

where d_2, the second digit, is any digit 0 through 9 inclusive.

Benford concluded that certain digits appear more frequently than others as the first digit in multi-digit numbers. Like Newcomb, Benford did not have an explanation for this natural phenomenon. His data suggests that the digit 1 appears as the first digit in a multi-digit number 30.1% of the time, the digit 2, 17.6% of the time, the digit 3, 12.5% of the time, etc.. But he did not illustrate any practical use of this observation [13].

Mark Nigrini, published his thesis in 1992 demonstrating that Benford's Law could be used to detect fraud and to detect rounded numbers [14]. Nigrini defined digital analysis as an audit technology designed to find abnormal duplications of digits, digit combinations, specific numbers and round numbers in corporate data. Benford's Law is used as the expected distribution of digits in accounting data. Digital analysis works by looking for abnormalities in four areas: digit and number patterns, round number occurrences, duplication of numbers and relative size of numbers [15].

By applying Benford's Law to the Greek public sector data, anomalies can be detected. While the first and second digit tests provide a high-level assessment, the first two-digit test provides a more detailed analysis as well as the first three and the last two digits tests. Regardless of the extent of digits analyzed, abnormal digit patterns can be reviewed for various types of Greek public sector data including investment sales/purchases, inventory unit costs, expense accounts and asset/liability accounts.

Also, one of the most common tests to perform is to check for duplicate payments in a payment history file. The Greek public sector auditor could test whether any payments were made to the same vendor by the same employee. All tests can easily be performed with no additional cost, using only a simple computer program, Active Data for Microsoft Excel.

Also anti-money laundering techniques can be used to detect and prevent occupational fraud. Money laundering is the process by which criminals conceal or disguise the proceeds of their crimes or convert those proceeds into goods and services. It allows criminals to put their illegal money into the stream of commerce, corrupting financial institutions and the money supply and giving criminals' unwarranted economic power [16].

The Bureau of Internal Revenue in USA developed several methods of proving a person had received income even though the bureau might have no direct evidence of this income. These techniques became known as indirect methods of establishing income. The most common of these methods for occupational fraud are net worth, bank deposit analysis and expenditure method or sources and application of funds. The net worth method is the most widely known and it adapts readily to nontax investigations of illegal income. It can be used when an employee has accumulated wealth and acquired assets with illicit proceeds. Doing this, will cause the subject's net worth to increase from one year to the next. The formula for calculating net worth is simple:

Assets:
Less: *Liabilities*
Equals: Net worth
Less: *Prior year's net worth*
Equals: Net worth increase (decrease)
Plus: *Living expenses*
Equals: Income (or expenditures)

Less: *Funds from known sources*
Equals: Funds from unknown sources

There is a resemblance of this formula to the balance sheet used in businesses. A net worth investigation has several stages, the first of which is the identification of the subject's assets, liabilities and living expenses.

Another well established indirect method is the bank deposits analysis. As with net worth method, the basis is to look for funds from known and unknown sources. According to this technique the subject's banking activity rather than assets and expenditures are analyzed. The ideas behind this method is that if we take all of the subject's bank deposits for a given period, subtract any transfers between accounts and then add any expenditures made in cash, we will know how much total income the subject must have had during the period [17]. The bank deposits calculation is as follows:

Total deposits to all accounts:
Less: *Transfers and redeposits*
Equals: Net deposits to all accounts
Plus: *Cash expenditures*
Equals: Total receipts from all sources
Less: *Funds from known sources*
Equals: Funds from unknown sources

Transfers between accounts and the money that is taken out and re-deposited are subtracted, because this type of churning doesn't represent income. Also, only expenditures made in cash are considered, because this was money spent, not deposited. Expenditures made by check are ignored.

There is also a third method to detect occupational fraud in the Greek public sector. The expenditures method compares the subject's known sources of funds during a given period. Any excess expenditures can only be examined by the subject having income from unknown sources. This method is simpler than the net worth analysis method and can be accomplished using only one period, where the net worth method must have a base year as a start. The formula used to compute net worth using the expenditures method is:

Known expenditures:
Less: *Known source of funds*
Equals: Funds from unknown sources

When illicit funds or assets have been acquired then one fact remains constant. Proceeds from illicit activities must be disguised in some way to avoid being discovered. Employees with illicit activities have developed many sophisticated techniques to hide funds or assets. They are trying to hide assets through currency hoards, safe deposit boxes, financial investments, insurance products and deposits to financial institutions. All these ways to hide cash assets must be audited to detect a fraudster employee.

Bribery frauds are another corruption scheme in the Greek public sector and involve payments to influence an employee to send business to the vendor making the payments. The frauds include kickbacks (return of a portion of a monetary sum received, especially because of coercion or a secret agreement), bid rigging (pre-arrangement of a bid to particular vendor instead of to the lowest bidder) and others. There are a few things to check, known as "red flags" such as a change in lifestyle of an employee, discovery of a relationship between an employee and a vendor and weak segregation of duties in approving vendors and invoices. Red flag of fraud is a common term associated with fraud identification and indicates that there is a potential for a fraud scheme. However, it does not necessarily indicate a fraud scenario has occurred.

The profile of employees who are involved in bribery schemes may include the following characteristics which are red flags: drug and/or alcohol addiction, personal financial problems, gambling habit, private debts, persons supported by the employee, extraordinary medical expenses, significant and regular expenses for entertainment and/or travel, Bribes may be disguised as "consultant fees" in which the consultants act as conduits for channeling the funds, less a nominal commission, back to the company official. Prevention methods include: i) rotating duties of approving contracts and/or vendors and bid responsibilities and ii) segregating duties of approving vendors and awarding contracts or approving invoices [6].

Also economic extortion in services such as Public Tax Revenues Department is another phenomenon in the Greek public sector. Economic extortion is the opposite of a bribery fraud. Instead of a vendor offering a bribe, the employee demands payment from a vendor in order to favor the vendor. Red flags and prevention methods are the same as for bribery. Red flags include complaints because if a particular vendor is being favored, then competing vendors may file complaints. Additionally, employee complaints about the service of a favored vendor may lead to the discovery of bribery and a conflict of interest. Suspicious activity also exists if a public servant/employee suddenly pays off a large loan with no plausible explanation of the source of funds or he collateralizes a loan with cash deposits.

Whistleblowing is one element that can make a small but useful contribution to the containment of fraud by encouraging employees to report illegal activities to the Greek public sector. Employees are normally unwilling to engage in whistleblowing because the commonest reason is that people often find themselves either being dismissed or effectively forced to leave and then find themselves unemployable. So it is vitable to have suitable legislation in place to encourage whistleblowing where existing systems are not working [18]. Restoring trust in the public sector must involve access to information to promote transparency, perhaps the most important weapon against fraud.

The threat of surprise audits, especially in currency or cash departments, may be a powerful deterrent to occupational fraud. An adequate reporting program should emphasize the negative impacts on job and profits, should support that there are no penalties for furnishing good-faith information and should actively encourage employees to come forward with information and reports of suspicious activity.

CONCLUSIONS

The chapter examines occupational fraud in the Greek Public Sector and the steps that can be taken to avoid and combat it. Businesses have learned at great expense that an insider can pose the same threat as a customer. It is essential in the anti money laundering field to have co-equal programs "to know your customer" and "to know your employee".

The deterrence of occupational fraud begins in the employee's mind. Employees who perceive that they will be caught when engaging in occupational fraud, are less likely to commit it. How much deterrent effect this concept provides, will be dependent on a number of factors, both internal and external. Internal controls can have a deterrent effect only when the employee perceives that such a control exists and it is for the purpose of uncovering fraud.

Implementing a Know Your Employee program and methods from anti - money laundering and anti - fraud field, relevant with fictitious payments to employees, payroll fraud, overbilling, bribery, corruption and economic extortion, can have a negative effect on occupational fraud. Using direct and indirect methods such as behavior profile of employees, Benford's Law, job rotation, segregation of duties and others, administration of Greek public sector can restore a climate of mistrust and reduce occupational fraud. But we must remember that internal controls alone are insufficient to fully prevent occupational fraud. Employee and citizen education is the foundation of preventing and detecting occupational fraud. Greek public sector should provide at least some basic antifraud training at the time employees are hired. No factor alone will detect and deter occupational fraud in the Greek public sector.

Our proposals offer important solutions for political analysts, politicians and society as a whole.

REFERENCES

[1] Newspaper *Kathimerini*, 5.29.2010.
[2] General Inspector of Greek Public Administration, *Annual Report* (2008) (In Greek Language).
[3] Transparency International, *Progress Report 2009: Enforcement of the OECD convention on combating bribery of foreign public officials in international business transactions*, Germany (2009).
[4] Eigen, P., *Policy Reform*, 5(4), 187-201, (2002).
[5] Cressey, D., *Other People's Money: A study in the Social Psychology of Embezzlement*, Montclair, N.J.: Patterson Smith, (1973).
[6] Singleton, T., Singleton, A., Bologna, J., and Lindquist, R., *Fraud Auditing and Forensic Accounting*, third edition, USA: John Wiley and Sons, Inc., (2006).
[7] Sutherland, E.H., *White Collar Crime*, New York: Dryden Press, (1949).
[8] Clinard, M.B., and Quinney, R., *Criminal Behaviour System: A typology,* New York: Holt, Rinehart and Winston (1973).
[9] Association of Certified Fraud Examiners, 2010 Report to the Nations on *Occupational Fraud and Abuse,* USA, (2010).
[10] Vona, L., *Fraud Risk Assessment: Building a fraud audit program*, USA: John Wiley and Sons, Inc.(2008).
[11] Wells, J., *Corporate Fraud Handbook: Prevention and Detection*, second edition, USA: John Wiley and Sons, Inc. (2007).
[12] Benford, F., *Proceedings of the American Philosophical Society*, 78(4), 551-572, (1938).
[13] Rosetti, C., *Using Benford's Law to detect fraud*, USA: Association of Certified Fraud Examiners, Inc. (2008).

[14] Nigrini, M., *The Detection of Income Tax Evasion Through an Analysis of Digital Distributions* (Ph.D. Thesis, University of Cincinnati), (1992).

[15] Shein, M., and Lanza, R., *Financial Statement Auditing, Fraud Detection and Cash Recovery using Active Data for Excel*, USA: InformationActive Inc.(2007).

[16] Nissman, D. M., *Follow the Money: A Guide to Financial and Money Laundering Investigations*, USA: Corpus Juris Publishing Co. (2005).

[17] Madinger, J., *Money Laundering: A Guide for Criminal Investigators*, second edition, USA: Taylor and Francis Group, (2006).

[18] Haynes, A., *Journal of Financial Crime*, 8(2), 123-135, (2000).

In: Greece: Economics, Political and Social Issues
Editor: Panagiotis Liargovas

ISBN: 978-1-62100-944-3
© 2012 Nova Science Publishers, Inc.

Chapter 12

INFO-COMMUNICATION GLOBALISATION AND THE GLOBAL INFO-CASH (GIC): A PRACTICAL WAY FOR GREECE TO EMERGE FROM THE CRISIS

George K. Gantzias[*]
University of the Aegean,
Department of Cultural Technology and Communication,
Lesvos, Greece

ABSTRACT

Nowadays digital transactions are part of our everyday life. The info-communication globalisation becomes a fact of life for civil society worldwide, involving many actors – politicians, activists, non-governmental organisations, info-communication firms, software providers and political parties. This raises obvious questions for the role of new communications technologies, the recent Greek crisis, the info-communication public sphere, participatory democracy and the digital form of currencies. As the info-communication public sphere gets more complex and chaotic, regular citizens/users/consumers are gaining access to digital entertainment, information and education anywhere and at anytime.

This chapter examines and analyses the role of the info-communication globalisation in recent Greek crisis. It introduces the info-communication public sphere and the participatory democracy as analytical 'tools' to examine the Greek crisis. Moreover, it analyses the Greek crisis together with the recent crisis in the USA. Finally, it strongly recommends that a practical way for Greece and the USA to emerge from the recent crisis is: to switch off the physical form of the Euro and dollar currencies, i.e. the cash payments using different currencies such as the Euro and the Dollar and switch on the digital form of single currency the Global Info-Cash (GIG), i.e. the info-cash payment using the digital subdivision of the Global Info-Cash, such as Info-CashGR and Info-CashUSA.

---

[*]E-mail address: ggantzias@aegean.gr or/and infogic@yahoo.gr

INTRODUCTION: THE CRISIS IS AN OPPORTUNITY FOR GREECE TO BE DISTINCTIVE

Digital technology has changed the traditional way in which we communicate, express our ideas, understand freedom and make transactions in our everyday life. In 2011, more than 50 per cent of the world's population had access to some combination of mobile phones, the Internet users are about two billion. The broadband subscribers are more than 100 million and the majority of transactions are digital in the global free market economy [1][2]. The broadband networks (wire and wireless) promote, on one hand, an increase in digital capital transactions and, on the other, a digitalisation of content and services in the info-communication public sphere [2][5][26]. In free market economy, instant capital transactions across geographic nodes that would have taken days and months to cross with physical means almost 'cancel' the concept of time as an obstacle or expense in the accounting books of the international companies. Recently, the increase of digital transactions are shaping the info-communication globalisation as new technologies and management expertise have reduced transportation and transaction costs and as tariffs and other human-made barriers to global markets are collapsing in the free market economy [5][7][8][22].

The Greek crisis is an opportunity, not a barrier, in that it provides the country with a platform from which distinctive solutions can emanate. Greek political and economic culture should be reformed due to recent monetary crisis in order Greece to be an active player in the info-communication globalisation [67][69][29]. This chapter examines and analyses the role of the info-communication globalisation in recent Greek crisis. It introduces the info-communication public sphere and the participatory democracy as analytical 'tools' to examine the Greek crisis. Moreover, it is trying to analyse the Greek crisis in combination with the recent crisis in the USA. Finally, it strongly recommends that a practical way for Greece and the USA to get out of the recent crisis is: to switch off the physical form of the Euro and dollar currencies, i.e. the cash payments using different currencies such as the Euro and the Dollar and switch on the digital form of single currency the Global Info-Cash (GIG), i.e. the info-cash payment using the digital subdivision of the Global Info-Cash, such as Info-CashGR and Info-CashUSA.

THE INFO-COMMUNICATION GLOBALISATION IN GREECE

Globalization has its origins in cultural, economic, political and social factors, as documented by scholarly analyses and scientific research in the field [11][[13][21]. The forces driving the info-communication globalization are not only the new technologies, the convergences of markets and the global network society but also regulation, public interest and the digital form of currencies (info-cash). This is in fact what separates, in size, speed and complexity, the info-communication globalization from other types of globalization [10][9][14][15][24].

Globalization and new technologies empower citizens / users / consumers to have access anywhere and anytime to the info-communication platforms by developing an info-communication culture to participate in the global network society [2][3][4][63]. According to the research "The Info-Communication Globalization, Participatory Freedom and the

Global Info-Cash (GIC)", *the info-communication culture is subject to both globally and locally cultural patterns which are:*

- Consumerism (signified by brands) - it refers to culture of consumerism which is directly related to the formation of global capitalist markets. Most countries now live under capitalism – sharing of market values and consumer culture.
- Networked individualism – it refers to a set of values and beliefs that gives priority to the satisfactions of individual needs and desires.
- cosmopolitanism (be ideological, political, or religious) – it refers to small but influential minority people – there is consciousness of the shared destiny of the planet we inhabit, be in terms of the environment, human rights, moral principles, global economics interdependency or geopolitical security.
- multiculturalism – it refers to existence of a multicultural global cultural characteristics by hybridization and remix of cultures from difference origins – as the diffusion of hip hop music in adapted version throughout the world or remixed video that populate YouTube.
- Communalism – It is a set of norms, values and beliefs that place the common goods over the individual satisfaction of its members on the basis of public interest principles.

These cultural patterns, the broadband networks and the info-com devices (i.e. mobile phones, tablets PCs, etc.) have been the causal dynamics of the Info-Communication globalisation. The digital revolution is the driving force for the domination of digital transactions, participatory freedom and the info-communication public sphere [5][28][27][40]. According to the research "The Info-Communication Globalization, Participatory Freedom and the Global Info-Cash (GIC)",

'the info-communication globalization is the type of globalization which is defined by the global culture, the net generation, the info-communication devises (all type of mobile phones, computers, tablet PC, etc.), the convergence of the internet and wireless communication, the info-communication public sphere, participatory freedom, regulation and public interest… in which all national economic, cultural and political systems become open, transparent and accountable and all national-states systems should behave according to the logic of the information accumulation and regulation.

Therefore, the info-communication globalisation is a dynamic process where there is transformation through digitalisation of social, political, economic and cultural systems – and attempts to encapsulate the present stages of the new communications technologies, concurrently with issues of regulation, public interest and participatory freedom[29][41][28][20][2].

THE INFO-COMMUNICATION PUBLIC SPHERE IN GREECE

Digital communication has become part of our everyday life, involving many local and global actors–regular citizens, activist, governments, information companies, communication companies and NGOs. (Non-Governmental Organisations) Social media like facebook and twitter increase shared awareness by publishing messages and opening democratic dialogues in the frame of info-communication globalisation [39][38][15][14][40]. The info-communication networks are online nodes (important online nodes are called 'online centres') where democratic dialogues and conversations are connecting citizens and governments, elected representatives, political parties and the net generation. For most people, life is recorded in fragmented narratives and the democratic conversation must be incessant if it is to be integrated in the info-communication networks [4][37][36][35]. According to the research "The Info-Communication Globalisation, Participatory Freedom and the Global Info-Cash (GIC)"

> 'The info-communication network's democratic dialogues and conversations are shaping a new type of public sphere, which we called 'the info-communication public sphere' (info-com public sphere). The info-com public sphere is created mainly by flows of massages among the citizens/users/consumers, though time and space in the global network society. The main characteristic of the info-com public sphere are:

> - Openness – opening participatory access to local, regional and global networks at anytime, anywhere, by anyone
> - Inclusion – a voice for all to express their opinion and ideas at local, regional and global levels,
> - Deliberation – making the most of citizens/ users / consumers needs in the info-communication globalisation
> - Responsiveness: listening and responding to citizens/ users / consumers fears and desires.

Nowadays, the main activities that shape and control our everyday life are organised by info-communication networks (i.e. the network of financial markets, international companies for valuating financial markets, the transitional NGO, international institutions, social movement, the social media, etc). Facebook and MySpace, along with other 'info-communication networks' such as Twitter, YouTube, Flickr and Bebo, exemplify the new type of public sphere in the info-communication globalisation. Recently, Facebook boast approximately 600 million active users, who on average day each spend 25 minutes on the site [25]. There are now about 5 million internet users in Greece (46.2 % of the Greek population), most of them active participants on the 'info-communication networks' such as facebook, Youtube, Twitter, etc [1]. In that digital environment, the Greek citizens/ users / consumers have the ability not to withdraw into isolation; on the contrary, they are participating actively in order to protect their info-communication rights [19][18][17][16].

In information and knowledge society, the info-communication rights cover a broad range: access to information, protection of participatory freedom, copyrights, digital exploitation of work, validity of transparency, digital signatures, crime in cyberspace, unlawful Internet content, protection of information of a private nature, the rights to make digital transactions and the rights to use the digital form of global currency (i.e. the Global Info-Cash) [68] [71]. The protection of citizens/users/consumers' rights must rely on the participatory approach in the info-communication public sphere. The participatory approach relies on global corporation, harmonization, participatory freedom and consensus in the info-communication globalization [28][23][6][19][23]. Google and Facebook as active platforms in the info-communication public sphere are introducing a new face of participation and freedom to all democratic systems around the world. Uricchio (2004) argues that "participation in these peer-to-peer collaborative communities constitutes a form of cultural citizenship' [31]. The first modern national republics such as the American Republic, the British parliamentary monarchy, etc. were forming a public sphere that Jurgen Habermas (1989) called 'the bourgeois public sphere'[32][33][34]]. That type of public sphere had a different character and preceded the digital revolution in society. Nowadays, digital technology marks a new type of the public sphere, the info-communication public sphere, which is characterized by networked collaboration and collective intelligence, anytime and anywhere [35][37][63].

The information and communication technologies permeate the way the Greek citizens/users/customers study, learn, educate, communicate, do business and access info-communication platforms, get informed and make payment transactions both globally and locally in the info-communication public sphere. Nowadays, Greek citizens/users/consumers show a significant degree of disappointment have informed by traditional media (newspapers, TV, radio, etc) and keeping up with the events by getting involved in compiling, sharing, filtering, discussing and distributing information and news. The Greek population is gaining greater access to information, more opportunities to engage in public speech, and enhanced ability to undertake collection action [59][56][41][75][48][77]. In the recent cultural and economic crises as the protest of "*Aganaktismenoi*" (indignants) in Athens demonstrated, these increased freedoms can help loosely coordinate citizens/users/consumers' demand for change.

The info-communication platforms such as Twitter, CNN, Aljazzira, Youtube have become platforms whereby people report what they are witnessing in virtually any part of the world. Classified documents are published in bundles online. Mobile-phone footage of the recent demonstration in Athens, uprisings in the Arab world described by the media as the 'Arab spring', tornadoes in U.S.A. and tsunami in Japan are posted on the info-communication platforms. Celebrities and world leaders, including Barack Obama [78] and Hugo Cháves [79], George Pappadreou [80], publish updates directly via social media. In addition, many governments around the world make raw data available through 'open government' initiatives in order to present themselves as more accountable and transparent. The Greek government is introducing info-communication platforms in the public sector, in order to improve communication with citizens/users/consumers and companies, and to promote transparency and accountability [42][41][59][57][69][47][77]. Moreover, the Greek government encourages active participation and participatory freedom in the info-communication public sphere by promoting the «Cl@rity» program. In particular, from *October 1st 2010, all Ministries are obliged to upload their decisions on the Internet, through the «Cl@rity» program. Cl@rity is one of the major transparency initiatives of the Ministry of the Interior, Decentralization and e-Government. Henceforth, the decisions of the public entities can not be implemented if they are not uploaded on the Clarity websites, each document is digitally singed and assigned a transaction unique number automatically by the system [42].*

Nowadays, the democratic institutions and political parties must become sensitive to the ways in which real people tell their stories and express their fears and desires. The Greek citizens are very disappointed with the political parties and they want to see an authentic relationship between 'speaking and being heard, input and output, touching the level and watching the wheel turn' [75][69][48][49]. In other words, according to the research "The Info-Communication Globalisation, Participatory Freedom and the Global Info-Cash (GIC)" 'the Greek citizens/users/customers do not want to be asked their opinions merely so that a government can claim that it has asked them for...Greek citizens/users/consumers do want to be asked and heard by the politicians when they are making decisions which are affecting seriously their everyday life'. The info-com public sphere empowers Greek citizens/users/consumers to:

- be independent from party politics,
- understand the serious role of the public interest in the decision making process,
- have access to appropriate sources,
- be well informed,
- set up an appropriate mechanism for structuring and displaying the decision-making process,
- articulate their ideas,
- protect their info-communication rights such as the participatory freedom, access to information, validity of transparency, etc'.

PARTICIPATORY FREEDOM IN GREECE

In the info-communication public sphere citizens/users/consumers from all countries around the world are asking for global accountability, global transparency, global regulations, global currency and global policies to promote democracy, freedom, public interest and regulation. In particular, any global policy to promote participatory freedom and public interest between government and citizens' success depends upon the extent that feedback loops are bidirectional and governments are willing and able to respond to them. The governments should encourage policies for participatory freedom and public interest by getting involved in online consultation and discussion. In particular, it is vital for the Greek government and its ministers to demonstrate their commitment to listening to and learning from the contributions that are made by the citizens and potentially the Greek diaspora, and to respond to them in a timely and transparent way [57][42][15][2][63]. The success of implementation of policies for participatory freedom is not dependent upon technical operations of the info-communication platforms (internet, mobile networks, etc.), but upon measures capable of enhancing democratic efficiency, transparency, accountability, regulation and public interest.

Internet freedom is a very important issue for the existence of the info-communication public sphere. Nowadays, Internet freedom contributes to develop global policies and global regulation for encouraging participatory freedom in the info-communication society. Clay Shirky (2011) pointed out that

'U.S. Secretary of State Hillary Clinton outlines how the U.S. would promote Internet freedom abroad... there are several kind of freedom, including the freedom to access information (such as the ability to use Wikipedia and Google inside Iran), the freedom of ordinary citizens to produce their public media (such as the rights of Burmese activists to blog) and the freedom of citizens to converge with one another (such as the Chinese public's capacity to use instant messaging without interference)'[45].

The info-communication technology – mobile phones, text messages, digitals currencies, social networking, the Internet – widens the circle of citizens/users/consumers to easily and inexpensively share ideas and aspirations [63][2][5][71][12][39]. According to the research "The Info-Communication Globalisation, Participatory Freedom and the Global Info-Cash (GIC)",

'the spread of new type of freedom, the 'Participatory Freedom' (PF), makes it harder and costlier to isolate the citizens/users/consumers from the rest of world and gives them ordinary tools to be active in the info-communication globalisation....'Participatory Freedom' (PF) should be considered as a fundamental democratic right that empowers citizens/users/consumers to be active both globally and locally in the info-communication public sphere'.

GREECE AND EURO: THE GLOBAL-INFO CASH (GIC) AS A FEASIBLE AND EFFECTIVE SOLUTION

Greece became a member of the European Communities (European Union) on 1st January 1981 and joined the euro in 2001. In 2009, the Greek Prime Minister George Papandreou announced that the Greek government's structural deficit was not around 6 per cent of GDP, but was over 12 per cent, which marked the recession in the Greek economy. In 2011, the Greece crisis is still in recession with the unemployment of 15.8 per cent and youth unemployment of about 40 per cent, although public sector salaries have been cut, taxes are going up, shops and businesses are closing and Greek banks are still waiting for good news to arrive from the global free market economy [47][75][66].

The need for reform of established institutions, markets, regulations and legislations in our society is not a new phenomenon. Thomas Jefferson, the third President of the United States, stated in 1816 that:

...both laws and institutions must go hand with the progress of human mind.As that become more developed, more enlightened, as new discoveries are made, new truths disclosed, and manners and opinions with the change of circumstances, institutions must advance also, and keep pace with the time.

This statement indicates how important it is for each country and particularly for Greece to keep up with the changes by reforming its economic, political, cultural, communication and legal systems when the time is right [67][65][57]. Almost everybody has a different perception regarding the right time for reforms in Greece. The fundamental question for reforming the traditional widely corrupt and dysfunctional cultural and political system in Greece is the following: Can digital technology bridge the gap between the government and the governed in Greece?

The digital technology can serve as a bridge for the gap between governments and governed in the info-communication globalisation. A large number of political leaders around the world have been enthusiastic as regards the advocacy of policies for the digitization of democratic systems and transactions. Most of them agree that governments should use new technologies such as the Internet to empower citizens and their governments to be more open and transparent in their decision-making processes [57][15][16][58][30][77]. The Greek Prime Minister George Papandreou in his speech to World Congress on Information Technology, 21 May 2004 pointed out that there is a growing pressure upon public administration at all levels to devise policies that will give substance to these aspirations. Recently, the Greek Prime Minister George Papandreou [80] pointed out that "We want a different Greece."

The global credit crises together with the recent Greek, Portuguese and Irish financial crisis marked the start of the visible part of the crisis in the European monetary system. According to Brendan Brown (2010) *'Right at the start the monetary union, and indeed even half-year before its formal start (from mid- to end- 1998) the founder members of the European Central Bank (ECB) took a serious of ill-fated decisions regarding the design of the monetary policy framework'[50].* According to the research "The Info-Communication Globalisation, Participatory Freedom and the Global Info-Cash (GIC)" *'the Greek crisis could not be so serious if the guiding monetary principle in the Treaty (the monetary clause) would have included not only the goal of monetary stability alongside the aim of price level stability in the long run but also a set of clear public interest principles for monetary union and a 'regulatory mechanism' for the single currency (i.e. euro)'.*

Furthermore, according to the above research *'the monetary policy was mainly a policy for establishing the euro as a single unit for making easer the transactions in EU markets and not as cultural asset for achieving political and economic convergence of the EU members states'.* In that respect the membership of the European citizen as a consumer or a businessman-investor in the European and global markets, although supported by the advantage of equal participation in the monetary system of a single European market economy, in fact, can not be implemented successfully without having support from backup systems, which have the authority to monitor, regulate and manage effectively and at the right time the single currency's (the Euro) cultural, political and social characteristics [67].

The recent crisis in Greece is not only economic but also cultural and political. According to the first president of the ECB, Wim Duisenberg, *'The euro is much more than just currency. It is a symbol of European integration in every sense of the world'[52].*

In 1st January 2002 Romano Prodi on the CNN claimed:

> 'The euro is not economic at all. It is a completely political step…the historic significance of the euro is to construct a bi-polar economy in the world. The two poles are the dollar and the euro. That is the political meaning of the single European currency. It is a step beyond which there will be others. The euro is just an antipasto'[53].

Moreover, Jason Manolopoulos (2011) pointed out for the time when Greece jointed the euro that '

> The total public debt was above 'maximum" of 60 per cent of the GDP, but the EU had water down this requirement through Article 104c(b) which simply required that the debt be in the process of falling and that it should 'approach the reference value (60%) at satisfactory pace'[55].

The European leaders, at that time, focused on spending more energy on meeting the single currency targets (i.e. monetary union, participation of Greece to the European elite club, etc.) rather than setting a clear set of public interest principles and a regulatory mechanism for achieving actual cultural, political and economic convergence. Nowadays, history repeats itself, and the European leaders are focused on spending more energy in meeting the targets to save the Euro and the collapsing European monetary system, rather than seriously exploring other possible solutions to the recent crisis, such the Global Info-Cash (GIC) solution described above [66] [29][72].

Recently not only Greece but also the USA is heavily financing consumption with debt. According to Mr Paul Volcker, former Chairman who was president of New York Federal Bank during the 70s crisis pointed out 'we borrow and borrow and continually spend and, so long as people are willing to lend, there is not sufficient pressure to do something about it in a timely way'[46]. According to Raghuram Rajan (2011) 'To see, why the United States has come to run such a large trade deficit, it is necessary to understand U.S. consumptions increased so dramatically…U.S. consumption increased from about 67 percent of GDP in the late 1990 to about 70 percent in 2007, financed largely with debt'[55] . In the info-communication globalisation, the loss of 'accountability in monetary systems' and 'the behaviour of governments to finance consumption largely with debt' together with the lack of global regulations, public interest principles, participatory freedom and a common digital form of global currency (i.e. GIC) are the main reasons for the 'snowball effect' of crisis in Greece, EU and USA [29]. In July 2011 the USA lost its triple A credit by the huge increases in the USA government debt level. According to Stephanie Kirchgaessner and Michael Mackenzie (2011) 'White house and Republicans leaders dashed to shore up support on Capitol Hill for a compromise to prevent a US debt default, even as the markets switched their focus to more bad news about the economy…The house of Representatives was expected to vote on Monday night on proposed legislation…increase the dept ceiling by $2,100bn until 2013' [60].

The traditional corporations that evaluate bonds or even States (rating agencies such Moody's, Fitch, etc.) have been making a lot of noise by promoting analyses for selective or limited default of the Greek economy and by focusing to more bad news about the economy in the USA. According to Aline van Duyn and Richard Milne, (2011) 'the rating agencies, have been actually in the fire since the financial crisis – after trillions of dollars of debt backed by risky US mortgages was rate triple A but ended up worthless. The Financial Crisis Inquiry Commission established by the US government in 2009 found that: 'the failure of credit rating agencies were essential cogs in the wheels of financial destruction'" [61]. Therefore, not only Greece but also the USA is very close to default on its government debt. So the 'crisis virus' is not a 'Greek originated virus' but a 'global originated virus' and 'European oriented virus'.

The possibilities of collapsing European monitory policy together with the emerging of the digital form of global currency, the GIC, are challenging seriously the duopoly paradigm of the world currency system (i.e. the US dollar and the Euro). The idea of "money as a creature of the State' is valid insofar as it will be adapted in the info-communication globalisation [22][23][72][51][38][44][30]. In more than 6.9 billion people in the world today, there are at least 182 current official or de facto currencies in the 192 United Nations member countries. In the recent monetary crisis 'the main currencies float and crush against each other like continental plates'[62]. Moreover, Zhou Xiaochuan (2009), governor of the People's Bank of China, the new power player on the global financial stage, recently argued: The desirable goal of reforming the international monetary system, therefore, is to create an international reserve currency that is disconnected from individual nations and is able to remain stable in the long run, thus removing the inherent deficiencies caused by using credit-based national currencies [64].

Asking the right question is half way to find a practical solution, to answer to it correctly is the other half way to get the right solution. Furthermore, to agree to implement the right solution is definitely the way out of the crisis. This is the step by step approach to get out of the recent crisis, both globally and locally. Nowadays, the government leaders around the world should be able to avoid keep asking themselves the wrong question for getting out of the recent crisis of free market economy.

- Which country is 'the guilty one' for the recent crisis of free market economy? In recent crisis the quility country is probably Greece, but it is the wrong question to ask when the recent crisis is a 'global oriented virus'.

The right question to ask them is:

- Is the right time for their countries to switch off the physical form of currencies (i.e. the method of cash payment, the Euro, the dollar, etc.) and switch on the digital form of single currency the Global Info-Cash (GIC) with its digital subdivisions (i.e. Info-CashGr, Info-CashEU, Info-CashUSA etc. - the method of info-cash payments) in their free market economy?

Moreover, the citizens/users/consumers in Greece and the USA should ask themselves an important question for understanding the role of digital revolution in the recent crisis, which is:

- What connects the info-com devices (i.e. mobile phones, tablet PCs etc.,) Greece, the USA and the rating agencies (Moody's, Fitch, etc.);

One answer to that question is the following: The info-com devices (i.e. mobile phones, tablet PCs etc.,) give the opportunity to the Greek and USA citizens/users/consumers to have access and use digital form of currencies (i.e. info-cash) by making secure electronic payments at anytime and anywhere[65][68][67]. The mobile phone base on digital technology for electronic payments (i.e. mobile phones within the contactless technology or special chips for payments are the digital wallets), the rating agencies are evaluating the markets by using digital information (i.e. they rely on digital technology to evaluate markets) and the Greek and the US governments are using 'open government' platforms to inform their citizens/users/consumers (i.e. digital communication in the info-communication public sphere). Therefore, digital technology is not only the main connection between them, but a good reason for governments of Greece and the USA to be different (i.e. changing their financial behaviours, financing their consumption only by their debt), in the info-communication globalisation.

In conclusion, economic policy in developed world over the past 20 years has been subject to one overriding principle: to avoid of recession at all cost. In free market economy the monetary policy was the 'tool of choices' in the 20th century. Nowadays, the recession is increasing and the role of both global and local regulations together with the principle of public interest is extremely important in reforming Greek economic, political and cultural systems. At global level the protection of public interest would be used as the main justification for setting up a global regulatory system in information society. Public interest arguments, for example, have been used as the main justification for setting up specific rules for regulatory bodies to operate effectively in the information society [28][72][29].

According to Frank Webster (2009)

'the information society marks a profound transformation in our ways of life cannot be supported on the basis of the quantitative indices that are typically advanced. There can be no doubt that, in advanced nations, information and communication technologies are now pervasive and that information has grown in economic significance, as the substance of much work, and in amounts of symbolic output'[70].

Recently the use of mobile phones as the digital wallets for electronic payments marks a profound transformation our way of doing our payments in the info-communication globalization. Furthermore, the digital payments would have an economic and cultural significance in the Greek info-communication public sphere [6].

CONCLUSION: IS THE GLOBAL INFO-CASH (GIC) A SOLUTION TO CRISIS?

In the info-communication globalisation the citizens/users/customers are using their mobile (smart) phones as digital wallets for paying their cups of tea or coffee. In UK there are different research projects for examining and analyzing the role of using mobile phones as digital wallets. According to the BBC *'consumers can already take advantage of digital form of money in the UK, if their credit or debit card is enabled - designated on Barclaycards, for example, with a wireless symbol'[73].* According to the Daily Mirror, 'there are more than 12 million contactless credits and debit card in circulation. David Chan, chief executive of Barclaycard Consumer Europe, said:

"This is the first time that customers can use their mobile to pay for goods and services in shops across the UK rather than using cards or cash. They'll be able to do this, safe in the knowledge that this is a secure technology brought to them by the biggest names in payments and mobile technology'[74].

Nowadays, the customers could have the info-communication right or a special permission from their banks (i.e. contactless credits and debit card) to use their mobile phone as a digital wallet for buying a cinema ticket, a sandwich or a cup of coffee without the need for a card or cash (physical form of money). The Payments Council, which oversees payments strategy in the UK, recent report pointed out that using the physical form of money could be a minority activity by 2050 [73].

The Greek banks are heading towards that direction of using the methods of digital payment, using mobile phones as digital wallets. Moreover, due to the recent crisis, the Greek government introduced legislation for allowing the Greek citizens/users/costumes to make payments using cash (physical form of money) up to the amount of 3000 Euros, above which Greek citizens/users/costumes are obliged by law to use their bank accounts or their credit or debit cards. This is one of the methods that the Greek government intends to encourage transparency for payment's transactions in the Greek market [29].

Therefore, all countries around the world and not only Greece need to reform their social, political, cultural and economic system by switching off the physical form of currency and switching on the digital form of global currency (i.e. the Global Info-Cash) as soon as possible. According to the research, 'The Info-Communication Globalisation, Participatory Freedom and the Global Info-Cash (GIC)'

'It is very expensive for governments to produce, manage, store, control and regulate the transactions using the money as physical form than using the money as a digital form in the recent crisis. In the info-communication globalisation the physical form of money is like a 'corpse with a perfume'...and the digital form currency (the Global Info-Cash (GIC) with its digital subdivision, such as the Info-CashGR, the Info-Cash EU, the Info-CashUS, etc) is a practical solution for all governments around the world who want to:

- cut spending,
- collect taxes,
- improve services and products,
- reduce their debt
- be transparent and accountable in their policy making
- introduce local focused and global ranged regulatory bodies

REFERENCES

[1]   Internet World Stats - http://www.internetworldstats.com/stats9.htm.

[2]   Manuel Castels, *Communication power* Oxford University Press, New York., (2009)

[3]   Tiziana Terranova *Network Culture: Politics for the Information Age*, Pluto Press, London, 39-75, (2004).

[4]   Castells, Manuel *'The Information Age: Economy, Society, and Culture'.* (1996-98) *1998* Oxford:Blackwell. *Volume I: The Rise of the Network Society (1996) Volume II: The Power of Identity (1997). Volume III: End of Millennium (1998)* Revised edition for volumes I and III (2000).

[5]   D. Tapscott, *The Digital Economy: Promise and peril in an age of networked intelligence*, McGraw-Hill, (1996).

[6]   Ulrick Beck, *What Is Globalisation?* Cambridge: Polity press, 17-77, (2000).

[7]   Frank Webster, *'Theories of the Information Society'*, Routledge, London, (1995)

[8]   George Gantzias *'The Info-communication Industry: Digital Markets, Global Services'*, Zeno Publishers, London, (1998).

[9]   Frank Webster (et.al.) (eds.) *The Information Society Reader*, Rutledge, London, (2004).

[10]   Ulrick Beck, *What Is Globalisation?* Cambridge: Polity press, 25 -77, (2000).

[11]   David Held and Anthonny McGrew, (eds.) *Introduction to Governing Globalization* Cambridge: Polity press, 5-21, (2002).

[12] Frank Webster (et. all) eds.*The Information Society Reader* (Routledge Student Readers) Routledge, London, (2003).

[13] Paul Hirst and Graham Thompson *Globalisation in Question*. Cambridge: Polity press (1996).

[14] D. Held, *Global Social Democracy*, in A. Giddens (ed.), "The Progressive Manifesto", Cambridge: Polity, (2003).

[15] K.Nash, *Global Citizenship as Showbusiness: the Cultural Politics of Make Poverty History*, Media, Culture and Society 30/1: 167–81, (2008).

[16] Crawford, J. and Marks, S. *The Global Democracy Deficit: an Essay in International Law and its Limits*, in D. Archibugi, D. Held and M. Kohler (eds), 'Re-imagining Political Community: Studies in Cosmopolitan Democracy', Stanford: California: Stanford University Press, 1998.

[17] Edward Herman and Noam Chomsky, *Manufacturing Consent,*: Pantheon Books, New York (1988).

[18] Noam Chomsky, *Deterring Democracy*, Verso, London (1991).

[19] Frank Webster, Information Warfare, Surveillance and Human Rights, in Kirstie Ball and Frank Webster (eds), *The Intensification of Surveillance: Crime, Terrorism and Warfare in the Information Age* (pp.90-111), Pluto Press, London: (2003).

[20] Frank Webster, *Cultural Technology and Policy Journal*, 1, 49-66. www.ctpj.

[21] info Salvator Babones *Studying Globalization: Methodological Issuses,* in George Ritzer 'The Blackwell Companion to Globalization" Blackwell, Oxford. 144-61, (2007).

[22] Peter Dicker *Economic Globalization: Corporations* in George Ritzer 'The Blackwell Companion to Globalization" Blackwell, Oxford. 291-306, (2007)

[23] Carolyn Warner, *Globalization and Corruption* in George Ritzer 'The Blackwell Companion to Globalization" Blackwell, Oxford, 593-609, (2007)

[24] John Dunning, *Governments, Globalization and International Business.* Clarendon Press, Oxford (1997).

[25] Bod Garfield, *Spectrum*, 48(6) 30, (2011).

[26] Gary W. Flake et al., *IEEE Computer* 35(3), 66-71, (2002).

[27] Martinelli, Alberto, *Journal of World-Systems Research* 11, 241-260, (2005).

[28] George K Gantzias, *The Dynamics of Regulation Global Control, Local Resistance: Cultural Management and Policy,* Ashgate, Aldershot, England, 37-44.,(2001)

[29] George K. Gantzias, *The Info-Communication Globalisation, Participatory Freedom and the Global Info-Cash (GIC)* (Forthcoming)

[30] John G. Ikenberry, *The Future of the Liberal World Order Foreign Affairs*, 90(3), 56-68, (2011).

[31] W. Uricchio, *Cultural Citizenship in the Age of P2P Networks* in Bondjeberg, I. and Golding, P. (eds.) 'European Culture and the Media" Intellect Books, Bristol, p. 140,(2004).

[32] Jurgen Habermas, *The Structural Transformation of the Public Sphere: an Inquiry into a Category of Bourgeois Society*, Cambridge: Polity, (1989).

[33] Jurgen Habermas, *Between Facts and Norms: Contributions to a Discourse Theory of Law and Democracy*, Cambridge: Polity, (1996).

[34] Edward S. Herman, *Cultural Technology and Policy Journal*, 1, 5-22. www.ctpj.info

[35] E Bell, *The blogs of war*, The Observer, 30 March. (2003).

[36] L. Kahney, *Internet Strokes Anti-War movement*, Wired, 21 January. (2003).

[37] Clay Shirky, *Foreign Affairs*, 90(1), 28-41, (2011)

[38] David Kushner, *Spectrum*, 48(6), 63-65 (2011).

[39] Bod Garfield, *Spectrum*, 48(6), 27-33 (2011).

[40] John Rennie and Glenn Zoprette, *Spectrum*, 48(6), 23-25 (2011).

[41] George Gantzias, *'Cultural Policy and Regulation in the Info-Communication Industry'* in Vernilos, N, et.al. (eds.) Cultural Industries, Kritiki, Athens, (2005).

[42] Transparency and Openness Policies of the Greek Government: http://diavgeia.gov.gr/en

[43] Herny Farrell and John Quiggin ,*Foreign Affairs*, 90(3), 96-103, (2011).

[44] Michael Spence, *Foreign Affairs*, 90(4), 28-41, (2011)

[45] Clay Shirky ,*Foreign Affairs*, 90(1), 30, (2011)

[46] Nicole Bullock, *Echoes of New York in 1975 as views harden,* Financial Times, p.5., (July 25, 2011).

[47] Gideon Rachman, *Greece needs a new political culture,* Financial Times, (July 25, 2011)

[48] Christos Lyrintzis, *West European Politics*, 7(2), 100-113 (1984).

[49] Christos Lyrintzis, *European Journal of Political Research*, 15, 670-83 (1987)

[50] Brendan Brown, *Euro Crash: The Implications of Monetary Failure in Europe,* Palgrave Macmillan, UK. p. 4, 2010.

[51] R. L. Hetzel, *Economic Quarterly*, 95(2), pp. 203-29, (2009).

[52] Jason Manolopoulos, *Greece's 'ODIOUS' debt*, Anthems Press, London, p. 46, (2011).

[53] Jason Manolopoulos, *Greece's 'ODIOUS' debt*, Anthems Press, London, p. 33, (2011).

[54] Jason Manolopoulos, *Greece's 'ODIOUS' debt*, Anthems Press, London, p. 55, (2011).

[55] Raghuram Rajan *Foreign Affairs*, 90(2), 109. (2011).

[56] George K. Gantzias and Kammaras, Dimitris *'Media'* in Graham Speake (ed.) Encyclopaedia of Greece and Helenic Tradition, Fitzroy Dearborn, vol.2, London, pp. 1020-23, (2000).

[57] George K. Gantzias, *'Report for Greece: Information and Communication* Technologies, Regulation Framework, Cyber-Security and Cyber-Crime, Public and Private Corporation, Rand, Information Society Technology Programme: DDSI: IST-2002-29202. (1998-2002).

[58] Ulrick Beck, *What Is Globalisation?* Cambridge: Polity press, p. 20-55 (2000).

[59] George K. Gantzias, K. *'Communication Systems in the 21st century: Reform and Public Interest'* in George K. Gantzias and Dimitris Kamaras *Digital Communication, New Media and the Greek Information Society: Convergence, 'E-Commerce and Portals,* Zenon publishers, London, pp. 11-56. (2000).

[60] Stephanie Kirchgaessner and Michael Mackenzie, *Dash to secure US debt deal*, Financial Times, p.1, (August, 2, 2011).

[61] Aline Van Duyn and Richard Milne, *Arbiters under fire,* Financial Times, p.7, (July, 25, 2011).

[62] Alfred P. Lerner, American Economic Review 37, 312, (1947).

[63] Frank Webster *The Information Society Revisited*, in Leah A Lievrouw and Sonia Livingstone pp. Handbook of New Media Social Shaping and Consequences of ICTs, Sage Publication, pp 22-34, (2002).

[64] Zhou Xiaochuan, *Reform the International Monetary System,* The People's Bank of China, 23rd March, (Retrieved May 21, 2009), (http://www.pbc.gov.cn/english/detail.asp?col=6500andid=178).

[65] George Mavros, *Digital Money will save us!* Social Issues, Imerisia, Economic Newspaper, 12/13 March 2011, p. 38-39 (http://www.imerisia.gr/article.asp?catid=12333andsubid=2andpubid=102955157#) (Retrieved July 13, 2011),

[66] George Mavros, *Cultural mine for the stability of Euro, Politics,* Imerisia, p.22, 8/05/2010, http://www.imerisia.gr/article.asp?catid=15459andsubid=2andpubid=28521152 (Retrieved July 13, 2011)

[67] George K. Gantzias *The Crisis is an opportunity to Greece: From Euro to Info-Cash,* Kosmos of Ependitis, *Economic Newspaper,* p. 20, (15 May 2010).

[68] George K. Gantzias *Cultural Politics, Sponsorship and Corporate Social Responsibility* Papasotitiriou, Athens, (2010)

[69] George K. Gantzias *Loss in the Crisis Era, Analysis,* Imerisia, p 43, (21/24 April 2011).

[70] Frank Webster *The Information Society Revisited,* in Leah A Lievrouw and Sonia Livingstone pp. Handbook of New Media Social Shaping and Consequences of ICTs, Sage Publication, pp 33, (2002).

[71] Leah A Lievrouw and Sonia Livingstone *Handbook of New Media Social Shaping and Consequences of ICTs,* Sage Publication, (2002).

[72] Keith Pilbeam *Finace and Finacial Markets, third edition,* Palgrave Macmilan, (2010) pp. 457-481.

[73] BBC, *Orange customers of Everything Everywhere get mobile payments* http://www.bbc.co.uk/news/technology-12287009 (accessed 27 July 2011)

[74] The Daily Mirror, *New mobile phone payment system,* http://www.mirror.co.uk/news/latest/2011/05/20/new-mobile-phone-payment-system-115875-23142805/ (Retrieved 27 July 2011)

[75] Jason Manolopoulos, *Greece's 'ODIOUS' debt,* Anthems Press, London, (2011)

[76] See more about the Global Info-Cash on the web sites, www.globalinfocash.com.

[77] The first site about Greek Elections is www.EklogesOnline.com and/or www.greekelections.com - democratic platform for exchanging ideas and views in the info-communication public sphere.

[78] Facebook (the political info-communication public sphere) - Barack Obama. http://www.facebook.com/barackobama;

[79] Facebook (the political info-communication public sphere) - Hugo Cháves; http://www.facebook.com/pages/Hugo-Ch%C3%A1vez/112591172085879;

[80] Facebook (the political info-communication public sphere) George A. Papandreou. http://el-gr.facebook.com/george.a.papandreou

In: Greece: Economics, Political and Social Issues
Editor: Panagiotis Liargovas

ISBN: 978-1-62100-944-3
© 2012 Nova Science Publishers, Inc.

Chapter 13

GREEK FOREIGN POLICY SINCE THE END OF WORLD WAR II

Charalambos Tsardanidis[*]
Institute of International Economic Relations,
Athens, Greece

ABSTRACT

The liberation of Greece from Nazi occupation in October 1944 gave birth to hopes that the country would find its pace and a new era would emerge despite the disasters brought by the war. These hopes were soon gone when, in December 1944, the first battles began in Athens between the forces of ELAS (Greek People's Liberation Army), and the British forces and Greek armed groups supporting the legitimate government of George Papandreou. This civil war which lasted until 1949, as well as the real commencement of Cold War in 1947 that is connected to the Greek civil war, have marked Greek foreign policy in a decisive manner. Greece had no other option but to join the West. This purpose of this chapter is to make an assessment of Greek foreign policy since the end of World War II.

INTRODUCTION

In the post-war era, Athens achieved security in two ways. The first involved participation in a traditional balance-of-power system: NATO membership, close relationship with the US and the second integration into the West. The effort to achieve economic development and to integrate into the Western European system was based on the view that Europe was Greece's 'natural space'[1].

The relationship with the United States, however, inevitably grew into a state of dependence and strong intervention in Greek domestic affairs by the United States [2], [3]. Since 1952, however, the most characteristic feature of Greek foreign policy is the dilemma

---

[*] E-mail address: sae@hol.gr

how it would be possible to reconcile the country's commitments to its allies with the successful outcome of the so called "national issues", such as the issue of the unification (enosis) of Cyprus with Greece. These issues also set the framework for the foreign policy of the Greek Junta (1967-1974) which attempted to succeed where democratic governments had failed, that is in solving the Cyprus problem. The final result was tragic, just as it had been for the military campaign of Greek forces in Asia Minor (1922). Turkeys' invasion of Cyprus in July 1974 led the country to national humiliation for the third time since 1897 and 1922.

FORGING A CLOSER RELATION WITH THE USA: 1945-1952

The prevailing conditions in Greece at the end of World War II led first to the British and later to the American intervention. While the Anglo-Soviet "percentages agreement" in October 1944 in Moscow took place without the involvement of the Greek leadership, the decisions for the Truman Doctrine in 1947 were made with the symbolic consensus of the country's parties with the exception of the Communist party. By implementing the Truman Doctrine, Washington gradually took over from London the responsibility for the financial support, modernization and training of Greek armed forces. Thus, Greek foreign and defense policy identified itself with that of the West. Greece took part in the Korean War, joined the NATO in 1952, and signed its first defense agreement for the supply of military facilities to the U.S.A. the following year [4]. For the very first time in its modern history, Greece was given a territorial guarantee within the framework of an alliance with the great powers of the West. It must be noted that Greece had not had such a formal alliance even during the two world wars [5]. However, during the aforementioned period, representatives of the American embassy, the military and financial delegations were actively and directly involved with the formation of Greek governments and their policies [6]. The American embassy's intervention reached the level even in choosing the electoral system in 1952 brought about the highly-sought after political stability in Greece with the conservative government of Alexander Papagos coming to power.

THE DILEMMA BETWEEN THE COMMITMENTS TO THE WEST AND THE SATISFACTION OF NATIONAL ISSUES: 1952-1967

Both the conservative Papagos government and the subsequent Karamanlis governments were soon faced with an important dilemma. While the main goal of Greek foreign policy was the development of a closer relation with the West, the promotion of the Cyprus problem and the deterioration of Greek-Turkish relations since 1955 demanded greater flexibility and initiatives in foreign policy, such as for example a closer relation with those Arabic countries, like Egypt and Syria, that supported the Cypriots' demand for the right of self-determination. These countries, however, did not belong to the West and followed an anti-American policy.

On the other hand, the Soviet Union offered Greece support within the realms of the U.N. Neither Papagos' nor Karamanlis' governments were able to respond positively. Athens believed that the Soviet Union was trying to take advantage of the Cyprus Problem and the disharmony it had created within the Atlantic alliance.

Great Britain and the U.S.A. approached the Cyprus Problem in a negative manner. As a result, Greek public opinion began manifesting a strong dislike for the West, which in turn produced the danger of raising demands for redefining the principal directions of Athens foreign policy. The atmosphere in the interior of Greece was aggravated even more during the Cypriots' liberation armed struggle (1955-1959), a consequence of the repression policy applied by Great Britain in Cyprus.

The Zurich-London agreements and the establishment of the Republic of Cyprus in 1960 did not allow Greek foreign policy to let go of that dilemma as Nicosia became an active member of the Non-Aligned Movement, developed close relations with Moscow and its policies did not always coincide with Greek diplomacy. As a result, Greek foreign policy started to falter between the necessity to support the positions of Cyprus –especially within the framework of the U.N. and NATO–, and the maintenance, on the other hand, of close relations with the West, despite the fact that neither close relations with the U.S.A. nor the participation in the Atlantic Alliance seemed to safeguard the country from the intensifying Turkish aggression in Cyprus [7].

In the same period after an initial period of hesitance, on whether Greece should join the European Free Trade Association (EFTA) or not, it was decided that signing an Association Agreement with the EEC was the appropriate course of action for a number of financial and political reasons. Firstly, the EEC dynamics showed that it would be the nucleus of the European unification process. Secondly, this step would ensure the country's future participation as a full member. Third, Greek agricultural products would find their way to Western European markets setting the country free from the growing dependence on Eastern European countries. Moreover, financial help would be secured, and lastly, and most importantly, Greece's connection to the EEC was in accordance with the foreign policy agenda concerning the West. In fact, this connection would not only have political and military aspects but also financial ones. On the other hand, however, this Association Agreement with the EEC would not only strengthen the country's ties with the West but it could also act as a future starting point for raising Greece's unilateral dependence on the U.S.A. For this reason, the government of Karamanlis made sure that at the same time they developed close relations with France which had already started differentiating from the U.S.A. and stating that Europe should have an independent defense and foreign policy from the U.S.A. The Association Agreement was signed in Athens on 9 June 1961 and entered into force in November 1962 following its ratification.

THE FOREIGN POLICY OF THE GREEK MILITARY JUNTA: 1967-1974

The greatest problem for the military dictatorship was its relations with the EEC and the Council of Europe. The EEC decided to partly freeze the Association Agreement on issues concerning the supply of financial assistance and harmonization of Greek agriculture with the Common Agricultural Policy (CAP), while tariff dismantling proceeded normally according to the provisions of the Agreement. Serious reports of violations of fundamental human rights by the Greek Junta were brought before the Council of Europe and Athens, faced with the prospect of expulsion. Athens decided to withdraw from the Council of Europe in December

1969. However, the forced dictatorship on 21 April 1967 did not significantly alter the general principles of Greek foreign policy. Nevertheless, two important shifts took place. The first was forging closer relations with the U.S.A., while the second concerned the pursued policy on the Cyprus problem.

At first, the forced dictatorial regime was seemingly treated by the U.S.A. with a certain severity, such as refusal to supply heavy weapons and threats to cut off all economic and military assistance. However, the necessity of using the American bases, especially those in Crete, after the Arab-Israeli six-day war which resulted in a strong Soviet military presence in Egypt and the subsequent war of attrition of 1967-1971 between Egypt and Israel, made Washington reconsider its stance. The U.S.A. not only did not condemn the junta regime but were essentially the only western country that openly supported it [8]. Only near the end of the Papadopoulos dictatorship when Spiros Markezinis was appointed Prime Minister and with the prospect of free elections, did the new non-elected government attempted to counterbalance the close connection with the U.S.A. by making overtures towards Middle East and the Balkan countries.

In this context, the Greek government, also taking into consideration the reaction of the Arabic countries against the agreement permitting American ships to use the port of Elefsina, refused to allow American aircrafts to take off from the military base in Elefsina in order to transport war materials to Israel, while the same did not apply for the American bases in Crete.

The second shift in Greek foreign policy concerns the Cyprus problem. Soon it became obvious that the Greek military junta had chosen to follow a virtually threefold policy on the Cyprus problem. While in its public statements it gave the impression that it supported an independent and sovereign Cyprus, behind the scenes it undermined the Cypriot government by encouraging the political forces that opposed the Cypriot President Archbishop Makarios and also accused him –through the Greek officers in the Cypriot National Guard– of being against Enosis. At the same time it followed a third policy towards Turkey, encouraging the prospect of a direct Greek-Turkish dialogue. These three courses of action appeared conflicting and mutually exclusive but only on the surface. In reality, they aimed to oblige Makarios into accepting the Athens decision for direct contact with Turkey either by weakening him politically, or overthrowing him by force, or even by putting pressure on him to accept obligations in the intercommunal talks which began between the Greek Cypriot and Turkish Cypriots in 1968.

The Greek positions regarding the need for concessions, de-internationalization of the Cyprus problem, placing it within the framework of the allies and solving it with a direct Greek-Turkish dialogue were contrary to the stance of the Cypriot government. Thus the already bleak atmosphere of Greek-Cypriot relations became even obscurer and reached its worst when President Makarios, misjudging the intentions of the new Greek junta led by Ioannidis, proceeded to a head-on aggressive gesture.

On 2 July 1974, he sent his famous letter to Greek President Gizikis in which he openly accused the Greek government for its overall stance on the Cyprus problem and, especially, for its support of terrorism and all illegal organizations acting in Cyprus. He also demanded the immediate recall of all Greek officers, thus causing the reaction of the military regime in Athens with the coup of 15 July 1974, which in turn provoked the Turkish invasion on 20 July 1974 [9].

THE COURSE OF EUROPEANIZATION : 1974-2000

Following the events of 1974, Greek foreign policy had to face a new reality with three specific dimensions: first, the changes that took place in the international context and which were characterized by a movement towards economic depression and a shift of the international system from strictly bipolar to loosely bipolar; the second dimension concerned the policies that Athens had to formulated on the Cyprus problem and the Turkish aggressiveness in the Aegean,which had already began in 1973; the third dimension regarded the consequences on foreign policy of the dramatic changes which occurred in the interior and especially in the political system of Greece.

Since the fall of the dictatorship, Greek foreign policy can be divided in three periods: the 1974-1981 period, the 1981-1993 period and the 1993-2010 period. Each of these periods had its unique characteristics and its own achievements and failures.

1974-1981: The Period of Mild Readjustment and Application of a Multidimensional Foreign Policy

The main feature of this period is the establishment of a new Greek foreign policy that did not violate the basic principle of the post-war era that Greece "belongs to the West". Foreign policy was formulated on the basis of a common consensus among the political parties on the following principles: first, that Greece ought to follow a multidimensional foreign policy [10]; second, that the danger for national security came from Turkey and that, due to the western policy on the Cyprus problem and the Greek-Turkish relations, there was a significant divergence between the interests of Greece and those of its allies [11]; third, that Greece ought to preserve a functional security relationship with the United States based on mutual interests. Such a relationship "would be a valuable asset in times of severe local and regional challenges" [12]. However, the problem for all governments since 1974 remained how to apply a multidimensional foreign policy in the context of realistic and practical politics.

The greatest achievement of Greek diplomacy is without a doubt the country's accession to the European Community. Very soon, the newly elected conservative government of Nea Demokratia realized that the only way for the country to escape, if not wholly at least to a great extend, from the aforementioned dilemmas was to become a full member of the EC, which would in turn become the main factor determining Greek foreign policy.

It had been argued that Greece's accession to the EC would ensure the following considerable advantages for its foreign policy:

- It was the only possible option that would allow Athens to maintain its strong links to the West on a political, financial, cultural and defense level
- It would absolve Greece from past dependencies by making it an equal member to all large European E.C. Member States and with an equal vote. It would offer Greece the possibility to consolidate its international negotiating position and ability through the mechanism of European Political Cooperation (EPC) that is responsible for the coordination of Member States' foreign policies.

- Accession would prevent foreign forces from intervening in Greece's internal political developments
- For a country like Greece, pestered by Turkey's demands for expansion, E. C. accession would, on the one hand, offer support from a system of political solidarity and, on the other, it could oblige the E. C. to adopt a clearer stance on issues of vital importance for Greece
- Finally, Greece as a member of the E. C. would be able to give a wider scope to its foreign policy since in the eyes of the Arabic and Balkan countries the country's presence in the E.C. would take new proportions [13].

However, accession negotiations were considerably hindered mostly by the European Commission's effort to stall accession by invoking the problems in Greek-Turkish relations, and by the fact that countries like France and Italy –while clearly in favor of Greece's entrance into the Community– could not overlook the consequences that Community enlargement would have on their agriculture. The completion of negotiations was achieved mostly as a result of the Greek Prime Minister Konstantinos Karamanlis' political intervention, thus making Greece the tenth member of the E. C. in January 1981.

Greek foreign policy also succeeded in vigorously promoting its relations with Middle East countries, while refusing to recognize Israel *de jure* even after the E. C. accession. There was also a marked improvement with all Balkan countries and Athens took the initiative for a multilateral Balkan cooperation, be it only on matters of low politics, whose first conference was convened on 26 January 1976 in Athens. Furthermore, Foreign Minister George Rallis' visit to Moscow, in September 1978, inaugurated a new era for the development of Greek-Soviet relations.

However, Greek foreign policy experienced serious difficulties concerning both Greek-Turkish relations and the Cyprus Problem. On the field of Greek-Turkish relations, despite achieving, with the help of the Greek-American lobby, the embargo of American arms to Turkey and the bilateral talks that took place, tension culminated in the summer of 1976 when Turkey openly challenged the Greek continental shelf. As for the Cyprus Problem, there seemed to be no light at the end of the tunnel despite the fact that Greek as well as Cypriot diplomacy had succeeded in internationalizing the Cyprus Problem and having positive resolutions in the U.N. Security Council and the General Assembly.

NATO and U.S. relations were the most difficult test field for Greek foreign policy. Greece's withdrawal from the integrated military structure of NATO on 14 August 1974 offered Turkey the opportunity to enhance its strategic importance a few months after the Arab-Israeli war of 1973. Moreover, when Athens expressed its wish to rejoin the military sector of the Alliance in 1975, Ankara attempted to profit and would not agree without a prior restructuring of the operational control areas in the Aegean. Finally Greece managed to rejoin NATO only in 1980 [14].

As for the U.S.A., the main difficulties stemmed from the fact that Washington did not get actively involved to such a degree as to induce Ankara to change its politics both in the Cyprus problem and the Greek-Turkish relations [15]. Regarding the Cyprus Problem, the American government did not take the initiative until November 1978 with the Nimetz plan, which however was rejected by the Cypriot government [16]. At the same time, negotiations for the review of Greek-American defense agreements were on a thin line as Greece had linked the maintenance of American bases to the demand for preserving the 7 to 10 ratio of American military help towards Greece and Turkey respectively.

1981-1993: From the Delimitated Diversifications to the Shift towards European Union

The Socialist Party's (PASOK) victory in 1981 set the scene, given its programmatic commitments, for a radical shift in foreign policy such as Greece's withdrawal from the E. C. and NATO, the adoption of a stronger stance against Turkey, the consolidation of Third World relations and the rapid development of relations with the Eastern Bloc countries [17]. However, PASOK as a government implemented a policy of adaptation, even gradual, of Greek foreign policy to the international circumstances [18]. Therefore, on the issue of Greece's accession to the E.C., the new socialist government restricted to submitting demands for a partial review of the accession terms and also signed an agreement for the maintenance of the U.S. bases in Greece [19].

During the period 1981-1985, Athens adopted an independent but pragmatic political stance on the country's essential interests [20]. However, on international issues –regarding mostly the broader relations between West and East– Greek policy diversified from that of the West. The diversifications concerned among others: Jaruzelski's dictatorship in Poland; the deployment of Cruise and Perishing missiles in Europe; the establishment of a nuclear-weapon-free zone in the Balkans; friendly relations with Libya, Syria and the Palestine Liberation Organisation; and the Six-Nation Initiative for disarmament. This policy of diversification seemed to have been dictated by the need to project to the Greek public opinion, especially the members and voters of PASOK, as well as abroad that Greece follows a genuinely multidimensional foreign policy [21], [22].

There were the following reasons for such behavior: first, to respond to the internal pressure that the Socialist government was receiving from its own supporters and especially the leadership of the PASOK (who wanted a more independent Greek foreign policy) As J.O. Iatrides notes " Papandreou's diplomacy served its intended purpose: It had a therapeutic effect upon the national psyche, as the general public came to believe that the sovereignty had been restored" [23] ; second, as a means to avoid pressure from bigger member states within the EPC framework; third, to prevent any EPC decision that might include a political, economic or other cost for Athens, regarding the Cyprus problem and its dispute with Turkey and fourth, as a means to distance Athens from Washington [24]. It was also dictated by the realization that smaller states should diverse from their allies on issues that don't directly apply to their security so as not to be taken for granted [25].

By 1985, however, Greek foreign policy was fully integrated in the mechanisms of the E. C. and began functioning not only as a restrictive mechanism which prevented the adoption of atavistic nationalist positions, but also as a field for expanding the possibilities of Greek diplomacy that came out of its participation in the E.U. According to Panayiotis Ioakimidis three main reasons seem to explain this change: a) the significant economic benefits that Greece had drawn from EC membership, b) Greece by participating in the EPC had strengthened its bargaining power in the dealing with its foreign policy problems and c) the socializing effect that personal involvement in the Community policy – making process had had on a number of key political figures in the anti- EC camp [26].

Another feature of foreign policy from this period was also the drastic change of Greece's position regarding the Greek-Turkish dispute. Until then, the only matter Greece was prepared to discuss with Turkey was the delimitation of the continental shelf in the Aegean. However, after the Greek-Turkish crisis in March 1987 and a subsequent meeting between the Greek Prime Minister Andreas Papandreou and his Turkish counterpart Turgut Özal in Davos, Greece proceeds to the inauguration of a bilateral dialogue with Turkey, leaving aside the Cyprus problem. But neither this strategy lasted for long as reactions from the country's public opinion finally weakened the "spirit of Davos" as well as Turkey's lack of responsiveness to the Greek initiatives [27].

In 1990 the conservative party Nea Demokratia was in power once again. This did not significantly affect the main orientation of Greek foreign policy, although Greece's immediate environment had been altered due to the fall of the communist regimes. Greece, however, did not manage to profit from these developments and expand its sphere of influence. "Greek foreign policy exhibited a rather peculiar combination: defensiveness and a strong sense of insecurity, coupled with a tendency to open up too many fronts, which might have been interpreted as a sign of strength if it were not simply the product of poor judgment" [28]. Greece opted for a more nationalistic and confrontational foreign policy as regards the former Yugoslavia in general, and as regards the "FYROM issue" in particular [29]. It was soon obvious that the rigid stance it adopted on the Macedonian question–although briefly successful within the E.U. framework where Greek diplomacy managed to extract some conditions in the Maastricht negotiation regarding the recognition of FYROM–, led to an impasse. As for the mediation effort of the Mitsotakis government in the war of Bosnia, it was not successful. Therefore, it became apparent that "the 'skopjenization' of Greece's foreign policy had the effect of diverting scarce resources and attention from other important and pressing issues"[30].

1993- 2010: The Period of Intense Europeanization

A basic feature of this period beginning in 1993, and which is especially obvious from 1996 when Costas Simitis is elected as Prime Minister, is that the level of Europeanization of Greek foreign policy is rising increasingly and it could be argued that Greek foreign policy is now adjusted to the E.U. more than ever since most aspects of the country's foreign policy are realized in the spirit of E.U. politics. This adjustment is made clear by the following:

First, Greek foreign policy "absorbs" fairly successfully the logic of European integration. Greece's position on any foreign policy issue seems to take into serious consideration the trends developed in the E. U.

Second, from a country that had serious reservations regarding the strengthening of EPC in the mid 80's, almost twenty years later Greece is becoming a fervent supporter of the "communitisation" of the Common Foreign and Security Policy (CFSP). In fact, during the intergovernmental conference for the Constitution of Europe Greece suggested a more essential development of CFSP with the provision of taking decisions by qualified majority and with certain safeguards, after a Commission proposal.

Third, the benefits from this course to europeanization for Greek foreign policy were many. First, Cyprus's accession to the E.U., which should be considered an important achievement for Greek diplomacy, although the Cyprus problem had not been solved; second, the connection between the progress made in the negotiations for Turkey's accession and the solution of Greek-Turkish issues; third, the pressure applied on FYROM by not making it possible for the integration negotiations to start unless a solution has been reached concerning the country's official name on the basis of a compound name *erga omnes*.

Greek policy toward the Balkans since 1995 can be summed up as trying to avoid becoming a part of the problem, and joining instead those who wished to be part of the solution. This change of policy was due to many factors, the most important of which were: First, the realization that, in order to avoid the isolation of the first five years of the post-Cold War, due mainly to its Balkan policy Greece should develop the deepening and widening of its ties with NATO and the European Union. "Greek foreign policy makers claimed that only the EU framework could provide the means for cementing peaceful relations in the region, mainly through an integration process that could bring about the same reconciliation as in the case of relations between France and Germany" [31]. Second, from the perspective of Greece, the economic problems of the Balkans, the renewed ethnic conflict and political decay, and the influx of illegal migrants were posing novel challenges, leading to the urgent necessity of contributing to the stabilization of the Balkan states' economies and political systems. Third, Greece recognized that the future of the Balkans lay in the development of regional cooperation schemes. Greece's opportunity as an EU member located in the Balkans is to bring the countries of this region into trans- European networks and projects which will facilitate economic change and development. Fourth, Greece's foreign trade, and above all its exports to other Balkan countries, increased fourfold between 1990 and 1996. Furthermore, Greek investment in the Balkans also increased spectacularly. It was becoming clear that Greece had major economic interests in the Balkans and that a new political approach reflecting them had become necessary. Fifth, Greece recognized the fact, if not the desirability, that its national interests were compatible with the existence on its northern border of a new state – FYROM – which was relatively stable, consisting mostly of Slav Macedonians and Albanians, despite the continuing political disputes between the two countries. This new Greek policy toward south-east Europe can be summarized as having as its strategic objective the gradual integration of south-east Europe into the new European architecture and the Euro-Atlantic institutions [32].

On the other hand, Greece's stance, since 1996, of projecting the E.U. as the first and foremost field of action for Greek foreign policy does not necessarily bear evidence to its sufficient Europeanization, as this shift was made in order mostly to satisfy its national interests and not contribute to the European integration. In various issues of direct interest for Greece– such as the Cyprus problem, bilateral relations with Turkey and the relations with the countries of South-Eastern Europe and the Mediterranean–, E. U. positions increasingly reflected Greek positions as Greek diplomacy taking advantage of its strong presence in the E.U. not only contributed to the formulation of E.U. positions but, also, in some cases, such as Cyprus's accession, it defined the policy ultimately adopted by the E.U. As Kalaitzidis observes " through multiple strategies, sometimes well thought out and at other times quite ad hoc, the Greeks have transformed the issues in their surroundings in the Balkan Peninsula and Turkey into a EU problem" [33] Indeed, in Helsinki European Summit (December 1999) the European Union stressed that Turkey's eligibility for EU membership depended on resolving two issues: its border conflict with an EU member state, Greece, and the Cyprus issue [34]. It seems that Athens "strategic outlook centred on a European Turkey that would restrict the involvement of institutions such as the armed forces in the country's decision making structures and foreign policy, a state of affairs that had been known to increase risks of escalation of disputes" [35].However, according to James Ker- Lidsay this change of policy was not simply a diplomatic tactic. Instead, it was a political strategy. "Athens aim was to put in place an entirely new approach that would emphasize that long term stability could only be achieved by drawing Turkey closer to Europe and by building and cementing bilateral ties" [36].

Neverhteless, Greece has not achieved a high level of Europeanization. This is simply because it does not follow automatically that European norms and values have become totally embedded in the Greek political system, including its foreign policy decision–making process. Greek foreign policy continues to address the same old 'narrow' national interests(known in Greece as the ethnika themata or national issues that is to say, mainly the Cyprus problem and Greek Turkish relations). Even if, since 1996, Greece has tried to promote them through the EU framework, it does not necessarily and automatically mean that it has Europeanized them, mainly because such a tactical shift is meant to better promote those traditional interests. For example, the main new development, of which the Conservative governments (2004-2009) were particularly proud, was the attempt to build a strategic partnership with Russia, based mainly on energy cooperation that put some distance between the Greek government and the United States [37].

Furthermore, the continued dysfunction of domestic factors and actors further strengthens the view that Greek foreign policy has not yet become Europeanized [38].On the other hand the current improvement of Greek –Turkish relations and the expansion of their bilateral economic transactions as Thanos Dokos argues "remain nascent and fragile and it seems that it constitutes the epi-phenomenon of the two states' actual relationship. Both countries have not moved from their firm positions regarding high politics' issues [39].

CONCLUSION

Greece emerged after the beginning of the cold war as a frontline state with multiple external fronts. Until 1952, joining the West was achieved mainly through forging a closer relationship with the United States. However, the Cyprus Problem which emerged in the mid-1950's did not only affect the general orientation of Greek foreign policy, it hadn't only caused a serious deterioration of Greek-Turkish affairs, but also gave birth to an anti-western feeling of fury in a large part of the Greek population, almost a few years after the end of the civil war.

In the same period the prospect of European integration was another domain which offered solutions to Greek foreign policy. Greek leadership, with the exception of the Left party (EDA), pursued the quickest possible involvement of Greece in the Europe. The dictatorial regime was initially kept in relative international isolation, manifested mostly by the countries of Western Europe –especially the Scandinavian ones–, while its relations with France were quickly restored.

The accession to the EC became a top priority for Greek diplomacy, while other major concerns were also the Turkish aggressiveness in the Aegean, the Cyprus Problem, Greek-American relations and NATO relations. Moreover, there was intense Greek involvement in the area of the Balkans, the Middle East and in its relations with the Soviet Union.

The effort of Europeanization became the main theme for Greek foreign policy since 1993. All other issues gradually started to connect and their outcome to depend on the degree to which Greek foreign policy, on the one hand, adapted itself to the developing common European foreign policy and, on the other, was able to successfully table these issues within the Community. Greece's membership of the EU was meant to guarantee a number of important advantages for its foreign policy: as the only way to maintain and consolidate its existing links with the West, be it at the political, economic, cultural or defense levels; as a means to go beyond historical dilemmas of the past among West and East, by allowing a *de jure* equality between Greece and all the other (West) European states, including the big ones. Subsequently, the European card could allow a lessening of Greece's dependence, real or perceived, on the U.S.A.;as a way of strengthening Greece's international bargaining power initially through EPC and later the CFSP; as a means to secure solidarity from other EU states in its difficult relations with Turkey's hegemonic demands (over the Aegean and in Cyprus);finally as a EEC/EPC and later EU/CFSP member state, Greece would add an important *atout* to its foreign policy especially in the Balkans and the Mediterranean, areas which have often acted as demandeurs of more European foreign policy action.

REFERENCES

[1] Hatzivassiliou E., *Greece and the Cold War*. Frontline State 1952-1967, London: Routledge (2006).

[2] Couloumbis T.A – J.A. Petropoulos- H.J.Psomiades., *Foreign Interference in Greek Politics,* New York: Pella Publishing (1976).

[3] Witneer, L.J, *American Intervention in Greece 1943-1949*, New York: Columbia University Press (1982).

[4] Couloumbis T.A., *Greek Political Reaction to American and NATO Influences*, New Haven: Yale University Press, 77-89 (1966).

[5] Hatzivassiliou E., *Journal of Contemporary History*, 30(1), 193-94 (1995).

[6] Amen M.M., *Journal of the Hellenic Diaspora*, 5(3), 89-113 9 (1978).

[7] Coufoudakis V., *Millenium, Journal of International Studies*, 5(3), 248-250(1977).

[8] Pollis A., *Millenium, Journal of International Studies*,4(1), 28-51(1975).

[9] Asmusen J., *Cyprus At War Diplomacy and Conflict during the 1974 Crisis*, London : I.B. Tauris (2008).

[10] Moustakis, F., *The Greek – Turkish Relationship and NATO,* London: Frank Cass, 34 (2003).

[11] Couloumbis T.A., *"Defining Greek Foreign Policy Objectives"* in H.R. Penniman (ed.) *Greece at the Pools*, Washington: American Enterprise Institute for Public Policy Research, 165 (1981).

[12] Constas D., "Challenges to Greek Foreign Policy: Domestic and External Parameters" in D. Constas- T. G.Stavrou (eds), *Greece Prepares for the Twenty – First Century*, Washington DC: The Woodrow Wilson Center Press, 86 (1995).

[13] Tsakaloyannis P., "Greece: Old Problems, New Prospects" in C. Hill (ed.), *National Foreign Policies and European Political Cooperation*, London:RIIA/George Allen and Unwin, 127-128 (1983).

[14] Rizas,S., *Southeast European and Black Sea Studies*, 8(1), 51–66 (2008).

[15] Iatrides J.O. *"Greece and the United States: The Strained Partnership"* in R. Clogg (ed.), Greece in the 1980's, London: MacMillan Press, 168 (1983).

[16] Mayes S., *Round Table*, 69(273), 81-87 (1979).

[17] Loulis J.C., *Foreign Affairs*, 7, 376-377 (1984).

[18] Coufoudakis V., *Journal of Greek Modern Greek Studies*, 6(1), 55-79 (1988).

[19] Verney S., "Greece and the European Community" in K.Featherstone – D. Katsoudas (eds), *Political Change in Greece*, London:Croom Helm, 1987, pp.253-270 (1987).

[20] Coufoudakis V., *Current History*, 81(479), 426-431 (1982).

[21] Tsakaloyannis P., "National Paper on Greece" in C.O. Nuallain (ed.), *The Presidency of the European Council of Ministers,* London: Croom Helm, 113 (1985).

[22] McCaskill C.W., "PASOK's Third World/non – aligned relations" in N.Stavrou (ed.), *Greece Under Socialism*, New Rochelle:A.L.Caratzas, 325 (1988).

[23] Iatrides J.O., " Papandreou's Foreign Policy" in T.C. Kariotis (ed.), *The Greek Socialist Experiment. Papandreou's Greece 19811-1989*, New York: Pella Publishing Company, 158 (1992).

[24] Tsardanidis C. – Stavridis S., *Journal of European Integration*, 27(2), 217-239 (1995).

[25] Platias A., *High Politics in Small Countries: An Inquiry into Security Policies of Greece and Sweden*, Unpublished Ph D. dissertation, University of Cornell, 218-19(1986).

[26] Ioakimidis, P.C., "Greece in the EC: Policies, Experiences, and Prospects" in H.J. Psomiades –S.B. Thomadakis (eds), *Greece, the New Europe, and the Changing International Order*, New York: Pella Publishing Company, 411 (1993).

[27] Coufoudakis V., "PASOK on Greek- Turkish Relations and Cyprus, 1981- 1989: Ideology, Pragmatism, Deadlock" in T.C. Kariotis (ed.), *The Greek Socialist Experiment.* Papandreou's Greece 19811-1989, New York: Pella Publishing Company, 175 (1992).

[28] Tsoukalis L., "Beyond the Greek Paradox" in G. Allison – K.Nicolaidis (eds), *The Greek Paradox.Promise vs Performance,* Cambridge, MA:The MIT Press, 171 (1997).

[29] Kalaitzidis, A., *Europe's Greece. A Giant in the Making*, London: Palgrave MacMillan 136 (2010).

[30] Tziampiris A., "Greece and the Balkans in the Twentieth Century" in T. Couloumbis- T. Kariotis- F. Bellou (eds), *Greece in the Twentieth Century*, London: Frank Cassm,146 (2003).

[31] Huliaras A. – Tsardanidis C., *Geopolitics*,11(3), 477 (2006).

[32] Tsardanidis C. – Stavridis S., "Greece.From Special Case to Limited Europeanization" in R. Wong - C. Hill (eds), *National and European Foreign Policies.Towards Europeanization,* London:Routladge, 115 (2011).

[33] Kalaitzidis, A., *Europe's Greece. A Giant in the Making*, London: Palgrave MacMillan 147 (2010).

[34] Tsakonas P., *The Incomplete Breakthrough in Greek –Turkish Relations. Grasping Greece's Socialization Strategy*, London: Palgrave MacMillan, 93 (2010).

[35] Kotzias N., "EU, Turkey and Greece: The paradoxes of Convergence" in O. Anastasakis - K.A. Nicolaidis – K. Öktem (eds*), In the Long Shadow of Europe Greeks and Turks in the Era of Postnationalism*, Leiden : Martinus Nijhoff, 268 (2009).

[36] Ker- Lidsay J., *Crisis and Conciliation. A Year of Rapprochement between Greece and Turkey*, London: I.B. Tauris 119 (2007).

[37] Keridis D., "Greek Foreign Policy: Past, Present and Future Strategies" *The Constantinos Karamanlis Institute for Democracy Yearbook 2010*, 88 (2010).

[38] Tsardanidis C. – Stavridis S., *Journal of European Integration,* 27(2), 231 (1995).

[39] Dokos T., "Greece in a Changing Strategic Setting" in T. Couloumbis- T. Kariotis- F. Bellou (eds), *Greece in the Twentieth Century*, London: Frank Cassm,48 (2003).

PART III: SOCIAL ISSUES

In: Greece: Economics, Political and Social Issues
Editor: Panagiotis Liargovas

ISBN: 978-1-62100-944-3
© 2012 Nova Science Publishers, Inc.

Chapter 14

UNIONS AND LABOR MARKET ORGANIZATION IN GREECE

Stella Zambarloukou[*]
University of Crete,
Department of Sociology, Crete

ABSTRACT

The chapter focuses on understanding the main driving forces behind union and labor market organization in Greece. It concentrates on the period since the fall of the dictatorship in 1974, up to the present, but were necessary references are made to earlier periods. The particular characteristics of labor market formation and union organization are examined in light of the distinctive model of economic development followed in Greece and its turbulent political history. Greece has evolved during the post war period from a poor agricultural country to a modern service economy. The cost of this rapid change has been a highly segmented labor market and poor institutionalization of union organizations.

INTRODUCTION

Since the end of the civil war that succeeded World War II, Greece has evolved from an authoritarian or semi-authoritarian poor agricultural country to a democratic modern service economy. In addition it has joined the European Union, adopted the Euro as its currency and raised its GDP per person to slightly below the EU average. Nevertheless, at closer look, Greece differs in a number of ways from its European counterparts. Rapid economic development and long periods of authoritarian rule have left their mark on labor markets and union organization.

This chapter aims to describe the main features of labor markets and union organization in Greece and to decipher the major driving forces behind their evolution. Emphasis is placed

---

[*] E-mail address: zamba@social.soc.uoc.gr

on the recent period, since the establishment of democracy in 1974, but where necessary references are made to the immediate post war period. The first section highlights the main features of the economic model adopted in the post war period, while the following section examines how the latter has impacted on labor market formation. Next the main features of the union movement are discussed, and the major turning points in the industrial relations system and union organization are traced. Last attention is paid to the impact that the recent economic crisis has had on both labor markets and union organizations.

THE MODEL OF POST WAR ECONOMIC DEVELOPMENT

Greece is characterized by late and uneven development. Industrialization did not make an impact prior to the 20th century and never reached the levels achieved by other European countries. The latter holds true even when Greece is compared to the other South European countries with which it shares a number of common traits [1], [2], [3]. Up until the early 1970s Greece was still largely an agricultural country with 38% of its labor force in agriculture (see, table 1). Despite the sharp decline in agricultural employment in subsequent years, it continuous to employ 15% of the labor force which, is far above the EU-27 average that stands at 5,6%. In contrast industrial employment even at its peak during the early 1980s did not exceed 30%.

The model of economic development followed after the end of the civil war in 1949 was based on the suppression of wages through the containment of union activity and protectionist policies that minimized competition from abroad. While the state had an active role in the economy, mainly through the granting of subsidies and loans, it lacked a clear industrial strategy [4]. Growth in manufacturing involved on the most part low technology, traditional labor-intensive activities such as textiles and foodstuff. Construction constituted in many ways the driving force of the economy as the country had to be rebuilt following the devastation suffered during World War II, and the civil war that succeeded it, and the massive migration from rural areas to the cities that ensued. Construction continued to play a central role in the economy throughout the post war years and absorbed between a third and half of employment in industry.

One side effect of the model of economic growth followed was that paid employment did not rise to the levels encountered in other European countries. Regular paid employment remained below 50% of total employment until the 1980s and even today accounts for only about 62% of the labor force. On the other hand, self-employment remained at exceptionally high levels throughout the post war period and today is around 22% of the labor force, when in the EU-15 the average is close to 10% [5]. The remaining 16% is made up of small employers and family helpers.

While the composition of the labor force can in part be accounted for by the fact that agriculture continued to be an important source of employment until recently, the predominance of small family ownership in all economic sectors has played an equally important role [6]. With the exception of few large industrial and financial enterprises Greece's economy has been based on small family owned firms. Small ownership characterized all sectors from agriculture to industry and services, which in turn has encouraged growth mostly in labor-intensive low technology sectors. This has resulted in a dual economy, made up by a limited number of high to medium productivity large enterprises on the one hand and, on the other hand, numerous low productivity small economic units.

Table 1. Employment by Economic Sector (%)

	1971	1981	1991	2001
Agriculture	38.0	28.0	19.6	14.9
Mining	0.7	0.7	0.5	0.3
Manufacturing	18.2	20,3	16.6	11.5
Energy				2,2
Construction	8.1	9.6	8.5	8.1
Services	39.4	40.1	54.8	61.8

Source: ESYE, Population Census 1971, 1981, 1991, 2001.

Despite the 'weaknesses' of Greek manufacturing noted above, from the mid-1950s until the second oil crisis in 1979 Greece experienced high levels of annual economic growth (6-7%). The 'advantages', however, enjoyed by the Greek economy that led to the fore mentioned high annual growth rates were gradually lost after the collapse of the seven year dictatorship and the return to democracy in 1974. The granting of union freedoms led to labor mobilizations and substantial wage increases. In addition, following Greece's accession to the EU in 1981, protectionist policies were gradually relaxed and competition from other countries was intensified [7]. Governments, rather than confronting the structural problems facing industry chose to delay de-industrialization by nationalizing ailing firms [8]. Nationalizations began in the late 1970s but became much more widespread during the first term of the PanHellenic Socialist Movement (PASOK) in power (1981-85). However, the problems facing Greek manufacturing persisted and by the second half of the 1980s it became clear that de-industrialization could not be postponed further. Most manufacturing plants were technologically ill equipped and concentrated on traditional activities, which made them very vulnerable to competition from low-income countries. One after the other manufacturing plants either closed down or downsized. Employment in manufacturing declined sharply from the early 1990s and thereafter and is today around 12%.

Decline in agricultural and manufacturing employment was accompanied by a rise in service employment that came to represent more than 60% of overall employment. Tourism emerged as a major economic activity and accounts for approximately 15% of GDP and 18% of employment [9]. In addition, trade and transport, personal and social services have also grown in importance. The same does not hold true for business services that grew less compared to other EU countries, which comes to show that services are concentrated on activities that are not knowledge-intensive [10], [11]. Service growth in many ways replicated the model of economic growth observed in the early post war period in that it rested mostly on small-scale family firms and involved low technology and skills. While in the EU (15) 33,1% of those employed in services are in knowledge intensive services and 33.8% are in low knowledge intensive services, in the case of Greece the figures are 24.9% and 40,1% respectively [12].

The growth of services, during the recent period, did not totally make up for losses in employment positions in agriculture and manufacturing. As a result overall employment levels remained relatively low, almost five percentage points below the EU average [13]. While unemployment was sustained at low levels throughout the 1980s, in the 1990s it climbed above 10%, as a result of de-industrialization, the decline in agricultural employment and the continuing migration of the young to urban centers in search for work. Unemployment growth is also related to women's growing participation in the labor force. While female employment rates remain below the EU average they have risen substantially over the last 20 years, from 49.6% in 1990 to 57.5% in 2009.

THE DUAL STRUCTURE OF THE LABOR MARKET

While Greece followed the trend of other advanced countries and became a service-oriented economy, economic development continued to rest on small family owned firms. De-industrialization, the continuing decline in agricultural employment in combination with the persisting culture of 'familism' and the presence of an informal economy have encouraged the expansion of very small family owned firms in the service sector. SMEs make up 99,9% of all enterprises, while micro firms (less than 10 employees) constitute 97% of the total and employ more than 56% of the labor force in Greece (see, table 2). While, small and medium sized firms are mostly involved in traditional industrial activities, micro firms are mostly engaged in personal and commercial services [14]. These activities tend to be labor intensive and profit the most from the presence of low pay and informal or precarious work.

Greece has the largest informal economy in Europe, which is estimated at 30% of GDP. The informal sector usually acts in a complimentary way to the formal economy, by reducing the cost of products and services distributed in the market. Small firms owe in large part their existence to the presence of a substantial informal economy because this allows them to avoid taxes, social security contributions and state regulation [15], [16], [17]. As a result not enough incentives are created for the upgrading of products and services. This gives rise to a vicious circle given that, on the one hand, the presence of an informal economy encourages small firm creation and particular types of economic activities that are mostly labor intensive, while on the other hand, small firms in order to remain competitive are forced to function at the margins of the official economy.

Table 2. The distribution of firms by size, persons employed and value added

Type	Number of enterprises	Number of persons employed	Value added
Micro	97.1%	56.5%	21.1%
Small	2.6%	15.8%	19. 0%
Medium	1.1%	9.7%	17.8%
Large	0.1%	18.0%	42.1%

Source: Eurostat, *Structural Business Statistics*, Data Base, 2004 and 2005.

As shown in table 2, the smaller the size of the firm the lower the value added, which confirms that small firms tend to engage in less productive activities. For this reason they are profitable only if relatively cheap and flexible labor is available. This is indirectly confirmed by studies that show that the presence of large economic inequalities and poor employment conditions are correlated with the presence of a large number of small firms. Small firms pay less; provide worse working conditions and less security to their employees [14].

The presence of many small firms in combination with a large informal economy, have resulted in a highly segmented labor market, whereby different sectors of the labor force enjoy different rights and privileges. While Greece is often described as a country with strict labor regulation this description takes into account only part of reality. Core workers, and particularly those employed in the public sector or publicly owned enterprises, are protected by a complex web of labor regulation regarding firing and working hours in addition to enjoying (at least until recently) rather generous social security benefits. The above, however, is far from true for large sections of labor that are employed in small and micro-establishments. In small firms protection is much lower, and the use of informal work much more frequent. The latter is not so much the result of the lack of official regulation, but of poor regulation enforcement and the absence of unionization.

Two kinds of informal work can be found. Totally undeclared work and irregular self employed work performed by both low skilled workers and professionals. The latter type of work is very widespread in the construction sector. Informal or undeclared work is mostly found in agriculture, construction, hotels, catering and small scale retail as well as domestic services and caring for children and the elderly. Informal work includes unpaid family work, home working, unregistered casual or seasonal work, domestic work, and work in unregistered subcontracted workshops [18]. Where seasonal work is required informal employment is much more frequent [19]. While exact figures for undeclared work are unavailable it is estimated between 18-25% of total employment [20]. Women and immigrants are most likely to be undeclared workers. The flow of large numbers of immigrants in the 1990s gave new impetus to a number of labor-intensive sectors, particularly agriculture and construction and personal services [21]. On the whole, it appears that the availability of a large pool of labor willing to work for low pay and often without social security protection, has increased informal employment and sustained many small firms or traditional activities that would otherwise have been undermined by competition.

The rise in service employment has been associated across the Western world with the rise in precarious and atypical or non-standard forms of employment. In Greece non-standard employment such as part-time employment and contract employment has remained below the EU average. This was in part due to the presence of strict rules regulating work arrangements but also, because, flexibility in the market was provided by either totally informal work, or a disguised form of self-employment. However during recent years the use of atypical labor has become more frequent. This is particularly true of part time employment, which has risen from 4.4% of employment in 2000 to 8.5% in 2010, while the respective EU average in 2010 was about 20%. Contract employment has also increased somewhat over the past decade to around 12% of employment, and is currently about 2% points below the EU average [22]. On the whole atypical and precarious forms of employment have been estimated at 22% of the total. These include subcontracted workers, workers employed on a contract basis, part time workers and those earning less than the poverty threshold. If we add to the above those working in the black market economy, then about 40% of all employed work under precarious conditions [23].

The growth of atypical and precarious employment has accentuated differences between core workers and 'outsiders' and has resulted in employees having highly differentiated access to basic rights. Core workers enjoy relatively high protection from dismissal (or job tenure in the case of public employees) and substantial social security benefits. 'Outsiders' or peripheral workers enjoy little or no protection [21], [23]. Within each of the above broad categories, that constitute the basis for the dual structure of the Greek labor market, one can distinguish the presence of labor market sub-segments that enjoy different levels of protection and other benefits. On the one end, are those employed in public enterprises that enjoy life long job tenure, as well as private sector employees in large firms that, at least until recently were protected, by strict firing regulations. On the other side are those working in small firms that enjoy little protection in terms of firing and only minimum social security benefits. But worse still are those working in various forms of precarious labor, such as contract employment, temporary or part time work and the most vulnerable of all, those working in the black market economy that enjoy no social security protection at all. According to the most recent figures 25% of those employed are without social security protection [24]. Immigrants, women and the young seem to be the most likely to fall within the latter category.

While the rise of precarious employment is observed across the developed world, and is not particular to Greece, its impact tends to be greater due to the presence of a large number of very small firms and a large informal economy. The latter implies that this form of employment also involves to a larger extent non-declared work. Moreover, the underdeveloped nature of the welfare state in combination to the fact that social security benefits and health care provision are tightly connected to one's work status and social security contributions leaves outsiders with no social protection at all [25].

UNION ORGANIZATION: HISTORICAL BACKGROUND AND ORGANIZATIONAL STRUCTURE

The union movement reflects in a number of ways the structure of the labor market, given that those employed in the public sector and core workers in the private sector form the backbone of the union movement. One can in fact argue that the union movement, even if unwillingly, reinforces the segmentation of the labor market by supporting the demands of core workers while not being actively involved in trying to improve the position of those working at the margins of the economy. At the same time union structure is more than a mere reflection of labor market conditions. It is also the product of a long history of state suppression, political interventions and confrontation that have shaped its outlook and internal politics.

Wage and salary employees in Greece are organized in two major confederations. The General Confederation of Greek Workers (GSEE) represents all workers in the private sector and public companies, such as public transport and electricity, while the Chief Directorate of Public Employees Associations (ADEDY) represents all civil servants, as well as all employed in public education and the public health system. The GSEE has been in existence since 1918 and ADEDY since 1947. The government intervened in the GSEE soon after its creation to curb left wing influence within its ranks and in the late 1930s the Metaxas regime established a form of state corporatism, which left its mark on state-labor relations, for many years to come [26], [27]. Political interventions persisted up until the late 1980s, even though their intensity and effectiveness subsided with time. Control by the state of the union's finances was the most prevalent tool used throughout this period [28]. In addition, the collective bargaining framework legislated by law in 1955, which reaffirmed the state's role as arbitrator of all collective disputes and its right to impose compulsory arbitration on labor decisions, also remained in effect until the end of the 1980s.

State repression and efforts to infiltrate and control the union movement during most of the 20th century prevented genuine union autonomy or incorporation within the political system. Repression constituted union action by definition a political act so that politics and union activity became invariably linked. Political identity formed a major cleavage within society that cut across social divisions. The combination of low levels of industrialization, internal political divisions and efforts by the state to control the union movement resulted in union fragmentation, low institutionalization and a confrontational political culture [26]. Political divisions emerged as a major feature of the union movement even though organizational unity was maintained at the top. This, however, did not secure unitary representation at other levels of union organization given that, political conflicts for the control of the union movement predominant in the post war period. Partisan divisions became more formalized after 1974 as all political parties sought to extent their clientele through their presence within unions and formed union factions to achieve this end.[1]

Union organization formed a pyramid structure made up of three levels of representation. Primary unions, represented workers of a particular craft/ profession or industrial sector at the enterprise or local level. So called secondary unions were federations representing primary unions at an industry-wide, professional or craft basis, while local centers represented primary unions in a particular area. Finally the GSEE and ADEDY acted as an umbrella organization for all federations or local centers. The above complex structure resulted in a very large number of organizations that weakened the overall effectiveness of the labor movement and made it susceptible to outside influences.[2] Today there are 74 federations belonging to the GSEE and 46 that belong to ADEDY. In addition there are about 2500 primary unions belonging to GSEE and 1300 to ADEDY. Fragmentation today in part stems from the fact that industrial sectors are very loosely defined which results in each sub-sector having separate representation [29].

Collective agreements could be concluded at the national, industry-wide, and occupational levels, in accordance with the complex structure of union organization. The General Collective Agreement signed between the GSEE and the major employers' organizations determines minimum wages and salaries for all employees in the country.[3] The other agreements are signed between the most representative union and the respective employer organizations. The state, until 1990, had a strong role in the process and could intervene and impose compulsory arbitration. This contributed in unions addressing their demands more often to government than to employers. Moreover, it failed to create incentives

---

[1] The major union factions operating since 1974 are the 'PanHellenic Militant Labor Union Movement' (PASKE) that was affiliated to PASOK and the 'United Militant Union Movement' (ESAK) affiliated to the Communist party. Until 1981 the GSEE was under the leadership of conservative forces that however were not officially organized in a union faction. In 1981 The 'Independent Democratic Union Movement' (DAKE) was formed which was affiliated to the conservative 'New Democracy' party.

[2] Numerous organizations were formed, particularly during the immediate post civil-war period mainly to serve political or personal interests. It is estimated that following the fall of the seven-year dictatorship in 1974, there were about three thousand such organizations [26]. Even though in 1982 the GSEE register was cleared from unrepresentative unions, the problem of union fragmentation persisted.

[3] The major employer organizations are the Federation of Greek Industries (SEV), The Federation of Greek Professionals and Craftsmen (GSEVEE) and the Federation of Greek Trade (ESSE).

for either side to engage in dialogue thus sustaining the culture of confrontation that had been present from the inception of the labor movement.

FROM EXCLUSION TO MOBILIZATION: UNIONS IN THE POST 1974 PERIOD

Following the fall of the seven-year dictatorship in 1974, and the reinstatement of union freedoms, there was a partial return to pre-1967 practices aimed at maintaining state control over the GSEE leadership. This however did not prevent labor mobilization, on the contrary it politicized labor conflicts and accentuated divisions along partisan lines that cut across union organizations at all levels. Moreover some of the largest and most militant union federations came under left wing influence. Unions representing workers in public utility companies grew particularly strong during this period and were mostly under the influence of the socialist led union organization, PASKE. Not only did state intervention prove ineffective in curbing labor demands after the return to democracy in 1974, but it also led to the politicization of conflicts, which resulted in further unrest and strike activity.

The rise of PASOK to power in 1981 favored the further growth of organized labor. During the first period of socialist rule, up until 1985, close cooperation between government and the union leadership developed and unions managed to gain several concessions in exchange for their loyalty [30]. Union density peaked in 1982 with 36.7% of participation, and steadily declined thereafter to 28% [31], [32]. The highest participation rates were found in the public sector, public utility companies and the banking sector, where participation often approached 100%. These sectors formed the backbone of the union movement in the 1980s and thereafter, which enabled them to secure a number of benefits for their members. Their position was enhanced primarily by the following factors: (1) they were able to organize large strikes and bring about considerable disruption within society given that they performed key services. (2) They developed a close relationship of exchange with political parties, and in particular with PASOK that was in power for most of the 1980s, which gave them access to the decision-making bodies of public enterprises. (3) Competition between organized political forces to gain influence within the major federations, prompted governments to give into their demands.

In contrast unions in the private sector were weak. With the exception of a brief interlude after 1974, when the so called factory movement emerged, the small size of enterprises did not favor unionization and unions remained disadvantaged vis-a-vis employers. Within this context, it is not surprising that most labor mobilizations targeted the government and its economic policies rather than employers. This strategy proved by and large successful, as centralized collective bargaining made possible the betterment of the position of labor during the second half of the 1970s and the early 1980s, and average incomes rose substantially.

The deterioration of economic conditions during the second half of the 1980s put to the test the privileged relationship established between the union leadership and PASOK. The increase in public debt and poor economic performance meant that wage and salary growth could not be sustained at the same levels. The government used its prerogative to intervene in collective bargaining arrangements to impose austerity measures. Labor unrest ensued as a result and the GSEE leadership refused to endorse the incomes policy of the socialist government. While this crisis was resolved by putting aside union leaders that opposed the government's policy, it opened the way for change to take place at a later stage. By the end of the 1980s several factors contributed in shattering the relationship established between political forces and unions and called into question the institutional framework governing organized labor and collective bargaining.

The Transformation of Collective Bargaining and Attempts at Concertation

In the 1990s we witnessed a relaxation of political interventions within unions, an increase in their financial autonomy and institutional role, the transformation of collective bargaining and the first attempts at concertation between social partners and the government [33].

In year 1990, following a series of economic scandals, a coalition government was formed between all major parties that opened the way for the transformation of industrial relations arrangements. The most significant change was brought about with the introduction of law 1876/199 which abolished compulsory state arbitration as a means of resolving disputes and replaced it by a system of mediation. Arbitration remained an option only if requested by both employers and unions or unions alone. This satisfied a long-standing demand of left wing political forces that participated in the coalition government. Two other changes introduced by the new law are noteworthy: one, it made possible the signing of enterprise agreements in firms with over 50 employees and two, it gave precedence to industry-wide agreements over craft or professional agreements.

The decision to change collective bargaining arrangements must be viewed as the outcome of a series of events that led to the de-legitimation of government interventions within union organizations [26]. (1) The worsening economic conditions faced from the late 1980s onwards, meant that governments could no longer secure continued improvement in employment conditions. Government disengagement from collective bargaining was a way to avoid direct confrontation with unions. The union leadership, on the other hand, had less to gain from government's involvement. (2) A series of political scandals shattered the socialist party in the late 1980s that pushed the union leadership to seek ways to distance itself, even if temporarily, from party influence. (3) Employers on their part also favored the state's disengagement from collective bargaining because they believed that this would lead to the de-politicization of conflicts, which would facilitate dialogue with unions and put confrontation aside.

The abolition of compulsory arbitration did in fact help to promote consultation between employers and union organizations in the 1990s, possibly because neither side could now rely on state interference to resolve disputes each time they reached deadlock. Thus the climate of confrontation that dominated the previous period was put aside and the bargaining process assumed greater relevance and scope. Indicative of this is that while previously General Collective Agreements signed between the GSEE and major Employers' organizations applied for one year, from 1992 onwards agreements signed covered a two-year period. In addition the number of issues negotiated in collective bargaining increased and no longer focused exclusively on pay issues but included demands related to work organization, e.g. hours of work and safety and hygiene at work [34]. Last collective agreements were reached on the most part without resorting to state arbitration. While in the 1980s agreements reached by arbitration formed on average 42% of the total number of agreements signed (at all levels), during the following decade collective bargaining arbitration agreements constituted about 14% of the total [35]. It is also important to note that since the new law on collective bargaining was introduced no National Collective Agreement was concluded through the arbitration procedure. On the whole the new law helped to de-politicize conflicts and, for a while at least, it seemed as though the reaching of agreements through consensus was possible.

The other major change brought about by the new law was that industry-wide agreements gradually gained prominence over occupational agreements. This provided a partial remedy to the problem of union fragmentation, which had restricted unions negotiating capacity and accentuated inequalities between different segments of labor. Another significant feature of the new law was that coverage was provided to all employees of a particular sector, irrespective of whether the employer was a member of the organization signing the agreement or not. This provision was particularly beneficial for those employed by small firms that lacked union representation [29]. At the same time, this provision also secured employers from unfair competition from non-organized employers.

While at the institutional level the role of unions was enhanced this is less true of their real bargaining power. Government efforts to abide by the Maastricht criteria, continuing de-industrialization and privatization of formerly nationalized enterprises along with rising unemployment, had an overall negative impact on union's bargaining strength.[4] An indication of the above is the decline in union membership and strike activity that has been witnessed, particularly from the mid 1990s onwards [36]. Moreover, union mobilizations in the 1990s were primarily of a defensive nature and aimed to stall government plans to privatize public companies as well as efforts to reform the social security system and reduce social benefits. It is however interesting to note that while there was a significant decline in the number of strikes and the hours lost striking by the end of the 1990s, Greece continued to have a high strike rate compared to other European countries. While there is no record of the number of strikes during the first decade of 2000s, in a European company survey, conducted in 2009, 45% of employee representatives reported some kind of strike incident in 2008, which was the highest recorded among EU countries and comes to show that strike propensity remained comparatively high [37].

The relative moderation exhibited by unions during this period can be interpreted as an attempt to reaffirm their institutional role at a period when their real bargaining capacity was declining. In addition, the EU rhetoric on social dialogue and cooperation influenced political discourse in Greece and both political and union leaderships appeared eager to adjust to EU practices [38]. The government wished to capitalize on the above developments so as to promote a series of changes in labor relations in line with the Lisbon targets that aimed to increase labor market flexibility and combat unemployment. In 1997 the government invited social partners to discuss measures that would improve growth, competitiveness and employment. Seven months later a 'confidence pact' was signed, which affirmed the willingness of both sides to introduce measures that would combat unemployment. While on the symbolic level this was important, in real terms the agreement did not deliver major changes. In years 2000 and 2001, the government invited social partners to participate in

---

[4] Unemployment rose from 4% in 1981 to 7.5% in 1989 and to 10% in 1995 and remained above 10% for the rest of the decade In 2002 unemployment fell for the first time slightly below 10%, at 9.6%, only to rise again in subsequent years. National Statistical Service of Greece, *Greece in Numbers*, several editions.

tripartite concertation, in order to reach an agreement over the reform of the social security system and the rules regulating labor relations with the aim of inducing greater flexibility in work arrangements. Both attempts failed and the government ended up passing far less extensive reforms than initially planned.

The failure of concertation in part reflects the lack of trust between social partners in Greece as well as the absence of a culture of dialogue [39]. It also shows that such trust is hard to build at times of retrenchment. At the same time, the failure to achieve reforms by consensus needs to be understood as a by-product of the internal political divisions present within the union confederations. Political factionalism deters the majority, within the GSEE or ADEDY respectively, from agreeing on measures that are unpopular among sections of organized labor, as this would inevitably lead the opposition to challenge their decision and question their leadership status.

Centralized Bargaining Put to the Test

Despite the fact that, as we have seen above, the new law adopted in 1990, gave at first a new breath to the institution of collective bargaining and initiated a period of greater consultation between employers and unions, hopes that this would lead to a new period of concertation between social partners, soon collapsed. The failure to agree on reforms during the previous period, along with a decline in the growth rates of the Greek economy, contributed to the questioning of the value of centralized bargaining from a section of employers. While this did bring about immediate institutional changes, developments during the first decade of the new millennium prepared the way for decentralization to take place at a subsequent stage.

Even though the law passed in 1990 facilitated the signing of enterprise agreements, their numbers remained relatively small. In a survey study conducted among Greek firms, in the early 2000s, it was shown that 84.5% of firms based their wage rates and salaries on industry-wide agreements and only 0.5% on enterprise level agreements [40]. This is understandable given the small size of Greek firms. It suffices to say that in the vast majority of firms, unions cannot be formed as they employ fewer than 21 employees, which is the minimum union membership required by law for an enterprise union to be established. Nevertheless, during the 20 years that the law has been in effect there has been a gradual increase in the number of enterprise agreements signed. While on average, 121 enterprise agreements were signed every year between 1990-99 the number rose to 192, during the following decade 2000-09 (OMED, 2010), which indicates that a shift towards more decentralized bargaining was underway.

While the legal framework that was in place, in combination with the small size of many enterprises, made a shift towards decentralization very difficult in practice, employers did not hide their growing skepticism over the value of centralized bargaining. This is most clearly expressed in statements made on the part of the Hellenic Federation of Enterprises (SEV). For one, it supported that bargaining legislation should be modified, so that local agreements could be signed providing wages below the threshold placed by national collective agreements in areas with high unemployment, as a measure to stimulate economic activity. In addition the vice president of SEV in an interview in 2007 stated that industry-wide agreements should apply only where there are no enterprise agreements [41].

The first real challenge to the institution of industry-wide bargaining came, however, from the banking sector. In 2006 the managers of the six largest banks announced their intention not to take part in negotiations for an industry-wide collective agreement, but that instead each bank would sign a separate agreement with the union organization representing its employees. They rested their claim on the argument that technically they were not organized in a federation and thus not obliged to sign an agreement covering the whole sector. This caused the immediate reaction of the Greek Federation of Bank Employee Organizations (OTOE), which was one of the largest and most powerful union federations in the country. The nationalization of most major banks after 1974 meant that management was susceptible to political pressure and often gave in to union demands. However, from the late 1990s onwards the liberalization of the sector and the privatization of most banks [33] shifted employers' outlook, who now sought ways to disengage from the process of centralized collective bargaining. Banks had now to operate in a competitive environment, where government priorities did not play a major role in their decisions [42]. As argued by them in their letter, explaining the reasons for refusing to enter an industry-wide agreement, the system of collective bargaining was outmoded as it did not take into account the different needs and interests of each bank [43]. Even though in the end banks were forced to return to the bargaining table and, following concessions made on the part of OTOE on opening hours, a two-year industry wide agreement was signed, the same problem reemerged two years later with employers once again refusing to sign an industry wide agreement.

By and large, the following factors account for the change in attitude observed on the part of a large section of employers. One, the failure to reach consensus on major reforms promoted by government and supported by employers, cast doubt on the extent to which tripartite or bipartite cooperation could bring about the desired reforms, which in turn influenced negatively their viewing of centralized bargaining. Second, they became concerned over the continuing rise in incomes. Real incomes rose by about 19% during the period 2000-5, while productivity rose one percentage point less [44]. Moreover, despite the fact that wages grew less in manufacturing, increasing competition from Eastern European countries created pressure for a reduction in wages. Last, but not least, the liberalization of a number of sectors e.g. banking and telecommunications, changed employers priorities and encouraged them to find ways to bypass the powerful unions representing employees in these sectors.

Despite the shift in mood on the part of employers, during this period, the institutional framework remained intact. The political climate did not favor a change in the direction proposed by employers, given that neither of the two major parties: PASOK or New Democracy was willing to endanger their ties with union organizations. The above largely explains why a number of reforms that were on the agenda of successive governments during the first decade of the century remained incomplete. However, the severe debt crisis that became evident in 2009 spurred a series of developments that brought about radical changes and resulted in far more extensive reforms in labor regulations, collective bargaining and social security legislation than ever anticipated.

THE RECENT ECONOMIC CRISIS

The global economic crisis that erupted in 2008 made its impact felt in Greece a year later and expressed itself as a debt crisis that brought Greece on the verge of bankruptcy in 2010. Public debt rose to 126,8% in 2009 and the deficit climbed at 15,4%. The combination of the world economic crisis and the state's debt crisis has had a severe impact on the economy and resulted in the closure of many enterprises and the rise of unemployment to unprecedented levels. The lending crisis that ensued, led the government to turn to the EU and the IMF for a 110 billion-bailout loan. The loan was accompanied by a series of obligations on the part of the Greek government that involved the reduction of public spending and the adoption of measures aimed at inducing greater flexibility in the labor market in order to facilitate economic growth and competitiveness. The joint effect of the measures taken to deal with the debt crisis and the recession placed tremendous pressure on labor markets and by extension on union power.

As part of its obligation the Greek government adopted a series of strict austerity measures in 2010 that included: cutbacks in wages and pensions and shrinking of public sector spending. In addition it committed itself to introduce a number of legislative measures that aimed to enhance flexibility in labor relations and wage setting. Cutbacks in public spending involved a reduction in pay for all employed in the public sector that ranges around 10-30% of their salaries. Contract employment in the public sector is to be reduced by 50% while a maximum of one public employee can be hired for every five that retire. Last but not least, a reform of the social security system has been introduced that reduces pension benefits for all employed, raises the retirement age to 65 and cuts public health spending. In addition the new legislation passed aims to reduce some of the inequalities that exist between different categories of employees.[5]

The cuts in public spending and in the remuneration for all employed in the public sector has for the first time in the post war period affected negatively the position of core workers. This in and of itself places pressure on wages in the private sector to fall. Poor economic conditions and fear of unemployment has forced many in the private sector to accept a reduction in their income rather than endangering loosing their job. These tendencies have been reinforced by recent reforms introduced by the government that have relaxed restrictions on the firing of employees and reduced the severance pay for those laid off.

In 2010 law 3863/2010 was passed in parliament, which introduced major changes in the rules governing firing procedures and determining minimum wages and other work arrangements. The most important changes brought about by the new law are the following:

- It shortens the notice period required for dismissing white-collar workers, which amounts to an indirect reduction in their severance pay by 50%.
- It lowers the thresholds for collective dismissals. While previously firms with 20-200 employees could not dismiss more than four employees per month the threshold was raised to 6 for companies with up to 150 employees. In larger companies the threshold was set at 5% of staff while previously the threshold was between 2-3% for

---

[5] The above measures proved inadequate to solve Greece's debt crisis. In October 2011 new measures were legislated that among other things call for further reductions in salaries of public sector employees and pensions. In addition the way has been opened for the firing of public sector employees. The above were a precondition for a new bailout loan that is to be provided on the part of the EU and the IMF in addition to a voluntary 'haircut' of Greece's debt by 50%.

firms with more than 200 employees.

- It decreases the minimum wage for workers less than 25 years old to 84% of the minimum national wage set by the National General Collective Agreement, while for those under 18 it is set at 70% of the minimum wage.[6]

In addition to the above, two major reforms were introduced in collective bargaining arrangements both of which aimed at enhancing flexibility in wage setting. Both changes are in line with the suggestions made by the Hellenic Federation of Enterprises during the previous years. The first stipulates that 'special enterprise agreements' gain precedence over industry-wide general agreements, or even the General Collective Agreement setting minimum wages as long as the firm can demonstrate that such a move will allow it to avoid redundancies. The second major change introduced concerned the abolition of the privilege enjoyed by unions since 1990 to unilaterally resort to arbitration when, bargaining negotiations reached deadlock or, employers refused to negotiate. In practice this means that unions can no longer force employers to join the bargaining table. Given that most often it was weak unions of the private sector that found recourse in arbitration, when employers were unwilling to enter bargaining negotiations [45], they will suffer the most. However, this does not mean that former union strongholds will not be affected. On the contrary, the example of the banking sector indicates that employers are likely to seek ways to disengage form industry-wide bargaining in sectors that have undergone extensive liberalization and where employers face powerful unions.

The repercussions from the fore mentioned reforms are already visible as many organizations representing employers at the industry-wide or occupational level are refusing to come at the bargaining table to sign new collective agreements once their term expires. Given that if a six-month period passes after a collective agreement expires it seizes to be legally binding and new employees can be hired on the basis of personal agreements only, means that existing employees can be coerced into signing personal agreements with lower wages or salaries from those enjoyed until then, or otherwise they risk loosing their jobs. According to one estimate about two thirds of SMES adopt this practice [46]. There is thus a growing tendency not only for enterprise agreements to gain precedence over industry-wide agreements but for collective agreements to be replaced by personal agreements.

The Impact of the Crisis on Labor Markets

The recent austerity measures introduced by the government to reduce public expenditure worsened an already bad economic climate and led to greater recession. As a result many firms closed down or downsize while unemployment soared to 17%, at the time of writing. In addition during the last year so called atypical forms of work rose disproportionately. While this tendency was already evident before the crisis, developments during the past two years have accelerated the process of change and led to a sharp increase in atypical forms work, such as part-time and shared employment, that until recently were not particularly widespread.

---

[6] This was revised a year later so that those under 25 could earn 80% of the minimum wage.

Table 3 below indicates the number of new full time, part-time and shared-time contracts signed during the first two months of 2011 as opposed to 2010, as well as the number of existing full time contracts that have been transformed into either part-time or shared time contracts.

Table 3. Type of labor contracts undertaken during the first two months of 2010-2011

Year	New labor contracts			Existing Full-time Labor contracts transformed into either P-T or S-T		
	Full-time	Part-time	Shared-time	Part-time	Shared-time*	Shared-time**
2011	43900	24611	8263	5645	4556	1130
2010	79932	27857	6783	1887	373	40
% Change	-45,08	-11,65	21,82	199,15	1121,45	2725,00

*With the consent of the employee.
**Without the consent of the employee.
Source: Ministry of Labor and Social Insurance, Inspection Body, "The Shift in Employment Contracts during the first 2 months of 2010-2011", Press release, 6/4/2004, http://www.ypakp.gr/

As shown in table 3 above shared-time and part-time positions have become much more prevalent during this last year. The number of new, full time contracts, were reduced by 45% in 2011 compared to 2010, while new part time contracts were reduced by 12%. In contrast new shared-time contracts have increased by 22%. As a result the ratio of new full time positions to part time has decreased from slightly less than 3:1 to 2:1, while the ratio of full time positions to shared positions has decreased from 10:1 to 5:1. In addition, during this last year there was a sharp increase in the number of full time positions transformed into either shared or part time positions. As shown in table 3 the number of existing positions that have changed from full time status to part time has almost tripled during the first two months of 2011, compared to the same period in 2010, while those that have been transformed from full time to shared time increased more than ten times over.

The changes observed over the last year, reveal that employees, given the growing economic uncertainty and the lack of job prospects, are increasingly willing to accept more precarious working conditions. This is accentuated by the fact that the legal framework now provides greater freedom to employers to fire workers while collective bargaining arrangements have been weakened. Even though this process affects all segments of labor, as general conditions are deteriorating for all employed, including those that until recently were considered relatively privileged, those in precarious positions are the most exposed to the crisis. However, as unemployment rises and prospects worsen more and more people find themselves in a precarious position.

The Response of Unions

While the new measures introduced by government, have met the opposition of unions, which have staged large protests and strikes, they have been unable to halt the reform agenda.

This comes to show that their real bargaining power has been severely reduced as a result of the crisis. While the latter is largely the product of poor economic prospects, it is also related to the fact that union's power until recently rested primarily on the ties formed with political parties and pressure exercised on governments. However, under the existing circumstances the political leverage that unions can exercise has been severely diminished. The current debt crisis, along with the fact that the government is committed to follow a particular economic and social program, has deprived the union movement from its strongest weapon, which was its close relationship with political forces and its ability to influence social and economic policies.

At the same time, failure during the previous period to build solid institutions of consultation and tripartite policy making, has pushed unions in a defensive position whereby their role is restricted in trying to defend previously acquired rights. However, under the present circumstances this strategy is almost doomed to fail. This is particularly evident by the fact that unions so far have been unable to halt most reforms adversely affecting those working in public enterprises that make up the backbone of the union movement. Given the latter, as well as the fact that in the coming years public sector employment will shrink, we might expect unions' influence to subside.

CONCLUSION

Late economic development in conjunction with the persistence of traditional activities in the economy has led to the formation of dual labor market. On the one hand core workers, and particularly those working in the public sector, were highly protected and enjoyed more advantageous social security privileges that those in the private sector. On the other hand, the use of informal or atypical employment was very frequent, particularly in small family owned firms. This section of the labor force formed the 'outsiders' who enjoyed little or no social protection.

Union organization reflects on the one hand, the labor market structure and on the other, the turbulent political past of Greece. The small size of the working class and the dual structure of the labor market resulted in the union movement over-representing employees in the public sector. The latter was also the product of a relationship of exchange formed between organized labor and political parties in the post 1974 period, which has led successive governments to grant those working in the public sector and in public enterprises a series of concessions.

Political interventions within unions have left a legacy of union factionalism that has resulted in a highly confrontational culture on the one hand, and strong dependency on political forces on the other. For most of the 20th century unions enjoyed low institutionalization and were not incorporated in the social policy making processes. Unions on their part often acted in support of particularistic interests of the most privileged sectors of the labor force, thus indirectly reinforcing labor market segmentation. While during the past two decades unions began to adopt a less confrontational stance and achieved greater institutionalization this development coincided with a period of diminishing union power and growing economic challenges. Unions responded by adopting a defensive position and resisted most reforms aimed at changing work regulations or social security provisions. This, however, has left Greece ill equipped to deal with the challenges of the recent economic crisis, not only because it had failed during the previous period to improve its competitiveness and soaring public debts, but also because failure to build institutions of consultation, led to the marginalization of unions during the current period.

Recent developments brought about as a result of the economic crisis are rapidly tearing apart the collective bargaining system that was put in place in 1990. While decentralization of collective bargaining could already be detected before the crisis, the extent and force with which change in this direction is taking place has no precedent. Moreover, emphasis on enterprise level bargaining leaves by and large those employed in small firms outside the bargaining process. This means further weakening of the institutional role of unions given that in practice they represent an increasingly smaller section of the labor force.

While a general deterioration in the position of labor has taken place, labor market segmentation continues and wide inequalities exist in terms of job security and social provisions; It is likely, however, that some of these disparities will be gradually alleviated particularly as public sector employees loose some of their previously acquired rights. In the private sector, on the other hand, jobs that in the past provided a high level of security increasingly do not, in part because firing restrictions have been relaxed and in part because high unemployment constitutes most employees dispensable. As a result, private sector employees will find themselves under increasing pressure to accept lower pay and longer working hours. Last, and perhaps most importantly, the model of economic development followed by Greece so far indicates that the new positions that will be created in the private sector will be of a precarious nature.

REFERENCES

[1] B. Amable, *The Diversity of Modern Capitalism*, Oxford University Press, Oxford (2003).

[2] O. Molina and M. Rhodes, "The political economy of adjustment in Mixed Market Economies: A study of Spain and Italy". In B. Hancké, et al. (eds) *Beyond Varieties of Capitalism. Conflict, contradictions and complementarities in the European economy* Oxford University press, Oxford pp. 223-252 (2007).

[3] K. Featherstone, "Varieties of Capitalism and the Greek Case. Explaining the constrains on domestic reform". GreeSE Paper No 11, Hellenic Observatory. Papers on Greece and Southeast Europe, London (2008).

[4] T. Gianitsis, "Transformation and problems in Greek industry". In S. Vryonis (ed), *Greece on the Road to Democracy: Form the Junta to PASOK, 1974-86, A.D.* Garatzas, New Rochelle N.Y (1991).

[5] ESYE, *Population Census Figures 1981, 2001*. Eurostat, Labor Force Statistics, Data base (2005).

[6] K. Tsoukalas, *State Society and Work*, Themelio, Athens (1987).

[7] Giannitsis, *Entry in the European Community and its Consequences for Industry and Trade*, Foundation of Mediterranean Studies, Athens (1988).

[8] Y. Caloghirou et al, "The political economy of industrial restructuring: Comparing Greece and Spain", *South European Society and Politics,* 5(1), 73-96 (2000).

[9] Association of Greek Tourist Industry, *Tourism and Employment,* SETE, Athens (2003).

[10] J. Singleman, "The Sectoral transformation of the Labor Force in Seven Countries", 1920-70, *American Journal of Sociology*, 83(5), 224-34 (1978).

[11] S. Zambarloukou, 'Is there a South European Pattern of Post-Industrial Employment?' *South European Society and Politics,* 12(4), 425-42 (2007).

[12] B. Felix, "Employment in high technology", *Statistics in Focus*, Eurostat (2006)

[13] D. Karantinos, "Recent Trends in the Labor Market". In A. Mouriki et al (ed) *The Social Portrait of Greece,* Social Centre for Social Research, Athens pp. 121-124 (2001).

[14] EC, "Observatory of European SMEs. SMEs in Focus 2002". Available at: http://europa.eu.int/comm/enterprise/enterprise_policy/analysis/observatory_en

[15] M. Baldwin-Edwards, 'Where Free Markets Reign: Aliens in the twilight Zone". In M. Baldwin-Edwards and J. Arango (ed) *Immigrants and the Informal Economy in Southern Europe* Frank Cas, London pp.1-15 (1999).

[16] EIRO, "Industrial Relations in SMEs. Country reports of Greece, Italy, Portugal and Spain". Available at   http://www.eiro.eurofound.ie/1995/05study/TN 99052015.html (1999).

[17] P.Liargovas, "The White Paper on Growth, Competitiveness and Employment and Greek Small and Medium Sized Enterprises", *Small Business Economics*, 11, 201-14 (1998).

[18] Ch. Cousins, "Women and employment in S. Europe: The implications for recent policy and labor market detections", *South European Society and Politics* 5(1), 97-122 (2000)

[19] N. G. Bermeo, "What's Working in Southern Europe?" In N. Bermeo (ed) Unemployment in Southern Europe: Coping with the Consequences", Frank Cas, London (2000).

[20] EIRO 'Industrial Relations and Undeclared Work. Country reports of Greece, Italy and Spain' (2004). Available at: http://www.eiro.eurofound.eu.int/thematicfeature8.html

[21] N.M. Karakatsanis, "Relying on Stop-Gap Measures: Coping with unemployment in Greece" in N.G. Bermeo (ed) *Unemployment in Southern Europe,* Frank Cas, London pp.240-62 (2000).

[22] Eurostat, "Labor Force statistics 2010" (2011).

[23] Mouriki, "The 'new proletariat': the precariously employed-the outsiders of the contemporary labor market". In M. Naoumi (ed) *The Social Portrait of Greece,* Social Centre for Social Research, Athens pp. 109-122(2010).

[24] SEPE (Labor inspectorate), "Inspection statistics of Labor Inspectorate for 2010", press release, 19/1/2011. Available at:
http://www.ypakp.gr/index.php?ID=tGhAuA7M19PICCDpandgt=1andyp= (2011).

[25] For a discussion on the South European Welfare state see, Ferrera M. "The South European Model of Welfare in Social Europe", *Journal of European Social Policy*, 6(1) 17-37 (1996)

[26] S. Zambarloukou, *The State and Union Organization in Greece, 1936-90: A Comparative Approach*, Ant, N. Sakkoulas (1997).

[27] G. Mavrogordatos, *Between Pityokamtes and Prokroustis: Occupational Organizations in Contemporary Greece,* Odysseas, Athens (1988).

[28] G.F. Koukoules, *Greek Unions: Economic Self-Sufficiency and Dependence, 1938-84*, Odysseas, Athens pp.13-54 (1984).

[29] Y. Kouzis, *The Characteristics of the Greek Union Movements. Divergence Convergence from the European Context*, Gutenberg, Athens (2007)

[30] M. Spourdalakis, *The Rise of the Greek Socialist Party*, Routledge, London and New York (1988).

[31] EIRO, "Greece: Industrial Relations Profile" (1999). Available at http://www.eurofound.europa.eu/eiro/country/greece_3.htm.

[32] S. Seferiades, 'Unemployment, Inforamlization, Trade Union Decline in Greece: Questioning Analytical and Prescriptive Orthodoxies'. In N.G.Bermeo (ed) Unemployment in Southern Europe, Frank Cas, London, pp.60-89 (2000)

[33] G. Pagoulatos *Greece's New Political Economy. State, Finance and Growth from Postwar to EMU,* Palgrave Macmillan, New York (2003)

[34] Mouriki, "Labor Relations and Social Dialogue in Greece: The Difficult Path from State Custody to Independence', in *The Social Portrait of Greece* pp. 145-52 (2001).

[35] Organization of Mediation and Arbitration (OMED), *Report on Work Results 1992-2010* (2010) http://www.omed.gr/el/index.php?module=pagemasterandPAGE_user_op =view_pageandPAGE_id=39andMMN_position=82:77.

[36] EIROnline, 'Greece: Strike figures examined', (2003). Available at: http://www.eiro.eurofound.eu.int/2003/02/feature/gr032102f.

[37] European Foundation for the Improvement of Working and Living Conditions, *European Company survey 2009*, Luxemburg (2009).

[38] Kouzis (2007) p. 14.

[39] S. Zambarloukou, "Collective bargaining and Social Pacts: Greece in Comparative Perspective", *European Journal of Industrial Relation,* 12(2), 212-229 (2006)

[40] Y. Kouzis, "The impact of EMU on labor relations", *Epitheorisi Ergasiakon Sheseon*, 18, pp 57-66 (2002).

[41] SEV "The green bible for the modernization of labor regulations inn face of the challenges of the 21[st]century" (2007) accessed at http://www.sev.org.gr/online/view News.aspx?id=990andmid=8andlang=gr on August 4 (2007).

[42] S. Zambarloukou, "Ownership Corporate Governance and Industrial Relations in the Banking and Telecommunications Sectors: The case of Greece", *Industrial Relations Journal* 41(3), 233-238 (2010).

[43] Ch. Karakioulafis, "Banking Sector Strife over Industry-wide Agreement", (2006) accessed at http://www.eurofound.europa.eu/eiro/2006/02/inbrief/gr0602105n.htm.

[44] Institute of Labor GSEE-ADEDY, *The Greek Economy and Employment*, Annual Report 2006. INE, Athens (2006)

[45] Koukoules, "Retrospect on a controversial past". In Kasimati (ed) *The Greek Union Movement in the End of the 20th century,* pp. 25-84, Gutenberg, Athens (1997).

[46] K. Papadis "Firms cut down on wages to save themselves", *To BHMA*, March 6, 2011.

In: Greece: Economics, Political and Social Issues
Editor: Panagiotis Liargovas

ISBN: 978-1-62100-944-3
© 2012 Nova Science Publishers, Inc.

Chapter 15

CORPORATE SOCIAL RESPONSIBILITY IN GREECE: CURRENT DEVELOPMENTS AND FUTURE PROSPECTS

Skouloudis Antonis and Evangelinos Konstantinos*
University of the Aegean,
Department of Environmental Studies, Lesvos Island, Greece

ABSTRACT

The objective of this chapter is to provide an overview of Corporate Social Responsibility (CSR) in Greece and denote challenges that need to be met in order to further promote socially responsible business behaviour in the domestic economy. Drawing from prior literature, the analysis is built around three basic questions in relation to the Greek context: How is CSR perceived by Greek business professionals? How is CSR practiced in Greece? And how strategic CSR can help overcome the downturn the Greek economy faces nowadays? The extant empirical work suggests that, while CSR in Greece appears to be developing, there is still scope for improvement and further diffusion of relevant practices. While some of the patterns shaping CSR in Greece have been analysed, much work still remains to be carried out in extending and deepening our knowledge in this part of Europe.

INTRODUCTION

While corporate social responsibility (CSR)[1] footprints in terms of relevant policies and practices are evident among all regions, the level of uptake and diffusion differentiates, since countries differ greatly in terms of their levels of economic development, legal-political systems, cultural standards and expectations concerning business conduct [1,2]. The

---

* E-mail: skouloudis@env.aegean.gr

[1] Despite the numerous - and often biased - efforts to define this key conception in the academic study of business and society relations, it has remained an elusive task. In this regard, for the purpose of this study we approached CSR as "a concept whereby companies integrate social and environmental concerns in their business operations and in their interaction with their stakeholders on a voluntary basis" according to the most frequently mentioned definition of European Commission's Green Paper.

downturn of the Greek economy came as part of a consequent phase of the 2008 global financial crisis. It emerged as an unwelcome challenge and a wake up call for sound structural reforms under drastic measures and, despite the implicit socio-political costs, it can serve as a catalyst for targeting a more sustainable growth model in the long run. In this respect, CSR awareness is still rather low in Greece and only few large companies have articulated a sound strategy to promote such activities [3,4,5]. A domestic firm's CSR agenda usually pertains to the responsibilities of the public relations, communications or marketing departments and is mostly narrowed to charitable contributions or community donations. Correspondingly, the adoption of externally developed CSR initiatives, guidelines and standards is limited and governance mechanisms towards a more socially responsible business conduct are scarce. On the other hand, however, the recent introduction of leading sustainability indices in Greece, (AccountAbility Rating, Business in the Community Index) suggests that CSR could make further headway in domestic business conduct and eventually lead to the diffusion of socially responsible investments in the domestic capital market in the long term.

With this in mind and drawing from extant literature, this chapter attempts to portray CSR in Greece. To this end, the paper is built around the three following questions:

- How are CSR and ethical business behavior perceived by Greek business professionals?,
- How is CSR practiced in Greece?,
- How can the endorsement of responsible business behavior from a strategic perspective help overcome the crisis Greece faces today?

The rest of the chapter is structured as following: The next section discusses managerial perceptions for CSR in the Greek context. The following section addresses the current developments on the three CSR aspects: a) the adoption of management systems standards, b) the participation of Greek companies in formal voluntary CSR initiatives and c) the promotion of corporate triple-bottom-line/CSR reporting. Next, propositions for sound CSR-related strategies in Greece are identified leading to concluding remarks.

MANAGERIAL ATTITUDES RELATED TO CSR – THE GREEK PARADIGM

A marked difference of economic development in Greece, compared to other developed countries, lies in its incomplete transition from a mercantile/familial economy to joint stock/corporate capitalism [6]. The slack of state protectionism, the deindustrialization of formerly unproductive industries together with the emergence of globalization which allowed Greek business to relocate to more favourable socio-economic environments, gradually led to a decline in domestic industrial activity. This industrialization decline, evident since the late 1980s, 'left no room for the domestic industry to impress its norms and ethics on economy and society' [7]. Stavroulakis further stresses that Greece, being a rural country for long period of time, still lacks business tradition and ethics [7]. He also notes that Greek business management is characterized by short-termism and resistance to change. While over the past few years the largest business organizations have embraced a long-term strategic intent [8], the majority of Greek firms tend to disregard as irrelevant any dynamic changes and innovative practices that can potentially emerge, and primarily seek to implement a low-cost/cost cutting strategy. Moreover, domestic companies are characterized by a highly centralized decision-making process; top management is involved in most decisions [9] and Greek managers exhibit little confidence in the leadership capabilities of other individuals, even though they praise participative management [10]. In this respect, Stavroulakis referring to the Greek management's orientation to rational/personal interests, comments that:

> '(...) rarely did the average Greek businessman demonstrate evidence of social conscience and responsibility. Promotion of national and social interests through business activity, as happens for example among Japanese entrepreneurs, may appear extraneous to their Greek counterparts (with the exception of a small portion of the business elite)' [7].

The Global Leadership and Organizational Behaviour Effectiveness (GLOBE) research programme [11] offers some very fruitful insights on the Greek managerial perceptions for CSR. According to the GLOBE findings, Greek managers desire institutional collectivism (the extent to which institutional practices at the societal level encourage and reward collective action) much more than business executives of most other countries included in the survey. This is indicated by the society 'should be' – what should be happening in Greek society – coefficient, 5.40, ranking Greece fifth out of 61 countries, a finding that suggests the strong individualism of Greeks. In contrast, societal in-group collectivism (the extent to which individuals should express loyalty to, pride of and interdependence with their families) is much more highly valued in Greece than a large number of participating countries. Likewise, Greek managers regarded the concept of power distance (which denotes whether power should converge at the upper levels of society and whether people should believe in the ability to question superiors) considerably higher than those of most other participating countries, revealing the centralization of power perceived by respondents as existing within Greek society (Table 1).

In this respect, Waldman et al. [12] suggest that nations which highly value institutional collectivism incorporate CSR aspects into the decision-making process and consider how managerial actions pertain to the concerns of the larger collective or society.

Table 1. The Global Leadership and Organizational Behaviour Effectiveness (GLOBE) research findings for Greece

Societal Culture Dimension	Society "As Is"	Country Ranking	Society "Should be"	Country Ranking	Difference between "As is" and "Should be"
	Score	Rank	Score	Rank	Score
Institutional collectivism	3.25	61st	5.40	5th	2.15
In-group collectivism	5.27	35th	5.46	41st	0.19
Power distance	5.40	21st	2.39	52nd	-3.01

Source: Skouloudis et al., [13] – adapted from Papalexandris [14].

Table 2. Adoption of voluntary standards and initiatives by Greek companies

	AA1000AS	SA8000	GRI Guidelines	Global Compact
Number of organizations (as of late 2010)	3	17	24	78

Source: Authors' own elaboration.

Contrarily, in-group collectivism does not predict social responsibility values, as CSR refers to more societal-level concerns and such concerns are beyond the realm of the in-group. These authors also note that in cultures where power distance is high (such as Greece), aspects of CSR tend to be devalued since 'when there is a strong belief in society that there should be distance among people in terms of power, relatively high-level managers who have the power (such as our respondents) may be more self-centered or lacking in concern for shareholders/owners, broader stakeholder groups, and the community/society as a whole as they make decisions'.

Furthermore, it should be noted that there is a considerable female under-representation in high managerial posts, and in power positions in general [15,16] in the Greek business community. In this regard, it has been found that masculinity has a significant negative effect on corporate social and environmental performance [17] and is negatively related to a firm's ethical policies [18]. With this in mind, under Visser's [19] continuum of CSR embeddedness in organizational culture (Figure 1), Greek firms are primarily engaged in charitable and promotional CSR, since, according to our overall experience with the Greek paradigm, it is very few companies which are actively endorsing CSR from a strategic perspective.

CSR Embededness in the Greek Business Sector

Management Systems Standards

As shown in Figure 2, there is a significant divergence in the number of ISO 9001:2000 and ISO 14001 certificates in Greece. This should be conceived in conjunction with what Neumayer and Perkins [20] point out, that ISO 14000 is relevant to communities, NGOs, regulators, and other non-economic constituents that need not have any business links with the certified firm. ISO 14000 can potentially affect a broader set of stakeholders, and hence could reflect the country's cultural values more strongly than ISO 9000. To this regard, Corbett et al. [21] report that firms adopting ISO14000 are more motivated by relations with authorities and communities than firms adopting ISO 9000.

Greek industries may be safely considered to be late starters in the international certification process. This slow response has been particularly observed for ISO9000 and ISO14001 quality systems by Lipovatz et al. [22] and Lagodimos et al. [23] respectively. The latter found that the bulk (approximately 75% of the total) of the ISO 14001 certified entities operate in manufacture while others are roughly equally distributed between services (15%) and commerce (10%). This distribution differs significantly from that of ISO 9000 certified enterprises where 55% represented manufacture, services and commerce having 23% and 22%, respectively [24].

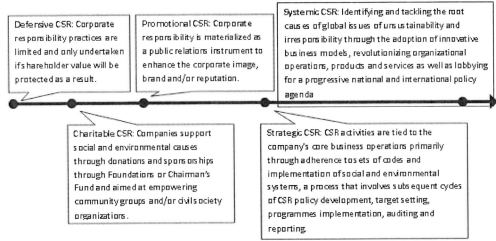

Source: Adapted from Visser [19].

Figure 1. A continuum of stages on the CSR embeddedness in business conduct.

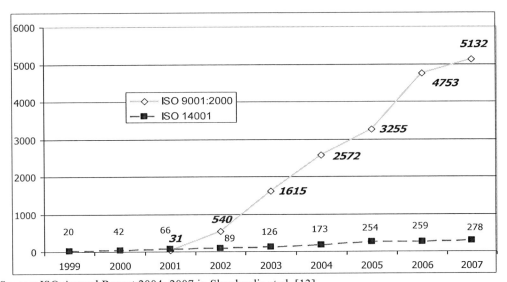

Source: ISO Annual Report 2004; 2007 in Skouloudis et al. [13].

Figure 2. ISO certifications in Greece.

These authors along with Tsekouras et al. [25] confirmed that in Greece there is an association of relatively large companies with ISO 14001/ISO 9000 certification and suggest that the degree of development of a sector certification culture (created by the previous adoption of ISO 9000) is a possible factor for EMS certification. Furthermore, the role of the state policy in Greece has been crucial in explaining organizational size as a factor for certification [23]; aiming to increase national awareness on quality and environmental issues, the implementation of standardised ISO management systems has traditionally been heavily subsidised by the Greek state, mainly through EU funds. While these subsidies primarily directed towards SMEs, given the size of Greek enterprises, nearly all can be classified as SMEs (according to uniformly applied EU norms). Consequently, the relatively larger firms (considered as more reliable) have been the prime beneficiaries, resulting in the association of with relatively large organizations. It is only recently that the problem has been understood and that real SMEs (based on specific criteria reflecting Greek enterprise norms) are obtaining access to state subsidies.

Kollman and Prakash [26] investigate cross-national variations in the implementation of environmental management systems standards (EMSS) and conclude that the characteristics of both domestic (business-government) relations and of international institutions advocating the standards (the EU and the International Organisation for Standardisation), need to be taken into account to fully explain the variations in the implementation of EMSS between different countries.

They suggest that the standards represent a new form of governance in which governments play a more limited role resulting in an extremely fragmented and decentralized form of policy making. However, this form of policy making has been slow to take hold in Greece. Indeed, Getimis and Giannakourou [27] stress the normative, rigid and legalistic form of Greek environmental policy, which is also evident in the low level of awareness of the various stakeholders, and thus explains both the low uptake of such standards and voluntary initiatives, as well as the fact that Greek companies appear to be less proactive than those in other countries (e.g. UK companies) [26].

The government in Greece has retained the right to policy making, with regional and local authorities having mainly a consultative role. NGOs, corporations or independent institutions have rarely been consulted and utilized in the formulation and execution of environmental policy reinforcing its normative, legalistic and mandatory nature.

Their exclusion from the process is the result of a widespread perception, that environmental policy making would be compromised if it involved NGOs or other independent institutions, as well as stemming from a fear on the part of bureaucrats that they might lose the privilege to maintain client based relations with companies. It this context, the administrative approach is in favour of command and control strategies rather than the development of self-regulation through proactive actions [27]:

> "The absence of a tradition of negotiation and debate both in the public service and in civil society, the low level of environmental awareness and of corporate ethics, and the particular characteristics of the Greek manufacturing sector (small and medium sized enterprises with few international connections), are some of the main features which have limited responsiveness to the EMAS Regulation" [28].

As of January 2011, 533 plants and facilities of 62 organizations operating in Greece have been certified under the EMAS regulation. What should be further highlighted though, is that 83% of those certifications belongs to facilities of three large companies while the remaining 17% (96 facilities) reveals the notably low level of EMAS penetration in the Greek industry.

In this respect, while the nature of environmental law in countries such as the UK or Germany seems to encourage companies to embrace voluntary initiatives, in Greece, environmental legislation appears to have the opposite effect [28]. Moreover, according to Heinelt and Toller [29], companies in Greece appear reluctant to publish corporate information:

"In Greece the obligation to publish an environmental statement under the EMAS rules is one of the factors that makes companies choose ISO 14001... The pursuit of their own interests by companies is viewed so negatively in Greek society that asking companies to make a voluntary contribution to environmental protection would not be understood by the general public. Publication in this setting of internal company data would only add more fuel to the fire" [30].

Endorsement of National and International CSR Initiatives

Greek companies prove to be at least reluctant to adopt and endorse voluntary CSR initiatives. Only three companies have certified their 2010 CSR reports according to the AA 1000 Assurance Standard while 33 organizations have indicated their adherence to the Global Reporting Initiative (GRI) Guidelines. Moreover, 17 facilities have been certified to Social Accountability 8000 (SA8000) Standard.

Furthermore, the number of organizations that have shown their commitment to the world's largest voluntary corporate responsibility initiative, the UN Global Compact principles, similarly was at low until 2007. Since then there has been an noticable growth in the number of business participants, while the number of stakeholders declaring their commitment to the initiative has risen respectively (Figure 3).

Recently (on November 2008), the Greek Business Council for Sustainable Development (BCSD) was launched. The BCSD is a member of the World Business Council for Sustainable Development - WBCSD's regional network. The 31 founding members – mainly industrial companies – have all signed a Code for Sustainable Development: a 10-point declaration on continuous improvement in economic, environmental and social performance.

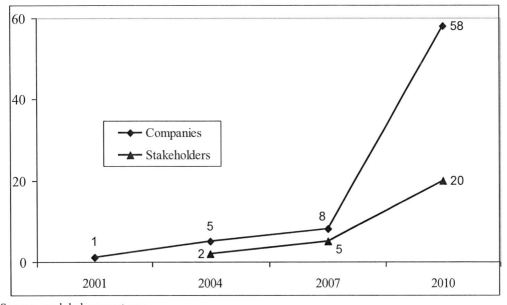

Source: unglobalcompact.org.

Figure 3. UN Global Compact participants in Greece 2001-2010.

To this regard, it should be mentioned that Titan Cement is the only Greek participant in a WBCSD sectoral project: the Cement Sustainability Initiative, a joint effort of 18 companies with the aim to develop common standards and systems to measure, monitor and report on health and safety performance, which the individual companies can then implement.

Table 3 shows the companies currently included in sustainability/CSR indices. Greek corporations are more oriented to the FTSE4Good indices. Midttun et al. [4] provides a reasonable explanation for this:

> "...Institutionalised orientations may also help explain the peculiar differences in industrial orientation towards different indexes. The fact that Nordic companies predominantly choose listings on DSJI, while many of the continentals and Mediterranean companies choose the FTSE4Good, presumably reflects different patterns of internationalisation. When Nordic and UK companies internationalise, they prefer listings on the New York stock exchange. Continental and Mediterranean countries, on the other hand, seem to be more oriented towards FTSE in London" [4].

It should be noted though that all major financial institutions are included in sustainability indices, proving that the Greek banking sector demonstrates robust corporate governance and risk management as well as high levels of environmental and social performance [30]. Moreover, compared to the number of Global Compact business participants, the number of Greek companies enlisted in such indices is considerably low. Again, Midttun et al. [4] neatly comment that:

> "...one might argue that the aggregated CSR indicators cover important distinctions in terms of CSR performance. While for instance it requires little or no effort to enter into the Global Compact and the GRI statistics, the SRI indices and the WBCSD involves significant demands in terms of performance and engagement. Thus, one might argue that the Global Compact and the GRI represent more of an indication of interest than an actual measure of performance. The DJSI and FTSE4Good, which measure real performance, should arguably be given greater significance. (...) Nevertheless Global Compact membership is gradually becoming more demanding and indicates a focus that is about to entail more and more screening of the firms' real commitment. The Mediterranean companies are quite active in this field and show clear ambitions with respect to future development" [4].

At a national level, a milestone in the diffusion of the CSR concept and supporting practices has been the formation of the Hellenic CSR Network, partner of the European CSR Network. The Hellenic CSR Network, based in Athens, was formed in June 2000 as a non-profit organization by thirteen companies and three business institutions. Its mission is to promote the concept of CSR to both Greek businesses and Greek society with endmost target to increase awareness on sustainable business practices. The Network aims at continuously updating and disseminate information on CSR; networking and collaborating with businesses, associations and other organisations, on all levels, for the exchange and dissemination of information; raising the awareness of the business community and the public on social action and the contribution of businesses on a local, national and international level; mobilising and developing partnerships for the promotion of social projects and the management of social issues; transferring, adapting and disseminating good practices in social cohesion and responsibility [31].

Table 3. Greek companies currently included in sustainability indices

FTSE4GOOD	Europe Index	Alpha Bank Bank of Piraeus Coca-Cola Hellas Cosmote Emporiki Bank EFG Eurobank Ergasias Bank Emporiki Bank Greek Org. of Football Prognostics Hellenic Telecommunications Org. 10.National Bank Of Greece
	Global Index	Alpha Bank Bank of Piraeus Cosmote EFG Eurobank Ergasias Bank Greek Org. of Football Prognostics Hellenic Telecommunications Org. National Bank Of Greece
DJSI	Dow Jones STOXX Sustainability	Coca-Cola HBC
	Dow Jones EURO STOXX Sustainability	Coca-Cola HBC
Ethibel Sustainability Index	ESI Excellence	Coca-Cola HBC Emporiki Bank
	ESI Pioneer	Emporiki Bank

Source: sustainable-investment.org, stoxx.com

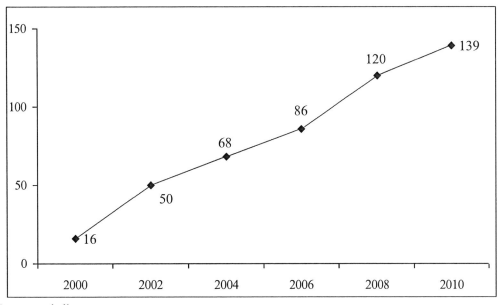

Source: csrhellas.org.

Figure 4. Hellenic Corporate Social Responsibility Network - core members 2000–2010.

Its current priorities include the collection of data on the social responsibility of Greek businesses; the increase of support given to business practitioners, especially small and medium-sized; the support and promotion of the "European Alliance for Corporate Social Responsibility"; the collaboration with public sector organisations; joint projects between its members for the management of urgent/sudden social or environmental changes; the creation of national network for the support of the principles of the Global Compact. Since its conception there has been a steady growth in the core-members companies of the Network which is quite promising (Figure 4).

Triple-Bottom-Line Reporting in Greece

The KPMG International Survey of Corporate Sustainability Reporting published in 2002 is the only global empirical study which included Greece in the sample. This survey examined the top 100 companies on the basis of their sustainability, non-financial reporting practices. Results confirmed that Greece has a relatively low reporting rate, with a mere 2% of the top 100 Greek companies publishing a report. However, 28% of those companies included health and safety, environmental or sustainability information in their annual financial reports.

Recent findings reflect that CSR accounting and reporting is still an unsystematic activity in Greece and most companies are at least reluctant to adopt such accountability practices [32,33,34]. In addition, Papaspyropoulos et al (2010) studied the extent of environmental reporting of the companies listed in the Athens Stock Exchange (ASE). The authors examined potential differences among ASE company sectors in terms of environmental reporting and opted for a segmentation of firms according to the comprehensiveness of disclosure. Their overall findings indicate a low extent of environmental accountability by domestic corporations and no difference either on the reporting practices between capitalization categories and sectors in ASE, or the environmental aspects that were covered. In addition, no relationship between the environmental sensitivity of firms and reporting comprehensiveness could be confirmed.

Domestic reporters tend to provide more typical disclosures concerning their profile and governance structure and less information on the 'hard facts' of non-financial dimensions of performance. Moreover, most of them disclose more information on labour practices, community donations and any CSR-related awards received during the reporting period, while only a few refer to their approach to crucial issues such as managing human rights-related performance, anti-corruption and anti-competitive behaviour procedures or clarifying whether fines/non-monetary sanctions were imposed on the organization for non-compliance with laws and regulations [34]. Such a major shortcoming of Greek reports reveals that this emerging instrument of corporate communication fails to address its key purpose: to promote stakeholder engagement and to discharge the organizational accountability towards the wider society. This is further confirmed by the fact that a mere 27% of the companies publishing a CSR report during 2010 verified the validity of all the disclosed information through independent assurance of the full report and included the assurance statement in the their report. While another 30% had only their reports third-party checked by experts, the rest either overlooked the issue of seeking assurance services or provided vague statements on future plans for external report verification.

Table 4. The cultural context of CSR communication according

Cultural context of CSR communication / Elements of CSR behavior	Latin-oriented context	Anglo-Saxon oriented context
Integration of CSR into the corporate strategy	The organization separates CSR activities from business operation and considers them to be discreet and part of the firm's disinterested generosity	The organization integrates CSR activities within its strategy, considering them a win-win approach
Media context and companies' reaction to it	The media are sceptical of companies that communicate CSR and, consequently, companies fear of media's negative criticism	The media tend to support businesses that communicate CSR and, consequently, companies do not fear their criticism.
Management tendency to take risks	Management thinks that it is too risky to build a corporate image on CSR activities because of the 'boomerang' effect emerging as soon as a problem arises.	Management perceives CSR as having a positive effect on corporate image and reputation since full disclosure is an important part of CSR strategy when the organization faces problems as well.

Source: Adapted from Birth et al. [36].

This absence of credible, verifiable information makes it difficult for customers, prospective employees, investors and pension fund managers, among other stakeholder groups, to make meaningful assessments and decisions about the CSR efforts of companies. Such evaluation processes get even more complex since companies often mix information on issues of legal compliance (e.g. mandatory employee health and safety measures and environmental protection procedures) with voluntary activities and programs to promote CSR. Tixier's [35] (in Birth et al. [36]) typology of CSR communication (Table 4) provide a useful interpretation of the Greek case. Under these 'lenses', Greek firms resemble a Latin-oriented approach of CSR communication with all the characteristics such an attitude encapsulates since, according to our overall experience with the Greek paradigm, it is only a handful of companies that is actively engaged in material external non-financial reporting.

REDEFINING BUSINESS MODELS IN TIMES OF ECONOMIC DOWNTURN

The low reform capacity and persistent weaknesses of the Greek economy did not appear to substantially affect official macroeconomic figures until the autumn of 2009, when other countries were striving to put forward bank bailouts and fiscal stimulus packages at that time. However, repeated revisions of the country's deficit and debt figures were at least disturbing; they undermined market confidence while increased the risk factor to other European peripheral countries and further tumbled the Eurozone in a period of intense turbulence. What had started as a crisis of private capital and profits from the other side of the Atlantic eventually transformed to a fiscal crisis of European Member-States [37]. Lacking in key respects, the domestic economy suffers from twin deficits: a budget deficit and an external current account deficit. It faces widespread tax avoidance and "legal" tax evasion [38] by Greece's over 900,000 private firms as well as evasion of social insurance contributions. It demonstrates sliding competitiveness potential and a comparatively unimpressive export performance because of inadequate product differentiation and penetration into foreign markets [39]. Likewise, inward foreign direct investment has been very low since the 1990s. Under such difficulties facing the Greek economy today, the redefinition of business models and attitudes can sharply add to the (re)stabilization of market flows and the promotion of a growth and development pattern built on the concepts of accountability, responsibility and trust. Redefining the management of domestic for-profit organizations towards a meaningful corporate social responsibility (CSR) agenda and the promotion of voluntary in nature (initially low-cost) business practices can result in win-win opportunities.

The dominating corporate culture in Greece pays lip service to practices above the minimum requirements of legal compliance, since domestic companies find it difficult to fulfil their formal legal obligations [29]. Corporate non-compliance with the legislative framework induces monetary and non-monetary sanctions or additional, stringent legal arrangements. From the stakeholder perspective, it can even lead to decreased market or investment shares, decreased attractiveness with employees or recruits, or negative media coverage. In this context, if the CSR agenda is liable to be merely captured by the public relations department of companies 'it is likely that a great deal of energy will be spent to a little effect' [40]. In contrast, under the 'lens' of strategic CSR, Greek companies would identify and assess the actual impacts of their operation, rather than the legal foundations for these impacts and whether the organization may be held legally responsible, something that indicates that in effective CSR there is not a strict distinction between law and fact [41]. Consequently, such a business behavior can lead to a shift of managerial attitudes which indicates a perception that informal, social norms are formal and legally binding, imposed by the various stakeholders of the firm [41]. It is also denotes the voluntary nature of effective corporate responsibility that urges companies to act beyond what the law dictates and engage in a self-regulating process. Fulfilling the expectations of governmental stakeholders (who are actually the agents of the public in promulgating standards of firms' behavior in the various business realms) makes it less imperative for the law to do more to contain the externalities of firms. It reduces the possibility of a more robust legislative intervention in the future and, therefore, provides better adaptation to conditions of uncertainty on future legislation and those requiring relevant compromises on behalf of the organization. Therefore, Greek firms should instill a climate that values the spirit of the law, as a set of codified ethics, in addition to the letter of the law. Clearly the adoption of strategic CSR implies the redefinition of values and policy goals that will guide organisations to be internally committed to legal compliance, and to move towards voluntary actions. Fostering such an organizational culture will underpin that they operate 'within the rules of the game' [42].

Moreover, since in the core meaning of the CSR concept relies in transformating existing business practices, it is rational to link it with business processes of organizational change and innovation. Innovation, in all its forms; from incremental (remodelling functionalities) to disruptive (breakthrough ideas), is a key factor for a company's survival and long-term growth [43,44]. Authors have pointed out that investing in CSR helps a company shape new capabilities and eventually apply such new knowledge to its conventional cost structure, organizational culture, resource allocation, tangible and intangible assets' management [45,46]. Kanter [47] coined the term 'corporate social innovation' to describe the turn firms should do towards social issues and utilize them as a learning laboratory for the identification of unmet needs and the development of solutions that create new markets. In this respect, Hockerts [48] proposes that corporate social innovation requires the creation of knowledge structures that result from investments in corporate social performance. In this context, the term 'knowledge innovation' has been coined to describe 'the exchange and application of new ideas into marketable goods and services, leading to the success of an enterprise, the vitality of a nation's economy and the advancement of society' [49]. By promoting effective stakeholder management Greek firms could contribute towards that direction as long as such practice would actually respond to stakeholders' needs and expectations. Such social responsiveness could develop a 'shield' that could embrace domestic companies to firmly hold their geographic presence and markets simultaneously and at the same time be profitable and effable. In other words, the ways in which Greek business organizations engage with the various social constituents is central to achieving two beneficial objectives: achieving competitive advantage through innovation and at the same time implementing a more sophisticated and deeply embedded form of organizational responsibility. Cohen and Levinthal's [51] discussion of absorptive capacity portrays such self-reinforcing behavior:

> 'If the firm engages in little innovative activity, and is therefore relatively insensitive to the opportunities in the external environment, it will have a low aspiration level with regard to exploitation of new technology, which in turn implies that it will continue to devote little effort to innovation. This creates a self-reinforcing cycle. Likewise, if an organization has a high aspiration level, influenced by externally generated technical opportunities, it will conduct more innovative activity and thereby increase its awareness of outside opportunities. Consequently, its aspiration level will remain high' [51].

Furthermore, the very nature of internationalization induces firms to engage in CSR for two basic reasons. First, because exporters need to entrench their reputation as good citizens in the eyes of host populations and, second, as a response to the new global governance system of international organisations (e.g. the Global Reporting Initiative, the Organization for Economic Cooperation and Development and the United Nations Global Compact) and other corporate 'watchdogs' and international constituents with strong public-interest agenda (i.e. asset management firms and NGOs) that promote responsible business behavior. Additionally, a growing number of consumers worldwide is increasingly aware of the implications of their purchasing decisions and consequently demand products that demonstrate sound environmental and social standards [52]. For instance, consumers now have the opportunity to take direct action to contribute to the reduction of greenhouse gas emissions by purchasing energy-efficient appliances or, likewise, through their purchasing behavior can help producers in developing countries make better trading conditions or to abolish forced and child labor.

Designing and implementing a 'total responsibility management' approach [53], where issues of stakeholder engagement combined with 'best practices' adoption - under the formulation of a core CSR strategy, can potentially contribute towards the internationalization of domestic products and services. Strike et al. [54] note the strong reputation of environmentally and socially responsible firms, with the various reputational resources to be crucial in the organization's relationship with its stakeholders [55]. Given that the notion of internationalization has been defined as an engagement in networks of interconnected business relationships with clients and suppliers [56], it has been argued that CSR-based reputation can prove important for developing and strengthening international network relationships and eventually facilitate future export success [57]. A company that promotes a 'CSR-supported export strategy' [57] can differentiate itself from the competitors and gain higher credibility. Such credibility is translated in reputational gains and a transition of the company's market orientation beyond the domestic borders [58]. The discrimination of non-native export ventures on institutional grounds (i.e. preconceptions, ethnocentric and political reasons) related to social and/or environmental dumping can be compensated by CSR-based reputation building at the firm level. In addition, product-level CSR reputational resources (defined by the reputation attributed on product differentiation employing CSR-related product features) and organizational-level CSR reputational resources (which strengthen customers' loyalty, advocacy and brand identification) are especially relevant to gain relative competitive advantages and difficult to imitate intangible assets. From the perspective of market apprehension, Greek exporters can utilize the feedback they receive from foreign markets and obtain essential CSR-related knowledge on how to transform and readjust the production processes and other operations. Again, Boehe et al. [57] provide a compelling example to outline such mechanism:

> "...firms that have not implemented any CSR-related strategies may face disadvantages in some international markets and consequently have lower (or negative) profit rates than those enjoyed by their competitors, especially in markets characterized by strong rivalry and customer bargaining power. Seeking to reverse their negative performance, these firms may observe their competitors, analyze their products or talk to international clients or consultants to understand why they are outperformed by their competition. Having learned their lessons, they may introduce products with CSR characteristics and related product and process improvements to enhance their performance in international markets" [57].

CONCLUSION

The very nature of modern business activity, regardless of firms' nationality, calls for an increase in CSR. The crisis itself was shaped around the lack of social responsibility and in favor of greed for excessive profits. On the other hand it is a wake up call for sound structural reforms under drastic measures and - despite the implicit socio-political or financial costs - it can serve as a catalyst for targeting a more sustainable growth model in the long run. However, it is managerial acumen, creativity and insight three essential components that will identify the value of responsible business behavior and transform current business practices to more viable, sustainable ones. Adopting a socially responsible business vision can result in win-win opportunities and mutually beneficial outcomes for the company and society (i.e. sustainable development).

While time will only tell how the Greek case will evolve, the role of the government is decisive in embedding strategic CSR to the domestic business community. Setting meaningful CSR standards equally reinforcing to legislation, capacity building for business associations to meet and audit CSR standards, developing incentives and rewards for compliance to socially responsible business practices are few aspects of the mediating role pertinent governmental bodies can play. The 110bn € bailout from the EU, co-sponsored by the IMF, and accompanied with a strict set of structural adjustment reforms, may solve the current fiscal and debt crisis. Still, the country needs to stand on its own feet and, in this context, redefine current production-business models and development plans.

REFERENCES

[1] Wotruba, T.R. *Journal of Public Policy and Marketing*, 16(1), 38–54 (1997).

[2] Hofstede, G. *Cultures consequences: comparing values, behaviours, institutions, and organizations across nations*. Thousand Oaks, CA: Sage Publications (2001).

[3] Tsakarestou, B. 'Greece: The experiment of market expansion'. In A. Habisch, J. Jonker, M. Wegner and R. Schmidpeter (eds.), *Corporate Social Responsibility Across Europe: 261–273*. Berlin, Heidelberg: Springer (2004).

[4] Midttun, A., Gautesen, K. and Gjølberg, M. *Corporate Governance*, 6(4), 369–385 (2006).

[5] Albareda, L., Lozano, J.M. and Ysa, T. *Journal of Business Ethics*, 74(4), 391-407 (2007).

[6] Louri, H. and Pepelasis-Minoglou, I. *Journal of European Economic History*, 31(2), 321–348 (2002).

[7] Stavroulakis, D. *MIBES Transactions*, 3(1), 147–156 (2009).

[8] Theriou, N.G. *Review of Economic Sciences*, 6, 145–160 (2004).

[9] Joiner, T.A. *Journal of Managerial Psychology*, 16(3), 229–242, 2000.

[10] Cummings, L.L. and Schmidt, S.M. *Administrative Science Quarterly*, 17, 265–278 (1972).

[11] House, R.J. and Javidan, M. 'Overview of GLOBE'. In House, R.J., Hanges, P.J., Javidan, M., Dorfman, P.W. and Gupta, V. (Eds.), *Culture, Leadership, and Organizations: The GLOBE Study of 62 Societies: 9–28*. Thousand Oaks, CA: Sage Publications (2004).

[12] Waldman, D.A., Sully de Luque, M., Washburn, N. and House R.J. *Journal of International Business Studies*, 37, 823–837 (2006).

[13] Skouloudis, A., K. Evangelinos, Y. Nikolaou and W. Leal Filho, *Business Ethics: A European Review* 20(2), 205-226 (2011).

[14] Papalexandris, N. 'Greece, from ancient myths to modern realities'. In J.S. Chhokar, F.C. Brodbeck and R.J. House (Eds), *Culture and Leadership across the World: The GLOBE Book of In-Depth Studies of 25 Societies: 767-802*. New Jersey: Lawrence Erlbaum Associates (2007).

[15] Galanaki, E., Papalexandris, N. and Halikias, J. *Gender in Management: An International Journal*, 24(7), 484–504 (2009).

[16] Mihail, D. 2006b. *Women in Management*, 21(8), 681–689 (2006b).

[17] Ringov, D. and Zollo, M. Corporate Governance: *The International Journal of Effective Board Performance*, 7(4), 476–485 (2007).

[18] Scholtens, B. and Dam, L. *Journal of Business Ethics*, 75(3), 273-284 (2007).

[19] Visser, W. *The age of responsibility:* CSR 2.0 and the new DNA of business, London: Wiley (2011).

[20] Neumayer, E., Perkins, R. *Environment and Planning*, 36(5), 823–839 (2004).

[21] Corbett, C.J., Luca, A.M. and Pan, J.N.. '*Global perspectives on global standards: A 15-economy survey of ISO 9000 and ISO 14000'*. ISO Management Systems, 1:January–February, 31–40 (2003).

[22] Lipovatz, D., Stenos, F. and Vaka, A. *International Journal of Quality and Reliability Management,* 16(6), 534–551 (1999).

[23] Lagodimos, A.G., Chountalas, P.T. and Chatzi, K. *Journal of Cleaner Production*, 15(18), 1743–1754 (2007).

[24] Lagodimos, A.G., Dervitsiotis, K.N. and Kirkagaslis S.E. *Total Quality Management and Business Excellence*, 16(4), 505–527 (2005).

[25] Tsekouras, K., Dimara, E. and Skuras, D. *Total quality management*, 13(6), 827–841 (2002).

[26] Kollman, K. and, Prakash, A. *Policy Sciences*, 35(1), 43–67 (2002).

[27] Getimis, P. and Giannakourou, G. 'The development of environmental policy in Greece'. In Heinelt, H., Malek, T., Smith, R. and Toller, A.E. (Eds.), *European Union Environmental Policy and New Forms of Governance, 289–294.* Aldershot: Ashgate (2001).

[28] Watson, M., and Emery, A.R.T. 2004. *Managerial Auditing Journal*, 19(6), 760–773 (2004).

[29] Heinelt, H. and Toller, A.E. 2001. 'Comparing EIA and EMAS in Germany, Britain and Greece'. In Heinelt, H., Malek, T., Smith, R. and Toller, A.E. (Eds.), *European Union Environmental Policy and New Forms of Governance*, 350–389. Aldershot: Ashgate (2001).

[30] United Nations Environmental Program - Financial Initiative (UNEP-FI). '*Scratching on the surface of sustainable finance: a survey on sustainable finance practices in Greece'*. UNEP-FI: Central and Eastern European Task Force. (2007)

[31] Hellenic Network for Corporate Social Responsibility. '*Organization, Mission, Activity, Members'*. Athens: Hellenic Network for Corporate Social Responsibility at: www.csrhellas.gr .

[32] Skouloudis, A. and Evangelinos, K. *Environmental Quality Management*, 19(1), 43–60 (2009).

[33] Skouloudis, A., Kourmousis, F. and Evangelinos, K. *Environmental Management*, 44(2), 298–311 (2009).

[34] Skouloudis, A., Evangelinos, K. and Kourmousis, F. *Journal of Cleaner Production*, 18(5), 426–438 (2010).

[35] Tixier, M. *Thunderbird International Business Review*, 45(1), 71-91 (2003).

[36] Birth, G., Illia, L., Lurati, F. and Zamparini, A. *Corporate Communications: An International Journal*, 13(2), 182–96 (2008).

[37] Schmidt, I. *Alternate Routes: A Journal of Critical Social Research*, 22, 71-86 (2010).

[38] Stathakis, G. *Synchrona Themata*, 108, January-March, 5-9 (in Greek), (2010),

[39] Athanasoglou, P.P., Backinezos, C. and Georgiou E.A. "Export performance, competitiveness and commodity composition", Bank of Greece, Economic Research Department, *Special Studies Division* (2010).

[40] Dine, J. Companies, *International Trade and Human Rights*, Cambridge: Cambridge University Press (2005).

[41] Buhmann, K. *Corporate Governance*, 6(2), 188-202.

[42] Friedman, M. *New York Times Magazine*, September 13, 122-126 (1970).

[43] Tushman, M.L. and Anderson, P. *Administrative Science Quarterly*, 31, 439-65 (1986).

[44] Tidd, J., J. Bessant and K. Pavitt, *Managing Innovation: Integrating Technological, Market and Organisational Change*, Wiley. Chichester (2005).

[45] Barney, J. Journal of Management, 17, 99-120 (1991).

[46] Russo, M.V. and Fouts, P.A. *Academy of Management Journal*, 4, 534-59 (1997).

[47] Kanter, R.M., *Harvard Business review*, 77(3), 122-32 (1999).

[48] Hockerts, K., "*Managerial Perceptions of the Business case for Corporate Social Responsibility*", CBSCSR Working Paper Series, Copenhagen Business School (2008).

[49] Amidon, D.M. *Innovation Strategy for the Knowledge Economy: The Ken Awakening*, Butterworth-Heinemann, Boston (1997).

[50] Chun, R., *Creativity and Innovation Management*, 15(1), 63-73 (2006).

[51] Cohen, W. and Levinthal, D. *Administrative Science Quarterly*, 35, 28–52 (1990).

[52] Chapple, W. and Moon, J., *Business and Society*, 44, 415–41 (2005).

[53] Waddock, S. and Bodwell, C. *Total Responsibility Management: the Manual*. Greenleaf Publishing, Sheffield (2007).

[54] Strike, V., J. Gao and P. Bansal., *Journal of International Business Studies* 37, 850–862 (2006).

[55] Coviello, N. and Munro, H. *International Business Review*, 6, 361-86 (1997).

[56] Johanson, J. and Vahlne, J.E., *Journal of International Business Studies*, 8, 23-32 (1977).

[57] Boehe, D.M., Cruz, L.B. and Ogasavara, M.H., "*How can Firms from Emerging Economies Enhance their CSR-Supported Export Strategies?*", Insper Institute of Education and Research, working paper 209/(2010).

[58] Knight, G. and Kim, D. *Journal of International Business Studies*, 40, 255-73 (2009).

In: Greece: Economics, Political and Social Issues
Editor: Panagiotis Liargovas

ISBN: 978-1-62100-944-3
© 2012 Nova Science Publishers, Inc.

Chapter 16

GREEK YOUNGSTERS' PERCEPTIONS OF MODERN GREEKS: AN EXPLORATORY STUDY

Chrysa Tamisoglou[*]
University of East Anglia, UK

ABSTRACT

This chapter reports the findings of exploratory research conducted in Greece aiming to identify what image the Greek younger generation has of modern Greeks. Nearly 200 children aged 12-15 participated in this research depicting modern Greeks' internal (psychological and personality) and external (physical) features. The methodological approaches used for data collection were focus group interviews and human figure drawing. Children were asked to draw a representative Greek person regardless of gender and to depict as many as possible internal and external traits in their drawings. Afterwards, they were stimulated to discuss their drawings in groups and to express their perceptions of modern Greeks. The findings of this study indicate that the younger generation perceives the national self through a critical lens attaching to modern Greeks not only positive characteristics but negative as well. They underline the direct link with ancient Greeks, the view that modern Greeks can rightfully be considered as European and the superiority of the national self in relation to some other nations. They point out that modern Greeks develop rather racist attitudes in regards to specific countries. The participants of this research also underline how social and political circumstances influence them in terms of the way they perceive their national self and suggest what should be changed in the social and political context in order for modern Greeks to develop a better state and national profile.

INTRODUCTION

How does a new generation form its ideas about its national self? Are young people born with a set of particular perceptions of what constitutes their national self or are their perceptions acquired in the social environment where they live? What do these perceptions

---

[*] E-mail address: C.Tamisoglou@uea.ac.uk

involve? Theorists who tried to provide satisfactory answers to these questions have focused on the nature of nation (e.g. [1], [2], [3]) and have underlined that the construction of each nation presupposes the cultivation of national identity to its members. National identity, on the one hand, concerns the way a nation is legislated and preserves its existence 'inspiring' its citizens to be an active part of it and, on the other hand, the way citizens sense and confirm their existence in a particular nation [4]. Although theorists do not agree on the way national identity is formed (for example, on the base of primordial attachments [5] or common cultural roots [6]), they concur that the cultivation of national identity involves mainly the younger generation. Therefore, a nation plans and implies several social, cultural, political, territorial and economical policies in order to secure the socialization of the younger generation of the nation as 'nationals' and 'citizens' [7], [8]. On the other hand, relevant literature suggests that the construction of national identity is close related to the sense of the 'other'. According to Kedourie [9] there is not only a 'we', an in-group in the foundations of a nation but a 'they', an out group(s) which we should be distinguished and remained separate. On the same path, Smith [10] supports the idea that each nation has to assert itself in contrast, and often in opposition, to other national communities. Further, Connor declares that '*a group of people become first aware of what are not ethnically before actually realizing what are they **are**'* [11: 333 emphasis in the original].

From a psychological point of view, relevant literature (e.g. [12], [13]) indicates that the way the younger generation perceives the world, itself and the 'other' is a cognitive process which is influenced by the conditions of the societal environment in which youngsters are brought up. In terms of the way children develop their ideas about, perceptions of and attitudes to 'national/ in group self' and the 'other/out group self', psychological research (e.g. [14], [15]) argues that from the age of 5-6, children can state some ideas and judgements about national self and other national groups which become more detailed and accurate by 10 or 11 years of age. At the age of 5-6, children's perceptions involve mostly typical physical features such as clothing, language and habits, and during middle childhood and onwards these features are expanded and entail also psychological and personality traits as well as political and religious belief. Additionally, the same research indicates that a) younger generation gains its knowledge about 'national self' and the 'other' through various political, social, cultural channels such as the political system of a state, its economic condition, family and the media and b) younger generation's ideas about its national 'self' and 'other' does not change considerable during the next years of its life.

Taking into consideration the above, this chapter reports and discusses the findings of an exploratory research which tries to gain insights into Greek children' ideas about the 'national self' and the modern Greeks. What do Greek youngsters think of and how do they describe a typical Greek person? What is their image of their national self? According to children' ideas, what are the typical physical, psychological and personality traits of the modern Greeks? Does the notion of 'other' play a role in the construction of their national self? How do gender and age influence the way children identify a modern Greek person? What do young people think about the state they live in and how they judge the national profile of their country? These are some of the issues this chapter tries to touch upon and draw insights.

At this early stage, it should be mentioned that this chapter does not aim to generalize its findings but to explore young people's perceptions and impose questions for further examination. Also, the presentation of the research and its findings has been adjusted to the limitation a chapter in a book imposes.

Methodological Design

Considering the psychological research discussed above, the target population of this research was children of 12 to 15 years of age. However, not all Greek nationality children of these ages participated in the research. Since the research was conducted at schools (places where children are gathered and can be investigated), the schools which participated in this study were selected randomly according to the Schools List provided by the Ministry of Education which enumerates each school of each level of each geographical area with a code number. Six schools which were located in North Greece (1 primary and 1 junior-high school from North-Western Greece, 1 primary and 1 junior-high school North-Central Greece, 1 primary and 1 junior-high school from North-Eastern Greece) were selected. In total, 192 pupils took part in this research and an almost equivalent number of boys and girls (93 boys and 99 girls). Since this study was an explanatory one, this size of the sample was judged appropriate.

The research was conducted at three stages. At the first stage, pupils were introduced to the scope, aims and the procedure of the research by the researcher. At the second stage of the research, pupils were asked to present their attitudes to, perceptions of and ideas about their national self. For this purpose, a visual technique was employed based on arts and, in particular, human figure drawing. Human figure drawing entails the presentation of a representative person who is of interest (in our case, a representative person from Greece) including his/her internal and external characteristics. The selection of the particular visual technique was made since a visual approach seems to facilitate and engage the participants of a survey [16]. In the same vein, the drawing activity is based on the arts-based paradigm in research. Art in research as Bochner & Ellis ([17]:508) state *can be representational, but it also can be evocative, embodied, sensual, and emotional; art can be viewed as an object or a product, but it also is an idea, a process, a way of knowing, a manner of speaking, an encounter with Others; art can reveal an artist's perceptions and feelings, but it also can be used to recognize one's own'*.

Additionally, psychological research (e.g. [18], [19]) has indicated that the act of drawing especially children's drawings represent children' internal reality, the internal qualities of objects, people and events and *reflect unconscious layers of their personality such as conflict, feelings and attitudes related to the self and significant others'* ([20]: 327). However, children's drawings and particularly human figure drawing is not only an individual creation and representation but embedded messages that disseminated by the social context in which children live. Dennis (1966 cited in [20]: 328) argues that drawing of people should be regarded as reflecting preferences and choices guided by social values to which a child is socialized.

Considering the above, children were given an A4 sheet and were asked to draw a Greek representative person (man or woman) in black and white colours. Youngsters were motivated to draw common and typical figures based on their experiences and knowledge. They were also asked to add symbols, objects, bubbles with characteristic phases and so on if they thought that these would help them to express their ideas. Children worked individually. When the drawing activity was over, at the third stage, children in groups of 4-5 discussed their drawings. This phase of the research aimed to investigate the way pupils portrayed the Greek national self and gain insights into their perception of the Greek nation. At this stage, the technique of focus group interview was used. The purpose of the technique is to '*provide insights into the attitudes, perceptions and opinions of participants*' ([21]:19). The group discussion of the drawings gave the opportunity to pupils to add comments on their own drawings and on others' as well as to raise objections to other pupils' ideas about the national self leading, in same cases, the discussion to a meaningful debate which helped the researcher to identify in depth pupils' ideas. Finally, the interviews were recorded with digital voice recorder and transcribed and the drawings were collected for further analysis.

Following the specific research design, 37 transcripts were collected and 192 drawings. The analysis of the transcripts was made by using NVIVO 8.0 (qualitative data analysis software). The analysis of drawings was based on the pattern of human figure drawing suggested by Bar-Tal & Teichman [20]. Bar-Tal & Teichman investigated pupils' ideas about national self on psychometric foundations and tried to identify how these ideas develop by age. For data collection, they used human figure drawings which were scored on structural and thematic variables. The aspects of structural analysis involved image complexity and image quality and the thematic variables dealt with the status, affect, behaviour and appearance of human figures. Since this study is not interested in the structure of the drawings (for example, proportions of limbs and distortion of a figure and/or complexity of human figure), the particular analysis was focused on the thematic aspects of the proposed pattern. In terms of thematic analysis, Bar-Tal & Teichman scored the drawings they collected according to attributed status, affect, behaviour and appearance. Attributed status included level of education or profession and figure size defined by length and width. Attributed affect entailed the rating of affect projected by the figure (negative, e.g. anger, threat; neutral, e.g. unspecified; positive, e.g. joy, happiness) and the number of colours used by children in a drawing. Attributed behaviour was linked with movement (human figure was presented as static or active), verbal expressions attached to figures (positive/neutral/negative content) and the decoration of a figure (the items that accompanied a figure). Appearance was related to the type of clothing (dressing code), to skin colour (light/dark), age (young/elder) and cleanliness (clean dirty). In the first phase of the analysis, the particular parameters were applied to a set of drawings in order to examine if they are applicable. This pilot examination showed that not all variables can be applied to the human figure drawings of this study. For example, the parameter 'movement' was not applicable since all human figure drawings presented as static figures and the age of figures can not be specified. Thus, the parameters that were used in the context of this study were:

A. Attributed status related to level of education or profession expressed by drawing (low level, e.g. garbage collector, unspecified, high level, e.g. doctor/businessman)
B. Attributed affect in regards to the figure's reflecting affect (negative, neutral, positive as defined above)
C. Attributed behaviour was examined under a) the content of verbal expressions that was stated in bubbles and attached to figures (negative/neutral/positive content) and b) figure decoration, the items that accompanied a figure (negative decoration e.g. bombs, guns; neutral when there was no decoration; positive e.g. flowers, home)
D. Attributed appearance related to type of clothing (negative e.g. old fashioned, ragged clothes, neutral e.g. classical dressing code, undefined, positive e.g. in fashion, rich clothes with accessories) and to body cleanliness (negative e.g. dirty face/body with smudges, positive e.g. clean and cared face/body).

The comments each child made for his/her creation of a particular human figure were attached underneath each figure. At the end of the comments, pupil's age and gender were mentioned.

Children's drawings and the accompanied comments were analyzed by the researcher and two coders (one teacher from primary school and one from secondary school) in order to secure, as far as possible, objectivity. An analysis protocol and a coding sheet were edited according to the parameters discussed above. Each teacher and the researcher evaluated each human figure individually stating whether the particular parameters attributed a negative or neutral or positive image. Additionally, the analysts would mention how they reached to their judgement, indicating relevant characteristics in the drawing and written expressions in pupils' comments. After this analysis, the judgements were compared and the inter-coder agreement was calculated[1].

PRESENTATION OF THE FINDINGS

Based on pupils' interviews and drawings, the national self was conceived with positive and negative characteristics which involve both internal and external traits. Concerning the external traits and modern Greeks' appearance, Greek people were depicted as modern. Women are dressed in modern and expensive clothes and with accessories and in-fashion hair style while men were dressed in ordinary dress code (Image 1). Participants commented that appearance is important for Greek people. 'Greek people like to be in fashion and pay attention to what they wear' (Int. 33). Considering men's ordinary dress code, youngsters discussed that Greek men, as well as women, 'they dress in expensive clothes but *they prefer more a 'free' style*' (Int.5). Although the majority of young people presented their figure as discussed above, 10% of the depicted Greek figures were dressed in traditional costumes (Image 2). Youngsters who chose to present their figures in this way commented that they opted for the particular dress code in order to show '*how much we are related to our heritage*' (Int. 19).

The majority of human figures (89%) were depicted with smiling and happy faces reflecting a positive image. Interviewees commented that the smiling and happy faces indicated that Greek people like having fun all the time and living their lives. They also compared this trait with the way people from other countries live their lives: '*We know how to enjoy our lives in contrast to people from other countries who keep working all the time and they do not know what life means*' (Int. 32). However, not all youngsters consider this trait positively. A small percentage of children (11%) think that the way Greek people like having fun and living their lives is a disadvantage. '*They always have how to have fun in their minds*' (Int. 12); so, Greek people do not like working and are indolent. '*Some Greek people work as less as possible and some others feel so lazy every time they have to go to work*' (Int. 36).

---

[1] Since there is no full agreement about the most reliable formula for the assessment of inter-coder reliability (Neuendorf 2002), in this analysis, the inter-coder reliability was calculated using the formulas developed by Cohen, Fleiss and Krippendorff. After the texts extracts have been categorized by the coders and the researcher, two consolidated files in which all categorizations were included were edited; one for each grade. These files were uploaded on the website: www.dfrelon.org where there is an online calculator of the most popular coefficients .The inter-coder agreement was above 0.800 in each case which, according with the creators of the formulas (Cohen 1960, Fleiss 1971, Krippendorff 2004) means that the reliability of the analysis is acceptable and we could proceed to the presentation of the outcomes.

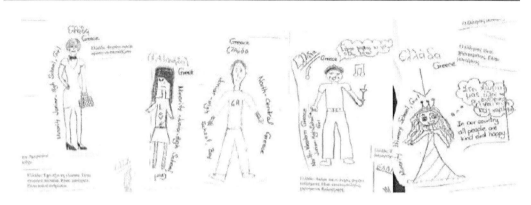

Image 1. Sample of female figures dressed in modern way and male figures dressed in ordinary clothes.

Image 2. Sample of figures dressed in traditional costumes.

Studying young people's drawings, it was noticed that the Greek flag accompanied 20% of all figures (Image 3). According to children's comments, the presentation of the particular element stood for the love Greek people have for their country. *'We are very proud of our country'* (Int. 11). They also discussed that as nation, *'we suffered and struggled but we managed to overcome hardships due to our love of freedom'* (Int. 29).

Another positive characteristic youngsters attached to Greek people was hospitality. Interviewees commented that Greek people are hospitable and respect travellers from other countries. *'It's a very old tradition which can be traced back to ancient Greece. Greeks have always been friendly to visitors, tourists and wanders'* (Int. 8). They also underlined that this trait distinguishes Greek people from the people of other countries. *'We are very friendly in contrast with people of other countries who do not care and do not help you'* (Int. 6)

It seemed that the ancient Greek civilization was not only responsible for Greek people's hospitality but also for the pride the children who were interviewed felt for their country's origins.

The particular youngsters defined themselves as descendants of the ancient Greeks underlining that this feature should be considered as integral part of the Greek identity. *'I am Greek, I have very important ancestors. I am proud of and admire the civilization my ancestors developed*' (Int. 4). The way some pupils drew Greek human figures demonstrated this pride and showed the link between youngsters and their ancestors (Image 4).

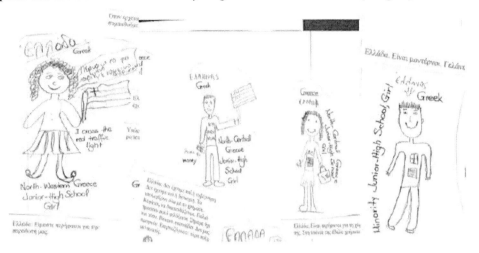

Image 3. Sample of figures depicted carrying or having the Greek flag on their clothes.

Image 4. Sample of figures presented as ancient Greeks.

Additionally, according to young people's comments, the ancient Greek civilization constitutes the reason that Greece should be considered as European country and its people as European because '*Greece is the cradle of civilization and democracy. The world has learnt from Greece. Despite our disadvantages, we had a great civilization*' (Int.2).

Further, European citizenship was a theme young people discussed while they tried to describe their national self. Although they declared that their country and its people should be thought as European, when they were asked if they felt European they stated that they have the sense that they are '*half European*' (Int.22). They identified as European the country which is very well organized at political and social level, is progressive and wealthy with a developed economy. They also indicated which countries exemplify the notion of 'European country': England, France and Germany. *'To be a European means to be civilized and organized as the British and the French. To obey the laws, to have a wealthy economy like Germany, to respect the environment'* (Int. 17). Comparing these countries with their own, participants stated that the way modern Greeks live has many things in common with these countries. However, many things should be done in order for their country to reach the standards these countries have set. *'I think Greek people are very close to the West Europeans. We are similar to the French, the Germans. Of course, we are not the same. We have a lot to do to be like them. We are behind them'* (Int. 24). According to participants' comments, the reason that Greece is behind these countries is the state's ineffective policy and its unreliable politicians. *'Politicians are interested in votes not in common good. They do not care about their country'* (Int. 20). *'The policy our government implies is not the appropriate one'* (Int. 23). *'Our society needs serious and effective reforms. We should stop being so selfish; we should care about others'* (Int. 31). But, at the same time, young people who were interviewed stated that *'it is not only politicians fault. Greek citizens vote for these parties. They should think more serious what they vote for'* (Int. 10).

The selfishness and the politicians' and state's policy ineffectiveness that interviewees commented on leads, according to their comments, to Greek people's disobedience of laws and official orders. *'When our politicians do not respect the laws they vote for what do you expect? The citizens would not obey them as well'* (Int. 30). Participants presented and commented on Greeks' people's disrespect for laws and commands in two ways: a) polluting the environment: Greeks are presented throwing away litter everywhere even in the case a bin is very close to them and b) smoking in places where smoking is forbidden showing that they do not care about the common good. Indicative is the figure presented in Image 5 which also depicted laziness and the importance of the past (history) - traits that have been discussed previously.

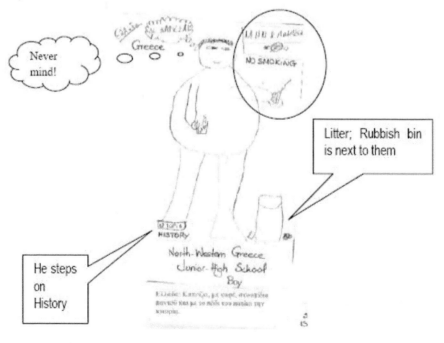

Image 5. Sample of figure which shows a man who is lazy and disobeys the laws.

Additionally, youngsters referred to this disadvantage comparing their country with other countries which are thought as 'expert' in this scheme. *'Greeks do not obey the laws like the Germans or the British'* (Int. 2).

The majority of the children interviewed (81%) added another disadvantage: Greek people's 'obsession' with money. According to the interviews, Greek people love and always think of money. *'They like 'easy money'* (Int. 27). *'They like to work less and earn a lot of money'* (Int. 15). Indicative are the children's drawings which demonstrate this 'love'; many figures present Greek people holding or having money (Image 6).

The feature that was mentioned in each interview and characterized as the most negative feature of the Greek people by interviewees, was the racist and xenophobic behaviour Greek people have towards people coming from some specific countries, especially from the Balkan peninsula. Young people admitted that they behave themselves such way: *'Bulgarians are very bad people. When I come across them in street, I change my direction'* (Int. 14). *'I do not want to have an Albanian as friend. We, the Greeks, we do not want to have any kind of affair with them'* (Int. 18). *'Yes, I am racist. I do not want them in my country. They are criminals'* (Int. 34). Explaining the causes of their xenophobic behaviour, they also discussed that this behaviour is a matter of phobic feelings, these people's poor living standards or derives from parental counselling. *'We are very racist. We behave badly to Albanians and we think of them as criminals and thieves. We do not want to speak or make friendship with them. We are afraid of them; they will kill or harm us'* (Int. 18). *'They are dressed in rags and smell awful'* (Int. 21). *'My mother told me to keep a distance from them'* (Int. 7). Nevertheless, participants stressed that they acknowledge that this behaviour is not right. *'I know it is not a good behaviour. But...'* (Int. 28) When pupils had occasionally a discussion with peers from a different background or saw a family in their neighbourhood coming from these countries, they argued that: *'They are like us. OK'* (Int. 11). It is also interesting that they defined this behaviour in terms of the country a person comes from. *'I am OK with a British person. Many of them come here in summer. We try to be hospitable to them'* (Int. 32).

Finally, in regard to the influence gender and age have on youngsters' ideas about modern Greeks, this exploratory study does not find that both parameters have any significant impact on children's perceptions.

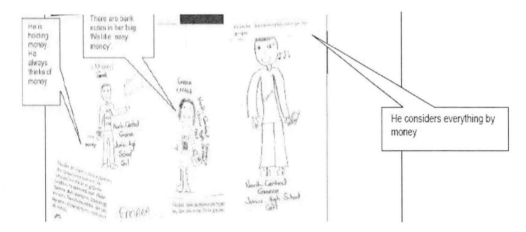

Image 6. Sample of figures holding money.

It was found that young people's perceptions of modern Greeks are the same no matter of the interviewee's gender. However, it was noticed that youngsters at the age of 15 was more capable to enrich their comments with arguments and examples than, for instance, children at the age of 12.

CONCLUSION

The presentation of Greek youngsters' perceptions of modern Greeks shows that youngsters identify their national self based on a net of internal and external, psychological and personality traits. Although participants' comments reflect a feeling of national in-group favouritism in the sense that interviewees are proud of and love their country, at the same time, their comments are critical and indicate a number of traits which are judged negatively.

More particularly, according to the findings, the participants' pride of their country derives mainly from the country's ancient past which seems to influence the modern Greek society until nowadays. Also, the country's ancient past seems to be the key for the country's European perspective and course. It is interesting that participants of this research did not refer to the modern Greek civilization and its contribution to the European civilization but they insisted on the ancient Greek past. The comment a 15 years old boy made is indicative: 'We keep talking about ancient Greece. What about modern Greece and its civilization? I do not know if we could discuss about modern Greek civilization and be proud of it' (Int. 26).

In the same vein, young people who participated in this research expressed a feeling of disaffection with the political system and the way modern Greek society functions. They underlined that, on the one hand, the ineffectiveness of the politic power influences the way Greek citizens react in their society and, on the other hand, the way Greek citizens perceive their citizenship has an impact on the way the political power is exercised. The participants of this research asked for a more organized society which sets the common and not the personal good in the front line, which respects its citizens and its citizens concern themselves with any level of their society. However, when they were asked to define and describe in details how they would like their society to be, they were not able to give specific guidelines because, as they stated, 'we are too young to be able to describe in details the society we would like. For sure, we would like a more just society' (Int. 13).

The notion of the 'other' seems to be influential over young participants' ideas about modern Greeks and their society. As shown in the presentation of the findings, youngsters compared their country's situation with other countries and the way their people developed their society. It seems that some countries, especially those from West Europe, stand as model for Greek youngsters. They argued that Greece and the Greek society should follow these countries' social settings to some extent in order for Greece to advance its national status.

However, discrimination could be detected in terms of the way the 'other' is perceived by young people who participated in this research. Based on the interviews, people who come from countries which are not considered as developed countries or part of the West Europe such as Balkan countries are thought rather negatively. This discrimination reflects young people's biases and stereotypes about these countries and their people. Considering that Greece is part of the Balkan countries and shares a lot with these countries such as culture and heritage, it needs further investigation into the origins of these biases and stereotypes. On the same path, it needs further examination how the perception that Greece is more close to West Europe is cultivated to Greek youngsters.

Finally, as stated previously, this study is an exploratory one and it does claim generalization of its findings. Nevertheless, it suggests that youngster's ideas about their national self is worthy investigation since it reflects a number of issues regarding country's profile and its society status. Additionally, it proposes a more expanded in size and depth investigation of young people's perception in order for the issues that this study touches upon to be further examined.

REFERENCES

[1] Kedourie, *Nationalism*, Hutshinson, London (1960).

[2] Smith, *National identity*, Penguin Books, London (1991).

[3] Gellner, *Nations and Nationalism*, Blackwell Publishing, Oxford (2006).

[4] Smith, *National identity*, Penguin Books, London (1991).

[5] Geertz, *The interpretation of Cultures*, Basic Books, Inc., New York (1973). G.

[6] Anderson, *Imagined Communities,* Verso, London (1991).

[7] Smith, *National identity*, Penguin Books, London (1991).

[8] M. Billig, *Banal Nationalism,* Sage Publications, London (1995).

[9] Kedourie, *Nationalism*, Hutshinson, London (1960).

[10] Smith, *National identity*, Penguin Books, London (1991).

[11] W. Connor, 'A nation is a nation, is a state, is an ethnic group, is a...', *Ethnic and Racial Studies,* 1, 4, 377-400 (1978).

[12] Bal-Tar, *Shared beliefs in a society: Social psychological analysis,* Sage, Thousand Oaks, CA (2000).

[13] Cullingford, *Prejudice From individual identity to nationalism to young people*, Kogan Page, London (2000).

[14] M. Barrett, H. Wilson, & E. Lyons, 'The development of national in-group bias: English children's attributions of characteristics to English, America and German people'. *British Journal of Development Psychology*, 21, 193-220 (2003).

[15] M. Barrett, *Children's knowledge, beliefs and feelings about nations and national groups*, Psychology Press, New York (2007).

[16] R. Chambers, 'Participatory Rural Appraisal (PRA): Analysis of Experience', *World Development*, 22, 9, 1253-1268 (1994).

[17] Bochner & C. Ellis, 'An introduction to the Arts and Narrative research: Art as inquiry', *Qualitative Inquiry,* 9, 506- 514 (2003).

[18] M. Koppitz, *Psychological evaluation of human figure drawings by middle school pupils*, Grune & Stratton, New York (1985).

[19] M.V. Cox, *Children's drawings of the human figure*, Erlbaum, Hove (1993).

[20] Bal-Tar & Y. Teichman, *Stereotypes and Prejudice in Conflict*, Cambridge University Press, Cambridge: (2005).

[21] R. A. Krueger, *Focus groups. A practical guide for applied research*, Sage, Newbury park, CA (1994).

In: Greece: Economics, Political and Social Issues
Editor: Panagiotis Liargovas

ISBN: 978-1-62100-944-3
© 2012 Nova Science Publishers, Inc.

Chapter 17

DEPICTION OF THE ROLE OF WOMEN ON THE ISLAND OF EVIA (GREECE): A SIGNIFICANT FISHING AREA

Joanna Castritsi-Catharios[1] and *Steriani Matsiori[2]*

[1]University of Athens, Department of Biology, Athens, Greece
[2]University of Thessaly, Department of Ichthyology and
Aquatic Environment, Volos, Greece

ABSTRACT

The role of women (and specifically those involved in the fisheries) on the island of Evia (Central Greece), the second biggest island in the country, was depicted through an extended survey. Evia is a significant fishing area, in terms of fishing fleets and number of fish farms. The field research was based on semi-structured interviews and on the usage of proper questionnaires. These were addressed to professional fishermen, owners of fish farms and conversion plants, women occupied in fish farms, local associations and local cooperatives.

The data collected refers to the economic situation of the family, the structure of the family, the social status and the educational level. Care was taken that the interviewed were covering a minimum of 5% in each category. Data was also used from the last National (Greek) census. The women on the island of Evia play a secondary role, in relation to males, in all fields of activity. The majority of fishermen's wives is not employed, but belongs to the category of assisting spouses. They have a lower educational level than their husbands, and their participation in public affairs is very limited. The women who are working do so, mainly in the primary sector (most commonly in the fisheries), and secondarily in the tertiary sector, usually in tourism or in the service field (in the urban areas). In fish farming, women are working independently from their husband's involvement in the field. Most of the women (59%) are workers, 27% are clerks in the offices and 14% are technological or scientific staff. In the cooperatives, the role of women is also secondary: they do not participate in the administration, being mainly involved in the production and marketing of the products.

---

[*] E-mail address: cathario@biol.uoa.gr & lyeco@hotmail.com

Introduction

The notion that women are not just marginal players, but active participants in the fisheries, is not new. Women play an important role in fishing communities all over the world since they are heavily involved in pre- and post-fishing activities. Currently, women contribute in multiple ways while their role includes: social and economic responsibilities and duties, both within and outside the family, including marketing, processing, and also the harvesting of aquatic products (FAO, 1988). Despite the important role played by women in the fishing sector, the social space they occupy has often remained invisible to researchers and policy makers (Bennett, 2005). Although, in the last years the issue of women in fisheries has become increasingly important, little information exists about women and their important roles in the fishery sector. Especially for Greece, little research has been done to investigate the important role of women in the fisheries and their socio-economic profile.

A study was carried out on the island of Evia (Central Greece), aiming to depict the role of women. Emphasis was placed in significant fishing areas, while priority was given to the women who, directly or indirectly, were related to the fisheries. Important data was retrieved through National and EU organizations (National Statistical Service, National Research Center, General Secretariat of Equality, etc.), while the bibliography approaching the same subject in different areas of the world was considered.

On an international basis, the largest number of individuals occupied in the fisheries is found in Asia (8.5%), followed by Africa (7%), Europe, South America, North and Central America (2% each), and Oceania (0.2%). Reliable data regarding women involved, directly or indirectly, in the fisheries is limited, although the role of women is significant. Previous research (1997), based on statistics from the fish processing industry in many EU countries, showed that Italy has the highest percentage of women workers (87%), followed by Portugal (75%), France (68%), Germany (55%) and Sweden (52%); while the United Kingdom (51%), Belgium (55%), Spain (55%), Netherlands (61%) and Greece (68%) have a higher percentage of men than women involved in this sector (Rana and Choo, 2001). On the contrary, Greece has the highest percentage of females (50%) in the aquaculture industry, followed by Finland (30%), France (23%), United Kingdom (15%) and Spain (7%) (Rana and Choo, 2001).

Women are usually working:

- In several fields of fisheries (paid or not), before or after the harvesting, including the contacts with the authorities. In some countries, more women than men are occupied in fish farming and inshore fishing (FAO, 2004).
- In the production of fish feed (FAO, 1988).
- In attending the children and implementing mental work within the family and in society (Nadel-Klein, 1988).
- In non-fishery sectors, increasing the family income and supplementing the varying income of their husbands' work (Tietze and Villareal, 2003).
- As members of fishery unions and organizations.

There is, on an international basis, a negative frame of mind against the involvement of women in fishing, strengthened by the fact that men consider themselves as more suitable and capable for fishing activities because of several factors (traditional structure of the fisheries, body strength, etc.). Women are considered as more suitable for auxiliary work, as it regards to fisheries. Bibliographical findings prove that:

- Men dominate the EU Consultative Committee on Fisheries and Aquaculture, comprised of a group of mainly big fishing industries (Gorez, 2000).
- In the Netherlands, only a few women are involved with actual fishing, 60% (approximately) of the women are involved in the decision-making regarding investments, finances and labor for the fishing enterprise; but despite their participation, neither receive a salary nor are they insured (Quist, 2000).
- In the eastern coast of Scotland, women are considered significant partners in the fishing business (due to their role they have in the decision making for the selection of the staff and the determination of the fishing policy), leading to a serious disagreement between males and females (Nadel-Klein, 1998).
- In N. Norway and Nova Scotia, women participate in family enterprises, but only in secondary activities (cleaning the vessel, preparing meals, etc.), supporting activities (purchase of equipment, listening to the relevant news, etc.), as well as in the management (recording the catches, payments, etc.) (Thiessen et al., 1992).
- In France, schools specializing in fishing studies accept girls as students, but very few of them are involved in technical works, while most of them are involved in marketing and management.
- Wives of fishermen in N. Carolina are discouraging their children from being involved in the fishery, resulting in a serious difficulty in staffing the fishing vessels with young people (Dixon et al., 1984).
- In Latin America, women have limited opportunities to get involved in training activities relating to technical aspects, micro enterprises and community organization, even in countries with experience in this area. Moreover, women in fisheries or aquaculture communities have no access to credit or co-financing systems for running their activities (Pereira, 2002).
- In India, women do not participate in the fishing activity, but they take care of the house. Also, they are involved in the selling of the catch (Norr and Norr, 1992). It has been estimated that women account for 25% of the workforce in fishing and fish farming, 60% of the workforce in exporting oriented fish and shellfish processing, and 40% of the workforce in domestic fish marketing (FAO, 2007).
- On the Fiji islands, as well as on other islands of the Pacific Ocean, women are moving away from the traditional fishing activities and taking part in the commercial side, establishing small-scale businesses. They are placed somewhere between the traditional "obligation" to participate in the fisheries and the modern needs of commerce (advertisement, promotion through internet, etc.) (Lambeth et al., 2002).
- Development and support systems have paid much less attention to the economic potentials of women in small-scale fisheries in West Africa. Women in developing economies, especially in Africa, lack access to services such as credit, fisheries extension, technology, information and basic education which are critical for shifting the patterns of fishery production or increasing output (Williams, 2000).
- Although women play a key role in the fisheries sector in Greece, there is limited information about them. The ultimate purpose of this study is to address the

important role played by women in the fishing sector in Greece, providing a brief introduction as to their actual role and status. The study was carried out on Evia Island.

Evia Island, and especially its coastal areas, constitutes a vital part of Greece. The role of women within the EU, of which Greece is a member state, shows a certain improvement in the last twenty years, and the effort is dynamically confirmed. The EU is contributing significantly towards this direction through treaties (Rome, 1957- Amsterdam, 1997), the five medium terms action programs, for the equality between the two sexes, and political decisions (Council of Lisbon - 2000). Greece has succeeded within the last twenty years to create favorable conditions for the women, through decisions of the parliament and within the frame of UN (convention for the deletion of all discriminations against women, protocol for the assurance of the women's rights, etc.). The efforts are mainly focused on the labor market, participating in the social life and the decision-making channels, and on the deletion of all structures and ways of thinking which lead to discrimination. The basic thought is associated with the conversion of equal rights, which are now consolidated, to equal chances.

MATERIALS AND METHODS

Greece has many of coastal areas, carrying a significant part of its population (urban, semi-urban, and agricultural). The Greek coastal line is 15.500 Kms, and its biggest part is habited and exploited. The Island of Evia was selected because it is considered as being representative of the country. Evia is the second biggest island of Greece, with a coastal line of 1094.641 Kms, 6.6% of the country. Evia has a significant fishing fleet (Table 1) and show other fisheries activities, most representatives being the fish farming (Table 2).

Table 1. Number (N) of vessels and individuals occupied

AREA	VESSELS		OCCUPIED PERSONS	
	N	%	N	%
Greece	19750	100	35177	100
Evia	1351	6.84	2998	5.96

Table 2. Number (N) of fish farms and individuals occupied

AREA	FARMS		OCCUPIED PERSONS	
	N	%	N	%
Greece	290	100	3371	100
Evia	39	13.45	533	15.81

In Figure 1 below, Evia Island is shown, the biggest fishing centers and auction hall of the island are marked (all registered fishing vessels of Evia are landing their product there and the offices of the fishermen unions are also located there).

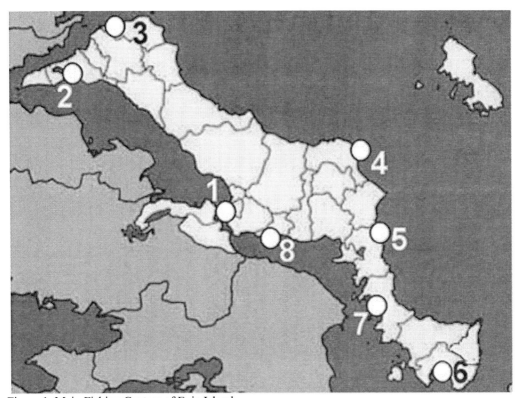

Figure 1. Main Fishing Centers of Evia Island
1: Chalkida (auction hall), 2: Edipsos, 3: Pefki, 4: Kymi, 5: Petria Beach, 6: Karistos, 7: Nea Styra, 8: Eretria.

Aiming to determine the socioeconomic status of the families involved with the fisheries, we focused our efforts on detecting the sources which would have recorded relatively reliable data. Tentative interviews were taken on different areas of the island and among authorized persons of cooperatives and fishermen unions, targeting to investigate the validity of the supplied data and to finalize the type and the content of the questionnaires.

A survey was conducted on women who were members of families of fishermen, working in fish farms or conversion plants, or members of relevant professional or other associations. We tried to cover a wide range of female activities in this coastal area.

Research in the field, which was fundamental for the implementation of this study, was based on semi-structured interviews and on the usage of proper questionnaires. Five different types of questionnaires were used, addressed to: professional fishermen, owners of fish farms or conversion plants, women occupied in fish farms, local associations, and local cooperatives. The data collected refers to the economic situation of the family, the structure of the family, and its social status and educational level. While it was emphasized that the questionnaires were anonymous and voluntary, care was taken that the interviewees would cover 5% in each category.

RESULTS

The prefecture of Evia (capital city Chalkida) participates by 2% on the population and by 2% on the country's GNP. During the last decade, the population of the prefecture was increased by 3.2%. The agricultural product corresponds to 2.7% of the national agricultural product, and to 12% of the total product of the prefecture. The corresponding figures for the product of the conversion are 3.7% (the 5th biggest figure in the country) and 22%.

Evia has the highest meat production (8% of the total Greek production), while it ranks as 5th in potato production (6% of the country). In general, during this period, the involvement in agriculture was reduced, although it remained at a higher level than the national average. The Gross National Product (GNP) has been increased in the same period and is higher than the average, while the income per capita is below average.

The active economic population was increased by 3.3% for Greece and by 1.8% for Evia. The unemployment was increased by 1.18%, against 3% in the territory. 66.7% of the active population of Evia is male (62.3% in the country).

The unemployment of women has decreased slightly by 0.7%, while it has increased by 1.4% for the country. The biggest percentage of employed people in the prefecture belongs to the group "Workers, Technicians, Operators" (38.4%); the group "Farmers, Stock Farmers, Fishermen" (17.7%); the group "Merchants, Salesmen", as well the group "Scientists, Craftsmen" (10.6%); the group "White-collar workers" (9.6%); the group "Services" (8.2%); and finally, the group "Directors, Executives" (1%). The largest percentage of women's employment comes under the group "Farmers, Stock Farmers, Fishermen" (18.7%); the group "Scientists, Craftsmen" (17.4%); "Workers, Technicians, Operators" (16%); "Merchants, Salesmen"; "White-collar workers" (15.8%); "Services" (11.7); and finally, the group "Directors, Executives" (0.5%).

Female illiteracy is considerably higher than that of the males, and the most significant differences are observed in the age group at least 50 years old, a fact that reflects a social mentality quite different from the present. A slight increase is observed in the percentage of women who finished a university.

The elaboration of the data obtained through the questionnaires leads to the following remarks:

Questionnaires Addressed to the Boat Owners

- Women are working as assistants in the fishing activity.
- 74.6% of the women are either illiterate or have just a basic-elementary education. This percentage is lower in the younger women.
- A small percentage of the women (11.9 %) are involved in social or public affairs by participating in associations or prefecture councils.
- 92.5 % of the women have to care for or nurse elder persons in the family.
- 79.1 % of the wives of the fishermen have no personal income.
- 26.3 % of the fishermen believe that women are more effective in open sea fishing, 31.6% in the aquaculture, 40.4% in the conversion industry and 1.8% in other sectors.

- 85.5% of the fishermen declared that they were willing to vote for women in national or municipal elections, associations, unions, etc.
- Fishermen believe that the participation of women in the fisheries is limited because they are occupied in housekeeping (26.6%), incapable (40.6%), less effective compared to men (7.8%), do not really want to be involved (9.4%) and because the traditional structure of fisheries does not allow for this (15.6%).
- Fishermen believe that women could be more actively involved in the fishery with the following prerequisites: increased salaries (47.5%), improved working conditions (21.3%), change of mentality by the male professionals (3.3%), proper distribution of the tasks in the house and the boat (13.1%), or better information and promotion of the participation of women in the fisheries (1.6%). Nonetheless, 13.1% of the fishermen do not see any chance for the active occupation of the women in fisheries.
- 91% of the fishermen declared that they are not willing to see their daughters occupied at the fishery.

Questionnaires Addressed to the Women Occupied in Aquaculture Plants and Conversion Plants in the Prefecture of Evia

- 10% of them are illiterate, 30% have an elementary school education, 10% have finished high school, 25% have finished the lyceum, 20% have a higher technological education, and 5% of them a university degree.
- 30% of the women had attended additional educational courses.
- 20% of the women were unmarried, 65% married, and 15% widowed or divorced.
- 85% of the women had no social activities, 10% were members of local associations, and 5% were members of municipal or prefecture councils.
- 90% of the women nurse or care for elder persons in the family.
- 15% of the women believe that the most proper branch of the fishery for women is in the open sea fishery, 30% in fish farming, and 55% in the conversion industry.
- All women working in aquaculture or conversion plants would vote for women as members in professional associations, or members of local, municipal and prefecture councils.
- The women occupied in aquaculture or conversion plants believe that the participation of women in the fishery is limited because: they are fully occupied with housekeeping (5%), they are not capable for this sector (40%), they are less effective than males (40%), and they do not really want to be involved with the fishing activity (15%).
- Prerequisites for an increased involvement of women in the fisheries are: increased salaries (65%), proper distribution of the tasks (25%) and their promotion (10%).
- 80% of those women declared that they are not willing to see their daughters occupied in the fishery.

Questionnaires Addressed to Cooperatives

- 80% of the women who are members of the cooperatives have an additional occupation (secondary or primary), while none of these women participate in the administration of the cooperative.
- 16.7% of the women are interested in participating in educational programs.
- 91.7% of the women consider that they do not participate in the decision-making in their work environment, 50% in their social environment and 91.7% within their family.

Questionnaires Addressed to Local Associations

- 75.4% of the women members of these associations are more than 40 years old.
- 4% of the women work in the primary sector, 11.5% in the secondary, 57.4% in the tertiary, while 29.8% are not working.
- 49.9% of women have an elementary school education, 32.7% have finished high school, 5.4% have a degree from higher educational institutions, 11.3% have a university degree and 0.7% of them are university post graduates.
- 90.4% of women were married, while 66.7% have one or two children.

CONCLUSION

The combined elaboration of the data obtained through the authorities, the questionnaires and the local survey leads to significant conclusions. It is quite clear that the women of Evia play a secondary role, in relation to males, in all fields of activity. The majority of fishermen' wives is unemployed, and belong to the category of assisting spouses, caring for the children and the house, and nursing the elder parents while they offer significant assistance to their husbands in fishing activities (Figure 2).

They have a lower educational level than their husbands, and their participation in public affairs is very limited. Those who are working do so in the primary sector, mainly (most commonly in the fishery) and secondarily, in the tertiary sector, usually in tourism occupations or in the service field (in the urban areas). The contribution of women to fishing activity is not recognized by the males: more than 40% of males consider the women as unable to work in this field. We should keep in mind that, in general, fishermen do not want to see their daughters occupied in the fisheries. What is encouraging is the fact that the male fisherman would vote for the presence of their wives in the local associations and unions, or in the local authorities. In fish farming, women are working independently of their husband's involvement in the field. 59% of the women are simple workers, 27% clerks in the offices, and 14% are technological or scientific staff. The majority of these women have never attended educational seminars. In spite of the fact that the time consuming occupation of fish farming (8 or more hours) does not allow for a secondary occupation, most of these women have the responsibility of housekeeping, the children and for the older members of the family.

Figure 2. Women working as assisting spouses.

In the cooperatives, the role of women is also secondary since they do not participate in the administration, being mainly involved in the production and marketing of the products. The administrators of the cooperatives are of the opinion that women do not participate in decision-making, either professionally or in the family. The data collected through the local associations shows that women in fisheries agriculture avoid participating in associations.

As a first stage, women should be properly informed and encouraged to become more active and to enter in the production field. It is imperative that the multiple roles of women should be considered in every measure to be taken: mother-, wife-, worker-, active citizen. The labor legislation should provide for better working conditions for women. The career orientation should be taken under consideration: the susceptibility of the female population and the traditional mentality does not approve of women going into the labor market. The establishment and funding of female-only cooperatives and associations will give impulse to their involvement in production and common affairs.

The funding of the female enterprising, as well as the actual enterprises, which promote the women's employment are effective measures against women's unemployment. The measures should not be limited to the working environment only, but should be extended in other fields, i.e. improvement and expansion of the care service to children and elder people. The introduction of part-time employment of women could be a measure for reconciliation between family and professional obligations.

All measures that would be taken must be followed-up and analyzed, as well as modified, according to the findings of that analysis. The need for equality in all fields- economic, political and mentality- is a matter of ethics and practice.

REFERENCES

[1] Bennett, E. *Marine Policy*, 29, 451-459 (2005).

[2] Dixon, R. D., Roger, C.L., Sabella J., and Marcus J.H. *Fishermen's Wives: A Case Study of a Middle Atlantic Coastal Fishing Community*. Sex Roles, 10, 33-52, (1984).

[3] FAO The Role, Status and Income-Earning Activities of Women in Small-Scale Fisheries, Peninsular Malaysia, Jahara Yahaya. FAO Project reports No. FAO-FI--MAL/86/005. FAO: Malaysia (1988).

[4] Gorez, B. A first step on the road to Damascus. (pp. 8-9) *Yemaya: ICSF's Newsletter on Gender and Fisheries* (2000).

[5] Josupeit, H. Women in the fisheries sector of Argentina, Uruguay and southern Brazil. *FAO Fisheries Circular*. No. 992. Rome: FAO (2004).

[6] Lambeth, L., Hanchard, B., Aslin H., Fay-Sauni, L., Tuara P., Rochers K.D., and Vunisea A. An Overview of the involvement of women in fisheries activities in Oceania, in M. J. Williams, N. H. Chao, P. S. Choo, K. Matics, M. C. Nandeesha, and M. Shariff, et al. (Eds.) *Global symposium on women in fisheries: Sixth Asian fisheries forum*, 127-142 Kaohsiung, Taiwan.

[7] Nadel-Klein, J. A fisher laddie needs a fisher lassie: endogamy and work in a Scottish fishing village, in: Nadel-Klein J., Davis D.L. (Eds), *To work and to weep*, St John's, 109-120, Newfoundland (1988).

[8] Norr, J. L., and Norr, K. F. *Society and Natural Resources*, 5, 149 – 163 (1992).

[9] Pereira, G. Women in fisheries in Latin America, in: M. J. Williams, N. H. Chao, P. S. Choo, K. Matics, M. C. Nandeesha, and M. Shariff, et al. (Eds.) *Global symposium on women in fisheries: Sixth Asian fisheries forum*, 175-180 Kaohsiung, Taiwan (2001).

[10] Quist, C. Vocal, independent, but still invisible. *Yemaya: ICSF's Newsletter on Gender and Fisheries*, 9-11 (2000).

[11] Rana, K., and Choo, P.S. Women in fisheries in the European Union, in: M. J. Williams, N. H. Chao, P. S. Choo, K. Matics, M. C. Nandeesha, and M. Shariff, et al. (Eds.) *Global symposium on women in fisheries: Sixth Asian fisheries forum*, 191-193, Kaohsiung, Taiwan (2001).

[12] Thiessen, V., Davis, A., and Jentoft, S. *Human Organization*, 51, 342-352 (1992).

[13] Tietze, U., Siar, S., Upare, S.M. and Upare, M.A. Livelihood and micro-enterprise development opportunities for women in coastal fishing communities in India – Case studies of Orissa and Maharashtra. *FAO Fisheries Circular*. No. 1021. Rome: FAO (2007).

[14] Tietze, U., and Villareal, L. (2003). Microfinance in fisheries and aquaculture: guidelines and case studies. *FAO Fisheries Technical Paper* No. 440. Rome: FAO.

[15] Williams, S. Economic potentials of women in small-scale fisheries in Africa. (2000) at http://www.orst.edu/dept/IIFET/2000/papers/williams.pdf

INDEX

#2

20th century, 60, 230, 254, 259, 268, 271
21st century, 48, 234

A

abolition, 45, 63, 65, 67, 261, 266
abuse, 210
access, xi, 17, 29, 93, 100, 101, 116, 119, 190, 217, 221, 222, 224, 225, 226, 230, 258, 260, 278, 305
accountability, 28, 29, 144, 183, 185, 212, 225, 226, 229, 282, 284
accounting, 17, 18, 179, 186, 188, 210, 214, 215, 222, 282
acquisitions, ix, 4, 115, 127
activism, 20
activity rate, 148, 155
adaptation, 243, 284
adjustment, vii, 3, 11, 18, 22, 26, 27, 31, 39, 50, 77, 93, 101, 189, 193, 244, 269, 287
administrators, 311
advancement, 198, 285
adverse conditions, 121
adverse effects, ix, 163
advocacy, 227, 286
Africa, 304, 305, 312
age, 19, 27, 55, 232, 234, 235, 265, 288, 292, 293, 294, 295, 299, 300, 308
ageing population, 126
agencies, 5, 126, 178, 180, 193, 229, 230
aggregate demand, 101, 126
aggregation, 165
aggression, 239
aggressiveness, 241, 246

agricultural sector, ix, 5, 163, 164, 165, 170, 171, 172, 173, 174
agriculture, 164, 239, 242, 254, 255, 257, 308, 311
airports, 54
algorithm, 165
analytical framework, 79
anatomy, 127
ancestors, 296
ANOVA, ix, 130, 152, 153, 154
aquaculture, 304, 305, 308, 309, 312
Arab world, 27, 225
arbitration, 259, 261, 266
architects, 55, 59
Argentina, 58, 74, 85, 312
armed forces, 238, 245
armed groups, xi, 6, 237
Asia, 238, 304
aspiration, 285
assessment, viii, xi, 5, 6, 71, 134, 135, 142, 144, 157, 174, 195, 202, 204, 215, 237, 295
assessment tools, 135, 157
assets, ix, 2, 4, 26, 57, 101, 102, 115, 116, 117, 118, 119, 120, 121, 122, 123, 124, 125, 126, 211, 212, 215, 216, 285, 286
assimilation, 47
asymmetric information, 117, 120
asymmetry, 78
atmosphere, 138, 239, 240
attitudes, xii, 6, 284, 291, 292, 293, 294
audit, 17, 124, 211, 214, 215, 217, 218, 286
Austria, 88, 98, 126
authoritarianism, 183
authorities, 2, 19, 20, 22, 27, 34, 42, 84, 125, 135, 142, 144, 180, 204, 276, 278, 304, 310
authority, viii, 4, 27, 33, 50, 184, 193, 199, 200, 203, 205, 212, 214, 228
autonomy, 20, 60, 184, 186, 259, 261
aversion, 52

314 Index

B

balance of payments, 79
balance sheet, 38, 116, 119, 120, 124, 216
balanced budget, 20, 38, 63, 67
Balkans, 243, 245, 246, 247, 248
bank failure, 115, 116, 117, 120
banking, viii, 1, 4, 13, 16, 53, 93, 115, 116, 117, 118, 119, 120, 121, 124, 126, 127, 191, 216, 260, 264, 266, 280
banking sector, ix, 4, 13, 16, 93, 115, 118, 120, 121, 126, 260, 264, 266, 280
bankruptcy, vii, 36, 61, 62, 64, 67, 265
banks, viii, 4, 16, 17, 20, 28, 47, 61, 115, 116, 117, 118, 119, 120, 121, 123, 124, 125, 126, 127, 179, 188, 192, 202, 227, 231, 264
bargaining, 43, 44, 117, 185, 189, 193, 243, 247, 259, 260, 261, 262, 263, 264, 266, 267, 268, 269, 271, 286
barriers, 27, 42, 58, 92, 149, 222
base rate, 96
base year, 216
basic education, 305
basis points, 73, 80
beef, 173
behaviors, 184
Belgium, 75, 80, 98, 99, 174, 304
beneficiaries, 48, 168, 169, 278
benefits, 3, 19, 24, 27, 36, 38, 41, 44, 46, 51, 52, 53, 54, 56, 92, 180, 183, 185, 199, 201, 243, 244, 257, 258, 260, 262, 265
bias, 29, 135, 150, 301
bilateral ties, 246
black hole, 38, 63
black market, 257, 258
Black Sea, 248
blogs, 233
Boat, 308
bond market, 191
bonds, 24, 38, 43, 61, 94, 97, 102, 103, 104, 109, 110, 111, 121, 123, 190, 229
bonuses, 185
borrowers, 116, 118, 120, 124
Bosnia, 244
Brazil, 312
breakdown, 12
bribes, 58
Britain, 47, 127, 134, 199, 239, 288
Buchanan, James, 31, 37, 59
budget deficit, 12, 14, 17, 52, 53, 88, 89, 92, 93, 94, 100, 103, 109, 126, 179, 180, 181, 186, 187, 192, 193, 204, 210, 284
Bulgaria, 190

bureaucracy, 15, 17, 22, 34, 39, 46, 47, 57, 59, 66, 184, 185
business cycle, 52, 53, 100
business environment, 131, 135, 202
business management, 274
business model, 284, 287
business processes, 284
businesses, 44, 52, 123, 130, 131, 132, 133, 134, 135, 138, 142, 143, 148, 149, 201, 216, 227, 280, 282, 283, 305
buyers, 117, 124

C

C4.5, 165
CAP, ix, 5, 163, 164, 167, 168, 170, 172, 173, 239
capacity building, 286
capital adequacy, ix, 4, 115, 119, 121, 126
capital flows, 179
capital inflow, 100
capital markets, 110, 116, 121
capital mobility, 100
capitalism, 37, 40, 49, 50, 51, 52, 54, 56, 62, 223, 274
Capitol Hill, 229
carapace, 42
case studies, 133, 312
case study, 134
cash, xi, 6, 20, 79, 119, 124, 212, 213, 216, 217, 221, 222, 230, 231, 232
cash flow, 80, 124
casinos, 1
casting, 60
catalyst, 18, 40, 178, 189, 190, 274, 286
cattle, 164
causality, 100, 101, 150
census, 255, 269
central bank, 78, 115, 188
central planning, 13
certification, 138, 139, 276, 277
CFSP, 244, 247
challenges, xii, 6, 18, 28, 38, 61, 82, 117, 123, 186, 241, 245, 268, 271, 273
chaos, 45
checks and balances, 183
chemical, 1, 170
Chicago, 68
child labor, 285
children, xii, 38, 257, 291, 292, 293, 294, 295, 296, 299, 300, 301, 304, 305, 310, 311
Chile, 19
China, 52, 62, 63, 67, 119, 229, 235
Chinese government, 119

Index

circuses, 37
cities, 28, 254
citizens, 38, 46, 48, 84, 186, 204, 210, 222, 224, 225,
    226, 227, 285, 292, 298, 300
citizenship, 225, 297, 300
civil servants, 55, 258
civil society, xi, 221, 278
civil war, xi, 6, 237, 246, 253, 254
civilization, 61, 296, 297, 300
classification, 198
cleaning, 119, 120, 305
cleavage, 259
clients, 26, 58, 286
climate, xi, 6, 14, 43, 209, 210, 218, 261, 264, 266,
    284
closure, 34, 123, 265
clothing, 292, 294
cluster theory, 130
clusters, 134, 144, 148
CNN, 225, 228
coal, 47
coding, 214, 295
coercion, 59, 66, 217
coffee, 231
cognitive process, 292
coherence, 200, 206
Cold War, xi, 6, 237, 245, 246, 247
collaboration, 225, 282
collateral, 37, 57, 118, 124
collective bargaining, 43, 44, 193, 259, 260, 261,
    263, 264, 266, 267, 269
collectivism, 275, 276
commerce, 215, 276, 305
commercial, 51, 53, 116, 119, 122, 256, 305
commercial bank, 116, 119
commodity, 63, 288
Common Agricultural Policy (CAP), ix, 163, 164,
    172, 239
Common Foreign and Security Policy, 244
Common Market, 165, 196, 207
communication, xi, 6, 221, 222, 223, 224, 225, 226,
    227, 229, 230, 231, 232, 235, 282, 283
communication technologies, 225, 231
communism, 45, 60
communities, 36, 64, 67, 225, 276, 292, 304, 305,
    312
community, 14, 36, 41, 45, 64, 181, 184, 191, 192,
    201, 274, 276, 280, 282, 286, 305
comparative advantage, 44, 121
compensation, 20, 120
competition, 2, 13, 14, 16, 17, 22, 28, 29, 36, 40, 47,
    51, 54, 60, 72, 132, 133, 134, 138, 183, 187, 254,
    255, 257, 262, 264, 286

competition policy, 134
competitive advantage, 285, 286
competitive behaviour, 282
competitive markets, 2
competitiveness, viii, 2, 4, 16, 21, 29, 30, 43, 44, 48,
    63, 64, 67, 75, 87, 91, 92, 94, 99, 101, 110, 111,
    112, 125, 132, 134, 138, 139, 141, 142, 190, 193,
    202, 210, 262, 265, 269, 284, 288
competitors, 286
complement, 189
complexity, 132, 222, 294
compliance, 15, 16, 186, 212, 282, 283, 284, 287
composition, 118, 254, 288
computer, 215
conception, 273, 282
conference, 18, 242, 244
configuration, 184
conflict, 45, 47, 56, 65, 189, 192, 217, 245, 293
conflict of interest, 217
conformity, 64
confrontation, 54, 64, 67, 258, 260, 261
Congress, 178, 194, 228
consciousness, 36, 38, 40, 223
consensus, 14, 15, 26, 46, 49, 138, 182, 187, 193,
    196, 224, 238, 241, 262, 263, 264
consent, 267
consolidation, 3, 20, 26, 27, 42, 58, 63, 64, 67, 180,
    189, 191, 193, 243
constituents, 276, 285
Constitution, 2, 29, 60, 63, 244
construction, 17, 28, 64, 93, 156, 257, 292
consulting, 139, 213
consumer price index, 91
consumers, xi, 221, 222, 224, 225, 226, 227, 230,
    231, 285
consumption, 41, 56, 123, 125, 171, 173, 185, 188,
    229, 230
Continental, 280
control group, 135
controversial, 38, 41, 49, 271
convention, 218, 306
convergence, 14, 16, 17, 23, 82, 83, 92, 94, 96, 104,
    187, 188, 189, 201, 223, 228, 229
convergence criteria, 16, 92, 187
conversations, 224
conversion rate, 93
cooperation, 124, 181, 184, 191, 204, 242, 245, 246,
    260, 262, 264
corporate governance, 188, 280
Corporate Social Responsibility, vi, xii, 235, 273,
    281, 282, 287, 288, 289
Corporate Social Responsibility (CSR), xii, 273
correlation, 2, 89, 99, 100, 104, 105

correlation coefficient, 89, 99, 100, 104

corruption, x, 19, 20, 22, 29, 42, 46, 49, 58, 73, 124, 125, 179, 185, 186, 200, 209, 210, 211, 212, 216, 218, 282

cosmetic, 190

cosmopolitanism, 223

cost, xii, 6, 14, 15, 19, 21, 27, 49, 58, 59, 77, 80, 84, 91, 92, 99, 108, 109, 110, 111, 112, 116, 123, 167, 182, 184, 186, 190, 192, 193, 201, 215, 230, 243, 253, 256, 275, 284

cotton, 62

Council of Europe, 239

Council of Ministers, 190, 248

counterbalance, 240

covering, vii, xii, 3, 11, 79, 89, 165, 186, 264, 303

CPI, 16, 210

Craftsmen, 259, 308

creativity, 286

credit market, 124

credit rating, 5, 124, 178, 193, 229

credit squeeze, 52

creditors, 61, 121, 178, 187

creditworthiness, 62

crimes, 212, 215

criminals, 211, 215, 299

crises, 5, 42, 62, 115, 117, 118, 120, 124, 182, 190, 192, 205, 225, 228

crisis management, 191

criticism, 39, 48, 52, 198, 283

crowding out, 106

CSF, x, 163, 165, 166, 168, 172

cultivation, 292

cultural practices, 83

cultural values, 276

culture, 181, 183, 185, 222, 223, 234, 256, 259, 260, 263, 268, 276, 277, 284, 285, 300

currency, vii, xi, 6, 16, 17, 19, 26, 31, 33, 55, 58, 88, 92, 93, 100, 101, 118, 119, 126, 178, 179, 188, 189, 191, 193, 216, 217, 221, 222, 224, 226, 228, 229, 230, 232, 253

current account, x, 4, 75, 118, 125, 177, 178, 181, 189, 284

current account balance, 75, 118

current account deficit, x, 4, 76, 125, 177, 178, 181, 189, 284

current prices, 116, 126, 210

customers, 117, 122, 225, 226, 231, 235, 283, 286

cyberspace, 224

Cyprus, 12, 94, 95, 96, 98, 99, 100, 104, 112, 206, 238, 239, 240, 241, 242, 243, 244, 245, 246, 247, 248

D

danger, 59, 126, 239, 241

data analysis, 294

data collection, xii, 291, 294

data mining, 164, 165, 171

data set, 165, 214

database, ix, 129, 144, 165

deaths, 143

debt service, 180

debts, 12, 17, 20, 21, 24, 37, 59, 60, 73, 111, 126, 137, 138, 187, 188, 190, 217, 269

decay, 245

decentralization, 34, 204, 263, 269

decision-making process, 226, 228, 275

decomposition, 185

decoration, 294

deduction, 132

defects, 188

defensiveness, 244

deficiencies, 15, 20, 26, 77, 79, 81, 230

deficit, vii, viii, x, 4, 13, 14, 17, 18, 19, 20, 25, 26, 30, 33, 38, 39, 40, 41, 55, 57, 58, 60, 72, 79, 87, 88, 89, 91, 92, 93, 94, 96, 99, 100, 101, 103, 104, 105, 106, 108, 109, 110, 111, 112, 118, 125, 126, 177, 178, 179, 180, 182, 188, 192, 202, 210, 227, 229, 265, 283

deflation, 118

democracy, xi, 6, 12, 38, 42, 51, 58, 60, 63, 65, 69, 183, 184, 186, 196, 200, 221, 222, 226, 254, 255, 260, 297

democrats, 59, 61, 65

demonstrations, 48

Denmark, 80, 171, 190

dependent variable, 109, 152

deposit accounts, 213

deposits, 117, 119, 120, 144, 155, 216, 217

depreciation, 92

depression, 241

depth, 51, 52, 198, 294, 301

deregulation, 25, 55, 110, 116

derivatives, 63

destiny, 223

destruction, 3, 59, 186, 229

detection, 211, 214

deterrence, 211, 218

devaluation, 27, 61, 63, 92, 118

developed countries, 64, 67, 115, 274, 300

developing countries, 188, 285

deviation, 27, 38

dialogues, 224

diffusion, xii, 6, 49, 54, 64, 67, 223, 273, 280

digital communication, 230

Index 317

diplomacy, 239, 241, 242, 243, 244, 245, 246
direct action, 52, 285
direct investment, 284
directives, 38
directors, 56, 212
disappointment, 225
disaster, 51
disbursement, 213
disclosure, 119, 282, 283
discontinuity, 184
discrimination, 286, 300, 306
disequilibrium, viii, 4, 87, 99
disorder, 192
distortions, 39, 112
distress, 120, 127
distribution, 37, 40, 49, 101, 149, 157, 158, 159, 167, 168, 213, 215, 256, 276, 309
distribution of income, 101
divergence, 100, 241, 276
diversification, 243
diversity, 165
division of labor, 43
DNA, 288
domestic agenda, 23
domestic capital, 274
domestic demand, 82
domestic economy, xii, 6, 118, 273, 284
domestic factors, 12, 23, 246
domestic industry, 274
dominance, 103, 201
donations, 274, 282
donor countries, 193
donors, 206
Draconian austerity measures, viii, 33
draft, 2, 127, 206
drainage, 164
drawing, xii, 52, 63, 246, 274, 291, 293, 294, 295
dumping, 286
duopoly, 229
dynamism, 52, 62, 64, 66, 67, 186

E

early retirement, 28
earnings, 79
Eastern Europe, 239, 245, 264, 288
ECOFIN, 188, 190
ecological data, 164
ecology, 139
economic activity, 62, 100, 143, 186, 255, 263
Economic and Monetary Union, 55, 86, 92
economic change, 11, 245

economic crisis, vii, x, 1, 3, 12, 19, 36, 61, 65, 72, 74, 81, 93, 94, 95, 96, 99, 104, 117, 118, 178, 197, 198, 201, 202, 254, 265, 269
economic development, xi, 6, 72, 73, 237, 253, 254, 256, 268, 269, 273, 274
economic downturn, 40
economic growth, 39, 59, 60, 61, 130, 131, 133, 144, 185, 254, 255, 265
economic indicator, 73, 74, 80, 84
economic institutions, 77
economic integration, 88, 89, 101, 191
economic performance, viii, 4, 71, 72, 73, 80, 85, 92, 195, 260
economic policy, vii, 1, 2, 12, 15, 24, 28, 35, 36, 38, 39, 41, 48, 59, 64, 65, 66, 73, 80, 84, 182, 187, 196, 202, 230
economic power, 215
economic problem, vii, 33, 37, 80, 245
economic progress, 35
economic reform, 27, 44, 82, 182, 185
economic reforms, 27, 182
economic rent, 58
economic theory, 58
economics, viii, 26, 30, 32, 35, 48, 60, 64, 71, 84, 99, 182, 183, 193, 223
economies of scale, 131
ecosystem, 174
education, xi, 18, 22, 28, 35, 41, 45, 47, 131, 134, 144, 148, 155, 205, 218, 221, 258, 294, 305, 308, 309, 310
educational institutions, 155
educational programs, 310
EEA, 164, 171, 173, 174
egalitarianism, 46
e-Government, 225
Egypt, 49, 238, 240
elaboration, 199, 276, 308, 310
elected leaders, 58
election, 1, 2, 28, 46, 58, 62, 65, 94, 125, 183
electricity, 53, 258
elementary school, 309, 310
embargo, 242
embassy, 238
emergency, 55, 58, 190, 192
empirical studies, 88
employability, 29
employees, xi, 5, 15, 17, 28, 41, 58, 124, 139, 143, 151, 152, 183, 187, 203, 209, 210, 211, 212, 213, 214, 217, 218, 256, 257, 258, 259, 261, 262, 263, 264, 265, 266, 267, 268, 269, 283, 284
employers, 15, 43, 211, 254, 259, 260, 261, 262, 263, 264, 266, 267

Index

employment, 13, 19, 20, 25, 54, 80, 91, 143, 144, 148, 149, 150, 151, 152, 153, 155, 156, 157, 158, 190, 203, 213, 254, 255, 256, 257, 258, 261, 262, 265, 266, 268, 270, 308, 311

employment growth, 151, 152, 155, 156, 157, 158

employment levels, 256

employment opportunities, 54

empowerment, 31, 200

EMS, 277

EMU, viii, 2, 4, 14, 15, 18, 26, 30, 31, 71, 77, 78, 85, 92, 93, 94, 99, 100, 104, 110, 112, 181, 184, 185, 187, 188, 193, 195, 200, 201, 202, 204, 271

energy, 12, 26, 27, 28, 54, 228, 246, 284, 285

enforcement, 185, 189, 257

England, 233, 298

enlargement, 242

enterprise economy, 53

entrepreneurs, 1, 3, 275

entrepreneurship, 2, 134

environment, vii, ix, 5, 11, 12, 14, 15, 17, 18, 22, 45, 52, 61, 64, 67, 77, 111, 116, 124, 126, 129, 130, 131, 132, 133, 135, 136, 143, 144, 148, 149, 150, 155, 157, 163, 164, 173, 181, 190, 202, 212, 223, 224, 244, 264, 285, 291, 292, 298, 311

environmental aspects, 282

environmental awareness, 278

environmental change, 282

environmental effects, x, 5, 163

environmental factors, 131

environmental impact, 164

environmental issues, 277

environmental management, 278

environmental policy, 201, 278, 288

environmental protection, x, 29, 163, 172, 279, 283

environments, ix, 129, 131, 132, 133, 136, 137, 143, 274

EPC, 241, 243, 244, 247

equality, 247, 306, 311

equilibrium, 38, 103, 185

equipment, 139, 305

equity, 119, 126

erosion, 125

ESI, 281

ethics, 212, 274, 278, 284, 311

euphoria, 17

Europe, xii, 20, 30, 45, 77, 86, 134, 138, 164, 174, 178, 179, 180, 182, 189, 190, 191, 192, 193, 194, 195, 196, 197, 200, 207, 231, 234, 237, 239, 243, 244, 245, 246, 248, 256, 269, 270, 271, 273, 281, 287, 300, 304

European Central Bank, x, xi, 17, 31, 61, 62, 80, 85, 86, 126, 178, 187, 190, 197, 198, 209, 210, 228

European Commission, x, 25, 30, 31, 32, 81, 82, 83, 85, 86, 91, 95, 96, 97, 98, 107, 127, 161, 165, 178, 189, 190, 196, 197, 198, 202, 207, 242, 273

European Community, 77, 181, 200, 241, 248, 269

European integration, 12, 30, 178, 228, 244, 245, 246

European market, 149, 228, 239

European Monetary System, 86

European Monetary Union, 77, 181, 200

European Union (EU), vii, ix, x, xi, 2, 4, 5, 6, 11, 12, 13, 14, 15, 16, 17, 18, 20, 22, 23, 24, 27, 28, 29, 30,62, 65, 72, 73, 78, 79, 80, 82, 83, 84, 86, 88, 93, 94, 96, 99, 111, 129, 132, 134, 135, 137, 138, 142, 143, 144, 150, 157, 161, 162, 163, 164, 171, 172, 173, 177, 178, 179, 180, 184, 185, 187, 188, 189, 190, 191, 192, 193, 196, 197, 198, 201, 202, 205, 228, 229, 232, 245, 246, 247, 248, 253, 254, 255, 256, 257, 262, 265, 277, 278, 287, 288, 304, 305, 306, 312

Europeanisation, 82

eurozone membership, x, 5, 177, 179

everyday life, xi, 221, 222, 223, 224, 226

evidence, 19, 26, 27, 89, 131, 132, 133, 137, 142, 148, 150, 153, 155, 156, 201, 212, 213, 215, 245, 275

evolution, 43, 52, 66, 91, 194, 253

exchange rate, 14, 61, 92, 100, 118, 126, 178, 188

exclusion, 278

execution, 46, 278

executive power, 183

exercise, 57, 63, 67, 73, 171, 268

expenditures, 39, 55, 57, 63, 65, 67, 214, 215, 216

expertise, 44, 222

exploitation, 39, 64, 67, 224, 285

exporters, 61, 285, 286

exports, 72, 79, 91, 92, 126, 139, 186, 245

exposure, 115, 118, 121

expulsion, 52, 239

external constraints, 30

external environment, ix, 129, 285

external financing, 181

externalities, 134, 181, 284

extinction, 13

extraction, 15, 185

extracts, 295

F

Facebook, 224, 235

factories, 57

faith, 217

families, 275, 307

family firms, 255

family income, 304
farmers, 13, 58, 167, 168, 173
farms, xii, 173, 303, 306, 307
fear, 178, 182, 191, 265, 278, 283
fears, 180, 193, 224, 225
feelings, 293, 299, 301
fertilizers, 170
Fiji, 305
financial condition, 120
financial crisis, 3, 5, 11, 59, 60, 88, 115, 116, 118, 123, 125, 126, 127, 179, 182, 186, 189, 190, 193, 201, 204, 228, 229, 274
financial data, 165
financial fragility, 119
financial innovation, 120
financial instability, 178
financial institutions, 138, 179, 193, 215, 216, 280
financial markets, 93, 100, 103, 115, 116, 190, 192, 224
financial performance, 15
financial policies, 198, 202
financial programs, x, 5, 163, 171, 173
financial reports, 282
financial sector, 63, 101, 116, 117, 119, 202
financial stability, 94, 126, 190
financial support, 65, 138, 142, 144, 238
financial system, 63, 120, 124, 126, 127, 179, 190
Finland, 100, 192, 304
firm size, 143, 148, 149, 150, 156
fiscal deficit, 13, 20, 40, 41, 55, 57, 59, 61, 88, 99, 101, 125
fiscal policy, viii, 4, 17, 20, 38, 87, 88, 100, 109, 110, 111, 112, 177
fish, xii, 7, 303, 304, 305, 306, 307, 309, 310
fisheries, xii, 7, 303, 304, 305, 306, 307, 309, 310, 311, 312
fishing, xii, 303, 304, 305, 306, 308, 309, 310, 312
fixed exchange rates, 99
flaws, 79, 189
flexibility, 17, 27, 29, 43, 139, 238, 257, 262, 265, 266
flowers, 294
fluctuations, viii, 53, 87, 112
food, 173
food products, 173
Football, 281
force, 13, 24, 37, 40, 43, 50, 65, 91, 124, 125, 164, 179, 223, 239, 240, 254, 256, 257, 266, 268, 269
foreclosure, 121, 124
foreign direct investment, 284
foreign exchange, 79, 118
foreign policy, xi, 6, 237, 238, 239, 240, 241, 242, 243, 244, 245, 246, 247

formation, xi, 6, 21, 22, 28, 101, 138, 139, 143, 223, 238, 253, 254, 268, 280
formula, 214, 215, 216, 295
foundations, 31, 44, 46, 49, 63, 67, 72, 186, 284, 292, 294
fragility, 119
France, 2, 31, 75, 80, 94, 95, 98, 99, 100, 104, 112, 126, 183, 189, 191, 205, 239, 242, 245, 246, 298, 304, 305
franchise, 191
fraud, x, 5, 209, 210, 211, 212, 213, 215, 216, 217, 218
free market economy, 222, 227, 230
free trade, 92
freedom, 43, 45, 50, 56, 93, 152, 222, 223, 224, 225, 226, 227, 229, 267, 296
fruits, 50
funding, ix, x, 4, 5, 39, 41, 54, 73, 79, 115, 116, 118, 119, 125, 126, 133, 163, 165, 181, 311
funds, x, 17, 19, 20, 27, 63, 116, 118, 119, 120, 138, 163, 165, 167, 168, 170, 172, 173, 179, 186, 192, 201, 202, 211, 212, 213, 215, 216, 217, 277
fusion, 17

G

gambling, 1, 217
garbage, 121, 294
geography, 131, 148
geometry, 15
Germany, 2, 21, 61, 62, 63, 67, 69, 75, 96, 98, 99, 100, 106, 108, 109, 110, 112, 126, 180, 183, 189, 191, 193, 196, 205, 218, 245, 278, 288, 298, 304
gigantism, 55, 58
GIS, 165
Glass-Steagall Act, 116
Global Competitiveness Report, 31
global economy, 60, 62, 63, 67, 72, 178
Global Info-Cash (GIG), xi, 6, 221, 222
global markets, 193, 222, 228
global recession, 179
globalization, 6, 193, 204, 222, 223, 224, 231, 274
GNP, 37, 56, 308
goods and services, 13, 38, 44, 91, 186, 193, 215, 231, 285
governance, 3, 26, 32, 82, 83, 178, 181, 182, 185, 188, 189, 191, 192, 200, 204, 206, 274, 278, 280, 282, 285
government budget, 88, 89, 93, 99, 112, 179, 201
government expenditure, 26
government intervention, 119, 120, 261
governments, 2, 3, 5, 12, 13, 14, 18, 22, 29, 40, 42, 51, 55, 59, 66, 77, 78, 83, 100, 110, 111, 115,

116, 117, 118, 119, 177, 179, 180, 183, 188, 190, 193, 203, 204, 205, 206, 223, 225, 226, 227, 229, 230, 232, 238, 241, 246, 260, 261, 264, 268, 278

governor, 18, 229

grants, 18, 144

gravity, 14, 191

Great Britain, 47, 127, 239

Great Depression, 62

greed, 204, 286

Greek banking sector, ix, 4, 115, 120, 121, 126, 280

Greek Current Account deficit, viii, 87

Greek economy, vii, viii, ix, xii, 3, 4, 12, 13, 17, 30, 33, 36, 37, 39, 44, 47, 50, 53, 56, 58, 65, 66, 73, 74, 75, 79, 82, 88, 89, 93, 94, 115, 126, 132, 137, 138, 142, 143, 148, 171, 178, 182, 186, 189, 201, 202, 206, 227, 229, 255, 263, 273, 274, 283

Greeks, vi, xii, 6, 36, 57, 72, 186, 187, 203, 245, 248, 275, 291, 292, 295, 296, 297, 298, 299, 300

greenhouse, 285

greenhouse gas, 285

greenhouse gas emissions, 285

gross domestic product, 178, 181, 185

Gross Domestic Product (GDP), 12, 14, 15, 16, 18, 20, 22, 25, 26, 57, 73, 74, 76, 77, 79, 80, 81, 88, 89, 90, 91, 92, 93, 94, 95, 96, 97, 99, 100, 107, 108, 109, 110, 116, 118, 121, 125, 126, 164, 171, 178, 179, 180, 181, 185, 188, 202, 210, 227, 228, 229, 253, 255, 256

growth, viii, ix, xi, 4, 12, 14, 16, 17, 18, 24, 25, 26, 31, 39, 49, 54, 60, 61, 77, 78, 82, 87, 89, 91, 92, 93, 94, 108, 109, 110, 129, 130, 131, 132, 133, 134, 135, 136, 137, 138, 142, 143, 144, 148, 149, 150, 151, 152, 153, 155, 156, 157, 158, 159, 179, 181, 183, 185, 189, 209, 210, 254, 255, 256, 257, 260, 262, 263, 265, 274, 279, 282, 284, 286

growth factor, 144

growth rate, 18, 92, 93, 110, 138, 150, 151, 155, 156, 179, 255, 263

growth theory, 130, 148

guidance, 13, 29, 35

guidelines, 84, 274, 300, 312

H

harbors, 54

harmonization, 224, 239

harmony, 37, 59

Harvard Law School, 127

harvesting, 304

healing, 123

health, 22, 27, 34, 46, 123, 180, 202, 204, 205, 258, 265, 280, 282, 283

health care, 34, 204, 258

health insurance, 34

heterogeneity, 117

high school, 293, 309, 310

higher education, 45, 310

highways, 185

history, vii, xi, 6, 14, 30, 34, 36, 39, 49, 54, 58, 59, 60, 61, 100, 125, 138, 215, 229, 238, 253, 258, 298

holding company, 119

hospitality, 296

host, 285

host population, 285

hostility, 192

hotel, 1, 148, 257

House, 63, 67, 287

House of Representatives, 63, 67

housing, 124, 148

human, xii, 41, 50, 57, 59, 61, 130, 131, 138, 144, 148, 155, 157, 204, 213, 222, 223, 227, 239, 282, 291, 293, 294, 295, 297, 301

human capital, 130, 131, 138, 144, 148, 155, 157

human resource development, 138

human resources, 41, 213

human rights, 223, 239, 282

hybridization, 223

I

ICTs, 234, 235

ideals, 42

identification, 213, 216, 217, 285, 286

identity, 14, 89, 104, 193, 212, 259, 292, 296, 301

ideology, 50

idiosyncratic, 84

illiteracy, 148, 308

illusion, 3, 55

image, xii, 6, 37, 44, 48, 160, 283, 291, 292, 294, 295

imbalances, viii, 22, 87, 100, 101, 110, 112, 125, 157, 178, 189, 193

IMF, 23, 24, 27, 30, 31, 84, 94, 95, 97, 98, 111, 112, 113, 178, 180, 182, 186, 187, 188, 189, 190, 198, 202, 205, 265, 287

imitation, 42

immigrants, 16, 257

imperialism, 39, 40

imports, 55, 92, 100

improvements, 44, 286

inauguration, 244

income, 18, 27, 36, 40, 47, 51, 54, 58, 65, 80, 92, 100, 101, 102, 111, 123, 144, 185, 202, 213, 215, 216, 255, 265, 304, 308

income tax, 185

incumbents, 182
indecisiveness, 192
independence, 60, 93, 271
independent variable, 108, 152, 153, 154, 155
India, 52, 58, 305, 312
indirect effect, 120
individual rights, 60, 65
individualism, 183, 223, 275
individuals, 15, 44, 60, 63, 101, 181, 201, 211, 213, 214, 275, 304, 306
indolent, 295
industrial environments, 133
industrial policies, 134
industrial relations, 254, 261
industrial restructuring, 269
industrial sectors, 141, 259
industrialisation, 138
industrialization, 12, 14, 255, 256, 259, 262, 274
industries, 73, 79, 111, 117, 131, 132, 133, 134, 137, 138, 142, 143, 148, 274, 276, 305
industry, 13, 117, 130, 133, 134, 143, 148, 156, 254, 255, 259, 261, 262, 263, 264, 266, 269, 274, 278, 304, 308, 309
ineffectiveness, 34, 193, 201, 298, 300
inefficiency, 36
inertia, 36, 37, 45, 86, 184, 201
inevitability, 189
inflation, 12, 14, 16, 17, 60, 91, 92, 100, 108, 144, 178, 188
informal practices, 16, 201
informal sector, 185, 256
Information and Communication Technologies, 234
infrastructure, 45, 130, 138, 139, 144, 148, 156
injections, 62, 64, 67, 80, 124
insecurity, 111, 244
institution building, 85
institutional change, 72, 73, 201, 263
institutional economics, viii, 71, 84
institutional reforms, 34, 49
institutions, vii, viii, 1, 2, 4, 5, 24, 26, 27, 29, 32, 34, 42, 43, 45, 47, 50, 59, 60, 63, 65, 71, 73, 77, 81, 84, 116, 117, 120, 133, 134, 138, 139, 155, 182, 183, 185, 186, 189, 191, 193, 199, 200, 201, 215, 216, 224, 225, 227, 245, 268, 269, 278, 280, 287, 310
integration, viii, 12, 14, 17, 26, 30, 87, 88, 89, 96, 100, 101, 103, 104, 110, 111, 178, 191, 228, 237, 244, 245, 246
intelligence, 225, 232
interbank market, 120
interdependence, 112, 177, 186, 275
interest groups, 5, 28, 181, 182, 183, 184, 185, 187, 193

interest rates, viii, 4, 16, 18, 87, 89, 92, 93, 96, 100, 101, 102, 103, 104, 108, 109, 110, 111, 112, 117, 118, 123, 180, 181, 188
interest-based behavior, vii, 3, 11, 27
interference, 226, 261
intermediaries, 133
internal controls, 212, 218
internal growth, 130
international competition, 51
international competitiveness, 43, 139
international financial institutions, 193
International Monetary Fund, xi, 65, 116, 126, 178, 198, 209, 210
internationalization, 240, 285
intervention, 47, 64, 65, 118, 119, 120, 125, 183, 237, 238, 242, 260, 284
investment, x, 15, 27, 38, 88, 89, 91, 93, 99, 101, 104, 105, 111, 116, 118, 122, 123, 141, 142, 156, 163, 167, 168, 172, 188, 215, 245, 281, 284
investment bank, 116
investments, 54, 56, 138, 139, 141, 142, 148, 167, 168, 216, 274, 285, 305
investors, 56, 62, 101, 115, 117, 118, 120, 180, 192, 193, 283
invisible hand, 36
Iran, 226
Ireland, 24, 77, 93, 98, 99, 126, 171, 178, 187, 191, 196, 197
iron, 60
irony, 57, 58
irrigation, x, 163, 164, 172
islands, 54, 167, 170, 305
isolation, 224, 245, 246
Israel, 240, 242
issues, vii, ix, 5, 6, 11, 18, 23, 31, 46, 64, 72, 116, 129, 135, 139, 178, 182, 192, 223, 238, 239, 242, 243, 244, 245, 246, 247, 261, 277, 280, 282, 283, 285, 292, 301
Italy, 16, 60, 75, 80, 85, 94, 95, 98, 99, 100, 104, 112, 126, 178, 183, 191, 242, 269, 270, 304

J

Japan, 60, 62, 73, 126, 225
Jefferson, Thomas, 227
job rotation, xi, 5, 209, 218
joint-stock companies, 56
journalists, 49
judiciary, 183
just society, 300

K

Keynes, 59, 60, 61, 62, 68
Keynesian, 58, 59, 60, 61, 64, 65, 66, 88, 100

L

labor force, 91, 164, 254, 256, 257, 268, 269
labor market, vii, xi, 6, 11, 25, 43, 44, 66, 72, 193, 202, 253, 257, 258, 262, 265, 268, 269, 270, 306, 311
labor markets, 202, 253, 265
labor relations, 258, 262, 265, 271
labor shortage, 44
labour market, 17, 18, 19, 27, 148, 155
Laffer Curve, 69
landscape, 24, 35, 64
Latin America, 305, 312
Latvia, 190
laws, 2, 3, 20, 35, 196, 212, 227, 282, 298, 299
laws and regulations, 212, 282
lead, 13, 14, 19, 34, 36, 38, 45, 61, 62, 64, 66, 67, 73, 79, 92, 100, 104, 111, 126, 189, 191, 205, 206, 217, 261, 263, 274, 284, 306
leadership, 14, 33, 37, 45, 51, 52, 54, 56, 65, 73, 83, 182, 191, 200, 238, 243, 246, 259, 260, 261, 263, 275
learning, 164, 184, 226, 285
legislation, 16, 27, 164, 184, 198, 203, 205, 217, 229, 231, 263, 264, 265, 278, 284, 286, 311
lender of last resort, 125, 126
lending, 102, 103, 111, 116, 117, 118, 120, 123, 124, 188, 265
lens, xii, 6, 284, 291
level of education, 294
LFA, 166
liberalism, 29, 30, 37, 39, 40, 50, 51, 54, 66
liberalization, 27, 39, 65, 93, 118, 120, 177, 200, 264, 266
liberation, xi, 6, 237, 239
liberty, 31, 63
liquidity, ix, 2, 3, 4, 115, 116, 117, 118, 119, 121, 125, 126, 127, 179, 188, 202
Lithuania, 190
loan guarantees, 190
loans, viii, 4, 62, 115, 117, 118, 119, 120, 121, 122, 123, 124, 125, 189, 190, 192, 254
local authorities, 204, 278, 310
local government, x, 5, 53, 197, 203, 205
local government reform, x, 5, 197
locus, 199, 200, 205
Luxemburg, 86, 98, 271

M

Maastricht criteria, 14, 80, 93, 178, 201, 262
Maastricht Treaty, 18, 92, 93, 181, 191
Macedonia, 167, 170, 173
machinery, 167, 168
macroeconomic management, 13, 41
macroeconomic policies, 17, 73, 119
macroeconomic policy, 13, 199
magnetic field, 63
magnitude, 48, 77, 192
major employers, 259
majority, xii, 7, 16, 42, 45, 49, 53, 63, 67, 72, 108, 131, 142, 183, 189, 205, 222, 244, 263, 275, 295, 299, 303, 310
Malaysia, 312
man, 293, 298
management, vii, ix, 4, 5, 12, 13, 19, 37, 38, 39, 41, 42, 43, 46, 47, 49, 51, 59, 66, 115, 117, 119, 120, 121, 123, 125, 126, 139, 164, 177, 179, 182, 191, 193, 202, 204, 210, 211, 222, 264, 274, 275, 277, 278, 280, 282, 284, 285, 288, 305
manipulation, 2, 54
manufacturing, 130, 131, 134, 139, 141, 148, 254, 255, 264, 278
manure, 164
marginalization, 269
market discipline, 120
market economy, 12, 210, 222, 227, 228, 230, 257, 258
market failure, 134
market opening, 26
market segment, 268, 269
market structure, 268
marketing, xiii, 274, 303, 304, 305, 311
masculinity, 276
mass, 18, 29, 37, 40, 43, 44, 45, 50, 53, 191
mass media, 18, 29, 37
materials, 240
matter, 111, 121, 182, 198, 244, 299, 300, 311
mature economies, 127
maximum price, 1
media, 18, 29, 37, 183, 186, 224, 225, 226, 283, 284, 292
median, 151, 211
mediation, 184, 244, 261
medical, 217
Mediterranean, 141, 177, 194, 245, 247, 269, 280
Mediterranean countries, 280
medium of exchange, 61
membership, x, 5, 6, 12, 13, 18, 28, 177, 178, 179, 184, 185, 228, 237, 243, 245, 247, 262, 263, 280
mergers, ix, 4, 115, 116, 127, 139

meritocracy, 201, 205
Mesopotamia, 49
messages, 44, 224, 227, 293
metals, 62
methodology, ix, 4, 129, 198
microeconomic theory, 130
Microsoft, 215
middle class, 51
Middle East, 85, 240, 242, 246
migrants, 245
migration, 254, 256
military, 12, 238, 239, 240, 242, 243
military dictatorship, 239
military junta, 240
minimum wage, 40, 43, 259, 265, 266
minimum wages, 259, 265, 266
Ministry of Education, 293
mission, 117, 280
mobile phone, 222, 223, 227, 230, 231, 235
modelling, 131, 135
models, ix, 4, 130, 135, 148, 149, 150, 152, 153,
154, 155, 156, 164, 206, 284, 287
modernisation, 82, 84, 138, 139
modernization, viii, 4, 29, 33, 34, 38, 42, 48, 71, 83,
84, 86, 179, 195, 202, 238, 271
momentum, 36, 45, 53, 60
monetary policy, 61, 93, 111, 178, 228, 230
monetary union, 14, 18, 77, 191, 228
money laundering, xi, 5, 209, 215, 217, 218
money supply, 215
monopoly, 14, 15, 28, 45
Moon, 289
moral hazard, 119, 120, 121, 123, 125, 188, 192
Moscow, 238, 239, 242
motivation, 85, 211
multiculturalism, 223
mutations, 53
MySpace, 224

N

Nash equilibrium, 185
national debt, 193
national identity, 14, 292
national interests, 77, 191, 192, 245, 246
national policy, 188
national security, 241
nationalism, 301
nationality, 286, 293
NATO, 237, 238, 239, 242, 243, 245, 246, 247
natural resources, 14
negative consequences, 48, 62
negative effects, 3

negative relation, 88
neglect, 120
negotiating, 43, 241, 262
negotiation, 19, 27, 44, 244, 278
net exports, 91
net private savings, viii, 4, 87, 105
Netherlands, 14, 75, 126, 304, 305
networking, 227, 280
neutral, 294, 295
NGOs, 224, 276, 278, 285
nitrogen, 165, 170, 171, 174
Nobel Prize, 59, 60
nodes, 191, 222, 224
non-respect of the rule of the law, vii, 1
normative neoclassical framework, viii, 4, 71
Norway, 118, 119, 305
nucleus, 239
nutrient, 174

O

Obama, 60, 61, 62, 63, 64, 67, 225, 235
Obama, Barack, 60, 62, 225, 235
obstacles, 47, 48, 60
Oceania, 304, 312
OECD, 13, 15, 18, 30, 31, 88, 94, 164, 181, 185,
195, 204, 218
officials, 18, 46, 118, 180, 183, 198, 207, 211, 218
oil, 12, 53, 62, 63, 92, 118, 138, 255
old age, 19
open economy, 126
operating costs, 123
operations, 62, 66, 121, 226, 273, 286
opportunism, 35
opportunities, 36, 43, 49, 53, 54, 181, 186, 212, 225,
284, 285, 286, 305, 312
optimism, 20, 104
Organization for Economic Cooperation and
Development (OECD), 13, 15, 18, 30, 31, 88, 94,
164, 181, 185, 195, 204, 218, 285
organizational culture, 276, 284, 285
organize, viii, 4, 33, 38, 260
organized labor, 260, 261, 263, 268
overgrazing, 164
ownership, 14, 18, 29, 47, 50, 53, 119, 125, 133, 254
ownership structure, 133

P

Pacific, 305
Pakistan, 58
paper money, 61

paradigm shift, x, 5, 197, 198, 199, 200, 205
parallel, 43, 47
paralysis, 42, 45
Parliament, 27, 194
participants, xii, 125, 188, 192, 224, 279, 280, 291, 293, 294, 298, 299, 300, 304
participatory democracy, xi, 6, 221, 222
paternalism, 55, 59, 60
pathology, 15
payroll, 27, 212, 213, 218
peace, 138
peer review, 188, 189
penalties, 42, 217
pension reforms, 26
pensioners, 38
performers, 150
perpetrators, 211
personal development, 133
personality, xii, 291, 292, 293, 300
personality traits, 292, 300
physical features, 292
plants, xii, 255, 278, 303, 307, 309
platform, 203, 222, 235
Poland, 190, 243
policy choice, 22, 182, 198
policy fragmentation, ix, 129
policy initiative, 124
policy instruments, 134, 199, 203, 204, 205
policy levels, 134
policy makers, 73, 80, 133, 182, 193, 245, 304
policy making, 72, 131, 134, 138, 232, 268, 278
policy options, 127
policy problems, 243
policy reform, 32, 182, 189
policymakers, 189
political clientelism, vii, 1, 58
political force, 14, 240, 260, 261, 268
political instability, 206
political leaders, 14, 37, 54, 64, 73, 191, 227
political parties, xi, 28, 186, 187, 200, 201, 221, 224, 225, 241, 259, 260, 268
political party, 39
political power, 300
political system, x, 5, 17, 27, 44, 81, 82, 84, 177, 182, 183, 191, 193, 223, 227, 241, 245, 246, 259, 273, 292, 300
politics, vii, 3, 5, 11, 15, 16, 22, 26, 30, 34, 37, 41, 42, 43, 45, 47, 52, 60, 64, 65, 82, 83, 84, 182, 183, 184, 191, 192, 193, 226, 241, 242, 244, 246, 258, 259
pollution, 164, 170

population, 36, 40, 49, 54, 126, 136, 143, 144, 148, 155, 164, 178, 187, 199, 222, 224, 225, 246, 293, 306, 308, 311
population density, 144, 155
population growth, 49
populism, 65
portfolio, viii, 87, 89, 101, 106, 109, 111, 121, 122, 123, 124
Portugal, 16, 24, 74, 75, 77, 79, 80, 94, 95, 98, 99, 100, 104, 112, 126, 178, 187, 191, 270, 304
positive relationship, 89
potato, 308
potential output, 17
poverty, 40, 47, 257
present value, 18
president, 228, 229, 263
President, 64, 227, 240
prestige, 38, 54
prevention, 182, 217
price index, 91
price mechanism, 60
price stability, 16, 93
primacy, 43
primary school, 295
primary sector, xii, 7, 303, 310
principles, viii, 55, 62, 64, 71, 223, 228, 229, 240, 241, 279, 282
private banks, 16, 17, 117
private firms, 13, 138, 284
private investment, 89, 91, 93, 104, 105, 138, 148
private ownership, 119
private sector, viii, 4, 28, 33, 36, 38, 41, 48, 54, 58, 63, 89, 93, 94, 96, 101, 102, 103, 106, 110, 111, 121, 123, 124, 125, 131, 138, 186, 258, 260, 265, 266, 268, 269
privatization, vii, 11, 15, 16, 17, 26, 27, 37, 38, 45, 50, 51, 52, 53, 54, 55, 65, 183, 184, 187, 204, 262, 264
probability, 212, 214
procurement, 17, 201, 203, 205
producers, 285
professionals, xii, 257, 273, 274, 309
profit, 27, 40, 44, 52, 123, 242, 244, 256, 280, 284, 286
profitability, 2
profiteering, 64, 67
programming, 38, 138, 142, 143, 144, 148
project, 14, 17, 19, 41, 52, 78, 83, 178, 182, 189, 243, 280
proliferation, 53
property rights, 2, 22, 58, 60, 63
proposition, 47, 56, 205
prosperity, 35, 41, 49, 50, 62

Index   325

protection, x, 3, 14, 20, 36, 37, 163, 172, 201, 224, 231, 257, 258, 268, 279, 283
protectionism, 182, 193, 274
public administration, x, 5, 28, 34, 54, 181, 183, 186, 197, 200, 201, 202, 203, 204, 205, 228
public administration reforms, x, 5, 197, 201, 202, 205
public affairs, xii, 7, 303, 308, 310
public concern, 46
public concerns, 46
public corporations, 57
public debt, 14, 18, 40, 48, 55, 56, 57, 59, 60, 61, 63, 64, 67, 73, 79, 80, 88, 91, 92, 94, 95, 99, 102, 103, 126, 127, 180, 181, 182, 187, 200, 210, 228, 260, 269
public education, 258
public employment, 13
public enterprises, 15, 16, 20, 30, 202, 258, 260, 268
public expenditures, 39, 63, 67
public finance, 18, 20, 26, 29, 31, 55, 58, 59, 118, 179, 184, 188, 190
public goods, 181, 182, 186, 193
public health, 258, 265
public interest, x, 3, 37, 42, 177, 183, 186, 222, 223, 226, 228, 229, 231
public life, 42
public markets, 183
public officials, 218
public opinion, 15, 16, 37, 40, 48, 78, 239, 243, 244
public pension, 19
public policy, 132, 182, 184
public safety, 1
public schools, 3
public sector, viii, x, 3, 4, 5, 13, 15, 16, 17, 19, 22, 26, 27, 28, 29, 33, 36, 37, 38, 39, 40, 41, 53, 54, 55, 57, 58, 61, 65, 84, 89, 92, 93, 94, 125, 139, 180, 183, 186, 187, 191, 203, 209, 210, 212, 213, 214, 215, 216, 217, 218, 225, 227, 257, 258, 260, 265, 268, 269, 282
public service, x, 22, 27, 197, 198, 204, 206, 278
public-private partnerships, vii, 3, 33
publishing, 203, 224, 282

Q

quotas, 143

R

radio, 225
rate of return, 102
ratification, 239

rating agencies, 5, 126, 178, 193, 229, 230
rationality, viii, 4, 33, 36, 38, 59, 60, 66, 184
reactions, 19, 48, 49, 244
reading, 72, 73
real estate, 26, 118, 121
real terms, 21, 41, 91, 262
reality, viii, 50, 52, 54, 55, 56, 61, 63, 65, 67, 71, 72, 73, 79, 80, 84, 189, 200, 240, 241, 257, 293
recall, 240
recalling, 34
reception, 131
recession, 11, 20, 24, 26, 27, 62, 64, 67, 94, 111, 118, 125, 178, 179, 185, 227, 230, 265, 266
reciprocity, 181, 182
recognition, 35, 36, 187, 244
recommendations, iv, 84
reconciliation, 213, 245, 311
reconstruction, 34, 44, 46
recovery, 14, 55, 61, 127, 204
recovery plan, 204
redistribution, 41, 58, 65
redundancy, 20
reform, vii, x, 3, 5, 11, 12, 15, 17, 18, 19, 20, 22, 23, 26, 27, 28, 29, 30, 31, 32, 34, 35, 38, 40, 42, 44, 45, 46, 47, 48, 51, 65, 74, 82, 83, 94, 127, 164, 182, 183, 184, 187, 189, 191, 193, 197, 198, 200, 201, 202, 203, 204, 205, 206, 218, 227, 232, 234, 235, 262, 263, 265, 267, 269, 274, 283, 287, 298
reformers, 35, 41
regional clusters, 148
regional cooperation, 245
regional economies, 148
regional policy, 133
regionalization, 164
regression, 45, 164
regression model, 164
regulations, 29, 42, 55, 66, 134, 190, 192, 201, 212, 226, 227, 229, 231, 258, 264, 268, 271, 282
regulatory bodies, 231, 232
regulatory changes, 116
reintroduction, 45
rejection, 42, 62, 105
relative size, 153, 215
relaxation, 20, 62, 261
relevance, 28, 116, 261
relief, 34, 40, 41, 92
remodelling, 284
rent, 2, 22, 24, 26, 29, 35, 58, 81, 83, 183, 184, 185, 193
reporters, 282
representativeness, 135, 143
repression, 239, 259
reputation, 78, 283, 285

requirements, 16, 38, 51, 64, 102, 103, 121, 124, 187, 284
reserve currency, 178, 230
reserves, 119, 188
resilience, 23, 201
resistance, 16, 26, 29, 192, 274
resolution, 46, 119, 165, 180, 186, 189, 193
resource allocation, 285
resource availability, 130
resource management, 204
resources, 13, 14, 22, 29, 34, 35, 41, 44, 47, 54, 120, 125, 183, 185, 204, 206, 212, 213, 244, 285
response, 5, 20, 30, 117, 120, 179, 181, 182, 186, 189, 190, 191, 192, 193, 198, 276, 285
responsiveness, 244, 278, 285
restrictions, 2, 29, 42, 52, 55, 135, 265, 269
restructuring, 13, 16, 30, 36, 38, 66, 202, 242, 269
retail, 118, 257
retardation, 49
retirement, 15, 27, 28, 31, 265
retirement age, 27, 265
retirement pension, 31
revaluation, 61, 62
revenue, 53, 55, 182, 202, 211
rewards, 54, 62, 286
rhetoric, 34, 39, 262
rights, 2, 20, 22, 36, 49, 50, 53, 58, 60, 65, 184, 223, 224, 226, 239, 257, 258, 268, 269, 282, 306
risk, ix, 4, 20, 56, 62, 63, 96, 115, 117, 118, 119, 121, 123, 125, 126, 164, 189, 191, 192, 266, 280, 283
risk management, ix, 4, 115, 125, 126, 280
risks, 119, 120, 121, 123, 246, 283
risk-taking, 115, 125
Romania, 190
Roosevelt, Franklin, 59
root, 72, 73, 82, 106, 108, 180
roots, 16, 105, 138, 206, 292
rule of law, 3, 28, 38, 42, 51, 59, 60, 186
rules, vii, 2, 3, 11, 15, 27, 28, 29, 30, 42, 78, 179, 185, 188, 191, 192, 199, 201, 231, 257, 263, 265, 279, 284
rural areas, 131, 254
rural development, 141
Russia, 36, 246

S

safety, 1, 119, 120, 187, 188, 261, 280, 282, 283
sanctions, 43, 192, 201, 282, 284
savings, viii, 4, 15, 87, 88, 89, 91, 101, 104, 105, 106, 118, 144, 155, 188, 203
savings banks, 118

Scandinavia, 127, 201
scarce resources, 244
school, 3, 37, 204, 293, 295, 301, 305, 309
science, 31, 35, 36, 52
scope, x, xii, 6, 14, 29, 79, 163, 172, 173, 242, 261, 273, 293
secondary education, 148
securities, 75, 117, 118, 190
security, 12, 18, 31, 139, 205, 213, 223, 237, 241, 243, 256, 257, 258, 262, 263, 264, 265, 268, 269
segregation, xi, 5, 117, 209, 217, 218
segregation of duties, xi, 5, 209, 217, 218
self-employed, 185
self-employment, 148, 254, 257
self-regulation, 37, 278
self-sufficiency, 60
sellers, 117, 124
seminars, 310
semi-structured interviews, xii, 303, 307
Senate, 63, 67
sensitivity, 165, 282
services, x, 1, 7, 13, 15, 17, 22, 27, 28, 38, 44, 91, 93, 94, 139, 185, 186, 193, 197, 198, 204, 206, 212, 213, 214, 215, 217, 222, 231, 232, 254, 255, 256, 257, 260, 276, 282, 285, 305
shape, 36, 56, 119, 187, 224, 284
shareholders, 40, 57, 121, 210, 276
shellfish, 305
shock, 22, 26, 78, 92, 100, 116
shortfall, 125
short-termism, 274
showing, 61, 170, 298
signals, 48, 188
significance level, 155
signs, 46, 108, 138
simple random sampling, 142
single currency, xi, 6, 16, 17, 101, 189, 221, 222, 228, 230
skilled workers, 257
skimming, 212
Slovakia, 98, 99
small businesses, 134
small firms, 156, 256, 257, 258, 262, 269
smoking, 3, 298
smuggling, 185
social activities, 309
social benefits, 24, 180, 262
social capital, 182, 194
social consensus, 187
social context, 293
social contract, 60, 186
social costs, 56
social environment, 291, 310

Index

social expenditure, 13, 24
social group, 200, 201
social interests, 275
social life, 41, 306
social network, 227
social norms, 59, 284
social organization, 50
social policy, 18, 35, 268
social resources, 35, 44
social responsibility, 6, 54, 273, 276, 282, 284, 286
social security, 18, 31, 205, 213, 256, 257, 258, 262, 263, 264, 265, 268
Social Security, 31, 163, 213
social services, 255
social status, xii, 211, 303, 307
socialism, 37, 42, 47, 49, 50, 51, 58, 65
socialist government, viii, 3, 4, 13, 18, 22, 24, 33, 57, 179, 200, 205, 243, 261
socialization, 35, 39, 119, 292
society, xi, 2, 3, 6, 13, 29, 34, 35, 42, 43, 44, 45, 46, 49, 51, 58, 59, 182, 183, 185, 186, 209, 218, 221, 222, 224, 226, 227, 231, 259, 260, 273, 274, 275, 276, 278, 279, 280, 282, 285, 286, 298, 300, 301, 304
socioeconomic status, 307
software providers, xi, 221
solidarity, 191, 193, 242, 247
solution, viii, 4, 5, 34, 42, 50, 62, 115, 116, 120, 121, 124, 125, 126, 127, 180, 193, 205, 229, 230, 232, 245
South America, 304
Southern eurozone countries, viii, 87, 89, 110
sovereign state, 191, 192
sovereignty, 77, 178, 182, 191, 243
Soviet Union, 42, 238, 246
Spain, 21, 60, 74, 75, 77, 79, 80, 94, 95, 98, 99, 100, 104, 112, 126, 171, 178, 191, 269, 270, 304
speculation, 80, 180, 190
speech, 191, 225, 228
spending, 26, 27, 29, 31, 55, 72, 94, 100, 111, 124, 179, 182, 201, 203, 204, 228, 232, 265
spillovers, 187
stability, 16, 60, 62, 63, 64, 67, 73, 78, 80, 92, 93, 94, 126, 133, 178, 190, 191, 228, 235, 238, 246
Stability and Growth Pact (SGP), 2, 78, 188
stabilization, vii, x, 3, 5, 11, 13, 14, 15, 16, 23, 46, 177, 181, 184, 189, 193, 200, 245, 284
stagflation, 31, 55
stakeholder groups, 276, 283
stakeholders, 273, 276, 278, 279, 284, 285, 286
state authorities, 22
state control, 16, 127, 138, 260
state intervention, 12, 14, 34, 46, 47, 65, 260

state of emergency, 58
state-owned enterprises, 20
states, 13, 14, 17, 24, 26, 45, 73, 77, 78, 80, 88, 132, 134, 137, 178, 182, 183, 188, 189, 190, 191, 223, 228, 243, 245, 246, 247
statistics, 20, 27, 106, 108, 150, 165, 270, 280, 304
statutes, 186
stereotypes, 300
stimulus, 184, 283
stock, 40, 43, 50, 51, 52, 56, 99, 102, 103, 116, 118, 119, 123, 212, 280
stock exchange, 43, 51, 56, 280
stock markets, 56
stock price, 123
stockholders, 119, 123, 124
stress, 124, 278
strictures, 189
strong force, 179
structural adjustment, 15, 18, 22, 92, 287
structural changes, 13, 31, 84
structural characteristics, 82
structural funds, 201
structural reforms, vii, x, 1, 3, 17, 18, 25, 65, 77, 82, 94, 197, 202, 274, 286
structure, vii, x, xii, 3, 4, 5, 22, 33, 40, 58, 100, 101, 123, 133, 138, 197, 205, 242, 258, 259, 268, 282, 284, 294, 303, 304, 307, 309
structuring, 139, 149, 226
submarines, 1
subprime loans, 117
subscribers, 34, 222
substitutes, 101, 116
substitution effect, 29
success rate, 212
supervision, 36, 84, 192
suppliers, 15, 17, 28, 183, 212, 213, 286
supply shock, 77
suppression, 254, 258
surplus, viii, 4, 25, 44, 55, 56, 87, 89, 92, 96, 99, 101, 106, 112, 118, 165, 170, 171, 181
surrogates, 148
surveillance, 182, 187, 188, 189, 190
survival, 12, 29, 62, 143, 144, 157, 284
survivors, 136
sustainability, 20, 73, 77, 83, 100, 179, 182, 190, 205, 274, 280, 281, 282
sustainable development, 81, 286
Sustainable Development, 194, 279
sustainable growth, 17, 274, 286
Sweden, 119, 120, 125, 126, 248, 304
synthesis, 37, 45, 138
Syria, 238, 243
systemic risk, 192

T

tactics, 46, 194
Taiwan, 312
takeover, 123
talent, 42
target, ix, 14, 45, 52, 129, 133, 136, 186, 200, 202, 280, 293
target population, 293
tariff, 60, 239
Task Force, 288
tax base, 179, 185
tax breaks, 63, 67
tax collection, 20, 185
tax evasion, 20, 185, 186, 195, 196, 201, 284
tax rates, 26, 56, 185
tax reform, 202
tax system, 185, 186
taxation, 24, 35, 36, 40, 47, 48, 55, 56, 57, 64, 65, 66, 192
taxes, 2, 20, 40, 55, 56, 63, 65, 67, 101, 111, 121, 122, 123, 144, 185, 186, 227, 232, 256
taxpayers, 118, 121, 124, 125, 144
teachers, 28, 84
techniques, ix, 5, 138, 149, 163, 165, 215, 216
technologies, 111, 222, 225, 227, 231
technology, 38, 44, 52, 53, 54, 215, 222, 225, 227, 230, 231, 235, 254, 255, 270, 285, 305
telecommunications, 16, 53, 148, 264
telephone, 53, 148
tempo, 21
tensions, 12, 15, 16, 82, 193, 242
territorial, 191, 238, 292
territory, 308
terrorism, 240
tertiary sector, xii, 7, 303, 310
testing, 28, 48, 105, 130, 131, 144, 150, 214
textiles, 254
Thailand, 88
theoretical assumptions, 199
third dimension, 241
Third World, 243, 248
thoughts, 49
threats, 240
time frame, 202, 203, 206
time periods, 89
time pressure, 200, 206
time series, 104, 106
top-down, 142
tornadoes, 225
total product, 173, 308
tourism, xii, 7, 27, 73, 79, 148, 303, 310

trade, 41, 48, 53, 55, 58, 61, 63, 66, 67, 79, 92, 96, 98, 99, 125, 134, 178, 182, 183, 187, 189, 198, 207, 214, 229, 245, 255
trade deficit, 79, 96, 98, 99, 125, 178, 229
trade policy, 182
trade union, 48, 53, 66, 182, 183, 187, 198, 207
trade-off, 58
traditions, 64
training, 133, 138, 139, 218, 238, 305
traits, xii, 254, 291, 292, 295, 298, 300
trajectory, 62, 66
transaction costs, 100, 189, 191, 222
transactions, xi, 93, 212, 218, 221, 222, 223, 224, 225, 227, 228, 232, 246
transcripts, 206, 294
transformation, vii, 45, 53, 199, 223, 231, 261, 270
transformations, 152
transmission, 77
transparency, x, 5, 29, 38, 42, 123, 183, 190, 197, 203, 205, 217, 224, 225, 226, 232
transport, 28, 50, 54, 204, 205, 240, 255, 258
transportation, 149, 222
Treasury, 63, 67, 119, 189
treaties, 306
turbulence, 39, 283
Turkey, 240, 241, 242, 243, 244, 245, 247, 248
Turks, 248
turnover, 56, 144, 149, 150, 151, 152, 153, 155, 156, 157, 158, 159

U

U.N. Security Council, 242
unemployment rate, 25, 91, 94
unification, 92, 238, 239
unions, 15, 16, 17, 19, 28, 29, 41, 58, 62, 84, 187, 259, 260, 261, 262, 263, 264, 266, 267, 268, 269, 304, 306, 307, 309, 310
unit cost, 111, 215
United Kingdom (UK), 21, 31, 118, 119, 60, 126, 161, 231, 234, 278, 280, 291, 304, 306
United Nations (UN), 165, 229, 279, 285, 288
United States (USA), xi, 6, 21, 58, 60, 61, 62, 63, 69, 77, 117, 119, 126, 127, 161, 178, 211, 215, 218, 219, 221, 222, 227, 229, 230, 237, 238, 241, 246, 248
universities, 3, 47, 132, 204
unprecedented economic crisis, vii, 1
urban, xii, 7, 50, 54, 130, 256, 303, 306, 310
urban areas, xii, 7, 303, 310
Uruguay, 312
uti, 104

V

valuation, 124, 188
value added tax, 186
variables, ix, 5, 72, 81, 89, 94, 99, 100, 101, 102, 103, 104, 105, 108, 109, 111, 130, 143, 144, 145, 148, 149, 150, 152, 153, 155, 156, 157, 188, 294
variations, 89, 99, 110, 278
VAT, ix, 129, 142
vector, 105
vein, 293, 300
velocity, 61
venture capital, 138
vessels, 305, 306
vested interests, 3
veto, 28, 29, 185
victims, 187
vision, 47, 73, 189, 191, 286
vocational education, 148
volatility, 182
vote, 42, 203, 229, 241, 298, 309, 310
voters, 35, 183, 243
voting, 53, 189
vulnerability, x, 39, 177, 182

W

wage increases, 13, 40, 41, 255
wage level, 44
wage rate, 263
wages, 15, 21, 35, 40, 43, 44, 58, 203, 213, 254, 259, 263, 264, 265, 266, 271
war, xi, 6, 12, 16, 29, 45, 46, 48, 60, 61, 62, 64, 67, 189, 193, 233, 237, 240, 241, 242, 244, 246, 253, 254, 255, 259, 265
war years, 254
Washington, 32, 127, 180, 238, 240, 242, 243, 247

water, 49, 53, 54, 164, 174, 228
weakness, 55, 124, 189, 201
wealth, 35, 37, 44, 49, 52, 58, 59, 64, 67, 102, 215
weapons, 1, 240
wear, 295
web, 160, 186, 235, 257
web sites, 235
websites, 225
welfare, 36, 58, 200, 201, 258
welfare state, 200, 201, 258
West Africa, 305
Western Europe, 30, 237, 239, 246
White Paper, 270
white-collar workers, 265
wholesale, 120
Wilson, Woodrow, 247
withdrawal, 242, 243
work environment, 310
workers, xiii, 3, 28, 35, 36, 41, 43, 44, 58, 257, 258, 259, 260, 265, 266, 267, 268, 303, 304, 308, 310
workforce, 305
working class, 268
working conditions, 257, 267, 309, 311
working hours, 257, 269
working population, 40
workload, 28
workplace, 61, 212
World Bank, 24
World War I, vi, xi, 6, 14, 59, 237, 238, 253, 254

Y

Yale University, 31, 247
young people, 291, 292, 295, 296, 297, 300, 301, 305
youth unemployment, 227
Yugoslavia, 244